# Raising Your Child's Inner Self-Esteem

## THE AUTHORITATIVE GUIDE FROM INFANCY THROUGH THE TEEN YEARS

# Raising Your Child's Inner Self-Esteem

## THE AUTHORITATIVE GUIDE FROM INFANCY THROUGH THE TEEN YEARS

Karen Owens, Ph.D.

PLENUM PRESS • NEW YORK AND LONDON

Library of Congress Cataloging-in-Publication Data

On file

ISBN 0-306-45084-4

© 1995 Karen B. Owens
Plenum Press is a Division of Plenum Publishing Corporation
233 Spring Street, New York, N.Y. 10013-1578

10 9 8 7 6 5 4 3 2 1

Printed in the United States of America

To my children:

To my recently married son, Gordon,
and his college sweetheart, Meade
and
to my recent college graduate, Eric

# Acknowledgments

A special thanks to a former developmental pyschology student, Kara Doran, who enthusiastically suggested my writing this book. To Linda Greenspan Regan, senior editor, Trade Division of Plenum Press, who insightfully recognized the importance of this book and offered many cogent comments and suggestions that helped to make this book a valuable source for parents and their children.

# Contents

# Introduction

Self-esteem refers to the extent to which we admire or value ourselves. Self-esteem derives from our attitudes, feelings, judgments, or evaluations of how capable, significant, successful, and worthy we are. Children—and adults—with high self-esteem are responsible and self-controlled, perceive themselves realistically, own up to their strengths and weaknesses, take pride in their accomplishments, and are not threatened by the successes of others.

Most parents recognize the importance of helping children develop positive self-esteem and place this as a high priority on their list of parental objectives. Parents recognize that if children see themselves as worthwhile, useful, lovable, competent human beings, they will be able to lead happy and productive lives. If, on the other hand, children feel worthless, unlovable, and incompetent, their lives will be plagued with self-doubt, self-pity, interpersonal ineffectiveness, and lack of success in all that they do. Without self-love, any solid and general growth of character and accomplishment is hardly possible. Nor is it possible to love others. "Indeed," says Robert Louis Stevenson, "he who loves himself, not in idle vanity, but with a plentitude of knowledge, is the best equipped of all to love his neighbors." A self-neglecting child shrinks from developing and asserting himself or herself because of uncertainty and mortification. To be healthy, at home in the world with a prospect of power, usefulness, and success, children must have healthy self-esteem.

Positive self-esteem is a basic need for every human being. Just as the body needs nutritious food to be healthy, so the personality needs esteem from others and from self to achieve emotional health. As parents, we want our children to develop healthy evaluations of themselves so that they may become successful, happy, well-adjusted adults.

1

Because the types of evaluations children have of themselves are learned, children themselves—as well as their parents, teachers, peers, and other significant people in their lives (persons whom they sense as being able to allay insecurity or intensify it and promote or diminish their sense of well-being)—play an important role in determining their self-esteem. No one is born with predetermined evaluations of self. Heredity influences self-evaluations only indirectly. Let's say that Ralph inherited a big nose, and he feels embarrassed and unattractive as a result of this physical characteristic. This inherited physical feature, however, does not, in and of itself, cause these negative feelings. Look at Jimmy Durante or Karl Malden—both had big noses, but this didn't, judging from their successes, cause negative feelings in them. So, it is how the individual, most importantly, and others judge this feature and how it is judged (positively or negatively) that will determine evaluations about this aspect of his or her physical self.

Children's self-evaluations tend to act as "information processors" in interpreting the experiences they encounter in their environment. That is, children's self-esteem influences how they *perceive* experiences in their environment and consequently how they act or *behave* in that environment. For example, Sarah has low self-esteem in the social domain; she believes that she is not very popular with the other kids in her class. As a result of this self-evaluation, Sarah will "see" only those aspects in her environment that fortify this negative evaluation of self. Perception is highly subjective and is always consistent with our self-evaluations. During recess one afternoon, Sarah notices that her friend Amy is playing with another girl, Julie. Sarah subjectively perceives this as Amy not being her friend anymore. (In reality, Amy may still like Sarah and want to play with her but, today, she chooses to play with Julie.) Sarah's perceptions, in turn, affect her behavior. She makes no overtures to join Amy and Julie in play, but rather, sits on the fringe of the playground away from the other children.

## Outer Self-Esteem

Children form their evaluations of self from two sources, outer and inner. Many years ago, Charles H. Cooley, a pioneer and expert in the field of self-esteem, referred to the outer, reflective component of self as the "looking-glass self," since significant others are the social mirror into which we look for information that comes to define the self.[1]

Each to each a looking glass
Reflects the other that does pass

Outer self-esteem is associated with how others have responded to us. If those experiences are positive, that is, if one feels loved and accepted despite imperfections, then the individual's internalized feelings about himself or herself will reflect this. Thus, children evaluate and value themselves in congruence with the general reactions of others toward them.

The origin of outer self-esteem lies in the complex interrelationships between children and others who comprise their environment. As such, one source of children's evaluations, the outer source, reflects the responses and appraisals of others. Children come to evaluate themselves from the "reflected appraisals" of others. Parents communicate powerful expectations that influence the development of children's self-esteem. For example, 3-year-old Burt's parents are highly critical of him and rarely praise him; they belittle his accomplishments and don't spend much time with him because of their own busy, hectic schedules. As a result, Burt begins to feel insignificant and unworthy, which leads to low self-esteem. Jamie, on the other hand, has parents who are warm, accepting, interested, and attentive. In this situation, Jamie tends to pick up a different message—"I am loved, I am a worthy person." This sets the stage for developing positive evaluations of self. Thus, children see themselves, more or less, the way others see and treat them.

The process by which an awareness of personal attributes is translated into children's self-esteem is shown in Figure 1.

Outer self-esteem develops from "others' perceptions of me," since children's evaluations are gradually abstracted from the ways other people have reacted to them. The conditions that children encounter in their environment, such as those in Burt's and Jamie's, contribute to a sense of success or failure, triumph or humiliation, and acceptance or

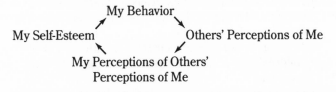

**Figure 1.** Personal attributes and children's self-esteem.

rejection and are ultimately determinants of their self-esteem. From personal experiences and the quality of those experiences with parents or peers, children mentally begin to construct evaluations of self.

Parents can help their children develop outer self-esteem by showing love, respect, and acceptance toward them. By expressing an "I love you, no matter what" kind of acceptance, children's self-esteem is strengthened. Professionals call this "no-strings-attached" form of love *unconditional positive regard.*[2] Unconditional love does not mean that the parents condone everything the child does. It does mean that, even though parents do not approve of children behaving in unacceptable ways, in their attempts to guide the child, love and caring are always there. Parental warmth, acceptance, and responsiveness—given unconditionally—are important for fostering healthy evaluations of self.

Initially, when children are very young (age 3 and younger), outer sources of self-esteem play a more important role in helping them develop in positive and healthy ways. During these early years, children need positive feedback from parents and thrive on arbitrary praise and approval bestowed on them by their parents.

## Inner Self-Esteem

Taken alone, this "looking-glass" orientation leaves us with an essentially passive and conforming view of human beings, one that emphasizes an external source (the opinion of others) as *the* substance of our self-esteem. Evaluative feedback from others is a powerful determinant of self-esteem, but it is not the only factor. Cooley's writings on self-esteem have been interpreted in a one-sided and distorted way; all the emphasis has been placed on outer sources of self-esteem. Cooley, however, also emphasized another source of self-esteem—an active, dynamic, *inner* self-esteem.

The inner source of self-esteem is based on children's self-evaluations derived from their *actual behaviors and competencies.* It is this active, dynamic, and more stable source of self-esteem—inner self-esteem—that also enables children to develop healthy evaluations of self. Inner self-esteem is not given to children by others, but is earned through children's developing competent behaviors and skills in socially valued areas.

Inner self-esteem is a child's belief in himself or herself and is based upon a sure knowledge of past achievements. Inner self-esteem is based on *self*-respect, *self*-acceptance, and *self*-love. As Cooley comments, individuals must feel that the final arbitrator is within and not outside them.[1] This is not to say that children should totally discount the environment. However, individuals should not be so dependent on the evaluations of others that they become chameleons, taking on the drab or bright colors of others' responses to them. Children need to direct their attention to how they appear to others *as well as inward* to self-evaluation. Highly sensitive children, however, are continually imagining how they appear to others and accepting this image as themselves. In short, a very sensitive child tends to become, for the time, his or her interpretation of what others think he or she is.

Children with high inner self-esteem are not so completely bogged down with others' evaluations of them that they fail to consider their self-appraisals and evaluations. Inner self-esteem is influenced more by internal or personal sources of evaluation, and the basis for such evaluations comes from successful performance of socially valued behavior. Though socially valued behavior is, of course, external to the child, the emphasis here is on the child's own inner perceptions of performance, capability, and worth within the context of behaviors externally valued. Thus, these children are not constantly worrying about how they measure up in comparison to others but tend to make self-comparisons and note their own personal improvement. Similarly, children with good inner self-esteem do not need constant praise from others as a form of encouragement and motivation but tend to derive their motivation from within and pursue goals because these goals are important to *them* and afford them enjoyment and pleasure.

Children with inner self-esteem have "outgrowing" minds. They are flexible thinkers and tend to be open to incorporating all kinds of new experiences into their self-pictures. In contrast, children who depend on outer sources of information about self tend to concentrate on working up old material, things that have happened to them in the past, instead of taking in new materials. These children have "ingrowing" minds. Imagine the energy it takes to limit new impressions and maintain old impressions that do not disturb the system to which a child has grown accustomed. An ingrowing mind wallows in the secure unity and stability of thought and character at the expense of openness and adaptability. Children need to develop outgrowing minds that are open to all sorts of impressions and eagerly take in new material.

Inner self-esteem is earned. In order for children to effectively master their environment, they must have knowledge about and training in developing socially valued skills and appropriate behavior, which requires effort and persistence on the parents' part, and, of course, on the children's part. With increasing age, children need to base their self-esteem on personal self-evaluations in addition to incorporating evaluations from others of their own competence and skills: academic skills, athletic and social skills, and other demonstrated competencies. Actual behavior and *real* accomplishments are the sources of inner self-esteem.

Inner self-esteem may be the more stable and cohesive sense of self. Outer self-esteem rises in environments that are perceived as favorable, and if the environment is perceived as unfavorable, self-esteem is lowered. Outer self-esteem may be so whimsical that it is impossible to foresee what turn it will take next. Children who are highly dependent on self-esteem from others are at the mercy of others and are very vulnerable. These children live in the frailest of glass houses, which may be shattered at any moment; in the case of children with low self-esteem, this catastrophe happens quite often. For example, Nancy has a very demanding teacher, who, at times, lavishes her with lots of attention (and Nancy feels good about herself); at other times, however, she ignores Nancy (and Nancy feels like a rotten person). These mercurial highs and lows hinge on the responses of others. Inner self-esteem is more stable because it has a solid base in children's actual character, behavior, skills, and competence. That is, children have the actual skills and competencies; they have experienced success, and, thus, someone else cannot instantly take inner self-esteem away from them. It has been realistically established and is based on their actual achievements. Inner self-esteem develops from actual achievements and success and stresses that children are active, creative agents, not just passive receptors, waiting like inert sponges to soak up others' evaluations of them. Table 1 highlights the differences between outer and inner self-esteem.

As children get older, inner self-esteem (demonstrated skills and competencies) becomes a more important component of self-esteem. Parents and others who initially bestowed arbitrary praise and approval on their young child begin to base their appraisals of the child and feedback given to the child on his or her actual competencies. Children who continue to receive generous narcissistic supplies of approval and recognition without doing much to earn them will enjoy an agreeable level of self-esteem, provided they never enter a harsher environment. But as children grow older, most do enter harsher environments, and they do

**Table 1.** Outer and Inner Self-Esteem

| Outer Self-Esteem | Inner Self-Esteem |
|---|---|
| Based on perceived reflections of others | Based on self-evaluations |
| Child perceived as passive agent absorbing feedback from others | Child perceived as active, dynamic, creative |
| Initially based on arbitrary praise bestowed on children by their parents | Earned through development of socially valued behaviors and skills |
| Tends to be unstable depending on how others treat them | Tends to be stable because it has a solid base in children's actual achievements and successes |

meet with more objective evaluations. A false sense of positive self-esteem may not be supported by peers and others later on.

If children are to maintain high evaluations of self, parents need to help their children develop the skills necessary to earn (through recognition of real accomplishments) both the positive evaluations of others and their own positive self-evaluations. If children have not had opportunities to develop areas of competence, their sense of self-esteem is very unstable.

There are certain competencies vital to developing inner self-esteem at each developmental level (infancy, early childhood, middle childhood, adolescence). That is, there are different developmental tasks, behaviors, and skills that need to be cultivated at each of these levels so that children will develop inner self-esteem and thus make a healthy adjustment to life. Parents need to be aware of the various skills and behaviors that are pivotal to helping children develop inner self-esteem. During infancy (from birth to age 2 years), foundations of inner self-esteem are built when parents and infants develop strong attachments, when parents help their infants develop a sense of trust in others, affectively communicate with their infants, and help their infants' emerging sense of self develop. During early childhood (ages 2–5), children's inner self-esteem is enhanced when they develop behaviors and skills that enable them to be self-sufficient, independent, and autonomous. Children in middle childhood (ages 6–12) have two very important developmental tasks that are vital to their inner self-esteem:

doing well academically and getting along with other children. Finally, adolescents (ages 12–18) need to develop a sense of autonomy while retaining a sense of connectedness with their parents; they need to develop a sense of who and what they are, and they need to achieve a comfortable body image.

## Multidimensional Self-Esteem

Children tend to make estimates of their self-worth in four important areas: academic, social, physical, and moral. Most experts agree that self-esteem cannot be adequately understood if this multidimensionality is ignored.[3] Children tend to evaluate themselves differently in various domains. One child may see herself as "worthy" in the physical domain because she is a terrific tennis player, but she may feel "unworthy" in the academic domain because she is getting a D in math.

When children first begin evaluating their self-worth, however, evaluations are generally global. That is, they are "all smart" or "all dumb," "very pretty" or "not pretty," and these evaluations change frequently. Billy, for example, can be smart one day because he knows how old he is but not smart the next day because he doesn't know the date of his birthday.

As children get older, self-esteem becomes multidimensional. Children tend to judge themselves in different domains: academic, social, physical, and moral. These domains are elaborated in Figure 2.

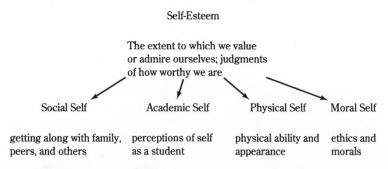

**Figure 2.** The domains of multidimensional self-esteem.

Among adults, only self-perceived competencies in areas that are valued by the individual will affect his or her self-esteem. For example, it's really important to Linda to be a good student, and if she doesn't do well in this domain, it will significantly affect her self-esteem. She doesn't particularly care if she is a good athlete, so if she is not, it will not affect her self-esteem. The importance of personally valued competencies was underscored by William James:

> I, who for the time have staked my all on being a psychologist, am mortified if others know much more psychology than I. But I am contented to wallow in the grossest ignorance of Greek. My deficiencies there give me no sense of personal humiliation at all. Had I pretensions to be a linguist, it would have been just the reverse. . . . So our self-feeling in this world depends entirely on what we back ourselves to be or do.[4]

Children, however, need to feel reasonably good about themselves in all these domains. Academic, athletic, and social competence and being a good and decent person are all highly valued and sought after by the majority of children in our culture. For those who choose to remain within this cultural mainstream, aspirations in these domains are likely to be high. Moreover, others, notably parents and peers, place a high value in these areas in our society. Therefore, it is extremely difficult for children and adolescents to discount the value and importance of doing as well as one can in each of these domains.

Doing well in each of these domains does not mean that every child must be the straight-A, Harvard-bound homecoming king or queen or the star athlete who receives the Good Samaritan award every year. It does mean that children strive to be the best they can be, are aware of their strengths and weaknesses, and take pride in their accomplishments. All normal children are capable of learning social skills that afford acceptance by others; academic skills that enable them to perform to the best of their abilities in school; physical skills so they can successfully execute average motor functions required to play games and sports; and moral skills that enable them to distinguish right from wrong.

Robert, to illustrate, is a C student, but he is persistent, tries hard, and doesn't give up when he gets frustrated. School work does not come easy for him, but he has developed good study skills that enable him to perform well within the average range. Robert has a wonderful sense of humor, which makes the other kids seek out his company. He is on the baseball team at school. While he is not the star player, the coach thinks of him as a very valuable player because of Robert's determination and tenacity to do well in the sport. Robert plays baseball because he really enjoys the sport, and he is always the first to compliment a team member who has executed a good play.

Martha is a B+ student. She is quite bright, and school work is easy for her. Martha, however, never seems to be quite satisfied with her work; she is a perfectionist and feels frustrated that she does not receive "As" in all her classes. Martha tries very hard to be accepted by the popular kids—she tries to associate only with those of the "in group." She emulates their interests rather than her own; tries to dress, talk, and act like the other girls; and joins the exclusive clubs to which these girls belong rather than the clubs of lesser status that hold more interest to her.

Which of these children has high inner self-esteem? Martha, who is successful, popular, talented, and bright, actually has low inner self-esteem; she is overly dependent on the approval from parents and peers, continuously compares herself to others, and pursues goals and interests of others, not her own. Robert, however, shows high inner self-esteem. He has developed good study skills that will help him as an adult; is well adjusted and secure; works hard; is persistent and responsible; and considers evaluations from others, but also depends on his own self-evaluations. He has developed skills and behaviors that enable him to feel good about himself socially, academically, physically, and morally.

I am always impressed, as I think we all are, with someone who is doing the best he or she can do (no matter what they are doing) and who takes a great deal of pride in what he or she has accomplished—a waitress, for example, who loves what she is doing and takes great pride in making the dinner a pleasant occasion; the newspaper boy who takes the extra time to place the paper on the front porch; the physically challenged child who participates in the Olympics for special children and beams with delight for having finished the race; the teacher who goes beyond reciting facts in her role as an educator. All of these are people with high inner self-esteem who are successful in achieving all that they can achieve. Their competence is not based on proving something to the world. Rather, they take pride and feel good in doing their best job for themselves. Can we ask for anything more when we see our children working and performing to the full extent of their ability and taking pride in their performances?

Being the best that we can be also involves helping children trust their own inner nature—an "accept me as I am" attitude. When I first started teaching at the college level, I felt I had to present the facade of a serious academic. Serious academics are reputedly distant, aloof, and lecture-oriented. But this is not me; this is not my style. A more casual and humorous atmosphere is more to my liking. I like having fun, even in an academic setting. So, I finally accepted this "inner nature" of mine and found teaching much more rewarding than when I was a pretend stoic. Children need to learn to do the same. As children get older, they need to develop an inner strength to accept and be content with themselves as they are. They need to hear, accept, and adopt the notion that "I am me, and I prize that differentness. I am who I am."

## Interaction of Inner and Outer Self-Esteem

Both inner and outer sources of self-esteem are interactive and interdependent, and both are necessary for high self-esteem. Outer self-esteem based on praise is more important to younger children. As children get older and feedback from parents and others becomes more dependent on children's actual behaviors and competencies, inner self-esteem takes on greater importance. Unfortunately, the more dynamic and significant dimension of self-esteem, inner self-esteem, has been almost completely neglected in self-esteem literature. Indeed, we've been brainwashed into thinking that how others evaluate and treat us is the only way we form ideas about ourselves. Many people, including educators and psychologists, still place a great deal of emphasis on outer self-esteem and believe that children's self-esteem is solely based on others' opinions of them.

As a result, most books and programs designed to help children develop healthy self-esteem, unfortunately, do not focus on inner self-esteem but rather, offer activities to help them build the reflective, outer, looking-glass self based on others' perceptions of them. For example, in a typical self-esteem activity, every child has a blank sheet of paper pinned to his or her back. Each child then moves around the room and has other members of the class write a positive comment or affirmation on his or her paper. The activity ends with each child reading these positive comments from others and then displaying them where everyone can see them. In these types of activities, children don't necessarily have to *do* anything to receive arbitrary praise from others.

How worthwhile are these activities? Not very. In fact, the overall results of intervention programs designed to enhance children's outer self-esteem (which most of them strive to do) show that they are ineffective in changing children's negative evaluations of self.[5] This is not to say that they are harmful, but they are not very effective either. Let's examine how children would be helped from an outer self-esteem perspective and from an inner self-esteem perspective.

Three-year-old Sandra was kicked out of nursery school. Sandra is incorrigible to say the least. She is nasty to the other children and often bites the other children (and teachers) when she does not get her way.

Ten-year-old Charlie is not doing well in school. What is most perplexing to his parents is that despite their efforts to help Charlie, he doesn't seem to care whether he does well or not. Charlie's mother asked if he had finished his math assignment, and Charlie said that he had. When his mother looked over his homework assignment, Charlie had written "I don't know" as his response to each of the problems on his homework assignment.

If we were working from an outer self-esteem perspective, Charlie's parents or teacher might say to him, "You are a bright student," or "You can do better if you try." Similarly, in Sandra's case, the teacher might put Sandra's picture on a bulletin board and have the students in her class write comments about what a swell kid she is. These strategies, however, are ineffective for several reasons: The children have not done anything to earn these comments, they probably will reject these "compliments" because they are inconsistent with their self-pictures, and we have not done anything to help them learn the behavior and skills needed to do better in school or become more socially acceptable.

In order to help Charlie, our ineffective learner, from an inner self-esteem perspective, we start by helping him develop the academic skills needed to do well. We would need to carefully examine and target the areas that are interfering with Charlie's academic success (lack of motivation and poor organizational skills, for example) and work out an individual plan for helping him succeed. We need to help Sandra develop social skills, such as communicating effectively with her peers and understanding their needs, as well as help her gain an understanding of how her behavior is making the other children feel. By developing their competencies, we change their self-evaluations from "I am not very smart" and "Other kids don't like me" to "I am capable" and "I am likeable," and, in turn, their self-esteem changes from positive to negative in these domains. Parents develop (or change) children's self-evaluations by helping them acquire the behavior and skills that they need to feel good about themselves socially, academically, physically, and morally. This gives rise to inner self-esteem.

## About this Book

It is my aim to help parents understand how high self-esteem is developed and how low self-esteem can be changed. Charlie and Sandra need a healthy dose of self-esteem, and learning how to administer this serum is one of our purposes here, but not just in the traditional sense of working on outer sources of self-esteem. Healthy self-esteem derives from feelings of one's own effectiveness and competence, one's sense of power or potency. We will be working on developing self-esteem that has a solid base in the children's actual character, behavior, and skills, which is the focus of the first part of this book.

We will also examine, in the first segment of the book, typical ways that children behave at various ages. By knowing what behavior to expect at different developmental levels, parents can structure their children's environment more effectively. For example, $2\frac{1}{2}$-year-olds are very rigid; they hate change and cannot make decisions. Knowing this, parents should stick to certain daytime routines and not offer these children too many choices.

Similarly, parents will learn that children have good stages when they are easy to get along with, followed by more difficult stages when the parent may wonder why he or she had kids in the first place. In general, 5-year-olds are very easy to get along with and seem very intent on pleasing their parents; 13-year-olds, however, are often extremely critical of their parents and argue for the sake of arguing. Knowing what to expect from children at various ages can also give parents some peace of mind in knowing that everything that goes wrong is not all their fault.

It is said that parenting is the most important profession, yet many parents have not received any training in this endeavor. It seems ironic that for most professions we have a minimal number of hours of required study, exams to pass, and degrees to be conferred before one is allowed to actively engage in that profession, but parenting does not require any training whatsoever. Many parents have commented, "If I only knew that earlier, I could have been a better parent." Informed parents, those who understand children and are knowledgeable about their development, will be more effective in their roles and subsequently will help their children become productive, well-adjusted individuals with healthy self-esteem.

Parents can also enhance children's inner self-esteem when they *create environments* that encourage and help children develop competent behaviors and skills in physical, social, academic, and moral domains, which is the focus of the second half of the book. Because the American family has changed significantly, conditions that foster children's self-esteem in the mid-1990s are quite different from what they were a few years ago.

Today's American family structure has changed from child-centered nuclear families to one-parent families, from one breadwinner to two. Today, two thirds of all mothers with children younger than 18 do at least some work outside the home, as do more than one half of all mothers with children under 5. In the past twenty-five years, the amount of time that parents spend with their children has dropped by 40 percent, from 30 hours a week to 17. For millions of American families, the second income means the difference between keeping or losing a tenuously maintained middle-class life.

The majority of parents are faced with many stressors and issues to be resolved. Like a pebble tossed into a pond sending concentric ripples as it hits the water, each decision parents make ushers in a whole new set of related issues and decisions. Parents today need to battle the rising costs of raising a family (a child born in the 1990s will cost $150,000 to raise to the age of 18, $100,000 more if the child completes his or her college education at a state institution). Along the same economic lines, couples today must decide (if they have a choice) whether mother should stay home with young children or work in outside paid employment. If the mother works outside the home, who will watch the children? What are the effects of full-time day care on infants and young children? Couples will also need to resolve division of labor issues. Who shall do what and when? Is there a 50–50 delineation of domestic chores and childrearing tasks in today's modern family? How do these changing lifestyles and patterns affect children's self-esteem? How can we enhance children's self-esteem in these situations? These and other important parenting concerns and issues will be addressed in the chapters that comprise the second half of the book.

To nurture self-esteem, parents need to be aware of effective styles and methods of disciplining. Family experiences greatly influence children's self-esteem—unfortunately, at times, in negative ways. Parental domination, indifference, lack of respect, disparagement, and lack of admiration and warmth are some of the ways in which children's self-esteem is lowered. Most of these parental behaviors are nonintentional and are made by parents who are not well-informed about children's development. Parents need to be informed about the important conditions in the home environment that nurture children's self-esteem. Thus, one important way to help children develop self-esteem is through effective discipline. We'll examine effective disciplining styles, the effects of punishment, the use of reinforcement, how children influence their parents, and effective and ineffective disciplining strategies.

Some children have particular needs and therefore require special conditions in order for them to develop self-esteem, and we will explore how parents can create conditions to enhance these children's inner self-esteem. We will discuss gifted children, children with handicaps, abused children, children with learning disabilities, and underachievers.

We can no longer think that the two-parent, white, middle-class family with two children and a dog named Spot is the typical family. Family lifestyles have changed significantly, as parents divorce, children live in single-parent families, and parents remarry to form blended families. The literature is inundated with negative information about the ill effects of divorce on children; how children living in single-parent families (usually headed by the mother) are doomed to face all kinds of problems, from dropping out of school to becoming delinquents; and the frailties and problems of living in a blended family. What is needed (and what will be emphasized in this book) is how parents can create positive conditions in these situations that will contribute to children developing healthy inner self-esteem. Similarly, we'll explore the conditions that foster self-esteem in less traditional families, those with same-sex parents, adoptive parents, and parents with an only child.

In addition to changing lifestyles, the mid-1990s are characterized by changing parenting patterns. Since more mothers are working outside the home, they are obviously spending less time with their children. Fathers, however, exemplary exceptions notwithstanding, rarely compensate by taking on increased responsibility. Thus, it is important for today's mothers and fathers to be aware of the conditions in a two-paycheck family that will not only help their children develop positive self-esteem but will also forge a stronger marriage.

Several decades ago, John B. Watson, the founder of the behaviorism movement in the United States, dedicated his first book on parenting with a cynical statement: "To the first mother who brings us a happy child."[6] (He believed this was an impossible feat.) The information that we now have about children would enable Watson to rededicate his book and allows me, with a great deal of confidence, to dedicate this book to the many *informed mothers and fathers* who will raise happy, well-adjusted children with healthy inner self-esteem.

# PART I  Inner Self-Esteem
## Building Children's Skills and Competencies

# CHAPTER 1  The Infancy Period
## Laying the Foundations for Inner Self-Esteem

During the infancy period, from birth to age 2, there are several developmental milestones that need to be cultivated to help infants form a firm foundation for inner self-esteem. One of the most important developmental tasks, in terms of self-development, is for the infant to develop a sense of self as a separate and distinct being. Learning that they are causal agents, that their actions have an effect on their environment, will, later on, give them a sense of control over their environment and what happens to them in that environment.

Moreover, infants and caregivers need to develop strong physical and emotional attachments so that infants will learn to trust, love, and feel secure with others when they are older. Raising children is about establishing positive relationships between caregivers and their offspring, and the optimal time to begin cultivating a solid relationship is in infancy. Learning communication skills that will enable the parent and child to experience positive feelings and mutually coordinated communiqués are a wonderful way to begin to establish these types of relationships.

You may be tempted to skip this chapter and read about older children because it's been quite some time since your child was an infant. After all, you don't need some guilt trip about what you should have done but didn't do when your child was an infant. This chapter is not intended to evoke guilt but, rather, to provide awareness of the entire self-esteem cycle. As such, this chapter is intended to serve as background information to shed light on older children. It is important to remember, however, that children are resilient and flexible. It's not as though you are walking down a one-way parenting boulevard and your child is doomed if you miss or overlook a certain parenting behavior. Helping a child develop a separate sense of self, trust and love in self and others, strong bonds with parents, and effective communication patterns does not occur over a weekend; rather, it is a continuous process. Moreover, the caring parent who reads this book probably didn't go too wrong during the infancy period—and, if not, we will discuss how you can undo any "mistakes" you may have made. First-time parents with infants, when reading this chapter, will discover the infant's amazing skills. Parents with older children may reminisce and capture some of the feelings they experienced when their child was very young. And those contemplating having another child might find this discussion useful.

## The Amazing Newborn

It was once thought that the behavior of newborns was entirely reflexive and that they lived in a world of confusing smells, sounds, and shifting shadows. We now know that this is not the case; the newborn has many amazing skills. At birth an infant's senses of sight, sound, touch, taste, and smell are nearly complete and improve rather rapidly in the first six months of life.

Infants have a fairly rigid distance of focus—approximately 10 to 12 inches. Most people don't know this, yet almost all adults (and children) will unknowingly accommodate the infant's limited field of vision by bending over close to the baby's face or bringing the baby close to their faces when communicating with the young infant. Research assessing the visual acuity in the newborn, or the ability to see clearly, has yielded mixed results. With normal acuity for adults being 20/20, estimates of newborn acuity range from 20/400 to 20/600, making the neonate legally blind in most states.[1] Acuity improves over the next several months. This slow development of the visual system, however, helps protect the infant from overstimulation. Visual acuity reaches adult levels by 6 months.

Before infants can actively explore their environment with their hands and feet, they are busy exploring with their eyes. When they encounter an interesting stimulus, newborns appear to explore the areas of greatest contrast. Newborns seem to be more sensitive to contrasting edges and contours, for example, the edge of a black line on a white background. Similarly, 1-month-old infants, when viewing a human face, scan the areas of most contrast—the hairline of the face, angles, and edges. It appears that young infants do not respond to or perceive total form, but instead react to some feature of the stimulus. At 2 months of age, children track an individual trait of the face such as a bright red mouth or shiny eyes.

Infants seem to have an inborn interest in looking at the human face.[2] Infants will stare as long as 20 minutes at a cardboard stylized face. However, when presented with a real face, the newborns appear surprised, look back at the stylized face, and return to look at the real face. When the real face continues to stare fixedly, the newborn looks worried, frowns, and turns away. The nonhuman or stylized face attracts the baby but does not carry this kind of expectation with it; the newborn, therefore, will stare at it for longer periods of time. Even at birth it appears that the newborn seems to prefer not only to look at the human face, but also has an expectation for interaction with it, a wonderful indication that we truly are social creatures from the moment of birth.

Newborns do not see colors but, rather, perceive their world in black, white, and gray. At birth, infants can see the difference between darkness and brightness. At approximately 2 weeks, however, infants will stare longer at certain colors, which indicates color recognition. Such preference suggests that the first color infants see is blue, followed by red, yellow, and green. By 6 months of age their color perception equals that of an adult.

The auditory system of the infant is fully functional from 5 months gestational age onward, which means that the infant has the ability to hear *in utero*. It has also been shown that it doesn't take a particularly loud sound to penetrate the womb and amniotic sac. Other than loud noises, the fetus may hear normal conversational sounds. Without being aware of it, parents may begin to sensitize the child to their voices even before a child is born. Perhaps this explains why babies recognize their parents' voices once they are born.

The auditory system is protected from overstimulation, and newborn infants have a high threshold for sound that decreases gradually over the first year of life. The softest sound that a newborn can hear is 10 to 20 decibels, approximately the amount you hear when you have a head cold. Infants are anywhere between 10 and 30 decibels less sensitive to sound than adults.

Infants can discriminate between loud and soft sounds and high and low ones. Young infants can detect nuances of sounds made in foreign languages that adults cannot hear. For example, Japanese babies have no trouble with the "L"–"R" distinction that their parents find difficult. Adults apparently have had long practice at learning not to hear many sounds that are not significant in their own language. This effect sets in early. Even at 1 year of age, infants have more trouble than they did earlier distinguishing sounds that are not used in their own language.

Smell is another way newborns gather information about their environment. Young infants have the ability to detect pheromones—chemical signals given off by others of the same species that communicate various messages, such as fear, identification, and so forth. Within two weeks of birth, for example, sleeping children will turn instinctively toward the breast pads worn by their own mother or a strange mother—food, any food, is essential.[3] A month later, however, one observes reduced head and arm movements in breastfed infants when their noses come into contact with breast pads worn by their mothers, signifying that the newborn can recognize the smell of his mother. This calming effect does not occur in response to odors from unfamiliar mothers.

Taste is a relatively simple sense in human beings, and the fine discriminations that we think we can make by taste alone, we actually smell. The neonate's sense of taste is reasonably well developed. Newborns display different facial expressions, tongue movements, and physiological responses for each of the four basic tastes of sweet, sour, salty, and bitter. Place food on the infant's tongue and you will find that she shows a preference for sweet substances. It has been found, for example, that when babies 2 to 3 days old are given a tiny amount of sugar water every time they make a sucking motion, the babies tend to suck more slowly and the heart rates tend to increase.[4] Why do they suck slower? Wouldn't you think they would suck faster? Perhaps babies suck slower in order to savor the sweeter liquid, and perhaps the excitement of tasting it increases the heart rate. Then again, perhaps the answer is not that simple.

Little research has been done on infants' perception of pain—after all, no one wants to hurt tiny newborns. However, if you have ever observed an infant's reaction to a blood test (usually done by pricking the baby's heel with a small stylet), you would assume, as he jerks back his foot and wails with anguish, that he is aware of pain. Similarly, after circumcision, a newborn's sleeping patterns are often disturbed, and there is a prolonged period of fussiness.[5] We know that babies are sensitive to touch, because most of the early reflexes are triggered by touching various parts of the body.

Excluding prenatal development, the two periods of greatest physical growth and development are infancy and adolescence. In fact, infants' physical development is so rapid that their size and skills appear to change daily. During infancy, the average child grows from 20 inches to 34 inches in length and from a birth weight of 7 to 8 pounds to a full 28 pounds. Weight changes during the first year of life are more dramatic than height changes.[6]

Much of the complex motor behavior children use later in life is exhibited in early infancy in the form of reflexes. These involuntary, autonomic responses are the building blocks of later motor behavior. By 8 months, children crawl, stand with help, use the thumb in grasping, and pick up small objects. Around 36 to 40 weeks, children can pull themselves up on furniture; by 48 weeks many children can stand alone and begin walking shortly thereafter.

In the beginning, an infant has no language other than crying. Although the newborn behaves in ways that can be very informative to the skilled observer or parent, there is no intention to transmit information and no expectation of any effect on the world as a result of this behavior. Obviously, the infant's cry may have a communicative value, but it appears that in the first nine months, this behavior is, from the infant's point of view, merely a built-in reaction to an internal state.[7] Although cries may not be purposeful, behavioral expressions of internal states may still be necessary for the establishment of later intentional communication systems.

The sound of a baby crying is not easy to ignore, nor should parents ignore the infant's cries. Crying is an important means of communication—the only means available to an infant. Something is bothering the infant; he may be hungry, frightened, cold, or just lonesome for you.

The notion still persists that if we've exhausted all possible things that could be wrong—that is, if we have changed, fed, checked to see if the infant is too warm or too cold, and so forth—the infant should be laid down gently, but firmly, to let it cry. Some parents have been told that if you pick up a baby and he or she stops crying, you will be encouraging the infant to cry in the future. In my opinion, that is nonsense! In fact, just the opposite occurs; the child cries less and learns to communicate with cooing sounds. As noted, crying is expressing a need. The infant may just need to be held. Letting the baby cry alone is a mistake. The comfort and security extended by a parent's loving arms is never wasted. The infant's need to be lovingly held when upset is as strong and important as the infant's need for food.

Children typically do not say their first words until approximately 10 to 12 months of age, but these words are preceded by a history of vocalization. By 2 months, infants have developed the musculature to produce certain sounds basic to language. With increased control of the tongue and mouth, a baby progresses from cooing to babbling to the one-word stage.

During the first two years of life, infants make major strides in the acquisition of knowledge about their social world. Behaviors such as fear of strangers, separation anxiety, formation of specific attachments, and the onset of communicative skills are all reflections of this. Although infants do not have friends in the usual sense of the term, it is interesting to note that play between familiar babies (those who have had regular contact with each other) is more interactive and their social behaviors more synchronized than between unfamiliar infants.[8]

Young infants have been neurally primed to be aware of and responsive to the emotional signals of their caregivers.[9] In other words, infants are prepared to respond affectively to others. Very young infants react in emotionally different ways to objects and people. When infants are presented with an object, for example, they will look intently at it, sit up straight, remain relatively still, and punctuate their fixed gaze with swiping movements and brief glances away. When presented with people, infants' postures are more relaxed and their movements are smoother. They become active at a slower pace and then look away for longer periods of time than they do with objects. Furthermore, infants give full greeting responses to people but not to objects. Simply stated, infants communicate with people and act instrumentally (not socially) toward objects.

Young infants can also discriminate the facial expressions of others. Infants will look more at facial expressions of joy than of anger. Infants as young as 10 weeks old react to maternal facial and vocal displays of anger with anger but have fewer angry responses when their mothers pose sadness. Moreover, infant reactions are even influenced by their appreciation of the context surrounding the event; for example, a mother wearing a mask elicits laughter, whereas a stranger wearing the same mask elicits distress and fear.

The emotional states of pleasure, rage, startlement, and distress appear in the first three months of life. The social smile, appearing at 3 months, may indicate pleasure, and laughter, appearing a month later, is thought to indicate delight. Affection and love for parents becomes particularly strong between 9 and 12 months of age. Fear, in the first months of life, is caused by loss of support (falling) and loud noises.

During the infancy period, children develop from activity-oriented thinking (thinking and doing at the same time) to symbol-oriented thinking (thoughts can be internalized, and infants can think before they act). The understanding that things and people continue to exist even when they are not present or when children cannot see them (object permanence) develops gradually over the first two years of life.

## Typical Behavior during the First Two Years of Life

In the first month of life infants attain a working physiological adjustment to their postnatal environment. They now breathe regularly and calmly since their heart has steadied. The most adaptive muscles are those of the eyes and mouth. A slight touch on the mouth will cause their lips to purse and make sucking motions. At 3 months, infants experience a brief period of disequilibrium; sleeping may not be smooth and they may experience feeding problems and exhibit crying spells. At 7 months, infants can sit with support and grasp and hold objects, and they will spend several moments during the day in active manipulatory exploration. Stranger anxiety may appear for some children during this period.

When infants are 12 months old, they are able to pull themselves to a standing position and cruise sideways as they hold to a support. Some 1-year-olds have acquired a few independent behaviors such as feeding themselves and cooperating for dressing. They enjoy expeditions outside the home. They love games like peek-a-boo and pat-a-cake. One-year-olds love audiences and will give command performances without much coaxing. They love to look at themselves in mirrors, sitting for long periods of time in front of the mirror gazing at their wonderful faces.

The 15-month-old child has limitless energy. She gets over, under, in, around, and through everything imaginable. She will only be happy in her playpen for a short period of time—approximately as long as it takes her to throw out the toys that are contained therein. Some children have given up the bottle and can awkwardly hold a cup.

By 18 months, the child can walk steadily and may run with a stiff, propulsive, flat gait. Many children begin to experience the first serious demands of parents. While disciplining efforts by parents have occurred earlier, many parents make a more concerted effort to direct their children's behavior. As the child approaches the second year of life, he moves from activity-oriented thinking to internal thinking. We see an explosion of vocabulary. Children are generally loving and affectionate.

## The Emerging Self

During infancy, the child's major task in terms of self-development is to learn to differentiate self from others and to come to see self as an active, independent, and causal agent. With time, children are better able to distinguish between people and things and between themselves and others. They begin to acquire an increased awareness of their personal identity and resources. Children notice that things from the outside world act on them, and they, in turn, act on and influence objects and people in their environment.

At first infants have a simple, poorly defined image of themselves and the world. The infant experiences a simple stream of impressions that gradually become discriminated as the child differentiates self or "me" from "not me." Margaret Mahler, a psychoanalytical theorist, suggests that infants are born with no sense of identity.[10] Their sense of self is totally fused with that of their caregivers, and it is only in the course of development that children develop a sense of their own boundaries and identities.

In the first month of life, continues Mahler, infants lack awareness of a nurturing agent. During this phase of self-development, physiological processes dominate, and there is a minimal responsiveness to the external environment. Between 2 and 4 months, the infant exists in a symbiotic fusion with the caregiver, unable to recognize a sense of separateness from mother. From 5 to 9 months, infants slowly hatch out of their symbiotic union with their caregivers and begin to form a sense of self as a separate being. From Mahler's perspective, this is not a sense of "who I am" but a sense of "I am"—that I exist as a separate, distinct entity. Key signs of this differentiation are infants' staring at their body parts. Infants seem mesmerized as they watch their hand open and close and their fingers wiggle. (They are only dimly aware that they are producing these actions.) Some infants stare for a long time to contemplate these newly discovered bits of self.

Around 10 to 15 months, when children are learning to walk, they learn to distance themselves from their caregivers. Later, at 15 to 22 months, children continue to practice moving away from their care-givers, with assurance that their caregivers will be there should they need reassurance and nurturing. Finally, between 22 and 36 months, children attain a distinct sense of individuality.

Several experiences contribute to the emergence of self as a sepa-rate and causal being, or "I," as it is sometimes called. Regular and con-sistent feedback between their actions and the effects of their actions are important experiences for the development of a separate sense of identity. In other words, infants learn cause and effect: If they do some-thing, a certain consequence or action will follow. The infant strikes at the mobile hanging over the crib, for example, gradually learning that the action of striking the object causes it to swing back and forth. Thus, they begin to realize that they are causal agents. Regular and consistent feedback provides the basis for establishing general expectancies about their world and their control over it. Such expectancies help infants dif-ferentiate their actions from the actions of others.

Social interactions with the caregiver provide extensive feedback and form an even stronger basis for the development of a separate sense of self than do actions with inanimate objects. The feedback given by mother provides a generalized expectancy about control over the world. Infants cry and their caregivers respond by picking them up and cud-dling them. Gradually, children learn that crying brings their caregivers. The consistency, timing, and quality of the caregivers' responsiveness to the infants' cues create powerful expectancies for the infants and their control of and competence in the social environment.

Developing a sense of control over one's environment has its rudi-mentary beginnings in infancy. However, as noted earlier, establishing the child's sense of control is an ongoing process. More will be said about establishing a sense of control in the chapters on early and mid-dle childhood.

## Self-Esteem in Baby Boys and Baby Girls

Different parental belief systems about boys and girls lead to dif-ferent ways of behaving toward them and to different self-esteem sys-tems in males and females. Newborns enter a world in which there are well-developed belief systems with associated expectations, hopes, and desires on the part of their parents. Perhaps the most well-researched issue concerns the beliefs that parents hold in connection with the sex of the child. Studies have shown that, even from conception, the baby elicits stereotyped sex-related responses and treatment because of its gender. Characteristics that are perceived as more masculine (e.g., big, sturdy, hungry, curious, vigorous, irritated) are more often attributed to the baby if it is believed to be a boy. Feminine attributes (e.g., pretty, cute, little, fine-featured, cuddly) are given to the baby if it is believed to be a girl. If the baby is active, it is believed to be a boy; if inactive, it is believed to be a girl.

Similarly, it has been found that parents describe their newborn sons and daughters in different ways.[11] Each baby in these studies had been routinely examined after birth by hospital personnel for physical and neurological characteristics such as muscle tone, reflexes, and irritability. No objective differences between males and females, even in size, were found. Yet, there are important differences in the way parents of girls and parents of boys described their newborns. The parents of the girls rated their babies as softer, more fine-featured, smaller, and more inattentive than did parents of boys. Fathers were particularly influenced by the gender of the child; they described their sons as firm, large-featured, well-coordinated, alert, strong, and hard. Men described their daughters as inattentive, weak, and delicate.

Moreover, parents tend to respond differently toward their sons and daughters during infancy. They tend to respond more quickly to a crying girl than a crying boy, offer "masculine" toys for boys and "feminine" toys for girls, and encourage more motor activity for boys and "nurturance play" for girls.[12] Parental belief systems and actions tend to be reflected in children's behavior. When given a choice of toys, for example, 19-month-old children consistently pick toys that are "appropriate" to their sex—boys choose trucks and little girls flock to the dolls.

## Building Inner Self-Esteem during Infancy

During infancy several of the child's needs must be met so that the infant's self-esteem will grow and develop. Physical needs notwithstanding, the infant's psychological needs fall into social and cognitive areas. In order for children to develop positive self-esteem in the social domain, infants must develop strong emotional bonds with their principal caregiver and learn to develop a sense of trust in others. Cognitively, infants need to be provided with a stimulating environment and the freedom to be curious in that environment.

## Building Strong Attachment Bonds

One of the most important developments during the infancy period is the formation of strong bonds of attachment between parents and children. Children who have developed a strong physical and emotional bond with their caregivers are considered securely attached; those children who have not developed strong bonds with their caregivers are referred to as insecurely attached. An important part of attachment research has centered on the quality of children's attachment to their caregivers, which has been consistently related to various aspects of children's functioning, including their basic survival, sociability, self-esteem, and cognitive abilities.

According to John Bowlby, a British psychologist, attachment between caregiver and infant is crucial to the infant's survival.[13] So important is this bond, Bowlby maintains, that situations that endanger the bond elicit actions on the part of the infant to preserve it. When these efforts are successful, the bond is restored. When they are not, sooner or later the effort wanes. Psychologist Rene Spitz, several decades ago, observed infants in institutions.[14] Although these infants were physically taken care of—diapered and fed—they did not have affectionate interactions with their caregivers. Some of these infants became very apathetic; showed an unsmiling, waxy gaze; and withdrew. In these extreme kinds of conditions, when young children are not exposed to consistent, loving treatment (are not held, touched, or caressed) or when they exist in an unstimulating, dull, affectionless world, they may fail to develop, may sicken, or may even die. Bowlby maintains, then, that the basic purpose of attachment is to keep children alive.

Important as its protective function is, attachment works in other ways to help children develop essential social and cognitive skills. Though theorists have their many differences, many approve of Freud's dictum that the mother-infant relationship is unique, without parallel, established unalterably as the prototype of all later love relations. All of children's later choices in the realms of friendship and love follow on the basis of memory traces left behind by these prototypes. A leading researcher in attachment, Mary Ainsworth, concurs by saying that children who do not form bonding ties as infants may suffer from a lifelong inability to establish and maintain deep significant interpersonal relationships.[15]

Bowlby suggests that infants and young children develop an *inner working model* of self and others. This is more than the learning of roles;

rather, children internalize the very nature of relationships themselves. Thus, in experiencing sensitive caregiving, the securely attached child not only learns to expect care, but also more generally learns that when a person is in need, another responds empathically. The inner working model that is formed during infancy and early childhood serves as the basis for the construction of subsequent relationships. The insecurely attached child develops a working model of parents as rejecting or inconsistently responsive. Either of these conditions could have deleterious consequences on their self-esteem and relations with others. Children who do not develop secure attachment relationships tend to see themselves as unlovable and others as rejecting and unresponsive. Insecure children will reenact aspects of their nonnurturant caregiver role in their interactions with each other.

In contrast, children who develop secure attachments are able to develop a sense of trust in themselves and others, which is vital to the development of inner self-esteem. Impressions of the infant, gained both from informal observation and empirical research, suggest that this trust emerges through numerous interactional activities between the caregiver and the child. As infants learn that parents are reliable and predictable, the sense of trust generalizes to other people and helps determine the quality of future interactions with others. According to Erik Erikson, learning that certain others can be relied on is the foundation for positive self-esteem.[16]

There is a vital link between quality of children's attachment to caregivers and developmental outcomes in social areas. Young children who have developed a secure attachment with their caregivers during infancy tend to be more socially active, are sought after by other children, exhibit more leadership qualities, and are more sympathetic to other children than same-age children who have not developed a secure attachment relationship with their caregivers.

Children labeled securely attached as infants tend to be more satisfied, more resourceful, and more able to be occupied when alone; have better relationships with people; and are more capable of age-appropriate behavior than children labeled as insecurely attached. Young children with secure attachments to their mothers play more harmoniously with peers than insecurely attached toddlers. Securely attached children are less likely to fight and more likely to share with others. Children with secure attachment histories tend to have many friends, more often select as partners other children with secure attachment histories, and experience deeper friendships.[17]

Compared to securely attached children, insecurely attached children are less competent, less sympathetic in interaction with their peers, more fearful of strangers, too dependent on adults, and more prone to behavior problems, including social withdrawal. Infants classified as insecure have been rated by preschool teachers as less empathic, less compliant, less cooperative, and exhibiting more negative emotions and less self-control than securely attached agemates. Boys classified as insecurely attached are seen by both peers and teachers as being less socially competent (more aggressive, showing more behavior problems) than are securely attached children.

Other studies have found no relation between attachment classification and problem behaviors during preschool, which may indicate that infants are neither made invulnerable by secure attachment nor are they doomed by insecure attachment to later psychopathology.[18]

The attachment classification of insecure-avoidant has been discussed most often as a predictor of future problems. These infants are unable to develop a complete sense of trust and confidence in mothers' availability. Many avoid interaction or contact with their mothers by averting their gaze, ignoring their mothers' solicitations, or actually moving away from their mothers. The child who uses avoidance to cope with stress is assumed to be masking anger. Jay Belsky at Pennsylvania State University suggests that this lack of trust in the attachment figure and the anger of the child in the insecure-avoidant class place children at risk for subsequent social difficulties, with lack of compliance, lack of cooperation, and increased aggressiveness.[19]

In the cognitive realm, attachment to the caregiver is seen as providing a secure and safe base from which the infant can move in order to explore the environment. Wariness provides the motivation to terminate exploration and seek proximity to the attachment figure when the environment is seen as threatening. Infants designated as secure differ significantly from insecure infants in their ability to use caregivers as a secure base from which to explore in the home.

Similarly, infants move and explore more freely and exhibit less negative emotions in a novel environment when in the presence of the attachment figure. Infants who are securely attached are more independent than insecurely attached infants and are thus more likely to leave their mothers' sides and explore the environment. This increased exploration, in turn, can produce a more intelligent child.[20]

Securely attached toddlers more often engage in symbolic play, are more enthusiastic and teachable in simple tasks, exhibit fewer frustration-related behaviors, and are more sophisticated in negotiating coordinated problem solving with caregivers than insecurely attached toddlers. These cognitive differences remain into the fourth year in exploratory tasks requiring social coordinations with caregivers and in academic tasks in which the caregiver teaches the child simple skills.

Young children who are classified as securely attached show increased effort during a competitive game with an adult (e.g., building a tower) following "failure" feedback (the adult's tower is bigger than the child's). In contrast, young children who are classified as insecurely attached show a corresponding decrease in effort as a result of failure feedback.

Evidence is not entirely clear as to why healthy emotional relationships can increase cognitive functioning. Although the results point to a relationship between quality of attachment and later cognitive competence, some caution is necessary in interpreting this relationship. It is unlikely that being securely attached causes children to be more intellectually advanced; rather, securely attached children may have some other factors in common:

1.  Mothers who have good relationships with their children may be especially encouraged to engage them and support them in solving problems.
2.  Children in these relationships may also be more competent and hence more willing to accept tutelage and maternal assistance.
3.  Children use stable emotional relationships as a base for exploring the wider world.

Evidence is accumulating from dozens of reports on numerous samples that secure attachment between caregivers and children may be correlated with children's later social and cognitive behavior.

## Developmental Progression of Attachment

Attachment between caregivers and children does not occur suddenly; rather, it develops gradually. Bowlby first distinguished four phases of the development of attachment and Ainsworth has elaborated on these developmental phases.[13] The first phase, known as the *initial preattachment phase*, occurs from birth to 3 months. The infant is attracted to all social objects and begins to prefer humans to inanimate objects. During the first three months of life infants do not form specific attachments. Anyone's warm arms and cuddles are welcome. Around 3 or 4 months, the *attachment-in-the-making phase*, infants begin to discriminate among the adults with whom they come into contact. Children make a clear distinction between familiar and unfamiliar figures, smiling and vocalizing more to familiar figures than to strangers. In the third phase, the *clear-cut-attachment phase* that takes place around 6 or 7 months, children develop specific, intense attachments, usually, but not always, to their mothers. Strong indications of this attachment are children's fear of strangers and separation anxiety.

Stranger anxiety begins around 6 months, reaches a peak at 8 to 10 months, and generally disappears around 15 months of age. Many babies show a pronounced fear of unfamiliar people. At the approach of an unfamiliar person, infants are likely to scream, bury their faces in caregivers' laps, or clutch dramatically at the caregiver. This is not a universal characteristic of infancy; its presence or absence is determined by a complex set of factors. Why are some children afraid of strangers and others not? It has been proposed that those youngsters who have been exposed to only a very limited variety of caregivers are more likely to show stranger anxiety. Cosmopolitan children who have been close to a diversity of people are less likely to show stranger anxiety.

Not only do children cry when a strange person enters the room, but they also become unhappy when a familiar person (mother or father) leaves the room. This desire for the familiar person to remain near makes its appearance at about 8 to 12 months and reaches its peak at about 2 years. This phenomenon has often been referred to as separation anxiety. Between the ages of 2 and 3 years, children generally become less fearful when their parents leave.

The intensity of separation anxiety is influenced by many factors. Young children are more likely to cry when left in an unfamiliar place, such as at a new babysitter's house. In addition, seeing mothers leave through an unfamiliar exit rather than a familiar one (e.g., leaving via the patio door rather than the front door) produces a more intense response. Leaving children with someone familiar produces less anxiety than leaving children with an unfamiliar person.

Ainsworth labels the fourth phase in the development of attachment the *goal-directed partnership phase* (7 months to 1 year).[15] Children begin to understand caregivers' goals, feelings, and points of view and are able to adjust their behaviors accordingly. In this phase, children become attached to more than one person. Multiple attachments occur as many young children show affectional bonds toward older brothers and sisters, grandparents, and regular babysitters.

## The Infant's Contributions to the Attachment Process

What pulls caregivers and infants together? This fascinating question can be answered by examining the interaction between them. Today, researchers recognize that caregivers and infants engage in a constant two-way flow of influence and that the relationship is an interactive one. Harmony depends on the adaptive abilities of both caregivers and children. Caregivers must be sensitive to the infants' behaviors, *and* infants must be socially responsive and provide feedback to the caregivers.

**Crying.**    Infants' cries have a uniquely potent and predictable effect on adults. Crying may communicate messages to adult listeners, even in the absence of parental experience. On hearing infants cry, adults experience physiological arousal and usually translate this arousal into an attempt to relieve the infant's distress. Picking up infants usually terminates the crying, which helps caregivers feel competent in their role. The distress–relief situation facilitates the development of an emotionally positive relationship and represents the origins of strong attachment bonds.

Moreover, these early and simple interactions centered on relief of infants' distress seem to advance the developing sociability of infants. If the distress–relief sequence is sufficiently predictable, infants may develop expectations concerning the probability of their caregivers' responses, permitting them to develop a sense of their own efficacy. Perceived control develops when infants recognize that they are able to elicit certain responses predictably from the environment.

**Gazing.**    Mutual gaze emerges sometime between the third and sixth week, just prior to the first social smile. The visual system provides one of the most powerful networks for the mediation of caregiver attachment. Mothers of blind infants, for example, report that they encounter more difficulties in feeling close to their infants when gazing is not possible.[21] Without the affirmation of mutual gazing, mothers feel lost and like strangers to their babies until both learn to substitute other means of communication. The general sequence of attachment, however, is the same for blind and sighted infants, although somewhat delayed for the former. Apparently, blind infants need to make use of other senses to organize early social relations. For example, when blind infants are able to respond to their caregivers through recognition of their touch or voice, bonding is strengthened.

Infants' gazing does have an effect on the caregivers' attachment to the children. The responses of fixation and visual pursuit are present soon after birth and rapidly become important in the infant–caregiver tie. For various reasons (developmental lags, poor vision), if children are unable to manage or maintain mutual gaze, caregivers are likely to feel estranged from them.

**Communicating.**    An essential principle of attachment is that parents must receive some response or signal from their infants, such as body or eye movements, to form a close bond. Exciting observations reveal that newborns move in tune with the structure of adult speech. When the caregiver and infant are observed "communicating" with each other, both the listener and the speaker are moving in tune with the words of the speakers, creating a type of dance. As the speaker pauses for a breath or to accent a syllable, the infant almost imperceptibly raises an eyebrow or lowers a foot. When infants are alert, they are ready to dance to mother's speech and movements.

**Smiling.**    During the first few weeks of life, smiles are seen during light sleep and drowsiness, rarely when the baby is awake and alert. These are called endogenous or spontaneous smiles because they bear no relation to the external world. Smiles occur when babies are aroused and then relax. As the baby relaxes, facial muscles relax too and for a brief moment a contented grin appears.

Social smiling is established between the second week and the second month of life. Smiles triggered by something in the external world are called exogenous smiles. The smile may be elicited by the sight of a toy or a human face, familiar or strange. At around 4 months, infants can distinguish between familiar and unfamiliar faces, smiling at the former and staring or frowning at the latter. This guarded reaction to unfamiliar faces, called wariness, and smiling at the familiar ones is a vital landmark in the development of attachment (perhaps more so for parents than for children). Smiling may serve to keep caregivers near infants; it is gratifying to the caregivers so they stay close, thereby ensuring that the infants receive the care they need. Not only are children's smiles produced by external stimuli, but for the first time they may also be instrumental; that is, they are produced in order to get a smile back.

**Locomotive Skills.**    Between 6 and 24 months, because of their increased locomotive skills (crawling and walking), infants now actively seek proximity to their caregivers. They begin to make purposeful efforts to stay close. Young toddlers also seek proximity by calling to their caregivers from another room, requesting assistance or company.

It can be seen that infants engage in certain behaviors that help them secure contact with those vital people in their environments who are necessary for providing protection, shelter, and food. The fact that such a small being can elicit positive (and negative) responses from parents tells us something about the powerful role that infants play in establishing attachment relationships.

## Caregivers' Contributions to the Attachment Process

Ainsworth's attachment theory is based on three premises:

1. During the first year of life, infants develop an emotional tie with the person who provides primary care.
2. The quality of this relationship is significantly influenced by the nature of interactions between caregivers and infants.
3. The quality of attachment between infants and caregivers sets up expectations (caregivers' availability and predictability) for future social interactions.[22]

Ainsworth maintains that it is the caregivers' consistent perceptions and accurate interpretations of the infant's signals and their sensitive and appropriate response to these signals that nurture the development of security. Synchrony is a key word in describing the type of relationship between caregivers and infants. Synchrony reflects an interactive experience between infants and caregivers; it reflects an appropriate fit between caregivers' and infants' behavior. Psychologists presume it derives from sensitive responsiveness and helps foster a state of social harmony. Caregivers of securely attached infants respond sensitively (promptly and appropriately) to their infants' needs. These sensitive parents are able to perceive and accurately interpret their infants' communications and are thus more responsive to their infants' needs. Conversely, insecure attachments are thought to develop as a function of caregivers' inconsistent or negligent perceptions, interpretations, and responses to infants' signals (i.e., insensitivity). Maternal intrusiveness, unresponsiveness, and inconsistency characterize interaction of insecure dyads.

## Sensitive Periods

Sensitive periods are timeframes during which an event must occur in order for desired behaviors to appear. For example, little chicks will bond with the first thing that they see moving, usually their mother. If chicks do not see their mother moving when they hatch, they will not bond with her. Some researchers maintain that there is a sensitive period for parent–infant contact, noting that the first few minutes or hours of life are crucial in the development of attachment. But there is a big difference between chicks and children.

Infants are in a quiet alert state for a period of 45 to 60 minutes immediately after birth. In this state infants' eyes are wide open, and they are able to respond to their environment. They can see; they have visual preferences and will turn their heads toward sounds. After this hour, the exhausted newborn sleeps for 3 to 4 hours.

Does the bond between mother and child begin during the first hour after birth? Most probably it *begins* then, but this hour is not the only time for developing bonding behaviors. After all, it wasn't long ago that it was common hospital practice to give the mother a brief glance at her child and then whisk the baby off to be checked, washed, and clothed. If this is *the* time for bonding then many of us who were born when this was the usual hospital procedure would not have formed secure attachments.

Of course, the same would be true for premature infants, and this is simply not the case. The attachment process is complex and ongoing. Bonding with premature infants, however, may be more difficult because these infants need special care and monitoring. Consequently, parents are often unable to touch, hold, feed, or play with their newborns. Parents are often forced into a supporting, peripheral position that makes bonding harder. In some cases of premature birth, there are difficulties in the formation of this bond because the physical problems and needs of premature infants interfere with a mother's attempts to interact with her child. For example, premature babies tend to be more irritable than their full-term counterparts. They show a lag in social smiling; are less ready to withstand the stimulation that occurs in playful, face-to-face interaction; and show more gaze aversion. They also sleep a greater proportion of the time and are less alert and responsive when awake. Their motor organization is poorer, and their states of arousal are less well-modulated. In sum, with premature infants, caregivers are faced with less adept social partners and need to be more patient in establishing strong attachment bonds.[23]

Premature infants need to be touched, rocked, or cuddled daily during their hospital stay. Those who receive this special care by a consistent caregiver have fewer apneic periods (short interruptions in breathing pattern), show increased weight gain, and show an advance in some areas of higher central nervous system functioning that persists for months after discharge from the hospital than their counterparts who have not received such treatment.

Parents need to know that, despite their size, many premature infants are strong little ones. Parents should discuss their fears and concerns for the health of their babies with their doctors. In addition, parents of premature infants need hospitals to provide flexible visiting policies, allow mother and father to share the responsibilities of caring for their infants, and offer not only advice for caring but also emotional support.

In the case of parent–infant attachment, sensitive periods are relative; that is, the length of time defining the sensitive period is more flexible. Bonding requires more than a brief exposure between parent and child. This is not to say that early and extended contact is unimportant. Babies develop best when in their earliest contacts with their caregivers they are given loving, responsive care. This emphasis on early bonding may create an expectation on the part of many parents that if they do not have this experience they have somehow failed and will never be fine parents. For all those who cannot or have not had these experiences, it is important to emphasize that the parent–infant relationship is a complex system with many fail-safe or alternative routes to the same outcomes. Its success or failure does not hinge on a few brief moments in time.

## Fathers and Attachment Relations

Only recently has the role of fathers in the attachment process been examined. A decade or so ago, researchers appeared to be content in assuming that the sole relationship enjoyed by young infants was that with their mothers. Increasingly, there has been a developing interest in the earliest stages of interaction, with observations of the father often beginning during his wife's pregnancy.

*The Prenatal Period.*    The expectant father, like the mother-to-be, shows a wide variety of reactions during his wife's pregnancy. The struggle for the expectant male during the prenatal period is to remain emotionally available to his wife and at the same time meet his own needs for feeling responsible and productive. In this regard, there is an association between the husband's responsiveness to his wife's pregnancy and her successful adaptation to it, which may help the mother feel more positive toward her newborn child. Moreover, fathers who attend prenatal classes have been observed to be more comfortable in giving care to their infants.[24]

*Birth Attendance.*    Fathers' potential role in childbirth has evolved from one of an unnecessary source of infection to an essential source of affection for both mother and newborn. Since the early 1980s, the concept of fathers attending the birth of their children has gained wide acceptance, and popular beliefs indicate that birth attendance plays a significant role in the development of father–child attachment. No conclusive evidence has been reported, however, that strongly suggests that bonding develops as a result of fathers' attending the birth of their child.

The emotional quality of the birth experience is the most significant predictor of the father's attachment to his infant.[25] While many fathers report pleasure and excitement at being present at birth, which can increase their feelings of self-esteem and self-worth, many find birth shocking and overwhelming emotionally. Fathers who attend their child's birth *and* experience positive emotions during delivery receive higher attachment scores with their infants than fathers who do not attend birth or who attend birth but experience negative emotions.

A father's presence at delivery is considered valuable because of his support of the mother during labor and delivery. When fathers are present, mothers relax more, experience less pain, and hence need less medication and have shorter labors.

Fathers' presence at birth has not been shown to have any long-term impact. Fathers who are committed to being involved with their children may show their commitment in many ways, including finding out about childbirth and attending classes, supporting their partner during pregnancy, holding and interacting with their newborns, and taking an active part in the day-to-day care of the infant. A father's presence may be seen positively by the mother as an indicator of father's acceptance of and interest in the child, and this may be built on in terms of parental closeness and joint interest in the child and the father's sense of competence around the child.

*Early Contact.*    Some researchers believe that the father must have extensive early exposure to the infant in the hospital, where the parent–infant bond is initially formed.[26] There is a lot of learning that goes on between mother and child in the hospital from which the father is often excluded. New mothers as well as new fathers must learn caring skills. The father needs to be included not only so that he will have the interest in and a feeling of closeness to his child, but also so that he can develop the kinds of skills that the mother is developing.

We have no conclusive evidence that attending birth and early extended contacts between father and infants promote strong attachment bonds. Some researchers, medical personnel, and the media, however, have overstated the benefits of birth attendance, saying that early contact leads to strong attachments between fathers and their infants. Although such a belief seems harmless if it increases fathers' involvement in child care and childrearing, it does create some problems if a large proportion of fathers feel guilty over missing their child's birth. We need to take a more balanced approach, one in which fathers, in consultation with their partners, choose, in all stages of the parenting process, levels of involvement that are consistent with their skills, desires, and perceived roles.

*A Preference for Father?*    Studies of infant–father attachment parallel those of infant–mother attachment; that is, they investigate infants' reactions to strangers and separations. In a stress-free home environment (when babies are not anxious or fearful) there is no indication that either parent can be described as a primary or preferred attachment figure. Across the second year of life, significant preferences for fathers occurred among boys. Girls are much less consistent—some prefer their mothers, some their fathers, some both parents or neither parent. The emergent preferences for fathers on the part of sons may be due partially to the tendency of fathers to be more attentive to their sons, especially immediately following birth and after their first birthday. Almost all children show some attachment behavior to both parents. It appears, however, that in stressful situations, when infants have a choice, they choose their mothers.

## Attachment beyond Infancy

Some mothers may have experienced more pain than elation when their children were born. Some mothers may have been ill or have suffered from other extenuating circumstances and as a result may have been unable to care for their child as well as they may have wanted to. Some fathers may not have read reams of psychological literature on caring for infants, and they may not have attended their children's birth.

In fact, some fathers (due to separation, divorce, business travel, military service, and so forth) may have been away from home more often than they were there. Some infants may not have been very cuddly, compliant, and responsive to their caregivers. If these or other situations occurred, it is important for these parents to know that the quality of attachment can change even when early attachment is poor or nonexistent.[27]

The quality of the parent–child bond can be strengthened in various ways. Parental nurturance is an important factor. Spending time with children, quality time as the phrase goes, helps establish positive bonds between children and caregivers. Even short periods of time (10 to 15 minutes a day) on a one-to-one basis with children is helpful. Parents can talk with their children about the child's concerns or what's happening in his or her life or just engage in fun, interactive activities.

Being responsive to children's needs as well as balancing your needs as a parent leads to sensitivity and stronger attachment bonds. In addition, receiving some practical and emotional support from community, religious, or civic groups may be important. This is particularly true if your child tends to be somewhat difficult, irritable, or noncompliant. Moreover, in these situations, parents need to be persistent in their affectionate overtures and exhibit high levels of patience. Finally, it is important to believe in your competence as a parent. If parents think of themselves as competent in their role, they are more likely to be sensitive and caring.

## Foundations of Children's Social Self-Esteem: Developing a Sense of Trust

Another important social need that must be met for future self-esteem is helping children develop a sense of trust. Beginnings of self-esteem relate to the development of trust in the primary caregiver. The goal of giving the infant a feeling of being loved and cared for is, according to Erik Erikson, the single most important goal in getting a child off to a good start in life.[16] Erikson proposed that human development consists of a series of periods in which some issue is particularly prominent and important. In his view, individuals experience a psychosocial crisis or conflict during each of eight psychosocial stages. A crisis is a turning point—a period when the potential for growth is high but when the person is also quite vulnerable. Erikson sees a crisis as a struggle between attaining some adaptive psychological quality versus failing to obtain it. Individuals negotiate each stage by developing a balance, or ratio, between the two qualities for which that stage is named. Successful negotiation of a stage, however, does imply the balance is weighted more toward the positive value than the negative value.

Successful resolution in each of these stages strengthens the ego and prepares the child to face the next crisis. Inadequate resolution invariably affects a person's ability to function and to cope. Failure or difficulty in establishing what is required at one stage does not condemn anyone to complete failure in the next stage, although developmental progress can be slowed or made more difficult to achieve. Thus, a crisis is not resolved once and then forgotten. Rather, resolutions of previously encountered conflicts are reshaped at each new stage of psychosocial development.

The first psychosocial stage, which Erikson labeled the "cornerstone of the vital personality," is known as "Basic Trust vs. Mistrust" (birth to age 2).[16] The infant's task is to reach out to the social environment for nurturance with the expectation that his or her longing will be satisfied. The degree of trust that infants develop depends on the quality of care they receive. Parents need to cuddle, play, and talk to their infants. They need to meet children's physical and psychological needs when they arise and remove discomforts quickly, so that children can develop a vital sense of trust that the world is safe and reliable. Moreover, parents need to have confidence in their parenting skills. Parents' confidence in themselves helps the infant establish feelings of trust and security in self and others. Infants who receive inconsistent and unreliable care from their parents develop a basic mistrust, which may lead, in adulthood, to a basic fear and withdrawal from interpersonal contact and a dread that one's social needs cannot or will not be met. An adult who experienced the conditions for trust during infancy greets the world with fundamental hope; one who did not greets the world with a sense of doom.

A sense of trust can be established after the infancy period. The best way to establish trust in older children is to mean what you say and follow through with what you say. If you say to your child that he can have friends over Friday night, you should keep that commitment. If you're going to make a Halloween costume for your daughter, you need to follow through. By establishing yourself as one who means what they say, children develop trust in your word. Being consistent is another factor that promotes trust. Consistency is a rather complex topic and for that reason we will be discussing consistency in more detail in

Chapter 6. Suffice it to say here that you can't condone a child's negative behavior one day (biting other children, for example) and then punish him or her for it the next. Establishing certain routines (when the
child wakes up, has lunch, goes to bed, and so forth) helps children feel
that their environment is dependable and that parents are reliable and
trustworthy.

## Foundations of Infants' Academic Self-Esteem

Infants' earliest intellectual needs can be met by providing them
with a stimulating environment: engaging in conversations; providing
a pleasant, interesting room with bright colors; taking them on walks in
their buggies—in short, treating them with intellectual respect. In the
early years of life, there are a variety of physical and social characteristics in the child's home environment that are particularly critical for
early cognitive performance.

Aspects of the physical environment that are positively related to
cognitive competence include availability of stimuli (particularly in the
first nine months of life). Infants need to be exposed to sensory stimuli
in their environment. Parents should provide their children with rich
sensory experiences and encourage active exploration of the sights,
sounds, and objects in their environment. Visual stimulation, for example, may be enhanced by providing young children with brightly colored objects for play such as a mobile. It should be designed to be seen
from below. Vary the mobile from time to time. Leave a safe, stainless
steel unbreakable mirror where it can be seen easily. Auditory stimulation comes from exposure to pleasant music and sounds. Music boxes,
record players, and tape recorders can be used to present all kinds of
music and pleasant sounds. For tactile stimulation encourage the child
to touch various kinds of textures—silk, wool, cotton, and so forth.
Stroking and touching your baby is important as well. Conditions that
deny the child opportunities for locomotor exploration or direct parent
restrictions on exploration tend to be negatively related to the development of early cognitive competence.

Variety of stimuli refers to changes in available objects. Parents
need to provide children with lots of different types of toys that are
geared to the child's developmental level. Toys to develop large muscles, such as tricycles, and toys to develop small muscles, such as peg
boards, are good choices. Variety of stimuli becomes more critical than
number of available objects as the child gets older. Responsivity of the

physical environment helps children develop their cognitive competence. Responding to their communiqués, listening when they talk, and playing interactive games are all examples of responsivity. Regularity of scheduling in the home is helpful; establish eating, sleeping, and playing routines. Evidence consistently suggests that high levels of ambient background noise, overcrowding, and home traffic pattern (number of people coming and going in the home) are negatively related to cognitive performance.

In addition, there are social-environmental factors in the home that are consistently and positively related to cognitive competence in the early years of life. Parental involvement appears to be important in the development of children's thinking abilities.[28] Engaging in playing games with your children, taking interest in your child's activities, and just having fun together promote cognitive competence. A high level of tactile stimulation (particularly in the first six months of life) promotes children's thinking abilities. Tactile stimulation involves holding, cuddling, stroking, and rocking children. Contingent responses to the child's distress (in the first year of life) enables children to develop their cognitive skills and involves consistently and reliably comforting children when they have a need. Finally, verbal stimulation (particularly after 12 months of age) helps children grow in cognitive ways. Talking with children and believing that your child can understand more than he or she can say is vital. Seek, above all, to communicate with your child. To understand is to be understood.

Optimal development occurs when parents do not pressure the child to learn, leave the child to deal with tasks that are somewhat difficult for the child to handle, and do not take over the tasks from the child. Similarly, adults need to adjust their level of interaction to the child's own level of competence.

Several psychologists have talked about enhancing children's cognitive development through stimulation. However, overstimulation is not a good practice. For example, it has been observed in spontaneous play situations that some mothers often overstimulate their infants, which results in infants decreasing their gaze time and their communicative efforts. Overstimulation in this sense means that mothers may continue to initiate interactions through talking, smiling, and touching their infants, even when the infant has turned away. Some studies have reported that mothers are interacting up to 90% of the time, whereas the infant is only looking 30% of the time.[29] Parental activity that is excessive or minimal may hurt the interaction. Parents may severely overload children with signals as they try to engage their infants in playful encounters. The child who is overloaded turns away and may resort to crying. If this overstimulation continues, the parent–child relationship may be seriously damaged. Therefore, parents need to engage in contingent stimulation, that is, stimulation related to the cues from the infant. When parents move at their infant's pace, it aids the infant's development and enhances cognitive abilities.

Consider the following interactive styles between two mothers and their infants: Mother and child are playing a delightful game of pat-a-cake; the infant turns away and sucks her thumb. The mother stops playing and watches her infant. Within a few seconds the child turns back and looks at mother with an inviting smile, mother moves closer and says, "So, you want to play another game." The game continues. After a short while the baby again turns away and stares without expression. Mother again waits. Soon the young infant turns back and they greet each other with smiles.

Imagine a similar situation; only this time when the young child looks away, mother gently brings the child's face to turn to hers and continues the game. The infant, however, does not interact and again turns away. Mother brings the infant's line of vision while clicking her tongue to gain his attention. The child begins to fuss and suck his thumb.

These different relational styles begin to establish an affective communication relationship. Good interaction is characterized by mutually coordinated states and positive affect. By contrast, poor interactions are characterized by miscoordinated interactions and negative affect. When the infant turns away it means that he has had enough and needs to calm down; it's his way of escaping by becoming perceptually unavailable. It is important that mother responds contingently to her infant's cues—when the child is looking away, mother should wait until the child is ready to begin communicating again.

Different emotional outcomes observed in happy and curious children, sad and withdrawn children, and angry and unfocused children are related to the affective communication system in which the infant participates. The achievement of mutually coordinated states between the infant and caregiver leads to positive emotions in the infant, whereas the infant experiences negative feelings when experiencing miscoordinated interactions.

The difference between children who are happy and curious and those who are sad and withdrawn can be related to the affective communication system. The achievement of coordinated states between mother and child results in positive affect and a desire to communicate further. These types of communication patterns help children become happy and curious. Poor interactive styles lead to negative affect; the infant experiences more distress, and eventually she will not want to communicate with mother. Infants who experience chronic miscoordinated interactions disengage from their mothers and become more withdrawn and sad.

As the infant gets older and becomes ambulatory, parents need to provide opportunities for children to express their naturally inquisitive nature by allowing them to engage in exploratory behaviors. The active, exploring child should spend only brief periods of time (10 to 20 minutes a day) in a playpen. Regular use of a playpen is a very poor child rearing practice in terms of meeting a child's intellectual needs. Reading children simple, entertaining stories and playing outdoors as much as possible to build on children's natural enthusiasm are some excellent ways to nurture a child's curiosity. Chapters that follow will also address how to build inner self-esteem in the academic domain.

## Summary

Infants do not exist in a world of reflexes and confusing sights and sounds, but rather, have a number of perceptual, sensory, and cognitive capabilities. In terms of self-development, the infant emerges from a symbiotic state with the principal caregiver to achieve a sense of separateness and distinction from others. The infant begins to perceive himself or herself as a causal agent whose actions affect others.

During infancy the foundations of self-esteem are beginning to form when infants develop strong attachment bonds with their parents, develop a sense of trust about their world and those who comprise it, and receive optimal stimulation when communicating with their parents. Parents who are sensitive, more child-centered, and nurturing, and who respond appropriately to children's signals (crying, gazing, smiling) will help their children establish firm foundations of inner self-esteem.

While infancy may be an optimal time to begin building foundations of inner self-esteem, parents with older children can begin building firm foundations for inner self-esteem beyond the infancy period. Being nurturing, caring, and sensitive to the child's needs promotes strong attachments.

# CHAPTER 2  Developing Inner Self-Esteem during Early Childhood

## Curious and Inquisitive Preschoolers

Two rich rewards of parenting in early childhood are the opportunity to view the world through the eyes of one's child and to be child-like (experiencing a renewed freshness with life). Children between the ages of 2 and 5 years are curious and inquisitive little souls; they have so much to learn and most don't waste any time in learning as much about their world as they can. Preschoolers have limitless energy—they get over, under, in, around, and through everything imaginable.

Children branch out socially as they learn to adapt to ever-widening social networks. Children become more involved with their peers. While they may initially play in a solitary fashion (playing alone with toys other than those used by peers) or engage in onlooker play (watching other children play), by the end of this period they interact cooperatively with other children in play situations. With their increased language abilities, preschoolers interact with others verbally rather than with objects. True give-and-take behavior begins. Many preschoolers have special friends, although these friends tend to change rather quickly.

In early childhood, most social exchanges occur in the setting of play, which generally involves engaging in a nonserious activity for the sheer satisfaction it brings. Most children spend countless hours at play, reveling in being silly and gleeful. According to preschoolers, friends are people who are "nice"; those who are "mean" are not friends. Trust is limited to faith in a friend's ability to play with the child's toys without breaking them. Children in early childhood begin to show pronounced gender-specific behavior. Boys tend to exhibit more independent and assertive behaviors; girls tend to be more passive and cooperative.

47

Emotionally, preschoolers tend to display fluctuating emotional states. In anger, the child may say "I hate you" and then return in a few minutes bright-eyed and ready for fun. They may be laughing and happy one minute and crying and miserable the next. Moreover, children tend to focus on one feeling at a time. For example, they are either "all loving" or all "unloving." It is not until the middle of the second year that the secondary emotions are observed. These emotions are sometimes called self-conscious emotions, for their emergence is dependent on the development of a particular important cognitive capacity: self-awareness. This new class of emotions includes embarrassment, empathy, pride, shame, and envy. In order for these emotions to be felt, children need to be able to evaluate their own actions and behaviors as good or bad.

Children's understanding of their world becomes greater during the preschool years. Just as the world of objects took on an increasing coherence and stability during the infancy period, the world that depends on symbolic representation—the world of socially shared meaning, categories, and relations—begins to take on a greater coherence and stability during the early childhood years. Preschoolers learn increasingly to represent the world mentally by means of memories, imagery, language, or symbols. Thus, there is a qualitative change when children move from action-oriented thinking to thinking based on mental representation.

Preschoolers' thinking is dominated by their perceptions; that is, children focus on that which strikes them first and most vividly. Thought at this cognitive level is highly dependent on immediate, visual experiences. For example, children think they have more money when they are holding six pennies versus one dime. As a parent, you may want to try this exercise to see how dependent on perception preoperational thinkers are. Take two tall, thin glasses of the same size and one glass that is short and shallow. Fill both of the thin glasses with equal amounts of a dark liquid (tea or soda). Ask your child if there is the same amount of liquid in each of these glasses. (Child will answer "Yes.") Then, before the child's eyes, pour the contents of one of the tall glasses into the short, shallow glass and ask if there is the same amount of liquid in these glasses. The preoperational thinker will answer, based on his perceptual thinking skills, that there is more liquid in the tall glass.

Children in early childhood are delightfully egocentric in their thinking. They are the *raison d'etre* of the universe. The egocentrism of these young children leads them to assume that everyone thinks as they do and that the whole world shares their feelings and desires. This sense of oneness with the world leads naturally to their assumptions of magic omnipotence. The world is not only created for them, but they can also control it. The sun and the moon must follow them when they go for a walk; they can make it snow by frantically dancing around in circles. They do not feel that they need to justify their own statements. Why should they, when all the world shares their thoughts and feelings?

One of the major milestones of this period is entering elementary school. Several developmental patterns can be observed in children in kindergarten. At school, the kindergartner has a short attention span and for that reason cannot concentrate for a long period of time on one structured activity. Some children feel rather insecure in a large group environment; some will continue to wear their hat or coat (a little something from home) until they learn to feel comfortable in the group. Five-year-olds begin to show a new understanding of causal relations.

Morally, children adopt parents' beliefs unquestioningly; their moral reasoning tends to be motivated by avoiding punishment from those who make the rules. They learn to distinguish right from wrong and to live with parental restrictions. Their moral behavior is based on specific, unchanging rules that they believe to be fixed and eternal. Their evaluations of whether another's behavior is right or wrong are judged in terms of the physical consequences of the act (breaking fifteen cups accidently is worse than breaking one cup on purpose).

Early childhood is a time of growing sophistication in the physical and motor areas. The body becomes more agile and controlled, and gross and fine motor development improves rapidly. Physically, the protruding stomachs, chubby cheeks, and double chins (all those endearing things grandmothers love) disappear. Children in early childhood display different ways of behaving as they grow from loving and affectionate 2-year-olds to imaginative and creative 5-year-olds (with a few demanding periods in between).

## Typical Behavior in Early Childhood

As noted earlier, understanding children's behavior at various age levels can be quite beneficial to parents. But these developmental norms break down when they are interpreted too closely by parents. Just because a child turns 3 years old, for example, does not mean that he automatically begins to behave exactly like the descriptions offered.

Each child adds his or her own special twist of individuality to these norms.

As children enter their second year, they tend to spend a little more time engaging in one activity. With this added maturity comes a calm willingness. Two-year-olds usually attempt to do what they can do and do not try too hard to do the things they cannot manage. They are generally loving and affectionate.

At $2\frac{1}{2}$ years, children may not be as easy to get along with as they were a few short months ago. They tend to be rather domineering, demanding, explosive, rebellious, tense, and rigid. They like to engage in ritualistic behaviors. That is, there is a certain way to do things and they do not like to deviate from that pattern. They like taking the same route to a familiar destination or having the same stories read over and over. Trouble brews when someone interferes with their ritualistic procedures. Generally, $2\frac{1}{2}$-year-olds have a hard time waiting for anything. Moreover, they have a hard time choosing between two alternatives. The child may spend 20 minutes deciding whether she wants to drink juice or milk if the choice is offered. So it is best for parents to make most of the decisions. It is generally wise to use techniques to get around the child's rigidities, rituals, and indecisiveness.

Unlike the $2\frac{1}{2}$-year-old, 3-year-olds tend to have an easygoing attitude toward life. They are no longer quite as rigid, dictatorial, and domineering. They don't need the protection of rituals and do not insist on doing everything their way. At $3\frac{1}{2}$ years, a child's behavior is marked by insecurity and incoordination. In language, children may begin stuttering; in motor areas they may begin stumbling and falling; in emotional areas they may constantly display their insecurity by asking, "Do you love me?" or complain that parents don't love them. Socially, they may have difficulties in relations with other people. They may exhibit this tension by biting their nails, sucking their thumbs, twisting their hair, or in facial and other tics.

While $3\frac{1}{2}$-year-olds are somewhat insecure, 4-year-olds seem overly brash and confident. (Nature seems to have this awkward way of going to extremes as the child develops.) Four-year-olds display a great deal of demanding, threatening, and commanding behavior. They tend to be blunt, bossy, belligerent, and rambunctious. They frequently whine, complain, and cry and are subject to fits of rage. The $4\frac{1}{2}$-year-old is still trying to sort out what is real and what is make-believe. Their mixture of reality and imagination can be quite exasperating to parents. They are a little more self-motivating than they were earlier. Now they can start a job and usually stick with it until they are finished with less need for parental control. These children love to discuss things and enjoy long conversations with others. Their play is less wild than at 4 years of age perhaps because they are able to tolerate more frustration before they explode.

Five-year-olds are wonderfully reliable, stable, calm, and friendly individuals. They are still homebodies, with mother holding the central place in their world. While they may be making some overtures toward independence, in general, they are usually content to obey mother's requests and try to live up to her expectations. This age is most satisfying as far as the parent–child relationship is concerned, because the 5-year-old endeavors to please and above all be a good helper.

Five-year-olds are imaginative, often highly dramatic and creative beings. They find it great fun to indulge in tall tales, role playing, and imitating adults. While they love fantasy and make-believe they usually are able to make a distinction between the two. Large-muscle development (using their arms and legs) is strong, and thus, they love games with lots of movement and physical activity. Lack of fine motor development (using their hands and fingers) is apparent in the child who has difficulty staying between the lines when coloring, drawing geometric shapes, or cutting with scissors.

## Development of Self during Early Childhood

Toddlers who have achieved an understanding of themselves as separate entities are able to use self-referential terms ("Tommy tired") and personal pronouns ("Me want cookie") and identify objects as belonging to them ("Blankie mine"). Recent work by Deborah Stipek at University of California at Los Angeles has shown that only toddlers who have achieved an understanding of themselves as separate entities are able to use self-referential terms and apply descriptive and evaluative terms to themselves.[1]

Young children are able to scan and respond to inner states. Toddlers, for example, can identify mood states and changes in mood. They occasionally share a memory or report a nightmare, all of which are examples of the toddler's awareness of mental activity and support the view that the toddler's self includes a private inner world. Distinguishing an inner self from the bodily self or outer self emerges between 3 and 4 years of age. After they have developed an understanding that they have private selves, children then set about the task of defining the characteristics of those selves.

What children think about themselves is dependent on the way in which they process information. For example, children in early childhood are in the stage of preoperational thinking, according to Jean Piaget.[2] During this stage, children can now think before acting; this is known as representational or internal thinking. For instance, before the age of 2 years, children are action thinkers; they think and do at the same time. If, for example, we observe a 15-month-old child trying to get her toy that is wedged underneath the couch, we would see her "think" as she acts. We would see her try to kick at it with her feet, then try to swipe at it with her hand, then use the handle of her toy lawn mower to finally free and retrieve the toy.

Sophisticated preoperational thinkers, however, can think first about how to unwedge the toy and carry out possible actions in their head before actually acting. This type of thinking is one of the great achievements of the preoperational child. Moreover, there is an explosion of vocabulary during early childhood. Children move from very simple two-word utterances to elaborate, complex sentences. As a result of these milestones in the cognitive domain, which result in more sophisticated thinking, we see a rapid growth in the number of self-descriptions children form about themselves.

Children's evaluations of self tend to derive from what they observe about themselves and require no probing or sophisticated analysis on their part. Young children generally attend to the overt, exterior, public aspects when evaluating the self rather than to underlying qualities or feelings. Young children are better at evaluating themselves than they are at evaluating others, possibly because of their egocentric outlook.

Children in early childhood are particularly aware of physical characteristics (strong, weak), social identity (boy, girl), and physical features (blue eyes, brown hair). In particular, children focus on facial features associated with gender and age. That is, they find it especially easy to tell themselves apart from children of the opposite sex and from older persons. Children between the ages of 2 and 3 are likely to organize their self-images around physical features and motor performance. ("I have big feet. I can run fast.") Children between the ages of 4 and 5 tend to describe themselves in terms of bodily activity rather than in terms of body parts. When children between the ages of 4 and 5 are asked to say things spontaneously about themselves, most of their responses are action statements. ("I can catch a ball" or "I can hop on one foot.")

Similarly, young children do not differentiate themselves from their physical surroundings. That is, they are, in an important sense, what they own and where they live. They do not differentiate the outward, observable aspects of the person from the inward, covert aspects. A person is how he or she looks and behaves. In early childhood, youngsters do not differentiate traits about themselves. For example, when labels such as good or bad first become available to children, they describe themselves as "all good" or "all bad"; they do not believe they can be both at the same time.

Do young children have fairly consistent pictures of self? Or are their self-images inconsistent and constantly changing? University of California at Davis psychologist Rebecca Eder found that when $3\frac{1}{2}$-year-olds and $5\frac{1}{2}$-year-olds are presented with a set of statements representing several personality characteristics in random order, they are consistent in selecting the same traits and characteristics over several trials, suggesting that young children have somewhat consistent self-images.[3]

In addition, children in early childhood tend to evaluate their abilities in a very direct way. Because motor accomplishments predominate children's activities, competence is defined by direct feedback from obvious successes or failures. Objective standards and physical realities dominate children's evaluations of self. They don't compare themselves to others, because they are egocentric in orientation and preoccupied with their own point of view rather than that of others. Moreover, children live within a limited social environment (limited exposure to others in a variety of settings) that does not yet foster appreciation of social standards. So self-esteem of younger children is not affected by relative comparisons.

Children less than 6 years of age base their self-evaluations on the "absolute standard" of completion of tasks. As greater cognitive sophistication develops (increased memory skills; appreciation of past, present, and future; ability to take the perspective of others), social comparison becomes possible. With the lessening of egocentrism and the development of skills that allow them to understand things from the perspective of others, children have the ability to imagine what significant others think of them. The term self-consciousness incorporates the consciousness of being judged by others, which, in turn, causes one to be conscious of the self that is being evaluated.

## Self-Esteem in Boys and Girls

Are the following personality traits more characteristic of boys or girls, or both?

- Independent
- Acts as leader
- Doesn't cry easily
- Curious
- Sensitive
- Cuddly
- Talkative
- Feelings easily hurt
- Good at sports
- Adventurous
- Helpful
- Confident

Children in early childhood show many pronounced "stereotypic" behaviors. Many of these gender-specific behaviors are learned from their parents. In your responses, were characteristics such as cuddly, talkative, feelings easily hurt, and helpful checked for girls, while does not cry easily, curious, adventurous, and independent were checked for boys? Many parents have rather traditional ideas as to how boys should behave and how girls should act, and children, in part, as a result of their parents' belief systems, learn to act in ways that are traditionally appropriate for their gender. Extensive literature has documented that parents socialize their boys and girls differently in terms of behaviors that are rewarded through physical contact, communication style, amount and type of play, choice of toys, clothing, affection, and so forth.[4]

Parents, teachers, and other adult models tend to reward activity, independence, and assertiveness in boys, while passivity, cooperation, and compliance are rewarded in girls.[5] Parents tend to associate physical ability or athletic skill with boys, together with getting dirty, being rough, and taking interest in toy cars, trucks, and tools. Traits considered appropriate for girls are gentleness, interest in clothes, and pleasantness toward others. Thus, these young children receive some fairly clear information from parents on which to build "masculine" and "feminine" images of self.

Parents continue to encourage "appropriate" behavior for both genders through their selection of the quantity and types of toys, the colors and types of clothing, and the colors and motifs of children's rooms. Parents provide boys with more sports equipment, tools, and large and small vehicles. Girls are provided with dolls, fictional character toys, children's furniture, and other "nurturing" types of toys.[6] Girls more often wear pink and multicolored clothes; boys wear blue, red, and white clothing more often. These different environments and preferred activities have an effect on the development of dissimilar self-esteem for boys and girls.

Toys have properties that bring out particular types of behavior in children and their parents. Thus, play with gender-typed toys may be the source of some observed behavioral gender differences in self-esteem. For instance, masculine toys such as trucks and adventure figures promote motor activities. Masculine toys (trucks and cars) are associated with developing eye-hand coordination and active thinking skills. When parents interact with their children while playing with these masculine toys, one observes relatively low levels of questions and more distance between parent and child, thus promoting more independent behavior. In contrast, play with feminine toys (dolls) elicits closer physical contact and more verbal interactions in the form of comments and questions. As a result of the type of toys with which children typically play, boys and girls may learn to base their self-esteem on different attributes. Boys' self-esteem may center on being independent and creative thinkers. Girls, on the other hand, may learn to base their self-esteem on being nurturing and dependent.

These patterns of interaction are not related to the child's gender but rather the type of toy with which the child and parent are playing. Fathers and daughters playing with trucks display more distance and lower levels of talking; mothers and sons playing with dolls show closer contact and more communication.[7] These marked differences in children's and parents' behaviors associated with different toys give support to the hypothesis that sex differences in self-esteem and behaviors are in some measure associated with differences in the toys with which girls and boys typically play.

Sex differences in the development of self are apparent very early in life. In early childhood, girls have, as a rule, more social sensibility; they care more obviously for social image and reflect upon it more. Boys are more taken with muscular activities and construction, and their imaginations are occupied somewhat less with persons and more with things.

These differences may not just be the result of a unilateral tendency on the part of parents and other social agents to use differential socialization practices; innate behavior based on gender may also contribute to the differences in socialization practices. For example, young boys have been observed to be more active and disruptive in their behavior than girls; they are more likely to show greater resistance to control and are less likely to be responsive to adult directives, both at home and at school, thereby more frequently eliciting critical, negative reactions from adult caregivers.

Still, the way parents differentially treat their sons and daughters may be due to the children's behavior as much as to the parents.[8] Since fathers tend to be the primary socializers of gender roles, they and their preschool sons and/or daughters were observed in a "waiting room" with a one-way mirror. The room had several tempting but potentially disaster-producing objects: a vase with flowers, a plastic pitcher filled with water, and so forth. Daughters were more content to sit on their father's lap for longer periods of time and played more quietly with the toys that were in the room. Boys, however, were more active, were not content to be held, and were fussier. The results of this study seem to indicate that it may not simply be fathers who encourage stereotypic behaviors toward their children. It appears that boys and girls differ from one another in the behavior they exhibit in the presence of their fathers, and this may play an integral role in the socialization practices of fathers as well as mothers.

While boys and girls may have received differential treatment from their parents, genetics and hormones (in particular, testosterone) play a role in determining children's masculine and feminine ways of behaving. But, the jury of genetic experts is still out; as more studies are done, a more finite answer as to the role of environment and genetics in gender-specific behavior will be forthcoming.

There are some things that parents can do to help boys and girls develop less stereotypic and more balanced feminine and masculine ways of behaving. Parents of girls can dress them for active play (not for watching on the sidelines) in bold, bright, very washable colors, not always pastels. Encourage interest in and use of nonsexist toys—toys that will allow manipulation of objects and active problem solving. Parents don't necessarily have to discourage quiet time, but they should make sure that other options are available. Take advantage of programs that might interest your little girl—Suzuki lessons, karate, sports. Try camping, nature walks, exploring, museum hopping, and traveling with your daughter. Parents of boys can let sons know it's okay for them to feel and express emotions. Fathers can share their emotional life with their sons and also be a model for accepting both successes and failures. Encourage boys to accept their strengths as well as limitations.

Developing inner self-esteem transcends the gender of the child. As Plato stated so many years ago, we need to relate to children in ways that stimulate their potentialities for growth, no matter what their gender. That is, parents need to help their children develop the skills that will enable them to *fulfill their potentialities*.

## Building Inner Self-Esteem during Early Childhood

Children's inner self-esteem is enhanced when parents engage in certain types of behaviors, which involve recognizing their child's temperament and creating a sense of trust and security in their children. In early childhood, behaviors and skills that are valued center on the development of a sense of autonomy (independent, free-thinking, responsible, and self-directing behavior); self-sufficiency; development of morally competent behaviors (honesty, caring about the welfare of other human beings); and controlling feelings of anger.

In order to accomplish these goals, members of a family need to establish basic commitments to each other: Parents need to provide warmth and nurturance to their children; they need to provide opportunities to encourage the development of individuality; and, finally, parents need to facilitate children's sense of control, confidence, and competence. These goals are vital for all children in all family situations. While it may be difficult for parents to manage financial, physical, or psychological hardships, it is not impossible.

During early childhood, though parental love continues to contribute to self-esteem, an important second component of self-esteem emerges. As children grow older, the criterion on which self-esteem is based changes from unconditional positive regard from the child's parents to actual behavior.[9] During this transition, self-esteem becomes more influenced by internal sources of evaluation, and the basis for such evaluations comes to focus on successful performance of socially valued behaviors. The ability to succeed in these pursuits becomes a measure of one's self-esteem. In order for children to develop inner self-esteem, parents need to help children believe that they have some power over their lives. Parents should not interpret this statement to mean that the child has all the power and becomes the ruling despot. Many of us have observed children in some families who dictate to the parents how things shall be run. This is not good for the child or parents. Parents cannot be the tyrannical rulers, either. Parents need to be firm but fair in establishing rules and regulations. When parents impose many restrictions and do not allow the child an input, or parents do not offer explanations for rules and disciplining measures, a child's sense of power or self-control is low and so is his self-esteem.

When parents are firm but fair in exercising their control, monitoring their children's behavior and following through on requirements, children's sense of control over their lives tends to be high and their self-esteem is as well. The critical factor appears to be whether parental control is accompanied by emotional support, commitment to the child's welfare, and an open interchange of ideas between parent and child.

Building socially valued behaviors and skills begins by discovering and capitalizing on your child's strengths. Every child has some strengths. As you begin to look for them, you'll find many more, and as you do, you give your child an exceptionally good basis from which to develop his or her talents. Permit a personal example, which shows how parents can look for strengths in their child's behavior. When my son, Gordon, was $3\frac{1}{2}$, he came dashing into the house asking for a pail and a broomstick. The people who lived a few houses down from us were having a concrete driveway poured. Gordon asked one of the construction workers if he would fill his bucket with cement. Gordon lugged this bucket home and plunged the stick into the center of the bucket. Curious about what he was doing, I asked him. "I'm making my very own tetherball game," he replied. (In tetherball, a ball is attached to a string which is fastened to a pole. Children use paddles to swing at the ball.) How creative, what great initiative; and he followed through with this project. *Parents need to help their child identify their own competent behavior.* Gordon was told, after making his own tetherball game, "How creative you are, what a great idea! That was a hard project, and you finished it all on your own." Here were some tangible behaviors and some great strengths that he was exhibiting. Today, Gordon shows these strengths. When children are helping others, parents should acknowledge that by saying, "What a helpful person you are." There are numerous situations when parents can capitalize on their child's strengths by labeling them for him or her.

When parents offer their children play materials that provide both a challenge and potential for success, children are likely to acquire feelings of competence. Encouragement and statements of confidence in the child's ability to succeed are important boosters for self-esteem. Along with encouragement, children sometimes need specific instruction. When children learn the skills needed to interact successfully with their peers, succeed in the academic domain, become morally competent, and become as physically skilled as the majority of their peers, they develop healthy self-esteem.

Help children be their own evaluators of their progress. If they are learning to draw or print, have them examine their earlier endeavors and notice how they have improved. Charting progress can be done in the other domains as well. Give them a special place in their room where they can display, for their own viewing pleasure, their works of art or recognition and rewards received in school. Have a chart entitled "Things I do well" and help the child make note of these wonderful achievements.

## Recognizing Children's Temperament

A child's individual differences in expressing emotions refers to his or her temperament. It is the apparently innate inclination toward a consistent style of emotional response in many different situations. Temperament refers to an early or stable pattern of emotional response or the child's intensity of emotional response. Most researchers agree that temperament includes individual behavioral differences in affective expressiveness, motor activity, and stimulus sensitivity.

Three temperament clusters or categories—easy children, difficult children, and slow-to-warm-up children—have been identified.[10] Easy children are characterized by predictability and regularity in behavior, are usually positive in mood, are low or mild in the intensity of their reactions, and usually try positive approaches to new situations. For example, the child who initially feels fearful in a new nursery school setting but fits in within a few days would be classified as having an easy temperament.

The difficult child is characterized by the opposite pattern of behavior. Difficult children are moody and intense, react negatively to new people and situations, frequently express negative moods, sleep poorly, and cry often and loudly. Little Charlie, who bites other children and does not learn to like or adapt to school, is a child with a difficult temperament.

Slow-to-warm-up children adapt slowly to new situations, are reluctant to participate in activities, and are negative in their moods. Unlike difficult children, who are prone to temper tantrums, slow-to-warm-up children are reluctant to express themselves. The child who is initially fearful in a new school setting and is still having difficulty several weeks later is a slow-to-warm-up child.

The view that temperament is present at birth, rigidly stable across time, and invariant across situations is no longer accepted by researchers in the field.[11] Results tend to support a view that children's temperament can be modified to a certain extent as a result of the experiences they encounter in their environment. Larry, age 4, is a slow-to-warm-up child who is fearful of meeting the dinner guests that his parents have invited to their home. Over time, because his parents entertain frequently, Larry may become somewhat more comfortable with his parents' new dinner guests. But it is doubtful that Larry will ever become the gregarious little life of the party on these occasions.

The idea that children with a difficult temperament are highly susceptible to future adjustment problems is no longer accepted. The impact of temperament on children's development appears to depend on whether a particular child's behavior coincides (goodness-of-fit) or doesn't coincide (poorness-of-fit) with his or her parents' environment.[10] In other words, the influence of temperament in shaping healthy or unhealthy development and functioning depends to some degree on environment.

Goodness-of-fit occurs when the demands and expectations of the environment are consonant with the child's capacities and characteristics. Shy Melissa has a slow-to-warm-up mother, which represents a goodness-of-fit. When this is so, healthy psychological development and functioning is likely. Poorness-of-fit, on the other hand, results when the child does not have the capacities or characteristics to cope adequately with environmental demands and expectations, as in the case of Chicago Bears fan Jack and his slow-to-warm-up son who would rather play quiet games such as chess. When this is so, excessive stress is likely to occur, and the child is at high risk for developing behavior problems.

Thus, goodness-of-fit indicates that the significance of temperament is not the child's particular attributes *per se*, but rather in the extent to which these attributes coincide with environmental demands. Moreover, the stability of temperament is a function of the interaction effects between temperament characteristics and the environment. Among Puerto Ricans, for example, a difficult temperament, characterized by high-intensity reactions, is highly regarded.[12] Because these temperamental characteristics are encouraged and reinforced, it is likely that children will exhibit these patterns of behavior for a considerable period of time. Similarly, among the Masai in East Africa, infants with difficult temperament, those who are fussy and irritable, are preferred because they will be the future warriors. Thus, in these situations the children's adjustment will be good, and the traits they exhibit are likely to be highly stable. These same kinds of behaviors, however, may not fit in other cultural settings. Because of this poorness-of-fit, the child's adjustment may be problematic, and the behaviors he or she exhibits may become modified to some extent.

Children who have a "difficult" temperament are not necessarily at an elevated risk for later childhood problems. Temperament affects development only in interaction with environmental forces. If the fit between children's behavior and parental values and expectations is a good one, children are likely to experience optimal development. By contrast, if the parents' values and expectations do not coincide with children's temperament, their development may not be optimal.

Thus, an important factor contributing to goodness-of-fit or poorness-of-fit may be the parents' subjective perceptions, because how parents perceive their children is likely to play a role in how they actually interact with them. Recognizing children's individual temperamental styles and more importantly accepting them is an important task for parents if optimal development is to occur for their children. Outgoing, aggressive, extroverted parents, for example, need to accept that their slow-to-warm-up child may not share the same attributes. Acceptance of a child's temperamental style helps to ensure a goodness-of-fit and optimal development and high self-esteem for the child.

## Establishing Children's Sense of Security

The childhood experience in the 1990s is quite different from that in times past. Some may comment that children's status has improved since children are no longer in service from dawn till dusk. While some experts may say that children never had it so good, others maintain that we are returning to the Dark Ages when children were not treated as special individuals. Tufts University professor David Elkind, for example, suggests that childhood is no longer considered a sheltered, special, and formative time and that we are witnessing "the disappearance of childhood."[13]

It doesn't take a social scientist's keen eye and experimental expertise to observe that children are growing up faster and faster. One can observe today how the language, games, clothing, sexuality, and taste of children and adults have become barely distinguishable. Precocious knowledge, independence, assertiveness, and "adultness" characterize many children today. On the sharp statistical rise are teenage suicide, pregnancy, alcoholism, drug use, child prostitution and pornography, truancy, and criminality. Why is this happening?

Elkind maintains that the changes in society and family lifestyles are prominent reasons for the disappearance of childhood.[13] The 1990s have witnessed a rise in the number of two-career families and a mounting divorce rate that has led to single-parent families. Moreover, the media place children and adults in the same symbolic world. Media, including books, films, and television, portray young people as precocious and present them in explicitly sexual or manipulative ways. The darker areas of sex, violence, and human aberrations are revealed all at once by media that do not and cannot exclude any audience.

Moreover, parents may believe that children should be readied for each new milestone in their development by being given systematic practice. Our preschoolers, for example, are given practice in the technical requirements of the reading process (known as "reading readiness") because in order to be prepared a child must read as soon as possible. The push toward early academic achievement is but one of the contemporary pressures on children. Another pressure on children is to be somebody—a superkid, a star basketball player, a tennis hero, and so on. In order to "be somebody," children need to begin developing these skills in early childhood. Sometimes they go to specialized training summer camps. Remember when kids went to camp to have a good time boating, swimming, hiking, and playing team sports just for fun? I'm sure that many children still do attend camps like these, but increasingly we are hearing that childhood should not be "frittered away" by engaging in activities merely because they are fun.

Parents need to realize that children are not their psychological equals and that children really don't flourish when treated as such. Parents should be encouraged to take a more authoritative role in the family and operate from the advantage of their superior knowledge. Such a parent is willing, in an accepting way, to reason and explain to children.

Children need to be protected from life's ugly vicissitudes. They need to feel the protectiveness of their parents. Under the parent's careful supervision, children can sense that they are separate, protected, and special. The value of children's exposure to evil, violence, injustice, and misery is questionable.[14] Today, as parents divorce and marry, struggle for economic survival, rail against political corruption, and agonize over depleting natural resources and ecological destruction, many make no attempt to shield their children from these complex affairs. Many parents believe that it is harmful not to expose children to these aspects of reality. Those who believe that protecting children is impoverishing them are making a questionable assumption—that children have the same ability to assimilate and utilize this knowledge and experience as adults do. Children need to feel secure in the certainty that children are children and adults are adults and that in spite of the "wretchedness" they might witness in their world, they can still remain separated from it and untouched by it. Children should be allowed the simple pleasures of play, imagination, curiosity, and pursuit of adventure, even in the most adverse circumstances. Developing a sense of security and feeling protected as a child are important components of inner self-esteem. Perhaps the recognition that a highly complex civilization such as ours cannot afford to shorten the period of nurture and protection of its younger members will restore a real childhood to the children of coming generations.

## Developing Children's Sense of Autonomy

During early childhood, children need to develop a sense of autonomy or independence. Erikson's second stage of development is known as "Autonomy vs. Shame and Doubt" (ages 2 to 4).[15] Children discover that they have a mind and a will of their own. To develop autonomy and a firm will in children, parents need to recognize children's needs to climb, open and close, push and pull, hold on and let go. Children increasingly demand to control their own behavior, but they do not have a keen sense of judgment about their capabilities; parents need to protect their children from excesses while granting them autonomy in matters they can handle. A successful resolution of this stage gives children the capacity to be loving and cooperative yet firm in dealing with others. Parental overprotection, lack of support, restricting freedom of movement, continuous impatience, or continually doing things for children that they can do for themselves can lead to children's developing a sense of shame and doubt which later may be expressed either in overcautiousness or in flagrant disregard of social convention.

Children of 4 or 5 years are ready to engage in constructive activities under their own initiative. Three major achievements, namely, increased social mobility, language development, and the expansion of imagination, set the stage for Erikson's third stage, "Initiative vs. Guilt." If explorations, projects, and activities are generally effective and rewarded by their parents, children develop a sense of competence. In later years, the child who manages this stage well is capable of engaging in self-initiated projects, trying new things, having a limited fear of failure, and imagining alternative solutions to problems. The potential problem at this period is guilt. If parents perceive their children's motor activity as bad, their questions as bothersome, and their play activities as stupid, children develop a sense of guilt over self-initiated activities in general. As adults they may either continuously try to prove themselves to others or may be hypercritical of everything concerning themselves and others.

## Teaching Children to Be Self-Sufficient

Children in early childhood who are allowed to feel pride and success in their efforts to care for themselves develop feelings of self-control and inner self-esteem. Parents play an important role in helping children develop self-regulation. In the early years of life parental behavior that enables children to develop self-regulatory behavior includes providing predictable routines, preventing children from experiencing overwhelming frustration, and responding appropriately to their bids for attention. In addition, parents need to present clear, consistent, and appropriate limits in order for children to develop rudimentary self-control. When appropriate and clear limits have been consistently set, toward the end of the second year, children are able to modulate their reactions, begin to comply with simple parental requests, and anticipate the need to inhibit certain acts (for example, not touching a dangerous object).

Children are also able to comply with parental expectations and can inhibit impulses even in the absence of external constraints. Advances in language development may also aid in self-regulation. Children may, for example, repeat the appropriate behavior, "You can't have a cookie until after dinner," which may aid them in inhibiting the specific but forbidden activity.

The rather complex routines that young children follow, such as playing cooperatively with peers and teachers at day-care centers, engaging in self-help behaviors, and apologizing for inappropriate behavior, suggest some internalization of appropriate behavioral standards. As children get older, they engage in more complex, adaptive, and more long-term self-regulatory behavior that involves self-reflection and planning strategies. They also acquire greater control over impulses and develop a keener awareness of socially acceptable behavior.

Individual differences in self-regulatory behavior tend to be associated with individual differences in parental childrearing strategies and children's personalities. Children tend to develop self-regulatory behavior when parents present clear and appropriate limits. Inconsistent, ambiguous, or harsh attempts at control tend to inhibit the development of self-control behavior in children.[16] Parental approaches to discipline, the strategies they use in solving problems, and the quality of the relationship between family members are also important variables in helping children develop self-control strategies. Individual differences in children's personalities also affect self-regulation. For example, children who are more irritable and more easily aroused may have difficulties developing self-regulatory behaviors.

As young children become more mature and more aware of their own individuality, they show an increasing interest in taking care of themselves. Young children want to do things by themselves, but because they are somewhat inexperienced, they need their parents' help in order to master various tasks. Teaching children these basic skills requires a great deal of patience. Teaching a child to dress herself, for example, and then waiting while she slowly and laboriously completes the task can be rather frustrating, particularly when it takes you only a few minutes to have the child dressed and ready to go.

In helping children become self-sufficient, it's a good idea to break down complex tasks into simple steps. We have done some of these tasks for so long that it's easy to forget how complicated they are. Do you remember when you first got behind the wheel of a car? There was so much to remember as you maneuvered the car around the block. Now, of course, you race across the highways on automatic pilot. When teaching a child a new task, try to break it down into nice easy steps. By doing so, the child has a greater chance of experiencing success, and as a parent you have less chance of experiencing frustration.

Clothes can be laid out in a foolproof way, so that it is easy for the child to get them on the right way the first time. Pullover shirts, for example, can be laid out with the front side down on the bed with the bottom toward the child. Then show him how to pick it up and pull it on, so it will automatically be the right way around. To don a jacket, put it down on the floor front side up, with the collar at his feet and the zipper open. Show him how to stoop down and stick his arms through the correct arm holes. Then have him stand up and swing his arms over his head and *voilà*, the coat is on. Make things as easy as you can when children are initially learning a self-help task. For example, when teaching your child to dress, keep shirts, pants, and underwear in drawers that he or she can reach.

Some children show an interest in choosing what they will wear. If you don't mind the mismatched tops and bottoms, let them choose. Or, if the combinations chosen by the non-fashion-minded child bother you, offer her a choice: "Do you want to wear the green or the blue blouse with this skirt?" Lots of compliments and encouragement for a job well done helps the child feel a sense of pride over mastering these important tasks. All of us like to receive recognition from others for our accomplishments, and small children benefit as well from parents' positive acknowledgments.

The key to training children to be self-sufficient is waiting until the child is ready to learn. When the timing is right, children actually teach themselves. Let's discuss toilet training as a case in point. The term implies that the parent "trains" the child to perform this task. This is simply not the case. Parents need to see toilet training as the child's own learning process, to be achieved by the child in accordance with his or her own maturation. Around the age of 2, children will train themselves in a relatively short period of time.[17] Trying to train a child much before the age of 2 is generally quite difficult. When parents are unable to wait and consequently impose toilet training as their idea, children see it as an invasion.

A toilet-trained child is sometimes seen as a measure of successful parenting, and for this reason and perhaps convenience, parents begin before the child is ready. Then the scene is set for failure. Power struggles between the parent and child will make this toilet-training period a stormy and unpleasant one. A child's need to become independent at his own speed is important. The child must be mentally capable of understanding the usefulness of this skill and physically capable of achieving it. Mastering these skills should be the child's own success, not the parents'. When children successfully develop the behaviors and skills necessary to master these skills that make them self-sufficient, inner self-esteem soars.

## Developing Morally Competent Children

Teaching children to respect others and to be honest, compassionate, and altruistic promotes high evaluations of self in children. Their level of moral reasoning is an important factor in determining how they will act in certain challenging situations. Higher levels of moral reasoning are superior to lower levels, because children are not dependent on others telling them what to do but act in moral ways because *they* want to. How do children develop from a lower level of morality based on parental constraint to a higher self-imposed morality?

In the past, churches and schools played a pivotal role in fostering children's moral development. Now, with religious influence declining and schools not really sure how to teach values, parents play a key role. One of parents' primary purposes is to serve as role models for their children. Children will try to emulate parents who treat others with respect and help others in need. Just a few days ago, the doorbell rang in the middle of the afternoon. On the steps stood a young mom and seven excited and eager 4- and 5-year-olds who were on a scavenger hunt. I was presented with a list of needed items and an explanation from one of the 5-year-olds that they were "getting things to give to people who have no homes." I was able to find a few of the items on the list and deposited them into their large cloth bag. "Wow! What a great job you kids are doing. Just look at all the good things we have so far for our homeless people," commented the young mother to the children. They all jumped up and down—they were smiling and exploding with moral self-esteem. What a great lesson they were learning.

Encouraging children to do something nice for someone else and discussing with them what they did and the positive way it made them feel will also help to promote morally conscious children. Several months ago, my teenage son, Eric, returned home with such a great smile on his face that I thought something *really* spectacular had happened to him. "Guess what!" he blurted. "Someone paid my toll on the interstate for me. What a great person. I feel so good. I'm going to have to do that for someone else." That's the thing about doing something nice for someone else, it not only makes you and the recipient feel good, but the receiver of this good will is likely to do something nice for someone else.

By living in accordance with the same basic rules that are expected of the child and by allowing the child a reasonable role in decision making, the parent can be an example of reciprocal morality. Giving children opportunities to participate in decision making promotes a higher level of moral reasoning.[18] Parental discussion style has an influence on children's level of moral reasoning. The parental discussion style that is most effective in promoting children's moral development involves eliciting the child's opinion, asking clarifying questions, paraphrasing, and checking for understanding.[19] The children of parents who rely on an informative discussion style, that is, directly challenging the child, critiquing the child's position, and lecturing, have lower levels of moral reasoning.

Children who exhibit higher levels of moral reasoning tend to have parents who are verbal, rational people who encourage warm, close relations with their family. The parents tend to promote a democratic style of family life, with a fair consideration of everyone's point of view. A democratic home requires more freedom of choice for the child and more time for the parent to discuss, when necessary, the choices made and to evaluate the consequences with the child.[20]

There is also a possible relationship between children's levels of moral reasoning and various disciplining techniques.[21] There are three broad types of discipline:

1. *Power-assertive techniques* (physical force, deprivation of material objects or privileges). Example: "As long as you live in this house, you will do as you are told."
2. *Induction* (explaining the possible consequence of the child's behavior). Example: "I can't allow you to hit your younger brother. That really hurts him."
3. *Love withdrawal* (ignoring child, threatening to leave child, explicitly stating dislike for child). Example: "I don't know why I ever had kids, they're so exasperating."

Power-assertive techniques are associated with lower levels of moral reasoning in children, while induction is associated with higher levels. Love withdrawal is rather ambiguous, perhaps because the anxiety it induces can operate in two ways. It can lead a child to conform in order to please the parent and maintain emotional harmony or refuse to conform in order to annoy the parent. In either case, it is not a good method.

Having family meetings in which problems are discussed and solutions are agreed upon by the family members involved helps children develop moral self-esteem. If two siblings, for example, are constantly arguing, the family can meet to have the concerned parties talk about ways to bring about a truce or at least a cease-fire. Discuss moral dilemmas (those that actually happen to your children or ones proposed by you) with your children. Have your children generate solutions to these dilemmas.

According to Piaget, moral development cannot take place when parent–child relations are one-sided and authoritarian.[2] Piaget believed that children cannot develop a true sense of justice when adults are strong and demanding and children feel weak and inferior. In these kinds of situations, children know what they are and are not supposed to do, but the rationale for conformity is often not understood, nor is there the sense of working out some arrangement for mutual benefit. Hence, adults who insist upon complete control short-circuit the process of building in their children a deeper understanding of cooperative arrangements.

Interactions with peers promote the development of moral reasoning. As children get older and attain a relative equality with adults and older children, they gain the confidence to participate with peers in decisions about applying and changing rules on the basis of reciprocity. The mutual give-and-take, which occurs among peers who have equal status, fosters a reciprocity of cooperation (each child has the freedom to enter into cooperative agreements and each must be satisfied with the agreement for it to be effective). Peer-group experiences help move children away from moral realism, in which rules are seen as external, constraining forces arbitrarily imposed by adult authority figures, and toward the notion of morality based on principles of cooperation and mutual consent. Morality, then, develops from acquisition of autonomy, emerging from the need to get along with others.

Social participation in groups appears to be another way to advance children's level of moral reasoning.[22] Boys and girls who are leaders and members of extracurricular groups such as Boy Scouts, Girl Scouts, or athletic teams tend to reason at higher and more advanced levels of moral reasoning than those who are not members of such responsible, organized groups.

## Helping Children Control Anger

It has been said that unrecognized and unexpressed anger can cause depression, aggressiveness, sarcastic and demeaning behavior, or highly volatile behavior. While the study of some emotions such as distress and fear has been widespread, the study of anger has not. It does seem paradoxical that anger research has been so limited, because several researchers have reported that anger seems to occur more frequently among children than fear, jealousy, and other emotions. Janice Stapley at Monmouth College suggests that anger is the most commonly experienced negative emotion in young children[23] and that unexpressed anger leads to future adjustment problems. Learning to recognize anger and deal with it effectively is vital to inner self-esteem.

Experiencing anger in moderate and resolute form is not only normal but essential. Yet it appears that early in life children are indoctrinated against being angry. When a child complains of unhappiness or expresses a positive emotion, parents are all ears and encourage the child to communicate with them. When children express anger, that is, when they respond assertively, parents often admonish them or reject them for doing so. Perhaps anger is taboo in our society because we are afraid these feelings may ultimately lead to violence. Violence is anger that has gotten out of control and is expressed with the intent to physically hurt someone. There is great concern about the violence and aggression we observe in our society.

Anger is an arousal state that is primarily socially instigated, often under conditions of threat or frustration. Early anger reactions may be caused by objection to routine physical habits (dressing and eating), disagreement with peers over possession of toys, loss of possessions, minor physical discomfort, changes in routine toilet training, arrival of a second baby, and conflict with parents over authority.

In younger children, responses to anger frequently involve the venting of angry feelings (particularly for boys) or active resistance, whereby children attempt to defend themselves in nonaggressive ways (particularly for girls). For example, children may display anger by shoving a child who has grabbed a toy or they may throw tantrums when their mother turns off the television at bedtime.

As children get older there is a shift from wholehearted and violent reactions to a more subdued response. With increasing maturity the child learns to express his or her anger verbally. By the time children reach school age, most have learned to control overt reactions of anger. An older child's response may take the form of sulking, staring, swearing, and the old silent treatment.

Teaching children that anger is bad or refusing to recognize anger in children does not teach them how to deal effectively with angry feelings. What we are teaching them is to hide, cover up, disguise, or deny the existence of these feelings. When children are continually told that it is wrong or bad to display angry feelings and are punished for their fits of anger, they become obsessed with feelings of guilt and fear. They often repress their emotions until the tension becomes unbearable and shows up in some worse form of behavior. Because these feelings have been bottled up inside, causing a buildup of anger, some children may become overwhelmed by them.

You may have found on days when several frustrating incidents have occurred that toward the end of the day you erupt with fury. You may yell, insult, and hit below the belt. Afterwards you feel guilty, sad, and perhaps a little childish and vow next time that you will be more patient and have more control so that you do not have a repeat performance. When we find no release from angry feelings we become oversensitive to anger-provoking incidents. We may overreact to certain events by becoming more angry than is warranted. We have accumulated so much anger that only a little more is needed to trigger off an explosive reaction. Unexpressed, unrecognized feelings of anger do not dissipate but begin to accumulate.

It is by understanding that angry feelings are a natural and necessary part of life that parents can help the child learn how to control anger. While most of us may not like being angry, we cannot ignore it in ourselves or refuse to recognize it in children. To keep our anger feelings from erupting into harmful actions, we need to acknowledge them before we can learn to deal effectively with them. Those who have grown up being unafraid of angry feelings, those who are aware of their angry feelings and see them as being natural emotions, those who feel they can control angry feelings rather than be at the mercy of these feelings are the ones who can apply their energies to change the cause of anger and engage in planned and effective action.

Parents must make a distinction between angry feelings and angry acts. Children often have angry feelings and cannot control them, but children must learn to control angry acts. While they should be free to express their feelings, they must learn to refrain from engaging in violent behavior. Expression of angry feelings can help them learn to cope with this emotion so that it does not become too much for them or for parents to handle.

Parents should acknowledge the child's angry feelings. ("I know you are angry with Danny for breaking your toy.") Assure the child that this feeling is normal. Set firm limits on the physical expression of anger; the child needs to internalize these limits. ("But I cannot allow you to hit him.") The child must learn that certain actions are not permitted. Give the child a constructive release for anger. ("Show me how angry you are by hitting this pillow as hard as you can.") Children need to be inhibited in violent actions such as hitting other children, hitting parents, being cruel to animals, and destroying property.

Whenever possible, parents should try to calm down before reacting in an anger situation. They should avoid acting when their emotions and physical state of arousal are at their peak. When we react while we are still fired up, we often say and do things we are sorry for later. It's best not to respond to a child's wild outburst with one of your own special tantrums. When anger is met with more anger, a vicious cycle is set up, and anger-producing behavior increases rather than decreases.

Generally, it is best when parents do not hold anger grudges toward the child for long periods of time. Children feel loved when adults are affectionate toward them; they feel rejected when parents are angry. After the anger incident, parents should be able to be warm and affectionate again.

## Summary

Self-images in early childhood are based on children's physical features, gender identity, physical characteristics, and motor skills. Children between the ages of 2 and 5 years evaluate their abilities in very direct ways and use objective standards of judgment (whether they have completed a task or not) rather than using social comparisons for self-evaluation. Young boys and girls are further socialized to engage in rather traditional masculine and feminine ways of behaving.

Children develop inner self-esteem during the preschool years by becoming more independent, learning skills that will enable them to become more self-sufficient, acquiring skills that will enable them to develop morally competent ways of behaving, and learning how to cope with anger. For optimal development to occur, parents need to recognize and accept their child's temperament (easy, difficult, slow-to-warm-up) and establish children's sense of security by helping them feel protected and safe.

# CHAPTER 3  Developing Inner Self-Esteem during the School-Age Years
## Social Self-Esteem

## The School-Age Child

School-age children are no longer babies. The ups and downs of the preschool years lie behind them, and the demands of adult life are still a long way off. The middle childhood years, however, bring their own special challenges. In middle childhood a child is taken out of the home and thrust into a new location with a group of new peers. This stimulates the child's mind in a world of sophisticated knowledge as well as the child's body in the atmosphere of new sports and games. Camaraderie takes on new meaning.

In general, middle childhood (ages 7 to 12 years) is a time of concreteness. Children are concrete thinkers who are highly dependent on actually manipulating objects or being able to concretely imagine them when they are solving problems. They have little capacity for abstract thinking.

On a social level, children's all-consuming interest in their parents subsides, as they withdraw their emotional energy from adults and begin to unite with their peers. Middle childhood is characterized by a shift from egocentrism to sociocentrism, a shift from initial awareness of self to an awareness of others, and also a shift from self-satisfaction to concern for the satisfaction of others. Children are busy with the process of blending into the social fabric.

During middle childhood, children develop a spirit of group-mindedness and social consciousness. They become quite concerned about what others think of them. There is an overwhelming importance of doing what the gang does, of being competent, of being liked by the rest of the class. The adequacy of their self-images is based on the reflections they perceive from the peer group and on how well they master the specific academic and social tasks required in school, at home, and among their peers.

Their "Keep out!" signs reveal their need for privacy and their identity with the peer group. They seek ways of expressing their individuality, independence, and separateness and need to escape from the adult world. Shifting from a dependent role to a more independent one is still a gradual process, and children often vacillate between these two poles. At times, they may attempt to assert their independence by resisting adult control, reacting negatively to rules and regulations, or accusing their parents of treating them like babies. At other times, they may want to slip back and take on the comfortable, dependent role.

Their emotional life revolves around actual situations rather than the more fanciful world of early childhood. Children tend to worry about their grades, promotion to the next grade, and what other people think about them. Eleven- and 12-year-olds, in particular, tend to worry more than others about being popular. Temper tantrums may be exhibited by children during middle childhood if they do not get their own way. Some resort to sudden explosions—stomp to their rooms, scream, cry, or yell, and slam their bedroom doors—to punctuate their anger. Others may respond in a more sophisticated manner, giving parents the old silent treatment as they retire to the seclusion of their rooms.

Morally, life is viewed from a black-and-white perspective. Rules of the game are of paramount importance, and certain behaviors are viewed as totally right or totally wrong. Children in middle childhood usually accept the family's views on moral issues. Parents expect children to be responsible for their behavior. Children clearly show an awareness of right and wrong and are generally able to follow the straight and narrow. Many children do not understand and are shocked by white lies, injustice, and the many inconsistencies of adults who may demand a standard of behavior from the child that they do not practice themselves. Children are both bewildered and resentful when parents or other adults try to introduce shades of gray into their strict standards of values or behavior.

## Typical Behavior during the School-Age Years

Parents may find that their 6-year-old is not quite the same calm little person that he or she was at 5 years of age. At 6 years, children are branching out; it is a rambunctious, feisty, expansive stage. Children are trying, so it seems, to do everything possible at once, as they thrust from the secure world of their homes to explore new worlds outside the home. Mother is no longer the center of the child's world—now the child wants to be the center of everything. He wants to be the best, the most important, and mothers are relegated to second place. Children are the center of their own world and may become quite demanding. It seems that mother cannot do anything right. More often than not, she gets blamed by the child for everything that goes wrong in her child's world.

Six-year-olds tend to be ambivalent little souls characterized by opposites and extremes. At times they are at their best when company arrives; at times they are at their worst. At times they are loving; at times they are angry. They can be bold and brash and, then, childlike and babyish. They are able to be "strong" in front of their younger siblings while getting a tetanus shot and at other times wail their hearts out because they skinned their knees, convinced that they need surgery for the wound.

Most children now spend a full day in school. They marvel at their academic accomplishments and take great pride in receiving stars and smiley faces from the teacher. The child is proud of these recognitions of success. Because school can be a more sedentary place with less time for activity than in preschool, children need opportunities to release pent-up energies when they return home.

Physically, 6-year-olds are stronger and more skillful than they were at 5 but still have trouble with skills requiring fine motor coordination. Their vocabulary is rapidly expanding, sometimes in ways that are not appreciated by parents, for many children begin to incorporate expletives and "bathroom" language into their personal communiqués. Six-year-olds are rather inflexible; they want everything to happen in a certain way and often make rigid demands on others. They have a hard time accepting criticism; they have to be right, they have to be the winners.

After the expansive, vigorous activity seen in 6-year-olds, 7-year-olds seem quite pensive, silent, and somber. It's almost as though they need a break from the exuberance of their sixth year and need to mull things over for a period of time. They are in a focal period in which they like to be alone more often and perhaps "reflect" on their life. Another reason for the quietness observed at this age is that they are moving from the world of fantasy to the world of reality. Many children are questioning what is fantasy and what is reality. Doubts about whether Santa Claus or the tooth fairy or the Easter Bunny are real fester and many learn that they are not. Because of their more reflective, contemplative needs, 7-year-olds require a private place in the home that they don't have to share with anyone else.

Seven-year-olds are easily disappointed when things don't turn out as planned. They cannot understand why, for example, one cannot drive in a raging blizzard to get the stickers mother had promised. They tend to want their way most of the time. If they are playing a game with their friends and their friends don't want to play using the child's new rules, many children of this age just simply say, "Well, then I quit. I don't want to play your stupid game."

At this age, children are not especially adventurous and many prefer to engage in quiet activities such as watching television, reading, or doing puzzles. They are not quite as self-centered as they were when they were 6; they may even listen to someone else's side of the story. Children at this age are also somewhat insecure, with many firmly believing that their parents prefer their siblings to them. They often notice what the parents do for the sibling ("Dad fixed my brother's bike") and not what the parent does for them ("Dad never fixes my bike").

Eight-year-olds leave behind their more serious, withdrawn, and inward stage of 7. They have further consolidated the self they were meditating over at 7 years and now are ready to burst forth with vigorous, exuberant experimenting. They are ready to tackle all sorts of activities with gusto, bravado, and verve. Eight is an expansive stage physically, emotionally, and mentally. Eight-year-olds are often hurried, careless, noisy, and somewhat rebellious individuals. They often run instead of walk, slam doors, and talk loudly as if the whole block needs to hear what they have to say. We see more confidence in 8-year-olds; they tend to try new activities and tend to follow them through to completion.

Eight-year-olds are great collectors of anything from stickers to baseball cards to beer cans. While parents may not enjoy having their house smell like the Budweiser brewery, collections offer children a sense of pride in ownership and status among their collecting counterparts and even help them with organizational skills. Eight-year-olds are truly motivated by money. Their allowance, however, should not be used as a motivational tool to do chores. This is their money and they are responsible for it. Whatever their allowance is supposed to cover (lunch money, new toys, etc.), they have to learn to manage it so they can pay for these items. What parents can do is list "bonus chores," chores that are above and beyond the call of duty, such as washing windows or cleaning the basement and offer children additional money if they want to do these extra chores.

Eight-year-olds are careless and often lose possessions such as jackets and shoes. Their relationship with mother may not be very smooth since 8-year-olds tend to be somewhat critical and argumentative. (Can adolescence be far off?) Eight-year-olds are the best excuse-makers around; they have excuses for everything from not doing their chores to not doing their homework. They are ready for action and are fast-paced—they eat, play, and talk fast. They are great conversationalists and love to talk to anyone who will listen.

As the 8-year-old bolts out the door, the 9-year-old enters with a great deal of adultlike poise. The phrase "he's 9 going on 39" is applicable to this age group. Nine-year-olds are moving away from mother to establish relationships with peers. There is a greater detachment from parents; 9-year-olds have a strong loyalty to and interest in their friends. They are social creatures and love being with their friends as often as possible.

The key word describing 9-year-olds is independence. They no longer want (or tolerate) being treated like babies. They like to feel that they can do things for themselves and tend to resist authoritarian commands. (It is, however, okay for them to be bossy and authoritarian in their actions toward others.) The 9-year-old is not the expansive, buoyant person she was at 8, but more like the quiet, introspective 7-year-old. Once again, children sift and sort their experiences and evaluate themselves in light of those experiences. Their new powers of self-appraisal are deeper and more discriminating now.

Many children are quite capable of carrying out their responsibilities independently, provided parents are not expecting them to do more than they are capable of doing. Nine-year-olds, however, are quite critical of themselves and may feel they are too fat or too thin, too tall or too short, and so forth. Nine-year-olds can be extremely self-conscious. The slightest problem, whether it be one too many freckles or wearing glasses, may prevent them from actively entering into social activities.

At 9 years children get a better hold of themselves; they seem more together than when they were 8 years old. Eight-year-olds are more dependent on receiving recognition and support from their parents and are not terribly self-motivated. (Money motivates them more than anything.) Nine-year-olds acquire new forms of self-dependence and self-motivation; they are not as money-mad nor are they too dependent on praise. Nine-year-olds like to be trusted, like being on their own, and relish in being given new freedoms, such as being responsible for their allowance. They tend to be fair-minded, somewhat business-like, and quite responsible.

Ten-year-olds appear to be in a stage of predictability, comfort, and calm. They are relaxed and casual and are able to take most things in stride. Of course, there are the usual differences of opinion between parent and child regarding bedtime, cleanliness, punctuality, and everyday mishaps, but in general, 10-year-olds are agreeable, content, and compliant. Unlike the critical 9-year-old, 10-year-olds are happy with their mothers and proud of their fathers. In general, it is a period of equilibrium; they are very easy to get along with.

Many 10-year-olds have a steady set of friends; boys tend to have five or six boys that are their "best friends;" girls tend to form triads, which may lead to some friction. Two of the friends may decide to form a dyad leaving the third girl out temporarily; these dyad relationships frequently switch between the three girls. Ten-year-olds love to hear secrets but are not always very good at keeping secrets told to them by others, and this may be a main reason for girls' switching loyalties in their best friends. Girls are more aware of interpersonal relationships than are boys. They are very aware of their clothes, hairstyles, and overall appearance.

Contentment with self at 10 years turns to supercriticalness at 11. Children are aware of their faults and resent criticism from others. Eleven-year-olds tend to be somewhat pessimistic and more often than not believe that things are likely to go wrong. Their favorite thing to do is be with their friends, and they are not terribly enthusiastic about doing things with their parents. In fact, 11-year-olds are quite critical of adults. More often than not, they rebel at routine and resent being told what to do. Eleven-year-olds tend to isolate themselves from their parents. "Do not enter" signs may be posted on their bedroom doors to ward off "intruding" siblings or parents. They are very sensitive to criticism.

Being popular is important to children at this age, particularly for girls. In order to be accepted, they want to dress, talk, and act the way their friends do. As a result, 11-year-olds are quite conforming. Friendships become more stable at this age, and many of these children have a circle of friends that tends to remain quite constant. The "cliques" that are formed at this age tend to last into high school and beyond.

Twelve-year-olds are more accepting of their parents and even, on occasion, may enjoy being with the family. They do make a clear distinction of their world of peers and the adult world. Often forgetting that their parents were once kids themselves, they frequently think that parents couldn't possibly understand what they are experiencing in their world. They are quite self-reliant, responsible, and mature. Those who have begun their growth spurt (around 12 years for girls; around 13 or 14 for boys) may be more moody, restless, and lazy.

Twelve-year-olds are also conformists, and copying what everyone else is doing takes on importance. Girls tend to have crushes on boys and consider being popular with boys their number one goal. While some boys may show an interest in the opposite sex, most are content to play baseball and stick with their same-sex peers.

The proposition that the peer group becomes the predominant reference group for the child may be measured by the degree to which the child conforms to group norms. Twelve-year-olds appear to be the most conforming, reflecting the significance of peers. In other words, with children's increasing integration into the peer group between early childhood and late childhood, they grow to value it with increasing importance.

It should be pointed out that while peers and family influences play a significant role in determining children's level of self-esteem, peers tend to be less influential than the family. This is so because when children begin to incorporate nonfamily influences into their self-pictures, they are at a more cognitively advanced stage and therefore are less helpless. That is, the evaluations and standards of nonfamily agents are more amenable to scrutiny by children's higher intellectual faculties. By contrast, the evaluations and standards of the child's family, incorporated at an earlier, less advanced age, tend to be accepted without critical judgment. This is not to say, however, that negative images formed in the earlier years cannot be changed.

## Development of Self in Middle Childhood

While a child's evaluations of self are continually growing and changing, they begin, during middle childhood, to solidify and resist changes that disturb their evaluations of self. Sometime between the ages of 8 and 9 years, children begin to develop a relatively stable view of their capacities in many areas. Once children's self-evaluations begin to jell, they tend to behave in accordance with their preconceived notions of themselves. Children's subjective evaluations of themselves become the core element in structuring their behavior. This means that they try to protect and preserve the evaluations they hold of themselves; a need for internal consistency pushes them to resist and reject anything incompatible with their self-evaluations. Behavior must always be appropriate to their self-evaluations.

Thus, children's self-esteem tends to become more selective as to which features of their experiences are assumed to be self-referring. If an attitude or value seems to fit in, they are likely to adopt it. If it is inconsistent with their self-pictures, they are likely to ignore or reject it. Children tend to erect a perceptual barrier around themselves. Events that are new or that confirm the already developed self-evaluation readily gain admittance; others are denied or discouraged.

If, for example, one of Susie's self-evaluations is that she is disliked by others and someone tells her that she is a likeable person, she may resort to a number of ways to "reject" this information that is inconsistent with her self-evaluation. She may say, "This person doesn't know what he is talking about," or, "Wait until she knows me better and finds out what I'm really like." Children will twist and cram experiences into preconceived slots in an attempt to maintain consistency of self. Any value that is inconsistent with children's evaluations of themselves cannot be assimilated.

Because children have a strong tendency to defend their self-evaluations, they are apt to blot out any positive messages about their own competence if such messages are in conflict with an unfavorable picture of self. Individuals who believe that they are weak or stupid will cling to perceptions that bolster this unflattering picture and reject any suggestions that they may be strong or bright. To protect good self-esteem, they will strive hard or will select behaviors that preserve or enhance it. Children generally solve any dissonance between evidence about themselves and their judgment of a situation in which they are involved by retaining their customary judgment of themselves. Once they have formulated a particular self-evaluation, they proceed through life behaving according to their particular self-evaluations and expect the people in their environment to treat them accordingly. Thus, children's self-evaluations will be reflected in their actions and reinforced by the feedback they receive from others. Their experiences confirm their expectations, and a vicious or beneficent cycle is set up.

## Seeing What We Want to See

Children's self-evaluations influence the way they perceive their environment. They subjectively view their environment in ways that are consistent with their self-pictures. If a young child's self-evaluation is that the teacher doesn't like her (even though this may not be the case) she will "see" the teacher in ways that support this self-evaluation. The teacher, for example, may be passing back spelling papers, with a blank expression on her face that doesn't change as she returns the papers to her students. Our young child, however, "sees" the teacher differently; she sees her teacher give her a dirty look as she gives her paper back. Similarly, if children think they are social klutzes, they "see" others treating them like "third wheels;" if they feel unworthy, they "see" others treating them with rudeness and insult.

## Behaving in Ways Consistent with Self-Esteem

Children's perceptions, in turn, influence the way they behave. In other words, their evaluations of self become strong enough to help dictate their behavior; self-evaluation thus becomes an agent of socialization as well as a product of it. Children with negative self-evaluations seem to want others to think as poorly of them as they do of themselves. They attempt to produce in others the response they expect. If someone sees herself as unattractive to others, she behaves in a manner consistent with this self-image. She doesn't take time to fix her hair or wear fashionable clothes, maintains bad posture, and so on. Children who feel academically inadequate see themselves as unable to achieve and therefore behave in such a way that they really do fail to attain academic superiority. Such children have to make poor grades in order to be true to themselves, for it would be just as wrong for these children who believe themselves to be dumb in their studies to make good grades as it would be for children who define themselves as honest to steal. Children's self-evaluations (I am smart/not smart; pretty/not pretty; good at sports/not good at sports) influence their perceptions and, in turn, their behaviors. Once children have definite self-evaluations, they create experiences to fortify these evaluations.

During the school years, children classify their own positive and negative self-attributes in order to arrive at general feelings about themselves. Because these children are not capable of reasoning abstractly, their evaluations of self revolve around concrete, observable traits. Children's self-evaluations become more coherent, more complex, better organized, and more focused. Global evaluations of self ("all smart" or "all dumb") are replaced by differential evaluations ("smart in English, dumb in math"). With increasing age, portrayals of self shift from superficial, concrete qualities in middle childhood to more ephemeral and abstract features in adolescence.

During middle childhood, children's breadth of self-descriptions increases from a few physical qualities, motor skills, sex type, and age, which are the hallmarks of young children's self-pictures, to a number of new categories centering primarily on concrete and observable traits. Consider the following self-descriptions reported by a girl age 7 and a boy age 9.

> I am 7 years old. I have one sister. Next year I will be eight. I like coloring. The game I like is hide the thimble. I go riding every Wednesday. I have lots of toys. I like flowers—roses, buttercups and daisies. I like milk to drink and meat and potatoes to eat.
> I have dark brown hair, brown eyes, and a fair face. I am a quick worker, but am often lazy. I am good but often naughty. I am sometimes funny and sometimes serious. I am sometimes silly and stupid and often good.[1]

These descriptions can be categorized into "peripheral" and "dispositional" statements. Peripheral statements refer to appearance, identity information (such as name or age), routine activities or habits, possessions, details of life events, likes and dislikes, and social roles. Peripheral self-evaluations tend to be rather superficial, concrete, and are based on observable characteristics. Dispositional statements, which include personality traits, general trends in behavior, motives, needs, values, and attitudes, are more sophisticated, less superficial, and less concrete. As children get older, we see a shift from peripheral evaluations to more dispositional ones. Moreover, the most pronounced change occurs between the ages of 7 and 9.

Children also describe themselves using characteristics that distinguish them from other children.[2] For instance, children who are six or more months older or younger than the model age for their class are more likely to mention their age when describing themselves. Similarly, foreign-born children tend to mention their birthplace. Children report hair color, eye color, and weight much more frequently if these characteristics are distinct from those of their classmates. Apparently, then, older children exhibit high sensitivity to even small qualitative differences in particular characteristics, suggesting that children often define the self by characteristics that they sense will distinguish them clearly from others.

Children are also aware that they are distinct or different from others, not just because of physical differences but because they have different thoughts and feelings. The self is now defined internally as well as externally. As one 10-year-old commented, "There could be a person who looks like me, but no one can ever think just like me." They now see that the self can monitor its own thoughts. ("I can do well in math, if I really try.")

Children also tend to describe themselves in terms of their physical abilities relative to others, such as, "I can ride a bike better than my brother." This indicates that children are now distinguishing themselves in terms of their active abilities in comparison to others rather than in absolute terms, as they did in early childhood. As children progress through the elementary grades, evaluations are increasingly based on normative criteria (standard of average performances), and children begin to define competence in terms of social comparison.

Social self-evaluations make their appearance during the school-age years.[3] Who they are becomes intimately tied to the many other people around them. That is, children define the self in terms of traits they usually exhibit in their dealings with others: kind, friendly, tough, shy, and so on. Similarly, children refer to social group memberships in their self-descriptions. A child might say, for example, that he is a Boy Scout or a Catholic. This suggests that the social self becomes predominant during middle childhood and the active or the physical self becomes less important.

With increasing age, children assimilate into their picture of self the recognition or feedback received from their peers as well as teachers and other people of authority. Children begin to judge themselves through many experiences and interactions, gradually attaching more importance to their peers' evaluations of them.[4] Much of children's earlier interest with adults and parents subsides, as they withdraw their emotional energy from adults and begin to unite with their society of peers. Thus, children's gradual integration into the peer group is accompanied by a shift from a reliance on parents for evaluations of self to a reliance on peers. Unlike arbitrary praise and approval given by parents to their preschool-age children, however, evaluations from parents and peers during middle childhood is based on children's actual competencies. Thus, building inner self-esteem and acquiring appropriate behaviors and skills takes on an added importance during middle childhood.

## Self-Esteem in Boys and Girls

This is not to say that outer self-esteem, based on evaluations received from others, is unimportant at this stage. During middle childhood, children receive powerful external messages that influence their self-esteem and very often these messages are different for boys and girls. Parents, however, are not the only ones that influence the development of self-evaluations that differ according to gender. Children's outer self-esteem, during middle childhood, is differentially influenced by television and by teachers. Television, to illustrate, is embedded in the cultural fabric and tends to reinforce the values and the approved sex-typed behavior of our society. It continues to present to the child male and female stereotypes. How does television influence self-esteem in males and females? The most widely researched aspect of television and self-esteem in males and females is the nature of gender roles in television material seen by children.

There are markedly more males than females on television. Males are seen as dominant, aggressive, get-the-job-done people. They are more active, autonomous, and problem-solving. The roles they play are highly prestigious; they are usually doctors, lawyers, law enforcement officials, and the like. On prime-time television, 71 percent of the men are portrayed as professionals compared with 29 percent of prime-time female characters.[5]

Females are underrepresented in virtually every aspect of the television schedule and in every kind of programming seen by children.[6] Women fill only about one third of the roles in prime time and are most frequently seen as nurses, secretaries, or entertainers. In general, women are in marital, romantic, or family roles and are portrayed as more attractive, sociable, and rule-abiding. Women are usually younger than men. Women, more so than men, are likely to be romantically involved, performing homemaking activities for others, and engaging in child-care activities.

What messages are children receiving from television? A male should be powerful and have a good job. In trying to reach these goals he should be aggressive, try to remain unemotional, and be smart. A female should strive for marriage; the jobs she is capable of performing are mediocre and pay poorly, so she needs the support of a man. In order to achieve this goal, she must remain youthful looking and attractive and be warm and sensitive. Being impressionable, children, especially those watching massive doses of these programs, incorporate these stereotypes into their self-images and behave accordingly.

On a more problematic note, girls receive messages that in order to be successful women they need to be young and beautiful. Unfortunately, basing self-esteem on these rather superficial and fading commodities can cause problems as a woman gets older, when she may not be able to maintain her youthful appearance. Boys, however, receive messages that self-esteem is based on more substantial, more attainable phenomena, such as education and profession. At least, men have more control over obtaining these goals and they're not as vulnerable to losing them as they get older.

More subtle yet powerful forms of differential treatment may occur in the classroom. It appears that our educational systems still support a policy of training boys for individualistic behavior and girls for socially conforming behavior. Most teachers, however, are not aware that they are treating boys and girls differently and giving boys a decided advantage over girls.

It has been said that teachers respond more positively to their preferred gender. If so, whom do they prefer? In general, it appears that female teachers prefer male students.[7] Some teachers have pointed out that males are more honest, more willing to exchange their ideas, more willing to try new things, and, in general, are easier to talk to. The only reasons mentioned for liking girls is that they are obedient and thus do not present disciplinary problems.

Although girls are rated by teachers as being more hardworking than boys, boys have more interactions of all kinds with their teachers. Teachers make a distinction between high-achieving boys and average- or low-achieving boys. High-achieving boys have the most favorable interactions with their teachers and receive a great deal of praise from them. Teachers prefer high-achieving boys and will interact at a higher level and encourage continued responses from them.[8] Average- or low-achieving boys interact less frequently with their teachers and are criticized the most. Girls of *all achievement levels*, however, are treated alike. High-achieving boys have been shown to receive more praise than high-achieving girls at the elementary and high school level. Thus, the way teachers treat high-achieving girls may lead to lower levels of achievement among girls.

Teachers tend to prefer girls who act in dependent ways—ones who are quiet but attentive in class, do extra-credit assignments, follow directions, and obey rules. Thus, the submissive, achieving girls and the high-achieving, outspoken boys are preferred, and their behavior is rewarded by teachers. Teachers tend to pay more attention to boys and give them twice as much individual instruction on tasks as they give girls. Boys are rewarded more for academic achievement, and girls are reinforced for being dependent and staying close to teachers. Boys are encouraged to be creative and independent in their activities, while teachers are more likely to take over and complete a task for a girl.

Teachers tend to respond to boys when they are behaving aggressively but tend to ignore girls when they are behaving in an aggressive manner. Furthermore, teachers tend to respond and attend to girls' low-intensity demands. These responses teach boys that being physically assertive gets attention and teaches girls that talking gets attention. Thus, stereotypic masculine and feminine ways of behaving are perpetuated—boys are assertive and girls talk a lot.

## Building Inner Self-Esteem during Middle Childhood: Social Self-Esteem

Children's social relationships with peers most often develop through the school environment, and these relationships serve as the feedback source for the development of social self-esteem. Learning to get along with others, which contributes to social self-esteem, is vital to the child's future adjustment. Doing well in school, leading to high academic self-esteem, is another important task for children in middle childhood. The development of social understanding, the establishment of effective peer relationships, and school adjustment are some of the salient developmental issues that children need to master in the early and middle years of childhood in order to form high inner self-esteem. During the school-age years, a significant portion of children's inner self-esteem is based on these two developmental tasks. Thus, the school setting becomes the second most important environment in the development of self-esteem. School is second only to the home as an institution that determines children's self-images. Let's begin with children's social self-esteem.

It may be helpful for parents to measure their child's social self-esteem by having their child answer true or false to the questions in Table 2.

If your child's answers agree with 13 or more of the responses on the key, he or she has adequate social self-evaluations. If, however, they scored significantly below this number, they would profit from learning

**Table 2**. Social Self-Esteem Inventory

| | |
|---|---|
| 1. I like to make new friends. | 11. I wish I had more friends. |
| 2. I wish I got along better with other children. | 12. Friends usually follow my ideas. |
| 3. I often let other children have their own way. | 13. I am a good person. |
| 4. Most kids have more friends than I do. | 14. I wish I were more popular. |
| 5. I am an easy person to like. | 15. I am fun to be with. |
| 6. I am popular with the other kids in my class. | 16. Sometimes I am hard to be friendly with. |
| 7. Other kids pick on me. | 17. Often I don't like to be with other people. |
| 8. I usually play with other kids after school. | 18. Other kids often tease me. |
| 9. I don't play with kids very often. | 19. I sometimes feel lonely. |
| 10. It's hard for me to make friends. | 20. Sometimes I am not very friendly to other kids. |

**Key**

| | | | |
|---|---|---|---|
| 1. true | 6. true | 11. false | 16. false |
| 2. false | 7. false | 12. true | 17. false |
| 3. false | 8. true | 13. true | 18. false |
| 4. false | 9. false | 14. false | 19. false |
| 5. true | 10. false | 15. true | 20. false |

appropriate skills and behaviors in order to feel better about themselves in the social domain.

The peer group plays an important role in assigning status to its individual members, which strongly affects the course of children's socialization. Membership in a group seems to get structured into a hierarchy, from those accorded the highest status to those at the bottom of the popularity poll. It appears that even first-graders are quite capable of rating the children in their classes as well as ranking their own position in the power hierarchy. Most young children appear to agree, for example, about who are the smartest, most liked, and most disliked children in their classes, and these perceptions remain quite stable during the school years.

What determines a child's status in the hierarchy? What determines a child's acceptance or rejection? Social acceptance and rejection are correlated with behavioral characteristics of the child. One observes distinct behavioral profiles of children with different social status.

## Behaviors Associated with Popular Children

Social science researchers have noted that across all ages, social competence is related to the same general set of behaviors. Social popularity and peer acceptance have been found to be related to athletic and extracurricular competencies and academic achievement. Children who are involved in sports and school activities and those who do well in their studies tend to be more highly accepted by others. Personality traits such as extroversion, honesty, cheerfulness, and cooperation have been noted as desirable personality traits found in popular children. Popular children are prosocial (sharing, giving, less egocentric) and tend to help set up rules and norms for the group.

The popular child tends to be more sociocentric than egocentric. That is, popular children tend to be thoughtful of others' feelings, be accepting of others, and show concern and interest in others. They are sensitive not only to the feelings of others but also to the effect their behavior has on others. They can analyze their actions and communications and adjust them so as to interact in a positive manner. For example, children with high social competence are more accurate at encoding emotions of others (anger, disgust, happiness, sadness) than less socially competent, same-sex peers. A high level of skill in understanding others' feelings is associated with social competence and, in turn, popularity. High-status children can recognize the affective expression of others and are thus better liked by their peers. Similarly, socially competent children tend to make accurate and constructive attributions for behavior ("I was tired today and not very nice to Mary; I'd better tell her I am sorry for what I said"), whereas socially incompetent children have a tendency to make self-defeating or inappropriate attributions for behavior ("I'm such a loser, I always say the wrong things to people.").

This is how researchers, based on empirical studies, have categorized popular children. Many of these studies, however, were conducted on younger children (preschoolers) and older children (adolescents). One gets a different impression when observing popular children between the ages of 9 and 14 years. They do not appear to be as prosocial or empathetic to other children. In fact, many of these children appear to be aloof (and, at times, cruel) to the feelings of others. In many cases, the so-called popular children are sarcastic, demanding, and dictatorial. Another correlate of popularity (not discussed by researchers) is money. Popular children tend to have access to many of life's material pleasures—expensive clothes, homes, and toys.

These types of popular children, however, tend not to remain popular as they grow older. Eventually, these children who callously neglect the feelings of others and depend on their material advantages to define their social meaningfulness fall from their fragile pedestals. Even in a materialistic society such as ours, many adults value friends for their loyalty, respect, sense of humor, and honesty—not for their designer clothing. We need to be realistic, however. Children are more superficial. One area that appears to be particularly important in children's social hierarchy is the clothes our children wear. Wearing outmoded clothes can inhibit a child's chance of acceptance by the other children, though it certainly shouldn't. However, as children get older, they are more likely to be able to express their self-image by wearing clothes they feel comfortable in and not follow the "popular" crowd.

## Developing Socially Competent Children

We are a social species; most of our happiness and fulfillment rests on our ability to relate effectively to others. Interpersonal relationships are essential for children's personal well-being, since many of their higher-level needs, those of status, respect, and self-expression, are satisfied by group recognition or thwarted by group denial. Children's progress in any area of endeavor is dependent on their social stability. At any age level a feeling of belonging is essential to functioning effectively. In fact, interpersonal relations play such an important role in children's lives that how children relate to their peers may be regarded as kind of a barometer of their level of adjustment to life in general. Therefore, helping children develop inner social self-esteem is very essential.

## The Role of Parents in the Development of Social Competence

Social competence refers to the

ability to function effectively in interpersonal transactions, in which the term "effective" means outcomes that are successful from the perspectives of all social partners. As such it encompasses skills and abilities relating to all aspects of interpersonal problem solving, from self-regulation of emotions aroused in social interaction, to the negotiation of solutions in interpersonal conflicts.[9]

As noted in Chapter 1, the foundations of social self-esteem are built in infancy. Infants who are securely attached tend to become socially competent when older. Securely attached children, for example, tend to display more positive feelings, empathy, and social competence and express less negative feelings than insecurely attached children.[10] Securely attached children tend to be described as having more friends and behaving more compliantly. Insecurely attached children are hindered in their development of social competence by the fact that their parents tend to be insensitive and unresponsive, emotionally unavailable, poorly attuned to social situations, and unable to anticipate others' behaviors, the consequences of these behaviors, or the outcomes of their own actions.

The parent–child relationship plays a powerful role in helping children develop socially competent behavior.[11] Consistencies in past experiences influence future interactions by providing frameworks for interpersonal understanding and guidelines for responding to others. It appears also that the type of relationship children have with their mothers is generalized to other relationships. In Bowlby's terms, this relationship creates an inner working model that becomes the prototype for other relationships. Generalizations formed from past relationship experiences provide children with expectations of their relationships with others. Similarly, knowledge from past relationships influences later relationship experiences because it affects children's perceptions of social encounters. Thus, parent–child relationships are the prime context for development of early social skills and social-cognitive processing.

The parent–child relationship serves at least three functions in the child's development of social competence:

(1) Parent–child interaction sets the stage in which many competencies necessary for social interaction begin to develop. This relationship furnishes the child with many of the skills needed to conduct relationships with other people, such as language skills and the ability to control impulses.
(2) The parent–child relationship constitutes emotional and cognitive resources that allow the child to explore his or her social and nonsocial environments. It is the safety net permitting the child to take the risk of venturing forth and a source of help in problem solving.
(3) The parent–child relationship is the forerunner of other relationships. It is in this relationship that the child begins to form the expectations and assumptions about interactions with other people and to develop strategies for protecting the self and attaining personal goals.[12]

Sensitive and responsive parents who are emotionally available, highly attuned to social situations, and socially competent in anticipating others' behaviors and the consequences of these behaviors tend to have socially competent children. Parents who lack these skills may be more preoccupied with their own rather than their children's needs. Consequently, they often fail to notice when their children are having difficulty with peers. In these situations, parents are likely to be ineffective teachers of social skills.[13] Sensitive parenting involves setting clear expectations, exerting rational control, communicating openly, and providing warmth and support. These kinds of parental behaviors are associated with social competence in children.[14]

It appears that parental involvement in organizing and managing children's social contacts is associated with positive peer relations.[15] Furthermore, the more mothers value and feel responsible for their children's sociability, the more their children are likely to demonstrate social competence in the classroom.[16] Mothers who tend not to believe as strongly in the importance of social skills have children who demonstrate less social competence. Mothers who do not recognize the importance of social relationships tend to have children who attempt to control the behavior of others, cry when trying to achieve their goals, and show indications of being hyperactive and distractable. Thus, parental involvement and strong beliefs in the importance of developing good social skills is associated with the development of socially competent behavior in children.

Optimistic parental interpretations of children's behavior appear to be associated with social competence in children.[17] Mothers with socially competent children tend to believe that social skills and lack thereof are caused by factors external to their children, such as parental teaching and the provision of opportunities for peer play. Mothers of children who do not demonstrate social competence tend to believe that the development of social competence is caused by internal factors (the child is born that way or is too insecure)

Mothers of socially competent children also tend to see their children's behavior more realistically than mothers of socially incompetent children. Danny's mother, for example, recognizes that he is displaying hyperactive, acting-out behaviors that his classmates find annoying, and thus, his chances of being liked by the other children have lessened. Danny's mother then tries to help him develop more socially competent ways of behaving. Peter displays similar types of acting-out behavior; yet, his mother continues to believe that he is just an active boy with no problems at all. When parents deny or excuse their children's socially incompetent ways of behaving, children have a poor chance of developing more appropriate social behaviors.

Differences in the frequency, intensity, and quality of parental involvement appear to be important predictors of children's social competence with peers. To illustrate, children's success with peers is associated with moderate levels of parental structuring and organizing, including the child in decision-making situations, and actual coaching and advice, focusing on group-oriented and nondisruptive play strategies.[18]

## Coaching

Parents can become coaches who verbally transmit rules of social behavior. The procedure consists of three basic components: verbal instruction of how to behave in socially acceptable ways, opportunity to rehearse or practice new social skills, and review of the child's progress in mastering these new social skills. For example, parents can target the behavior that the child needs to learn: how to enter a group, be attentive, share, follow rules, initiate entry in the peer group, meet expectations of the peer group, respond to failure, ask questions of peers, lead peers by offering useful suggestions or direction, offer supportive statements to peers, and so on. Then, parents teach the child how to master these skills. For example, Janine is not very polite to her peers and teachers. Her parents, then, can target some behaviors that will help her become more polite to others. Janine can be taught to share or cooperate, comfort a peer who is troubled, say thank you to a peer who has been helpful, and apologize when she has accidently hurt a peer. She should then be given opportunities to practice these skills with other children. Afterwards, Janine should meet with her parents (coaches) to review the skills she has been taught.

During coaching sessions, parents should be warm and approving, not critical and cold. After informing the child about appropriate ways of behaving and giving her opportunities to practice, parents will want to review the child's progress. This should be a positive review. Janine's parents, for example, can put a poster in her room titled "My Best Behavior Is: Being Nice to Others." Under this, parents should note the date and specific displays of the target behavior. (e.g., February 12—allowed a friend to play with Nintendo game). When Janine has performed three or four "nice to others" behaviors, her parents then should reward her with something that she desires, for example, an extra half-hour of television on Friday night, a trip to Ben and Jerry's for an ice-cream cone, or having a friend spend the night. The comments noted on the poster should be very specific, not global and general. ("Played well today" is too broad and meaningless.)

Coaching involves identifying the child's problem and providing some form of instruction regarding strategies for interacting with peers. Concepts that can be used include participation (how to get started and the importance of paying attention), cooperation (the importance of taking turns and sharing materials), communication (the importance of talking with others and listening), and being friendly and nice (the importance of smiling, helping, and encouraging others). Coaches can assist children by

1. Telling them why each concept is important to peer interaction
2. Asking for examples to assess children's understanding of the concept
3. Reinforcing the examples or providing suggestions when children have trouble finding their own examples
4. Discussing both the positive and negative behavioral examples that are important to interactions
5. Trying out some of the ideas in play situations
6. Assessing the situation afterward.[19]

Choose one particular behavior to work on at a time. When the child has successfully mastered it, move on to the next target behavior. Let's say a child is unpopular because he or she is constantly tattling on the other children. Some children delight in telling of other children's bad deeds and do so for various reasons. Some may engage in this behavior because they themselves may want to take part in the forbidden activity but manage to control their impulses. These children are seeking approval for not participating. If this is the case, parents may remark that they are glad the child is not participating, but that is all they should say. Other children may tattle because they have few friends, and they want to retaliate or get even for lack of friends. Others tattle for attention or to put others down to save their own shaky self-esteem.

Parents should ignore the child's tattling behavior. In addition, they need to work on the tattletale's relationship with others. Attention should be given for positive behaviors. Such children need to be coached so that they know the difference between reporting (Lisa fell on the steps and is hurt) and tattling (John is chewing gum). They need to see that in the former type of behavior they are helping someone, while in the latter they're doing harm. Coaching is an effective technique for helping children to learn to engage in behaviors that are positively perceived by their peers.

## Areas of Expertise

Parents can help their children find an area of expertise that is valued by their peers. By capitalizing on their hobbies, collections, skills, and interests, parents can help to stimulate their children's pride and positive recognition from other children.

## Doing Well Academically

Children who are not accepted by others tend to not do well academically. There is evidence that low achievement is partly responsible for these children's low social status. Studies have shown that tutoring rejected children in school subjects is just as effective in enhancing their social competence as training in social skills.[20]

## Becoming Less Egocentric and More Sociocentric

No one likes children who insist on having their way all the time, tell others what to do, and insist that other children follow their rules. It is important for parents to help children learn to subjugate some of their desires for the good of the group. Role playing may be an effective way to help children see how *they* feel when they are bossed around and never have a chance to do what they want to do.

## Communication Skills

Various communication skills have been found to predict social acceptance in middle childhood, and training in communication has been used successfully as a means of bolstering peer acceptance in school-age children. Three communication skills appear to be necessary for children in establishing effective discourse:

1. Ability to direct initiations clearly: Popular children can read a social situation accurately and then enter the group by making relevant conversation. ("I know how to play four-square, I can show you a cool way to throw the ball.") Children who become popular respond positively to the initiations of others. They re-

alize that going for a thing directly may not be the most effective way of attaining it. Children with low self-acceptance approach others in a more aggressive and dictatorial fashion.
("Hey, John, you're not playing well, I'll take your place in the
game.") When communicating they make irrelevant, disruptive, or negative comments to the other players. ("Greg, you're
such a klutz!")

2. Ability to respond clearly and appropriately to the initiations of
others: When others respond to the child, he pays attention to
what they are saying and offers a meaningful comment. They
exchange more meaningful information. ("I don't understand
the new rule you made, will you explain it to me.") Children
who are not accepted by others often speak in monologues,
that is, they don't respond meaningfully to what another child
is saying. ("I make the rules in this game because I know how
to play better than you do.")

3. Ability to reinitiate by providing responses that also serve as
new initiations: Popular children are more inclined to clearly
direct their initiations to specific listeners, speak to all the children involved rather than just one, respond appropriately to
others' initiations, and acknowledge others. All of these skills
contribute to coherent discourse and may be basic to successful
social interaction and subsequently children's peer acceptance.

## Chores

Children's lives need to be balanced with play and responsibilities.
Parents should not demand so many responsibilities that children have
no time for anything else. Children, however, who engage in activities
that make *important contributions* to their families and that are essential for the welfare of their families tend to be more prosocial in their relations with others and tend to exhibit more positive evaluations about
themselves.[21] Children often view chores as meaningless and thus are
reluctant to carry out their family responsibilities. If children are aware
of how much the family depends on them in doing these chores and
how helpful the child is to the family, children will be more dependable
and positive about doing their fair share around the house. Thus, children who, for example, help watch their siblings are performing an activity upon which the family depends. Children realize their important
contributions to their families and tend to feel that they are good peo-

ple. What children do for the good of their families is also good for their self-esteem.

## Flexibility in New Situations

New situations, such as a move to a new location, subject children to difficult circumstances. Children have to deal with "breaking into" existing social groups and cliques, which is not an easy task. Second, each new location may have a completely different set of behaviors that are valued by the children and that are exhibited by popular children. Fear (of the unknown) is a common emotion experienced by children who move frequently; it is unsettling, to say the least, when children don't know anyone and don't know what is expected of them.

Parents can aid children in these situations by showing them that they (the parents) are adjusting to the new situation. Parents need to act as flexible role models who can tackle the tasks that come from moving to a new location. If parents complain about the problems of finding a dentist or doctor, or where to shop, children will pick up on this negativity. Children who move frequently should be encouraged to engage consistently in certain sports or certain clubs. That way when they move to a new location they will continue to have some activity that they have done before and can enjoy in each new location, establishing threads of continuity. Parents can also help their children by talking to their child's new teacher about the community and what kinds of behaviors, games, and activities are considered "cool" by the other children.

# Behaviors Associated with Low-Acceptance Children

Childhood peer status has emerged as a significant predictor of later adjustment. The consequences of peer rejection may be so severe that they result in mental health problems in later life. Children's antisocial dispositions interfere with the development of academic skills necessary for effective learning and with the development of interpersonal skills necessary for forming effective peer relationships. Antisocial children's failure in childhood often translates to social failure in adulthood, that is, the development of socially inappropriate ways of behaving that lead to further rejection from others, academic underachievement, and difficulty in marriage and family relationships.

Children who for one reason or another are unable to establish peer relationships often develop considerable frustration and alienation. Too often they cling to unproductive and unskilled ways of reaching out to others, which results in continued rejection. If they lack social acceptance, their lowered social status causes them to feel inadequate, helpless, and alone. Much of the anxiety and stress children feel is produced because they feel they don't belong. In fact, it is impossible to find one study to refute the statement that children's general emotional adjustment is related to their general acceptance by others. Research consistently shows that the degree of emotional adjustment is associated with the degree of social acceptance throughout the formative years. For these reasons, it is important to identify socially unaccepted children and help them develop socially competent behaviors.

Children who are not accepted by others tend to fall into one of several categories:

1. Quarrelsome, domineering, and aversive with peers
2. Disruptive, defiant, and rebellious
3. Extremely passive and withdrawn
4. Bizarre or seriously disturbed
5. Physically or socially disadvantaged (e.g., low IQ, physical disability, unattractive)[22]

Children whose acceptance by others is low are categorized as neglected, socially withdrawn, rejected-aggressive, and controversial children.

Neglected children initiate fewer social approaches with peers and spend more time in solitary yet appropriate activity on the playground. They are often rated by peers as shy and more socially uninvolved than children of high popularity. These children are not highly liked or disliked by others and, in general, are not at risk for later adjustment problems.

Socially withdrawn children avoid participation with others; they compensate for their inability to find a place among their peers by remaining on the fringes. Shy children don't initiate, complain, demand their fair share, or stand up for their rights. They play by themselves, keep in the background, and try to remain inconspicuous.

Rejected-aggressive children tend to display more deviant behavior (conduct problems, low self-control). They show problems of argumentation, disruptive behavior, and lack of attention. The combination of aggressive behavior and rejected status increases risk for later development of externalizing disorders. There seems to be growing evidence that aggressive *and* disruptive behavior leads to children's future adjustment problems.[23]

Controversial children are just as aggressive and disruptive as their rejected-aggressive peers but they also tend to be more cooperative and more socially engaged with peers than are rejected-aggressive children. These children are sometimes nice to others and sometimes not so nice and, as a result, receive high negative and relatively high positive nominations from their peers. These children are less at risk for later adjustment problems than rejected-aggressive children.

## Neglected Children

Neglected children who seldom interact with others garner very little in the way of praise or hate in the peer group; they are simply "overlooked" by their peers. They have few friends but are not disliked by their peers. Neglected children tend to display less aggression and engage in more solitary play. They tend to receive fewer social overtures from peers than more sociable children. Neglected children tend to exhibit more egocentric speech and direct more of their utterances to imaginary companions or inanimate objects. They are less mature, less assertive, and more compliant or deferential.

Neglected children, however, exhibit no more problem behavior than popular children and are less deviant than rejected children. Further, neglected children are more likely than rejected children to improve their status over time; there is little evidence that these children are at risk for later disorders. Children who are neglected by peers at one time in one context are not commonly neglected at other times in other contexts. Furthermore, even though neglected children receive few best-friend nominations, they are as well liked by peers, on a rating scale measure, as children of average status.

Neglected children, however, are more likely to report not having a best friend and also report the lowest perceived social competence. Neglected children tend to display a generally negative pattern of self-perception including low efficacy and low social expectations. Many neglected children are categorized as socially withdrawn or rejected-withdrawn.

## Socially Withdrawn Children

Socially withdrawn children are outwardly submissive, never show signs of anger, have few friends, and appear lost in a nonreal world. Just as the body, if threatened, fights for life, so does the ego, if threatened, fight for survival. Aggressive children are willing to fight the forces around them with which they cannot come to an agreement on their own terms. Solitary children, however, appear to have given up the effort to adjust to the world of reality. They "adjust" by isolating themselves and thus blot out the annoying tensions of the world. In their world of fantasy, they are strong and loved. They experience no failure or disapproval and can achieve all their goals. The higher their level of anxiety becomes, the more they use fantasy as a protective device.

These shy children avoid other children by taking refuge perhaps in watching television, reading, or devoting their free time to developing special skills or hobbies. For example, they may spend an inordinate amount of time making complex and intricate drawings, building models, or working on a stereo set. Such activities, whatever they may be, further isolate them. Withdrawn children usually reject attempts on the part of a well-meaning adult to get them more socially involved. They don't respond to these adults because these children lack social know-how and have a fear of failure. Shy children are described as higher in anxiety and lower in self-esteem than their more confident counterparts.

**Causes for Withdrawal.** Children who avoid normal social contacts do so for many reasons. Some are motivated by physical weaknesses. Frail children with poor physical stamina may resist attempts to push them into active participation with others. In such cases, shyness is a defense mechanism; it helps them avoid strenuous activities that they feel unable to undertake. Sometimes physical factors, such as braces or being overweight, can cause feelings of shyness.

Shyness in the United States may be a result of cultural norms that overemphasize individual success. Moreover, in some schools, competition to get the best grades, be the most popular, or be the best athlete can be rather fierce. Some children seem to thrive on this type of competitiveness; others, particularly shy children, do not fare as well. Parents may encourage shyness in their children by adhering to traditional values of individual achievement, aspiration, and social approval as the primary measures of self-worth. These pressures for individual achievement may be greater for firstborn children.

Some experts maintain that shyness is not something children are born with but, rather, a learned phenomenon.[24] Some of the factors that may cause shyness in children are difficulties in school; unfavorable comparisons with older siblings, relatives, or peers; loss of usual social supports that result from frequent family moves or from sudden changes in social bonding due to divorce and death; and lack of experience in social settings.

Some shy children may be overwhelmed by all kinds of fears—of school, failure, rejection from their peers, and the future in general. They may decide, as a result, to give up trying to master their environment by retreating into a pleasant world of make-believe. Such children often feel inferior to others, and their withdrawal is a method of avoiding painful situations in which their awkward behavior becomes clearly visible.

Not surprisingly, shy children often develop feelings of anger and resentment. Unlike aggressive youngsters, they have difficulty relieving such tensions. Some cases of excessive shyness can be traced to problems in the home. A common reason for shyness in children is that they are simply imitating their parents' shyness. The two extremes of rejection and overprotection by parents may lead to shyness. Overprotected children become clingy and dependent. Often, their mothers try to anticipate their every need, fight their every battle, and suffer their every pain, thus robbing them of the freedom to develop their own emotional strength.

Other researchers have concluded that biological factors predispose infants to display shy behaviors.[25] Extremely shy children, for example, have significantly higher heart rates and heart variabilities than children who are not shy. In addition, shy children have higher levels of norepinephrine, a neurotransmitter that tends to rev up the sympathetic nervous system when children face unfamiliar, unpredictable, or challenging situations. Moreover, shy children tend to have higher levels of the hormone cortisol, which triggers a state of heightened bodily arousal (increased blood pressure, muscle tone, and pupil dilation) when trying to cope with challenging situations. Robert Plomin, a leading behavioral geneticist at Pennsylvania State University, asserts that heredity plays a larger role in shyness than in other personality traits.[26]

What are the life-course consequences of childhood shyness? Shy boys are more likely than their peers to delay entry into marriage, parenthood, and stable careers; to attain less occupational achievement and stability; and to experience marital instability. Shy girls are more likely than their peers to follow a conventional pattern of marriage, childbearing, and homemaking.

**Raising Inner Self-Esteem in Shy Children.**    Girls are more likely than boys to exhibit withdrawal and shyness.[27] Shy girls are likely to have low social self-esteem and tend to perceive themselves as poorly accepted by their peers. These girls are at risk for developing internal disorders, including social anxiety and depression.

Not all shy children, however, are "disturbed" and headed for disaster. Shy children, who are uncomfortable and miserable because of their shyness and children who have no friends will definitely profit from some help in overcoming their intense shyness.

The inventory in Table 3 may help parents to determine whether their child is too shy and will profit from professional help. Answering "yes" to even one or two of questions 1, 2, 5, 6, and 7 and answering "no" to one or two of questions 3, 4, 8, 9, and 10 may indicate that the child needs expert assistance in overcoming shyness.

Shy children need help to feel more secure and engage in social activities. Joining social organizations, particularly those to which parents belong, may help them feel more secure. When the mother or father is present, children feel more secure when participating in group activities. They should not, however, be pushed or forced into doing something they feel uncomfortable doing. Shy children's anxieties increase under pressure. Pressure for standards out of their range of capability may lead to further feelings of inadequacy and further withdrawal.

It is best not to start a campaign against children's daydreaming. For many children, this is their only release, their only way of arranging their environment to receive some pleasure. If at all possible, these children need to receive in reality the pleasure and the joys that they

**Table 3.**  Shyness Inventory

1. Does your child always play alone or stay by himself or herself both at home and at school?
2. Does your child go home from school day after day and stay by himself or herself reading or playing with toys in a solitary manner?
3. Does your child have at least one friend?
4. Does your child participate in after-school sports or belong to some club?
5. Does your child have many fears? (All children have fears, but a shy child is overwhelmed by many fears.)
6. Does your child seem lost in daydreams much of the time?
7. Does your child live in a make-believe world much of the time?
8. Is your child learning what he or she is expected to learn at his or her age?
9. Does your child seem happy?
10. Does your child have interest in different types of activities?

vainly seek in their imaginary activities. By encouraging these children to talk about things and experiences in their imaginary world, parents can perhaps help them channel some of these fantasies into real creative effort. For example, Mary's mother learns that one of her child's daydreams is that she is a good artist and that the other children think her work is wonderful. With this knowledge, Mary's mother can help her by giving her art materials and even lessons to help her actually achieve her daydream.

When disciplinary action is required, it is generally wise not to rush in and completely overwhelm the shy child. Quiet children are usually quite aware of what they're supposed to be doing and what the rules are. Furthermore, quiet children are very sensitive to negative appraisal and evaluation by others. A firm but gentle reminder is usually all these children need.

Various kinds of guidance, modeling, and practice in social skills seem to bolster the morale and self-confidence of children who think of themselves as shy. Individual children need to know about and be able to perform successfully a range of behaviors that are necessary for initiating and maintaining positive social interactions. Parents of shy children may want to visit the children's teacher and become familiar with what the children are doing and learning at school. Parents can also familiarize the children, when possible, with these skills and learning tasks at home. Perhaps, then, when these skills are introduced in school, the children will feel more comfortable and more confident in what they are learning in the classroom.

Parents can ask their children's teacher to give them the names of other children in the class who are also rather timid and shy. This will give the children more equal companionship. It is especially helpful to do this if a shy child seems to be dominated by an older, more aggressive sibling or neighborhood playmate.

### Rejected-Aggressive Children

The rejected-aggressive child exhibits high levels of aggressive behavior and displays more deviant behavior in a variety of settings. He is characterized with multiple social-skill deficits and subsequently, multiple difficulties in peer relations. He is at highest risk for developing disturbances later in life. Hostility combined with social ineptness and an inability to respond positively to peers are characteristics of rejected-aggressive children.[28] It is the combination of aggressiveness with the child's inability to respond positively and cooperatively with peers that appears to be most closely associated with peer rejection.

Unlike neglected and socially withdrawn children, rejected-aggressive children are actively disliked by their peers. Rejected-aggressive children tend to act in conceited (even though their self-esteem is low), disruptive, and silly ways. Additional attributes of the rejected-aggressive child are anxiety, excessive emotional dependence on adults, uncertainty, bitterness and sarcasm toward others, and social indifference. Further, rejected children are more likely to be low achievers in school, to experience learning difficulties, and to drop out of school than their socially accepted peers. In order for children to concentrate on their learning tasks and succeed in school, they need to feel some acceptance by peers.

Rejected-aggressive children have great difficulty seeing a situation from another person's perspective. They have been shown to be deficient in a variety of social skills, such as communicating emotions and needs accurately, responding to emotions and needs accurately, and responding to peers with appropriate attention or help. Rejected-aggressive children are more argumentative, disruptive, inattentive, imperceptive, and less prosocial. These children significantly overestimate both their social and behavioral competence, maintaining that they have hundreds of friends. Overestimating their competence may help to create a protective defense against realities that are too painful for children to fully acknowledge. With time, these transactions limit the child's opportunities for constructive social involvement with other children.

Aggressive children deliberately seek to harm or injure others and frequently resort to these kinds of behavior in different situations. Antisocial aggression has been characterized as one of the most prevalent, stable, socially transmittable, personally destructive, and clinically problematic behavior patterns. Childhood aggression is relatively stable over time and appears to place children at risk for subsequent developmental difficulties such as peer rejection.

Aggression can take various forms depending on the needs, goals, and emotions associated with it. Physically aggressive children meet others head on with their tactics of pushing, pulling, punching, and kicking. Or, their aggressions may be directed toward property such as destroying a book or carving designs on the furniture. Hard-boiled youngsters, commonly known as bullies, are examples of children who are expressing their aggression physically. Bullies tend to be either controversial or rejected children. Thus, the rejected bully collects many "liked least" votes and the controversial bully tends to collect many "least liked" votes from peers as well as "most liked."

Verbally aggressive children often resort to name-calling and making abusive statements to their peers. Physical aggression is not their style. Unlike bullies, children who tease other children usually do not have any intention of doing physical harm. Instead, they make their classmates feel uncomfortable by taunting them in malicious ways.

The number of girls who fall into the rejected-aggressive category is quite small; however, aggressiveness is as problematic for girls and contributes to later adjustment difficulties just as it does for boys. These girls tend to start fights more often and are more rebellious. While a certain amount of aggressive behavior may be tolerated and even accepted for boys, it is not tolerated in girls. "Highly aggressive behavior in preadolescence constitutes an essential stepping stone for later deviance, particularly for girls."[29]

**Causes of Aggression.**    Concerned adults may want to know the origins of aggression in children. Is aggressive behavior innate or learned? Although the research on both sides has been impressive, there is no final answer. Research does suggest, however, that biological-genetic factors, environmental factors, and cognitive factors all play important roles in shaping the development of aggression.

*Biological-Genetic Factors.*    It has been found that when female monkeys are given the male hormone testosterone, they become more aggressive (fighting behavior increases). While the relationship between hormones (testosterone) and aggressiveness in lower animals is quite clear, this is not the case for humans. The relationship between hormones and aggressive behavior in humans is complex. There does not appear to be a direct relationship between testosterone and aggressive behavior.

Some research also suggests that the hormone noradrenaline and a neurotransmitter, serotonin, are associated with aggression. High levels of noradrenaline are associated with risks such as over-arousal, rapid heartbeat, and increased tendency toward impulsive acts of violence. Low levels of serotonin are associated with risks of depression, alcoholism, explosive rage, and impulsive aggression.

It seems, however, that all that can be concluded from contemporary research is that biological factors interact with environmental factors in determining the extent to which aggression occurs. Hormones and neurotransmitters, then, should be viewed as part of a combination of determinants of aggression, rather than definite causes of aggression.

*Environmental Factors.* Environmental factors include the way parents contribute to building aggressive behavior in their children. Perhaps unknowingly, they may provide models of the very kind of behavior they want to discourage in a child. For example, parents may teach a child to become aggressive by being aggressive themselves. Children learn by identifying with their parents and imitating them.

Studies have indicated that parents of aggressive children reason less with their offspring and use physical punishment more than do parents of nonaggressive children. Punishing a child by physical means may bring results opposite to those intended, as exemplified by the following lines written by B. D. Grossman:

> My son is very aggressive
> He's always hitting other children
> I don't understand why . . .
> I hit him every time he does it.

Children of more power-assertive parents tend to be less competent with peers and more inclined to expect positive outcomes from unfriendly resolution of peer conflict. Aggressive exchanges continue for a longer time and more frequently in aggressive families than in normal families; they also tend to escalate in intensity.

Aggressive-rejected children tend to be found in families in which there is a high incidence of aggressive or coercive behavior on the part of both parents (threats, scolding, hitting) and children (yelling, hitting, defiance).[30] Both mothers and fathers of aggressive children are much more likely to initiate conflict against or in front of their children than are parents of nonaggressive children. Mothers' aversive behavior correlates positively with children's aversive behavior with peers. That is, mothers of aggressive children tend to be overly critical of their children, only see the negative things that their children do, and rarely, if ever, notice or praise good behaviors.

In addition, parents with aggressive-rejected children tend to be inconsistent in their use of punishment. This simply teaches children to be more persistent in their aggressive responses, because they have learned that eventually the parent will give in to their wishes. It has also been found that when parents tend to disagree about disciplining techniques, children tend to be more aggressive.

Parents in aggressive families are more likely to label neutral events as antisocial rather than prosocial. For example, when viewing videotapes of children playing, parents of aggressive children might view one child bumping into another as an aggressive, hostile act. Mothers of nonaggressive children, however, tend to see this same event in a more neutral and even positive way, as an accident or as an unintentional act. As a result of seeing events in a more hostile light, mothers of aggressive children often perceive that negative reactions by their children are warranted and even necessary. Rejected-aggressive children are less responsive to social stimuli, including social reinforcement and social punishment (threats, scolding), and show a significant delay in their interpersonal awareness and perspective-taking ability. These facts demonstrate the interactive nature of parent and child in the development of aggression.

Rejected-aggressive children report the least supportive relationship with their fathers of any group.[31] They tend to report receiving less love and affection from their fathers than popular, average, and neglected children. Their reports of relationships with mothers and teachers do not differ from those of other children. This finding fits well with other data showing tighter linkages between father–child relationships and peer acceptance than between mother–child relationships and peer acceptance.[32]

Variation in parental childrearing practices has emerged as an important factor related to children's functioning with peers. Success or failure with peers is influenced within the family primarily through parent discipline practices. Parents who are warm, responsive, and consistent disciplinarians have children who are more competent with peers than those parents who are harsh, rejecting, or excessively permissive. Parents of popular children show more positive emotions (cheerfulness, happiness, love) than parents of rejected children.

Peers also play an important role in the development, maintenance, and modification of aggression. Children will imitate aggressive peers. In fact, children may imitate aggressive behavior more often than passive behavior. In addition, it appears that nonaggressive children may learn to become aggressive in a peer setting. For example, a child who is constantly the victim of physical attacks from others, may, in order to avoid being picked on, lash out at others in an aggressive fashion.

Similarly, certain peer groups give greater status to highly aggressive children and thus may promote this type of antisocial behavior. In some peer groups, antisocial actions are highly valued and in other peer groups this type of behavior results in negative responses from others and virtual isolation from the peer group. Thus, in some groups, particularly those that give status to aggressive behaviors, children may be reinforced for their aggressions, which may increase in frequency. Other groups, however, may function to inhibit aggressive behavior by punishing or ignoring those children whose behaviors violate the group norms.

There is a cyclical, self-perpetuating process for aggressive boys in which an aggressive reputation leads to biased responses from peers, which elicits more aggression and in turn strengthens aggressive behavior. Josh is in the fourth grade and he is constantly picking on the other kids. He also does mean things like pull the chair out from underneath a child who is about to sit down; he also puts tacks on people's chairs. Since second grade, Josh has had a problem with taking things from other kids that do not belong to him. If a tack is found on the teacher's chair, or the milk money for the class is missing, Josh is usually blamed.

Thus, reputation and expectations within a peer group serve to maintain peer rejection. Peers become biased in their perceptions of a child and alter their behavior toward a child once they have identified that child as liked or disliked. This behavior, in turn, may lead the child to respond in ways that perpetuate peers' perceptions. Disliked children are held more accountable for negative behavior than are liked peers. Thus, social behavior tends to be perceived as a function of prior attitudes and beliefs about the child.

Rejected-aggressive children do not distribute their aggression evenly across all available peer targets but instead direct their attacks toward a minority of peers who serve consistently as victims. Children who are victims of aggression from others are likely to reward their attackers with tangible resources and signs of distress and are unlikely to punish their attackers with retaliation. Michael is a quiet boy and he wants to be accepted by the other kids. He is quite afraid of some of the boys in his class, particularly Evan, who picks on him all the time. Michael tries to appease Evan—he gives him stickers and treats from his lunch. But Evan just continues to pick on him and demands more gifts from him. Victims of bullies also tend to be rejected by their classmates and tend to be described by their peers as shy, passive, and overly compliant. In general, victims of bullying tend to have low opinions of themselves, tend to be anxious and insecure, and perceive themselves as being less well accepted than other children. Because Michael acts in such a sheepish, passive way toward Evan's persecutions, Evan continues to treat Michael that way. Teaching victimized children to respond to verbal and physical attacks in ways that aggressors do not find reinforcing (for example, to respond to teasing with humor or assertion rather than overt distress) may reduce the aggressive attacks.

The effects of television violence and aggression has been investigated more thoroughly than any other television issue. During their television viewing time, children between the ages of 5 and 15 will have witnessed some 18,000 violent acts. (These violent acts average one per minute in standard television cartoons.) How does viewing aggression or violence on television affect these children? Experts have repeatedly concluded that there is a small but reliable causal effect of television violence on aggressive behavior.[33]

For boys, a preference for viewing violence on television at age 9 is significantly linked to aggressive behavior ten years later. In fact, of the great variety of other socialization and family background factors that have been measured, viewing television violence is the best single predictor of aggressive behavior in late adolescence. The watching of violence is likely to have both an immediate and a long-term, cumulative effect on building aggressive habits.

Exposure to televised violence also tends to decrease the viewer's behavioral and physiological responsiveness to aggression produced by others.[34] For example, grade-school children, while watching "real-life" aggression on a television monitor (two boys fist fighting) were found to show fewer physiological changes (increased heartbeat, sweaty palms) than those watching an equally arousing but nonviolent championship volleyball game. This suggests that children become hardened to violence after seeing a great deal of it.

*Cognitive Factors.*    Rejected-aggressive children do not process information in the same way that popular or average children do. They tend to view their world in a very negative way. For example, when aggressive children are shown a series of videos in which a provocation occurs (two boys want the same toy), they see this ambiguous scenario in a hostile way. They may explain, when viewing this scene, that one boy took the toy from the other boy. In addition, they will give a negative solution to the problem. (The boy who had the toy first should push the other kid down and grab the toy.) Popular children, however, viewing the same situation may say that both boys see the toy at the same time and both want to play with the toy. Further, they will generate more prosocial solutions to the problem; for example, one boy should have the toy for 10 minutes and then let the other boy play with it. Similarly, rejected-aggressive children are more likely than popular peers to think that unfriendly strategies (e.g., commanding a peer) will be instrumentally successful.

In the classroom setting, rejected children display fewer task-appropriate behaviors (raising their hand to ask a question) and more task-inappropriate behaviors (blurting out comments) than popular children. They spend less time on assigned academic tasks and are observed to spend their time clowning around, daydreaming, or walking aimlessly around the room. These children quite frequently attempt to interact with other children during quiet work periods. These attempts lead to high rates of rejection from the other children. Apparently, the rejected child's peers think that these approaches are inappropriate.

**Consequences of Rejection.** Research on rejected-aggressive children suggests that it is having few friends in class *and* being widely disliked by the peer group that lead to behavior adjustment problems.

Children who are rejected in preadolescence tend to have more adjustment problems in adolescence than neglected, popular, or average-status children, as measured by encounters with the police, truancy, and being retained or suspended in school. Rejected children, with average to even above-average intelligence, are more likely than their peers to drop out of school. While the high school dropout rate for the nation is around 20 percent, the average dropout rate for rejected children is 54 percent.[35] Rejected children tend to exhibit a variety of problem behaviors both at school and at home. Longitudinal research suggests that these children continue to be rejected by peers over time and are at risk for a variety of adolescent and adult adjustment problems.

Children who are actively disliked or rejected by their peers seem to be at a heightened risk for a wide range of mental health difficulties. Although much more needs to be learned, the most clearly identified risk factors for psychopathology, delinquency, substance abuse, or all three appear to be (1) antisocial, rebellious, and defiant behavior; (2) poor peer relations; (3) poor academic skills; and (4) low self-esteem.

Children who are disliked by their peers are more likely to have emotional problems. Both loneliness and social anxiety are likely to be elevated among children who are low in peer acceptance, especially rejected-aggressive children. Rejected-aggressive children report feeling significantly more lonely than children in other peer status classifications. It is possible that children's reports of loneliness are implicit calls for help. In admitting loneliness, children are saying that they are unhappy with their social situation and wish it were otherwise. There also appears to be an association between low peer status and depression.

There is a modest stability for popular and neglected children, but higher stability for rejected-aggressive children. Stability is not simply due to the fact that the composition of the examined peer groups remains the same over time. Even in new groups with unfamiliar peers, children tend to retain their social rank.[36] For example, when unfamiliar boys of differing social status are brought together in play groups once a week for six weeks, within three weeks their social status in these new groups is similar to their social status in the classrooms. Boys who are rejected in school are similarly shunned by their peers in their new settings. Rejected children tend to remain that way. Therefore, it is important to identify children who persist in maladaptive behavior and help them develop more socially competent ways of behaving.

**Raising Inner Self-Esteem in Rejected-Aggressive Children.** Unfortunately, when children behave aggressively their behavior is often met with counteraggression by adults. In this situation, neither party reduces tension and neither learns to understand the other or solve the problem. The more parents deal with children in negative ways, the more aggressive children become. Children disciplined by parents with punitive tactics are more likely to use these same tactics in dealing with other children. No amount of punishment seems effective with these children. In fact, what parents usually consider punishment for normal children usually turns out to be a reward for rejected-aggressive children. The more parents punish aggressive children, the more they reinforce this behavior. For some children, this is the only way in which they receive attention and thus punishment becomes reinforcing.

These children usually have had their share of punishment; they don't need any more. Rather, they need firm help in controlling and channeling their aggressive tendencies. They need to realize that there are other ways to solve their problems than by bulldozing their way through life. When children behave aggressively in an abusive way, they must be shown that they are using their strength in misguided ways.

Parents can help aggressive children by making it abundantly clear that aggression is frowned on, stopping it when it occurs, but not punishing the children physically for that aggression. Although physical punishment may stop a particular form of aggression temporarily, it appears to generate a great deal of hostility in children, which leads to further aggressive outbursts at another time and place. The most peaceful home is the one in which parents do not tolerate aggression, especially toward themselves; and rely mainly on nonpunitive forms of control. The families in which children frequently show angry, aggressive outbursts are likely to have parents who tolerate aggression, administer severe punishment for it, or both.

The aggressive child should not be rewarded for aggressive acts. If, for example, he pushes another child down and grabs the child's football, he should not be allowed to keep the football. In situations like this, the parent should avoid sermonizing or punishing the child for taking the football. Rather, the parent should retrieve the football (ignore the aggressing child), return the football to the other child, and give *him or her* more attention.

It is best, whenever possible, not only to ignore aggressors when they are victimizing others but also to attend to them when they are displaying cooperative behavior. Parents need to target deviant and prosocial behaviors, ignoring the former and rewarding the latter. By doing so, parents will see a decrease in their children's aggressive behaviors.

Another promising approach to treatment of antisocial aggression is to focus on identifying children's thinking patterns. As noted earlier, rejected-aggressive children seem to see others' behavior as more negative and to think that hostile strategies toward others are effective. Parents can help their children see how their behavior is affecting other children. Role-play situations, in which parents tease, interrupt, or say something sarcastic to the aggressive child and then explore how that makes him or her feel, are helpful. Parents need to help their aggressive child see the consequences of his or her behavior and how others react or feel about that behavior. Parents can help them experience how other children really feel and discuss how they can behave in more appropriate ways that children like.

Help them learn to interpret social cues. Is the peer acting benignly or is he intentionally trying to cause harm? How do we know this? If two boys are observed pushing each other what clues should the child look for? (Both boys are smiling so they probably are having fun, not being mean to each other.) Help them to see neutral acts as neutral, not hostile.

Help them search for alternative responses. Should he hit back? Should he go to an adult for help? Rejected-aggressive children, asked to generate possible responses to aggressive provocation, initially give competent ones, but their subsequent responses are less so compared to those of nonaggressive children. Have them explore many different ways of responding in various types of social situations.

## Summary

During middle childhood, children's evaluations of self become more concrete. In addition, children's self-esteem influences their perception of their environmental experiences and in turn their actions and behavior. Perceptions and behavior are always consistent with children's evaluation of self.

Parents can help their children develop socially competent behavior by teaching them effective communication skills, coaching them to behave in socially appropriate ways, giving them an area of expertise, helping them do well academically, and encouraging them to belong to social organizations.

During the ages of 6 to 12 years, learning to get along with others is an important developmental task. Children's social statuses have been categorized into the following groups: popular, neglected, shy-withdrawn, controversial, and rejected-aggressive. All children, even shy-withdrawn, quiet, gentle ones, need at least one friend. A child who has no friends, never plays with others in school or at home, daydreams excessively, and seems overwhelmed by fears will profit from professional help. Parents can help their shy children by joining a parent–child club to help them feel more secure in group situations. Shy children need to receive some pleasure and joys in their real world that they may be experiencing in their fantasy world. By encouraging shy children to talk about things and experiences in their imaginary world, parents can channel fantasies into real creative effort. Practicing social skills with their parents can help sensitive children become more adept when interacting with others. Parents can arrange for their child to meet with other shy children in the class to provide more equal companionship.

Children who are particularly vulnerable to adjustment problems later on are rejected-aggressive children, who tend to be consistently defiant, rebellious, and disruptive in a variety of settings. Rejected-aggressive children do not need physical punishment to shape them up. The best homes are those in which parents do not tolerate aggression and do not act aggressively with their children. Limiting the amount of television violence watched and monitoring friends, particularly if they condone aggressive ways of behaving, are positive things that parents can do to help their aggressive child. Focusing on the ways in which a child alienates others (sarcasm, physical aggression, poor communication skills, inappropriate behavior in the classroom) and using coaching and role playing to help him learn more socially competent ways of behaving are effective. Helping develop more adaptable, flexible, and positive thinking patterns is another significant way in which parents can help their rejected-aggressive child.

# CHAPTER 4 Developing Inner Self-Esteem during the School-Age Years
## Academic Self-Esteem

School is a social institution, reflecting the culture of which it is a part and transmitting to the young a world view as well as specific skills and knowledge. Children spend years in school as members of a small society in which there are tasks to be done, people to relate to, and rules that define the possibilities of behavior. Such experiences affect several aspects of children's behavior: their sense of self, beliefs about their academic competence, and their conceptions of a social system beyond the family.[1]

When children first begin school they are wonderfully confident about themselves. Most children begin school with positive feelings of being smart, capable, and eager to please. When children enter kindergarten, for example, they tend to underestimate the difficulty of a task, believing they can accomplish just about anything. They tend to hold and maintain high expectancies, are less apt to focus on negative outcomes, and view their ability as extremely high. In fact, most kindergartners and first-graders rank themselves at or near the top of their class (their ratings of their classmates mirror the teacher's ratings). What happens to these children?

When talking to children in fourth grade, for example, we encounter a number of children who hate school, who don't like to come to school, who don't try when they are in school. Why? What can parents do to help their children continue on a positive path and feel as good about themselves academically as they did as kindergartners?

**115**

To get an overall picture of your child's conceptions of himself or herself as a learner and how happy and satisfied he or she is in the academic setting, have him or her answer true or false to the questions on the academic self-esteem inventory (Table 4). If 12 or more of your child's responses agree with the key, his or her academic self-esteem is quite good. If, however, your child's score is significantly below that, he or she will profit from learning academic skills and competencies that will raise his or her inner academic self-esteem.

Experiencing more success than failure, feeling a sense of control over what happens to him or her in the academic setting, being organized, reading well, believing that effort is important and makes a difference in how well he or she does in the academic setting, doing homework, being motivated, being organized, and having parents who are involved with their children in academia, who have high expectations for their child, and believe that their child is capable in the academic setting are all factors that are crucial to the child's inner academic self-esteem, and in turn, his or her competence in that setting.

Before reading this chapter you may want to have your child answer the questions in Table 5. Encourage your child to be as honest as possible when answering the questions.

**Table 4.**  Academic Self-Esteem Inventory

1. School work is fairly easy for me.
2. I usually like my teachers.
3. I often get upset at school.
4. I usually get good grades in school.
5. I don't understand lots of stuff I am learning in school.
6. I forget most of what I learn.
7. I like going to school.
8. I am a good student.
9. My teacher thinks I am smart.
10. It takes me a long time to finish my homework.
11. I am proud of my work in school.
12. I usually don't understand my school assignments.
13. I am good at spelling.
14. My parents think I am smart.
15. I am good in math.
16. I like to read.
17. I am not doing very well in school.
18. I really don't care if I do well in school.
19. I look forward to going to school.
20. My friends think I am smart.

**Key**

| | | | |
|---|---|---|---|
| 1. true | 6. false | 11. true | 16. true |
| 2. true | 7. true | 12. false | 17. false |
| 3. false | 8. true | 13. true | 18. false |
| 4. true | 9. true | 14. true | 19. true |
| 5. false | 10. false | 15. true | 20. true |

**Table 5.** Academic Strengths and Weaknesses

Answer the questions by using the following point system:

| | |
|---|---|
| 5 points | This statement is always or almost always true of me. |
| 4 points | This statement is often true of me. |
| 3 points | This statement is sometimes true of me (about half the time). |
| 2 points | This statement is seldom true of me. |
| 1 point | This statement is never or almost never true of me. |

| | Almost Always | Often | Sometimes | Seldom | Never |
|---|---|---|---|---|---|
| **Success** | | | | | |
| 1. My teachers praise me for my good work. | 5 | 4 | 3 | 2 | 1 |
| 2. I do well in most of my subjects. | 5 | 4 | 3 | 2 | 1 |
| 3. School is a fun place. | 5 | 4 | 3 | 2 | 1 |
| 4. Even if something is really hard to do, I don't give up. | 5 | 4 | 3 | 2 | 1 |
| 5. I want to get good grades. | 5 | 4 | 3 | 2 | 1 |
| 6. I try hard to do well in school. | 5 | 4 | 3 | 2 | 1 |
| 7. I set high goals for myself in school. | 5 | 4 | 3 | 2 | 1 |
| 8. My parents are proud of my school work. | 5 | 4 | 3 | 2 | 1 |
| **Control** | | | | | |
| 1. If I try hard, I can accomplish anything. | 5 | 4 | 3 | 2 | 1 |
| 2. I am responsible for the grades that I receive in school. | 5 | 4 | 3 | 2 | 1 |
| 3. If I study hard for a test, I can get a good grade. | 5 | 4 | 3 | 2 | 1 |
| 4. I am responsible for my own behavior. | 5 | 4 | 3 | 2 | 1 |
| 5. Doing homework helps me to get better grades. | 5 | 4 | 3 | 2 | 1 |
| 6. The way people treat me depends on the way I act toward them. | 5 | 4 | 3 | 2 | 1 |

117

**Table 5.** (*Continued*)

| | Almost Always | Often | Sometimes | Seldom | Never |
|---|---|---|---|---|---|
| 7. My family listens to my opinion. | 5 | 4 | 3 | 2 | 1 |
| 8. Putting forth the effort to do well usually pays off. | 5 | 4 | 3 | 2 | 1 |
| **Organization** | | | | | |
| 1. I have a certain time when I do my homework. | 5 | 4 | 3 | 2 | 1 |
| 2. If I have a book report due, I plan out what I need to do ahead of time. | 5 | 4 | 3 | 2 | 1 |
| 3. I write out a schedule of the important things I need to do. | 5 | 4 | 3 | 2 | 1 |
| 4. I turn in assignments on time. | 5 | 4 | 3 | 2 | 1 |
| 5. I know what I have to do for each of my assignments. | 5 | 4 | 3 | 2 | 1 |
| 6. If I have an assignment due in three weeks, I start on it right away. | 5 | 4 | 3 | 2 | 1 |
| 7. I feel I have enough time to accomplish all the things I need to do. | 5 | 4 | 3 | 2 | 1 |
| 8. I am an organized person. | 5 | 4 | 3 | 2 | 1 |
| **Reading** | | | | | |
| 1. I read books for fun. | 5 | 4 | 3 | 2 | 1 |
| 2. I enjoy going to the library and checking out interesting books to read. | 5 | 4 | 3 | 2 | 1 |
| 3. I am a fast reader. | 5 | 4 | 3 | 2 | 1 |
| 4. Reading school books is interesting. | 5 | 4 | 3 | 2 | 1 |
| 5. I like to read. | 5 | 4 | 3 | 2 | 1 |
| 6. Most of what I read makes sense to me. | 5 | 4 | 3 | 2 | 1 |
| 7. I understand most of what I read in school. | 5 | 4 | 3 | 2 | 1 |
| 8. I can find the main points in reading an assignment. | 5 | 4 | 3 | 2 | 1 |

## Effort

| | | | | | |
|---|---|---|---|---|---|
| 1. If I try hard, I can do well in school. | 5 | 4 | 3 | 2 | 1 |
| 2. I believe that doing my homework will help me be a better student. | 5 | 4 | 3 | 2 | 1 |
| 3. I understand how to do my homework assignments. | 5 | 4 | 3 | 2 | 1 |
| 4. I enjoy learning. | 5 | 4 | 3 | 2 | 1 |
| 5. I can always get good grades if I want to. | 5 | 4 | 3 | 2 | 1 |
| 6. How well I do in school depends on how hard I try to do well in school. | 5 | 4 | 3 | 2 | 1 |
| 7. If I don't understand something, I will continue to try to understand it. | 5 | 4 | 3 | 2 | 1 |
| 8. I don't give up in school even when something that I am doing is difficult. | 5 | 4 | 3 | 2 | 1 |

## Motivation

| | | | | | |
|---|---|---|---|---|---|
| 1. I enjoy learning. | 5 | 4 | 3 | 2 | 1 |
| 2. I can study for long periods of time (an hour or more) when it is necessary. | 5 | 4 | 3 | 2 | 1 |
| 3. I like most of my subjects. | 5 | 4 | 3 | 2 | 1 |
| 4. I like most of my teachers. | 5 | 4 | 3 | 2 | 1 |
| 5. I believe that doing well in school is important. | 5 | 4 | 3 | 2 | 1 |
| 6. I don't get upset in school. | 5 | 4 | 3 | 2 | 1 |
| 7. School is fun. | 5 | 4 | 3 | 2 | 1 |
| 8. I look forward to learning new things. | 5 | 4 | 3 | 2 | 1 |

**Table 5.** (*Continued*)

| | Almost Always | Often | Sometimes | Seldom | Never |
|---|---|---|---|---|---|
| **Self-Evaluation** | | | | | |
| 1. I am happy with the grades that I am receiving. | 5 | 4 | 3 | 2 | 1 |
| 2. I am doing well in school. | 5 | 4 | 3 | 2 | 1 |
| 3. My teacher makes me feel that I am a good student. | 5 | 4 | 3 | 2 | 1 |
| 4. I like going to school. | 5 | 4 | 3 | 2 | 1 |
| 5. If I try hard, I will do well in school. | 5 | 4 | 3 | 2 | 1 |
| 6. School is fun. | 5 | 4 | 3 | 2 | 1 |
| 7. My friends think that I am smart. | 5 | 4 | 3 | 2 | 1 |
| 8. I think that I am smart. | 5 | 4 | 3 | 2 | 1 |
| **Parents** | | | | | |
| 1. My parents make me feel that I am a good student. | 5 | 4 | 3 | 2 | 1 |
| 2. My parents expect me to get good grades in school. | 5 | 4 | 3 | 2 | 1 |
| 3. My parents help me with my school work. | 5 | 4 | 3 | 2 | 1 |
| 4. My parents attend school functions (open house, parent–teacher conferences). | 5 | 4 | 3 | 2 | 1 |
| 5. We have books, magazines, and/or encyclopedias in our home. | 5 | 4 | 3 | 2 | 1 |
| 6. My parents are interested in how I am doing in school. | 5 | 4 | 3 | 2 | 1 |
| 7. My parents believe that I will be successful when I am older. | 5 | 4 | 3 | 2 | 1 |
| 8. Doing well in school is important to my parents. | 5 | 4 | 3 | 2 | 1 |

After your child has taken the inventory, add up his or her points for each of the categories and shade in each section on the bar graph (Figure 3) to the appropriate level. Examine the bar graph to gain an understanding of your child's strengths and weaknesses in the academic domain. Looking at the bar graph will enable you to target those areas that may be negatively influencing your child's academic success. The chapter will examine each of these areas that are vital to academic competence and discuss how you as parents can help your child acquire these skills, attitudes, and behaviors.

## Success and Failure

Does your child experience more success than failure in school? When children fail academically, they develop an "I don't care" attitude about doing well in school. Moreover, they engage in developing and repeating ineffective strategies such as not turning in assignments, not doing homework, and not trying hard to do well. These children frequently give up, particularly if they encounter difficulties in understanding their school work. Other unproductive strategies include setting unobtainable goals or exerting low effort and then making excuses for poor performance. Children who experience failure are particularly likely to develop unwarrantedly low expectations for success on academic tasks. That is, they are likely to develop expectations or levels of aspiration that are consistent with their past performances.

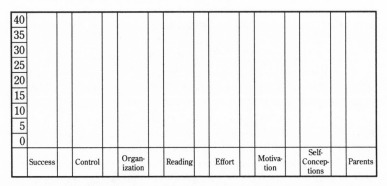

**Figure 3.** Strengths and Weaknesses in the Academic Domain.

Children exposed to frequent failure either set goals for learning that are so low they can attain them effortlessly, or they set ridiculously unobtainable goals. (Failing on an extremely difficult task has more face-saving potential then failing at an easy task.) They may resort to cheating or to failure-avoidance strategies (low effort or procrastination), because failure without effort is viewed as "failure with honor." They may attempt to gain self-esteem by acting out in class, thereby earning admiration from their peers. By their actions, these children are increasing the likelihood that they will continue to fail.

Moreover, when children are exposed to frequent failures, they may develop a feeling of learned helplessness. These children tend to feel they are unable to handle certain tasks; they perceive themselves as unable to surmount failure. They often put themselves down when they fail, yet when they succeed they are likely to say it was just luck. Children view experiences of failure as indicative of their ability, and as more of these experiences occur this view is continually reinforced.

Learned helplessness means that a child will avoid task situations that produce negative self-judgments. Martin Covington, an expert on self-esteem and academic achievement, maintains that when children don't do well in school and experience a feeling of learned helplessness, they engage in various "no effort" strategies in order to protect their self-esteem in the academic domain.[2] The child's sense of self-worth in the academic domain is based on the belief that his or her value as a person depends on the ability to achieve. High-achieving children gain their self-esteem from recognition and praise for their academic performance. In contrast, children who are not doing well academically are confronted with frequent failures and must attempt to protect their self-esteem through alternative modes of behavior, such as those just described. These children are not motivated to succeed but, rather, to avoid failure at all costs.

In short, *the need to avoid failure in order to protect self-esteem is one of the main obstacles to school achievement.* Academic achievement is best understood in terms of students' attempts to maintain a positive image of their own ability, especially when risking failure. Protecting one's sense of competence is the highest priority, higher than achievement itself. The strategies often employed by these children eventually lead to the very failures that they are attempting to avoid.

Children generally have good motives for their actions. Even those children who prefer failure to success in the classroom setting do so, as we have seen, for "logical" reasons. Understanding from the child's perspective why he or she finds failure more desirable than success is a starting point toward reversing the child's behavior.

Success is vital to maximizing the child's potential level of ability. As many of us know, it is extremely difficult or impossible to persist at a task for which failure is believed to be inevitable. A few years ago I decided to take piano lessons for the first time in my life. Since I was an adult, the piano teacher gave me some very difficult (so I thought) music for my beginning songs. I looked at the music and was intimidated by the hundreds of notes on the page. "How will I ever learn to play this?" I thought. It made me reflect for a moment about children who may not be doing well in math or spelling and then are presented with dozens of problems to solve or new words to learn to spell.

My progress in piano was quite slow, and my piano-playing self-esteem suffered. I reflected on children who rarely get positive feedback in the classroom and understood more clearly how they felt. I began to dread going to my piano lessons just as children who receive negative feedback in the classroom dread going to school. Have you ever had a job that you really hated? If so, then you have some understanding of how those children who are not doing well in school feel as they enter the classroom. Most of us hate to be in situations in which we feel incapable; conversely, most of us like to be in situations in which we feel capable and effective. Children are like that as well. They love to do things they do well and avoid doing things that they don't do well.

The child who discovers that he or she is good *at* nothing stands a good chance of becoming good *for* nothing. Children whose learning is not impeded by a sense of failure achieve significantly more. Enthusiasm for learning, active participation, and achieving one's potential level of ability are stimulated by success. Helping children to achieve success is vital to their academic achievement. Having them work with other more capable students, talking to the teacher about what needs to be done to help the child in weaker subjects, and breaking down tasks into simpler units may help the children experience the success that they need.

## Helping Children Develop an Inner Locus of Control

Feeling a sense of control over one's environment is vital to academic achievement. How much control does your child feel that he or she has over what happens in the academic environment? Children need to know that they are responsible for the caliber of work they are doing in school. Children who report that they control their outcomes in the academic setting are rated by teachers as more engaged in school activities and are higher in achievement and grades than those with less control understanding. The opposite is true of children who report that they have little control over academic outcomes.

Thus, an important motivational factor that affects children's learning and performance is their beliefs about the outcomes they might experience on academic tasks. These beliefs tend to guide their subsequent behavior. Children tend to attribute achievement outcomes to either internal or external causes. Children who attribute these outcomes to internal causes are said to have an internal locus of control.[3] These children tend to perceive a causal relationship between their personal actions in an academic situation and the resultant events. They might comment, "I know I can do well on the test if I study very hard." These children often credit themselves when they achieve. Students with an internal locus of control believe that they exercise more control over events and outcomes affecting them and, thereby, achieve more than do students with an external locus of control. Children with an inner sense of control feel more competent than those individuals who believe that life events are controlled by outside forces, a belief that may lead to feelings of helplessness and inadequacy.

Children with an external locus of control attribute events in their lives as beyond their control and usually achieve less. These children believe they lack the ability to do a task. ("I can't do this because I am no good at it.") If they achieve success in a certain task, they often attribute it to luck or some external circumstance over which they have little or no control. Furthermore, these children will devalue the success they may have achieved on a certain task and feel that the success certainly will not continue.

To shed further light on whether your child has an inner or outer locus of control have the child answer the sample questions from the Norwicki–Strickland Locus of Control Scale (Table 6).

Children who have eight or more answers that agree with the key tend to believe that they have little control over what happens to them. If that's the case, parents need to help their child develop an internal locus of control.

Students who perceive personal control over their own academic successes and failures show significantly larger achievement gains. Further, they have a more favorable attitude toward learning. Inner locus of control leads to accountability, taking responsibility for one's own be-

**Table 6.**  Sample Questions from the Norwicki–Strickland Locus of
Control Scale

Answer "yes" or "no" to the following questions.

1.  Do you believe that most problems will solve themselves if you just don't fool with them?
2.  Are some kids just born lucky?
3.  Most of the time do you feel that getting good grades means a great deal to you?
4.  Are you often blamed for things that just aren't your fault?
5.  Do you believe that if somebody studies hard enough he or she can pass any subject?
6.  Do you feel that most of the time it doesn't pay to try hard because things never turn out right anyway?
7.  Do you feel that cheering more than luck helps a team to win?
8.  Do you believe that your parents should allow you to make most of your own decisions?
9.  Do you feel that when you do something wrong there's very little you can do to make it right?
10. If you find a four-leaf clover do you believe that it might bring you good luck?
11. Do you often feel that whether you do your homework has much to do with what kinds of grades you get?
12. Have you ever had a good luck charm?
13. Do you believe that whether or not people like you depends on how you act?
14. Most of the time do you find it useless to try to get your own way at home?
15. Do you feel that when good things happen they happen because of hard work?
16. Do you feel that it's easy to get friends to do what you want them to?
17. Do you usually feel that it's almost useless to try in school because most other students are just plain smarter than you are?
18. Are you the kind of person who believes that planning ahead makes things turn out better?
19. Most of the time, do you feel that you have little to say about what your family decides to do and when?
20. Do you think it's better to be smart than to be lucky?

**Key**

The following answers indicate an outer locus of control:

| | | | |
|---|---|---|---|
| 1. yes | 6. yes | 11. no | 16. no |
| 2. yes | 7. no | 12. yes | 17. yes |
| 3. no | 8. no | 13. no | 18. no |
| 4. yes | 9. yes | 14. yes | 19. yes |
| 5. no | 10. yes | 15. no | 20. no |

havior. Children with an external locus of control do not show significant gains in achievement and have a less favorable attitude toward learning.

Older students tend to use outer locus of control solutions in an attempt to preserve their self-esteem. One of my students recently commented that she found her 3-hour-long class extremely boring because "the professor just reads from his notes; he never asks test questions from his lectures." These were her reasons for not doing well. Consequently, she cut class all the time. When children have an outer locus of control and blame outside forces for academic failure they are the ones that lose. A student with an inner locus of control would have been thinking, "What can I do to stay more interested in this class?" or "How can I study more effectively for this class?" This type of attitude and these types of solutions lead to higher achievement levels.

As children gain competence in a gradually widening sphere, they need to see themselves as causal agents and need to feel they have ability to control more of their environment. If children feel that success is caused by forces beyond their control, then success is meaningless and future success is seen as doubtful. The general conclusion is that students from first grade through college who have an internal locus of control have higher levels of achievement.

Helping children believe that they are active, causal agents will assist in improving their achievement level. Helping children feel that they can make things happen according to their intentions and wishes and that they can effectively deal with environmental and interpersonal demands will ultimately translate into self-confidence in their ability to realize personal and valued goals.

As parents you can help children develop a sense of control by answering their questions promptly, involving them in decision making, setting clearly defined rules (which contribute to a predictable environment), letting them make choices, and communicating to them that their opinions are worthy.

Developing an inner locus of control is vital to academic success. In fact, several researchers have concluded that an inner locus of control has a stronger relationship to achievement than all other school factors together.[4] Teaching children that they are responsible for their own behavior helps them to develop an inner sense of control. Having a child clean up spilled milk teaches more readily than words that one is responsible for his actions. One of the best ways that parents can help young children learn to develop an inner locus of control is through the concepts of natural and logical consequences and problem ownership.

## Natural and Logical Consequences

*Natural consequences* suggest to children that the world responds in an orderly fashion to their actions. Ideally, the disciplining experiences of children should follow as a natural result of their behavior. Parents can allow children to experience the natural consequences of their acts, which will provide an honest and real learning situation and help them develop an inner locus of control.

Natural consequences are those that occur when parents do not interfere at all, and at times it is possible to let that happen.[5] Natural consequences represent the pressure of reality without any specific action by adults; they always prove effective. It is most important to use words that convey to children that they have it in their power to take care of their problems and not that they must do what parents decide.

For example, say that your child refuses to eat. In the past, you have tried everything, reasoning, threatening, and bribing. What would happen if you let the child assume the responsibility for eating? What would be the natural consequence of not eating? Going hungry (without a lecture on the starving children of the world). The child won't keep this behavior up for long if you act genuinely unconcerned. Serve the dinner, for example, and make no comments. When everyone in the family is finished eating, remove the plates and again say nothing. Do not serve the child food until the next meal. If the child starts to groan and moan from hunger pains a few hours later, calmly and pleasantly tell the child you are sorry that she is hungry and that the next meal will be served in a few hours.

*Logical consequences* are those that are structured to fit a situation, when natural consequences are not immediately available or when they prove to be disastrous, such as in life-threatening situations. Adults need to structure events that logically follow the misdeed. If logical consequences are used as a threat or imposed in anger, they cease to be consequences and become punishments. The secret of effectiveness lies in the manner of application. It comprises a judicial withdrawal on the part of the parent that allows room for the logical sequences of events to take place.

Many times a logical consequence to fit the act will occur to a parent after a little thought. Parents merely need to ask themselves, "What would happen if I didn't interfere?" Toys destroyed are gone and not replaced. Clothes not put in the hamper don't get washed. If a child has not finished his math by the time the baseball team gathers, it is quite logical that he cannot join the team until he does finish it. Children who constantly run out into the street and are totally oblivious to the danger of cars must play inside or in the fenced backyard until they learn to stay out of the street.

Parents should remember that they are participants in a *learning* process, not a judicial one. Instead of being angry, parents should be understanding, sympathetic, and firm but fair. If they are, the chances of the child learning valuable insights that lead to the only workable method of discipline—self-discipline—are very good.

## Problem Ownership

Parents are often inclined to make too many of the child's problems their own. A child is not invited to a party, doesn't make the team, has a crush on a boy who doesn't like her, hates his teacher, or is suspended for missing two days of school; these are some common problems that children may encounter that parents believe are *their* problems. As such, parents assume ownership of the problem and intervene in order to solve the child's dilemma. Thomas Gordon writes that parents need to ascertain whether the problem is the child's or, indeed, the parent's.[6]

If the child's need is not being satisfied or he or she is upset about it, then it is the child's problem. It is not a problem for the parent because the child's behavior in no tangible way interferes with the parents' satisfying their own needs. If this is the case, the parent allows the child to own the problem and leaves responsibility for solving the problem with the child. Problems that children encounter when coping with their own life experiences should be the child's responsibility. The parent's role is to offer concern, care, and help. In such situations, parents should engage in active discussion in which they reflect the children's feelings back to them, for example, "It appears that you are upset about not being invited to Lynne's party" or "It sounds like you think that Mrs. Gates is not very fond of you." These communiqués help the child search for solutions to his or her problem. By allowing children to solve their own problems, parents not only strengthen their children's coping and problem-solving skills but accept their child as a separate and responsible person, which leads to an inner locus of control.

If the child is satisfying his or her own need but is also annoying his or her parent, then it is the parent's problem. When parents feel annoyed, frustrated, resentful, or don't like what the child is doing, the parent owns the problem. If, for example, the child is not doing chores around the house, is demanding too much attention, won't feed his pet, or interrupts constantly, it is the parent's problem. In these situations, parents should use "I-messages" to communicate their feelings.

Let's say that your child is pestering you to read him a story. You have just returned home from work and you're very tired and would like to have 15 minutes' rest before switching hats from "office person" to "parent." Telling the child, "You're being a pest," is a very poor way to communicate how tired you are. Children tend to decode this message as "I am a bad child." An I-message, however, such as "I am tired and would like to rest for a few minutes before we read a story together," is decoded correctly by the child as "Mom is tired." Because the child understands the message, he or she is more likely to comply. I-messages are quite effective in influencing a child to modify behavior that is unacceptable to the parent and is healthier for the child and the parent–child relationship. Table 7 summarizes the parent's role in situations when the child owns the problem and when the parent owns the problem.

## Being Organized

Lack of organization interferes with academic success. Helping children develop organizational skills will help them to be more effective learners. With younger children, make sure that the child's room is organized, that there is a place for frequently used items. Establish times for performing everyday activities: getting up for school, doing

**Table 7.** Problem Ownership

| When the Child Owns the Problem | When the Parent Owns the Problem |
| --- | --- |
| Child initiates communication | Parent initiates communication |
| Parent is a listener | Parent is a sender |
| Parent is a counselor | Parent is an influencer |
| Parent wants to help child | Parent wants to help himself or herself |
| Parent is a "sounding board" | Parent wants to "sound off" |
| Parent facilitates child finding own solution | Parent has to find his/her own solution |
| Parent accepts child's solution | Parent must be satisfied with solution |
| Parent primarily interested in child's needs | Parent interested in his/her own needs |
| Parent is more passive | Parent is more aggressive |

chores, and homework, for example. Reinforce children when they get things done on time. Use rewards to help children become more organized. (For example, "After you get ready for bed, you may watch a half hour of television.") Have them prepare items (books, clothing) that will be needed for the following morning. Parents and their children can work on a weekly schedule together and then post it on the child's bedroom closet door so that he or she can check it daily.

## Knowing What You Have to Do

Children should not be allowed to leave things in disarray. Discuss the project they may have been working on and have them make a list of the things that they need to do when they return to working on the project. Knowing what we have to do is a good part of the battle in tackling what we have to do. If children make notes of what they will begin with, they are better organized and waste less time trying to figure out what they should be doing.

## Organized Problem Solving

Children can become more organized if they follow this problem-solving method:

1.    Identify the problem: A book report due in four weeks.
2.    Identify goals: Write a five-page report.
3.    Develop strategies:
      Go to library and check out appropriate books. (week 1)
      Read and take notes on the books. (week 2)
      Write first draft. (week 3)
      Write final draft. (week 4)
4.    Carry out plan.

## Managing Time Successfully

Children can become more organized if they learn to manage their time successfully. Because time is so elusive, it is an easy commodity to ignore. Children can learn to manage time so that they don't waste it. Children need to approach time as if they are in control. When children say they don't have enough time, they may really be saying that they are not spending the time they do have in the way that they want. Time management gives children a chance to spend this valuable resource the way they want. The purpose of this exercise is to give children a tool to change the way they spend time and plan their time more effectively.

Time management has three important aspects: scheduling time for the "have to's" and planning time for the "want to's"; making sure that appointments or deadlines are not missed; and establishing where the time goes and where one wants it to go.

Children, with their parents' initial help, can start to control their time by becoming aware of how they spend their time. One way is for children to keep a daily log, hour by hour, of their activities for one week. Their log will give them a fairly accurate accounting of how they usually spend their time. Figure 4 shows a sample time plan.

Help your child make a quick estimate of his or her time commitments. How much time do they spend in class/school, studying, eating, traveling, socializing, talking on the phone, working, watching TV, and any other activities they can think of? Because their daily schedule on Tuesdays and Thursdays may be different from Mondays, Wednesdays, and Fridays, list the days of the week at the top of a page and have them jot down their schedule and then fill in the other activities they generally do during the week.

Have them look at the activities that have high payoffs, such as studying for an exam and attending class/school, and low payoff activities such as watching TV or talking on the phone. Help your child establish priorities.

Have them review for a few minutes the activities that they included in the inventory of how they spend their time. How many of the activities qualify as high priorities that are helping them reach their most valued goals? How many of their daily activities are low priorities and really could be discarded?

Take time to create a time schedule that is realistic and practical. Children should schedule their best study times for their most difficult subject areas. After a few weeks of working with your child on making a time log and following through with what they have scheduled, make it their responsibility for making and following their schedule.

# Reading

Reading is vital to one's success in school. Being a good reader leads to inner academic self-esteem. It's amazing, however, how many students find reading a drudgery and a chore. The first step into the

| Before 7:00 | Planned | Actual | Planned | Actual | Planned | Actual | TO DO LIST |
|---|---|---|---|---|---|---|---|
| 8:00 | | | | | | | |
| 9:00 | | | | | | | |
| 10:00 | | | | | | | |
| 11:00 | | | | | | | |
| 12:00 | | | | | | | |
| 1:00 | | | | | | | |
| 2:00 | | | | | | | |
| 3:00 | | | | | | | |
| 4:00 | | | | | | | |
| 5:00 | | | | | | | |
| 6:00 | | | | | | | |
| 7:00 | | | | | | | |
| 8:00 | | | | | | | |
| 9:00 | | | | | | | |
| 10:00 | | | | | | | |
| 11:00 | | | | | | | |
| After | | | | | | | |

**Figure 4.** Sample time plan.

world of reading is to develop a love for reading. This is particularly important for very young children. Expose your children to as many captivating books as you can. Let them see you reading books for pleasure. Take them to the library to check out books on their own. Read to children and have them "read" to you by telling stories from picture books.

It's interesting to note that children in Sweden do not have as many reading problems as children from the United States do. Sweden does not begin formally teaching reading skills until second grade. In kindergarten and first grade, children are exposed to many interesting and exciting books. They are encouraged to see the world of books as exciting, interesting, and fun.

It's a very good idea to have your child receive a thorough eye exam by an ophthalmologist before entering school. A significant percentage of children who have reading problems and are not doing well in school have vision problems.

After your child has begun to read, find some areas of interest that he or she has and check out books at the library. If the child is not too enthusiastic about reading, that is read the book to the child until the child begins to become engaged with the story, and then have him or her finish it on his or her own.

## The SQ3R System

Textbooks are read differently from books read for pleasure. Several decades ago, the SQ3R system (Survey, Question, Read, Recite, and Review) was designed.[7] Let's go through the steps that children need to follow when reading a chapter in their textbook. It's useful for parents to guide their children through these steps until the child has mastered them.

### Survey

Getting ready to read a chapter in a textbook should be like preparing to go on a trip, for which most people decide on a destination, consult a road map and travel guide, and plan their journey. Children should begin their journey through a chapter in their text by surveying the major topics in the chapter outline. Have them briefly look at each page, noting the number of key terms, the illustrations, and other special features. Have them read the chapter summary. Help them develop a sense of the most significant facts to gather from the chapter.

## Question

This step is essential in decreasing the amount of time children spend actually reading the chapter and in increasing the amount of time they have available for actively processing the information. Have them practice the skill of turning textbook reading into the search for answers to important questions. Have them make the major topic headings into questions.

## Read

Actively read one section of the chapter at a time; that is, actively search for the answers to their questions. Do not concentrate on reading every word on every page. Instead, focus on locating the important points that are made in each section. The payoff is in locating and paying attention to important information, material most likely to appear on tests.

## Recite

After children read, have them recite. Have them actively test their memory for what they have just read. After completing their search of the section, have them repeat the answers to their questions. If an answer escapes them, have them look for that information again. Have them look away from the page and try to summarize in their own words what they have just read. They should try to visualize each important term and give its definition. If they cannot recall a term, have them quickly rehearse the information and try again. Remember, recitation is a key step because they are practicing the very activity that will eventually be tested.

## Review

In this final step, children repeat the techniques of reciting, writing, and relating as often as necessary to assure themselves that they have mastered the information contained in the chapter. To be effective, their review must be active. They need to say out loud the answers to the questions; have them study with a friend and take turns quizzing each other.

# Believing in Effort

Children's sense of competence is based on their believing that their abilities are sufficient for academic achievement. Ratings in competence are close to the maximum in the early grades and decline after that.[8] Children with high perceived competence experience less classroom anxiety and have a higher preference for challenging work than those with low perceived competence.

Perceived autonomy or experiencing their behavior as under their control has also been linked to school competence. Parents who encourage their children to initiate and make their own choices rather than apply pressure and inducements to control the child's behavior have children who tend to do well academically. Parents who allow and support their children to develop a sense of themselves as individuals in charge of and responsible for their own actions, promote higher understanding, a greater sense of competence, and more perceived autonomy, which all lead to high academic self-esteem.

Children's conceptions of intelligence are also related to their perceived autonomy and academic achievement level. Young children give more social definitions of intelligence. Kindergartners and first-graders, for example, when asked to explain the "smartness" ratings they gave their classmates, tend to respond that smart classmates share their toys and smart classmates do not bite other children.[9] Even after children have begun to differentiate social and cognitive competence, they do not have a concept of intellectual competence that is as narrow as that of most older children. Many second- and third-graders discuss work habits (e.g., neatness, effort) to assess their own and their peers' ability in school.

Most importantly, young children do not differentiate between effort and ability. Young children tend to believe that ability is similar to a skill and that it is increased through one's own instrumental behavior, like practice or effort. Young children (kindergarten to grade 3), for example, insist that even when the child who achieved a higher performance outcome also exerted less effort, the one who tried harder, nevertheless, must be smarter. Subsequently, older children (and many adults) tend to perceive ability as a stable trait, unaffected by effort. Thus, these older children infer from identical performance outcomes that the child who exerts less effort must be the smarter.

Older children no longer conceive of intelligence as a repertoire of skills that can be endlessly expanded through their efforts. Rather, they learn to see intelligence as a global, stable entity whose adequacy is judged by their performance. Intelligence is thought of as fixed and un-alterable, something inherited. The concepts of effort and ability have been widely used in analyzing achievement motivation in U.S. children and children in other countries, particularly Japan and China. For years, researchers have been trying to discover the secret of superior perfor-mance, particularly in math and science, by Asian children. One factor that appears to account for these differences in academic performance levels is effort.[10]

Asian students hold very strong beliefs about effort. There is a say-ing in Japan, "Pass with four, fail with five." This means if you get five or more hours of sleep a night, you are not putting forth enough effort. Parents and teachers also believe in the power of effort. Teachers be-lieve that everyone in their classroom is capable of doing the work re-quired at each grade level, if they try hard enough. Thus, effort is a key variable that accounts for the higher achievement levels of Asian and American-Asian students.[11]

The development of the concept of ability as a stable trait is espe-cially important to understand because it has implications for children's behavior in school. Young children's persistence on academic tasks does not decline as a consequence of failure until the fifth or sixth grade. Several studies provide direct evidence indicating that the debilitating effect of failure is associated with the development of a concept of abil-ity as a stable trait.[12]

Additional studies have examined the power of beliefs about abil-ity (stable trait or influenced by effort) and its association with behav-ior and academic performance. When children associate ability with effort, their motivation levels and academic performance exceed those of children who see ability as a stable trait.[13]

When children see ability as an internal, stable factor that is fixed by innate factors, they react with feelings of shame when faced with fail-ure, which leads to poor performance. Expectations for future success are low. In contrast, children who interpret the same failure as caused by insufficient effort react with feelings of guilt, an emotion known to mo-bilize future effort and improved performance. For those who see failure as the result of improper effort, failure presents a challenge. For those who interpret it as evidence of inability or a lack of worth, it can be dev-astating. Failure can mobilize students to increase effort, but for those who view intelligence as nonmodifiable, it can drive them to despair.

The results of these studies suggest that a crucial variable for school success may be the child's and parents' notions of intelligence. Those who believe that effort in the form of persistence and hard work is the key component of intelligence achieve academic success. Thus, parents should use techniques that encourage children to attribute their failures to factors over which they have some control, such as effort, before self-defeating attributions occur. When parents and teachers are instructed to give children explanations that attribute their task failures to lack of effort rather than ability, the children's level of achievement increases.

## Doing Homework

The quality of educational programs offered, socioeconomic class, and parents' level of education and their interest in their child's academic success all appear to be important determinants of children's achievement level. These variables are not readily changeable. Is there a variable that is easier to change that will improve student achievement? It seems that increased study time shows a consistent effect on school achievement, as measured in the grades students receive in their classes. It appears that the number of hours of homework per week is substantially related to achievement.[14] Furthermore, the amount of time spent studying has a significant effect on grades.

An increase in time spent on homework has a positive effect on a student's grades, even after controlling for race, family background, and ability. Average grades and homework time have a strikingly strong relationship for all levels of ability. For example, students of high ability who study 1 hour a week receive mostly Bs and Cs, whereas students of comparable ability who study 10 hours a week receive mostly As and Bs. Homework time (the amount of time and effort one is willing to put in on studies), regardless of particular ability level, increases one's level of achievement based on grades received.

## Parental Involvement

How does your child perceive your involvement, level of expectation, and beliefs regarding his or her capabilities as a student? Remember, it is important to view these categories from the child's perspective. You may feel that you are involved, have high expectations, and believe in your child's capabilities, but if the child sees things differently than you do, you need to see these parental characteristics from the child's perspective.

High levels of involvement are associated with children's academic competence.[15] There are three types of parental involvement. One category of parental involvement, *cognitive/intellectual*, depends on exposing children to cognitively stimulating activities and materials such as books and current events. Children's mental abilities are enhanced in a home environment in which the parents provide rich sensory experiences and encourage the child's active exploration of the sights, sounds, and objects in their environments.

A second category is based on *personal* involvement, for example, attending parent–teacher conferences, plays, recitals, and open house, which indicates to children that parents care about school and enjoy interactions with children around school. The third category of involvement is parental *behavior*. Parents, for example, may participate in skill-building activities, such as helping their children with their homework. Parental behaviors, such as assisting children with their studies and stimulating greater competence through skill building, may have direct effects on children's academic achievement. Parental monitoring of the child's homework activities and their guidance has been shown to facilitate children's cognitive development and academic achievement. Guidance does not mean doing your child's homework. Rather, it is helping your child learn to organize, concentrate, and focus on getting the most out of homework.

Another possible impact of parental behavior, however, may be through the child's attitudes toward himself or herself in the academic setting. A child, for example, who perceives a parent as interested might also feel more competent in the academic setting. Parents' behavior may not affect the child through skill building, as has been traditionally assumed, but through its impact on children's attitudes and motivations about school and oneself as a learner. Children's attitudes and beliefs about their academic competence in school are powerful determinants of school success.

## Parental Expectations

The kinds of expectations parents and teachers have for children affect how children feel about themselves in academic settings, which influences the child's performance in class. Japanese children are taught very early in life that they must do well in school or they will suffer ridicule—ridicule that extends to the child's mother. So devoted are mothers to the educational success of their children that a new cultural institution has sprung up—the *kyoiku mama* (education mother). This role represents a completely self-sacrificing existence for Japanese mothers, one that involves full responsibility for their child's schooling. Mothers' high expectations lead to children's good performance in the academic setting.

Robert Rosenthal and Lenore Jacobson's research was the first to show the strong influence that expectations have on children's academic performance.[16] In their Oak School experiment a group of educators from Harvard University came in and told all the teachers, "We are going to go in your classrooms and we are going to give a test called the 'Harvard Test of Inflected Acquisition.' This test is going to measure which children in your classroom are most likely to show an intellectual spurt during the year that they are in your class. Because of the basic principles of the test construction, we are not permitted to discuss the test or test scores, but we'll point out the children who will grow academically this year to you."

The educators then gave some obsolete intelligence tests to the children and then proceeded to throw them out when the children were finished. Twenty percent of the children in each class were chosen by means of a table of random numbers, that is, their names were drawn out of a hat. The educators from Harvard then sat down with the teachers and read the names of the five children in each of their classes who were going to spurt that semester.

Many teachers expressed shock when certain names were mentioned, "Bernard! Bernard couldn't spurt if you put him in a cannon!" Nevertheless, the Harvard Test of Inflected Acquisition never lies. Every child on the list did show an academic spurt that semester. The "special" children, in fact, gained an average of 20 IQ points—the lower the grade level, the greater the IQ gain. What does this study show? In general, you get what you expect. If a parent or teacher believes that a child is capable, the child will be successful.

## Parenting Styles

Children with authoritative parents who are warm but firm and place high value on the development of the child's autonomy and self-direction tend to succeed at higher levels academically than children with authoritarian parents who tend to favor more punitive, absolute, and forceful disciplinary measures and place a high value on conformity and obedience. Permissive parents who are more passive in matters of discipline and give the child a high degree of freedom also tend to have children who do not do well academically. Children who describe their parents as behaving more democratically, more warmly, and more encouraging tend to earn higher grades in school.

## Mothers' and Fathers' Warmth

A mother's support and affection for her children, as shown in her physical and verbal responses to them and her positive regard for herself and her children, seem to have a significant positive influence on children's level of achievement. These supportive attitudes tend to release the child's ability to concentrate and master the learning tasks at hand.

Similarly, children who perform well academically appear to value their fathers' companionship. These children perceive themselves as similar to their fathers; fathers of high achievers are more accessible to their children and are democratic in dealing with their children. Paternal nurturance has been found to be positively related to children's achievement. High-achieving students tend to report that their fathers are more accepting and somewhat less controlling than fathers described by low achievers. Low-achieving children tend to describe their fathers as not allowing them to make decisions, giving them little control over what they do, and making them conform to fathers' rules and regulations.

## High Motivation

Some children just drift through their school years. They simply are not motivated and we all know that motivation is a key to success. How can parents help the unmotivated child? Parents need to encourage their children to initiate and make their own decisions. Children's explorations, new projects, and activities need to be recognized and rewarded by parents. Overprotection, lack of support, restricting children's freedom of movement, impatience, or continually doing things for children that they can do for themselves will block the development of this inner energizing motivational drive.

Sometimes motivation is based on outside sources, doing something for someone or something else. Children make good grades, for example, to please parents, keep a scholarship, and so forth. This is known as extrinsic motivation and sometimes it is quite effective. But, to be a highly motivated student, motivation must come from within; it must be important to the child. Every child has something that personally motivates him or her—intrinsic motivation brings them feelings of self-pride and satisfaction. What are some things that intrinsically motivate your child and why? How can you as parents help your child apply these motivational satisfactions to school?

## Believing the Child is Capable

One of the best ways to increase children's level of motivation is believing they are capable of doing the work that is expected of them in the classroom. In light of this information, parents must have or develop trust in their child, an inner confidence that their child will do all right in school. Children need parental trust in them and their ability to master school tasks in order to give them the confidence to actually do so. Doubts that they will succeed (these are, after all, the source of parents' worrying about their children's school performance) are utterly destructive to children's academic success.

Generally, it is neither laziness nor lack of interest that keeps children from applying themselves to their studies. It is their perception that their parents do not believe they can succeed. As a consequence, children may come to resent school and all it stands for, to hate school work to the degree that they actually are unable to do it. Who of us can attend to something we hate? *The conviction of parents that their child will succeed is what children need most in order to be able to do so.* It is the parents' trust in their children that enables them to create a sense of confidence in their own abilities.

This information is particularly pertinent to parents of children who are not doing well in school. Some parents go overboard, caring so much that their children do well academically that they become the ones who go to school for the child. They assume all responsibility for school work (because they know that their child will not). Moreover, in the quest to pull their child from this "motivational slump," they may resort to saying rather demeaning things to the child. ("Do you want to grow up to be a ditch digger? Well, you will if you don't study.") Many children actually believe in this lack of ability after they have been told this long enough by their parents and don't bother to study.

Avoiding negative labeling will help enhance children's self-esteem. Children's behavior directly coincides with the labels that are attached to them. Negative labels are incorporated into children's self-images and help to confirm negative views of self, leading to further maladaptive and unproductive behavior. If a word or label is attached to children long enough, they tend to become that type of person; the labels are verified by children developing that behavior, attitude, or feeling. Stressing the negative and labeling the unproductive behavior keeps the idea going and tends to "stamp in" the inappropriate actions. Thus, many children think of themselves as procrastinators, failures, lazy, incapable, and so on, because they are told time and time again that they are that kind of person. Positive labels (hardworking, responsible, creative) are also incorporated in the self and children learn to produce behavior that reflects these labels.

When parents fail to trust their children's capabilities or resort to negative labeling as a motivational tool, they destroy the child's academic self-esteem, sense of control, competence, and autonomy—important motivational factors that are related to children doing well academically.

Most parents worry about their children's academic progress because it relates to their children's future. It is important for parents to remember that the future to a child means tomorrow, or, at best, a few days from now. To a child, his or her "future" is incomprehensible and makes no sense. A parent's interest in their children's academic success is of paramount importance. But this interest needs to be promoted within the context of the here and now—this is how children live and how they understand their lives.

## Summary

Our society highly values achievement in school. Subsequently, when children do not do well academically, parents rightfully are concerned. A good education, to many parents, plays an important role in determining the child's future success in many areas. There are several skills, behaviors, and attitudes that are vital to developing inner academic self-esteem. One pivotal factor is experiencing more success than failure in the academic setting. A significant portion of children's academic self-esteem, because academia is so valued in our society, is based on their performance in school. When children experience more failure than success they engage in various "no effort" strategies (low effort, procrastination, not doing their homework, setting low or ridiculously high goals, not caring about school, and so forth) to protect their self-esteem. To children, the lack of effort becomes the reason for not doing well in school, not the lack of intelligence or ability; thus, a small shred of their academic self-esteem is preserved.

Children need to feel that they have some control over what happens to them in the academic setting. They need to learn that they are responsible for their grades, turning in their assignments, and carrying out the behaviors that are required to succeed in that environment. When parents use natural and logical consequences in disciplining their children and recognize problems that belong to their children and problems that belong to both parents and children, an inner sense of control is established. Moreover, children need to be organized, have a good motivational drive to do well, and see the importance of doing their homework assignments to enhance their academic self-esteem.

Parents need to become involved with their child's education; they need to provide children with stimulating activities and materials, help children with their homework (not do it for them), and be interested in the academic progress of their child. Parents need to have realistic expectations of their child and very importantly, believe that their child is capable of succeeding in the academic domain. By achieving in the academic area, the child has a solid basis for maintaining high inner self-esteem.

# CHAPTER 5  Developing Inner Self-Esteem during Adolescence

## The Autonomous Adolescent

The onset of adolescence is usually associated with puberty, a period of rapid change from 100 percent child to biological, sexual maturity. Within a few years of reaching puberty, the child is transformed into an adult, at least in physical appearance. Changes at puberty are grouped into two classes: those related to the development of male or female sexual characteristics and those related to overall physical growth, known as the growth spurt. In girls, the growth spurt begins about age 10 or 11, reaches its peak at about 12, and decreases at age 13, with slow continual growth for several additional years. Boys begin their growth spurt later than girls, beginning at around age 13, reaching a peak at 14, and declining at age $15\frac{1}{2}$.

Adolescents' thinking is marked by movement from reality to the realm of possibility; they move from the concrete operational thinking of middle childhood to the formal operational thinking stage. Formal operational thinkers are no longer preoccupied with systematizing and organizing what comes to their senses. At the formal level, actual props and points of reference are no longer needed. The adolescent has the potential to conjure up many possibilities or solutions to problems, both the very obvious and the very subtle. Adolescents now construe the world abstractly and hypothetically.

Socially, adolescents begin to compare their own views with those of society at large, and they realize that the social system in which they operate is a product of the shared views of the members of society. Friendships are seen as open relationship systems subject to change, flexibility, and growth. Trust is knowing that each partner helps the other and allows the other to develop independent relations. True close friends attend to the deeper psychological needs of each other.

During adolescence there is a change from defining friendship as a concrete, behavioral, surface relationship of playing together and sharing items to a more abstract, internal dispositional relationship of caring for one another, sharing one's thoughts and feelings, and comforting each other at a deeper level than during middle childhood. There is a greater emotional investment with peers during adolescence, evidenced, perhaps, by the increase in the amount of time that is spent with friends. Friendships no longer need to be so exclusive, as pairs of friends accept each other's need to establish relationships with other people. Whereas younger children tend to describe others in vague, global, and nonspecific ways (nice, kind, good, bad), adolescents have descriptions that are more precise and differentiated (cheerful, generous, considerate of others).

Girls tend to develop considerable intimacy in their friendships, more so than boys. Intimacy has most often been equated with telling one's problems and sharing one's feelings as well as the underlying belief that a friend will understand one's situation. The ability to establish close, intimate friendships becomes increasingly important during early adolescence. Moreover, adolescents who rate their friendships as intimate and satisfying are more competent, more sociable, less hostile, and less anxious/depressed and have higher social self-esteem than those involved in less intimate friendships.[1]

During adolescence, conceptions of friendships undergo a great deal of change, with three major changes:

1. Change from defining friendships in a rather superficial way as concrete, behavioral, surface relationships to more abstract, intimate relationships of caring for one another, sharing one's thoughts and feelings, and comforting each other
2. With increasing age, a shift from self-centered orientation of friends satisfying one's wants and needs to mutually satisfying relationships
3. A change from momentary or transient relationships to relations that endure over time despite occasional conflict.

Moral guidelines during early and middle childhood are seen as absolutes emanating from such authorities as parents or teachers; judgments of right and wrong are made according to concrete rules. During adolescence, however, such absolutes and rules come to be questioned, as the adolescent begins to see that moral standards are subjective and based on points of view that are subject to disagreement. Later in adolescence comes the emergence of reasoning that is based on such moral principles as equality, justice, or fairness—abstract guidelines that transcend concrete situations.

In the emotional domain, G. Stanley Hall wrote, several decades ago, that it is adolescents' "natural impulse to experience hot and perfervid states." Novelists, social psychologists, psychoanalysts, and anthropologists have noted similar descriptions of adolescent moodiness or emotionality. They view emotional states experienced during adolescence as being more extreme, changing more quickly, and being less predictable than those experienced at earlier and later periods.

The hypothesis that adolescence is a time of extreme emotionality needs to be separated from the broader hypothesis that adolescence it is a time of turmoil or "storm and stress." The storm and stress view captures adolescence as a very troublesome time with most teenagers experiencing extreme moods, a great deal of adjustment difficulties, as well as severe stress and conflict.

Some believe that adolescence is a particularly difficult time for both parents and adolescents. Parents tend to see adolescents as rebellious, confused, argumentative, and difficult. In many families, it's "us" (parents) versus "them" (teenagers). In general, despite the vast physical and psychological changes that occur during adolescence; it is not a period of extreme "storm and stress" for most teenagers and their parents. On the contrary, the great majority of adolescents report feeling globally happy with their lives, rates of psychiatric disorder during adolescence are not greater than in later periods of the life span, and the typical teenager does not experience a breach in relations with parents.

The absence of the general condition of turmoil among the majority of teenagers, however, does not disprove the more specific hypothesis that adolescents are emotional creatures. Wide emotional swings, including positive as well as negative emotional states, are a normal part of the adolescent experience. Adolescents report more occasions of both negative and positive emotional states. Parenting adolescents is a mixture of joy and frustration. Teenagers are exerting their independence, searching for a stable identity, and striving for social success as they transform from a child to a young adult. Fortunately, most teenagers (and their parents) are able, with a few bumps and setbacks, to make it through the adolescent years quite successfully.

## Typical Behavior during Adolescence

Thirteen-year-olds tend to be somewhat shy, somewhat moody, and not too communicative. They often prefer to withdraw from the family circle and go off by themselves. The "introversion" that parents observe in their 13-year-olds is a cardinal trait of this age group. Once again, as the child tended to do at ages 7 and 9 years, the young adolescent clarifies and organizes his or her experiences by inward rehearsals and self-examination. Thirteen-year-olds tend to be quite critical of themselves as they analyze their weaknesses and strengths. While they can be somewhat self-critical, they are also very sensitive to criticism from others. Thirteen-year-olds are rather sloppy, which causes some dissension between mother and child. They do not particularly like to participate in family get-togethers and tend to be embarrassed if seen with parents in public.

Thirteen-year-olds are more discriminating in their estimation and acceptance of companions. Girls form intimate relationships and tend to spend a good amount of time talking about their problems with each other. Boys, on the other hand, like to get together with friends so they can *do* something. Some 13-year-olds have begun to date, but many just enjoy going to casual parties or school dances. At 13, boys and girls seem to develop feelings of "neutrality" toward the opposite sex.

The shyness and touchiness of 13 gives way to a more expansive and robust 14. Fourteen-year-olds withdraw less and are better aware of themselves and their interpersonal environment. They are quite gregarious and prefer a variety of associates. Boys travel in groups without necessarily having a close friend. Girls are more likely to have two or three special friends. Boys show more interest in girls and many enjoy parties and dances. Fourteen-year-olds are able to recognize two sides of an argument or point of view, which may help them to be more considerate of others and more controlled in emotional situations.

Fifteen-year-olds tend to be indifferent to everything; they appear to be totally nonexcitable and rather apathetic. Fifteen-year-olds are not very outgoing, tending to keep to themselves. In fact, family unity may be at an all-time low, as 15-year-olds tend to be belligerent, defiant, and quite frequently threaten to leave home. These adolescents want to be treated as adults; they want to outgrow their dependence on their parents.

While 15-year-olds seem to be walking around in a fog, dissatisfied, uncertain, and even rebellious, 16-year-olds are more cordial, more tolerant of their family, and more worldly in general. They like to spend more time with friends than they do at home. But, when they are home, they tend to be more communicative than at 15. Similarly, they are not quite as touchy and moody as they were a year earlier. Many 16-year-olds no longer demand independence as they did before, easing the relationship with their parents. As 16-year-olds outgrow the sophomore slump, they may worry once again about doing well academically. They have a tendency to hide their feelings from their parents, choosing to confide in their friends rather than in their moms and dads.

Adolescence is a time when teenagers tend to be extremely critical of their parents. Many enjoy arguing with their parents just for the sake of arguing. Most teenagers are extremely self-conscious. They feel they are always "on stage" and that everyone around them is aware of and as concerned about their appearance as they are. It is this belief that constitutes the egocentrism of adolescence. In a sense, adolescents are continually constructing or reacting to an imaginary audience. It is an audience because adolescents believe that they will be the focus of attention, and it is imaginary because in actual social situations this is not the case. Adolescents, for example, are very conscious of the tiniest imperfections (a pimple on their face, bad hair) and feel that everyone notices these imperfections as well. This may explain, in part, why some teenagers are so highly critical of others and see even slight imperfections in others. The adolescent's desire for privacy may be a reaction to the feeling of being under the constant scrutiny of other people.

A second aspect of egocentrism is the experience of the personal fable. David Elkind uses this term to refer to adolescents' notions that their feelings and experiences are unique.[2] It seems impossible to them that an adult might know what they are experiencing or feeling. What looks like defiance or negativism in an early adolescent may often be the result of such an adherence to a personal fable. One consequence of the egocentrism may be unrealistic idealism. Piaget stated that "the adolescent not only tries to adapt his ego to his social environment, but just as emphatically tries to adjust the environment to his ego."[3] Thus, the adolescent may be highly interested in politics, religion, or educational reform and may develop ideas of an egocentric nature as solutions to problems in these areas. As the egocentrism of other periods gradually diminishes, so does the egocentrism of adolescence.

## Development of Self during Adolescence

During adolescence, self-evaluations become more analytical. ("I am basically a good kid, when I want to be.") Moreover, social relationships (getting along with others, being popular, having a boyfriend or girlfriend) are very important to most adolescents and play a big role in contributing to their level of social self-esteem. In addition, adolescents begin to develop a strong belief in their power and ability to control their environment.

The shift from physical, concrete evaluations of self to abstract, psychological evaluations that occurs during adolescence reflects cognitive advances in thinking and reasoning. Adolescents are able to think abstractly, reason about the hypothetical, and introspect. The emergence of formal operational thinking substantially affects the adolescent's self-esteem.

Adolescents begin to evaluate themselves more in terms of psychological traits (feelings, personality traits, relations with others) reflecting on an inner world of thoughts and feelings. ("I get along well with others because I am basically a friendly person.") Thus, with increasing age an individual's self-pictures become more abstract. Adolescents no longer judge themselves in terms of specific acts and qualities but, rather, in terms of abstractions and general evaluations. One self-evaluation might be, "I am not very popular with the in crowd, but I have my own circle of friends, so I am happy." In short, the self becomes less a pure perceptual object (dependent on observable traits) and more and more a conceptual trait system (dependent on feelings and relationships with others).

Why do adolescents, in contrast to younger children, assess the self and others in terms of a psychological interior (an inner world of thought and feeling)? The answer is found in the different cognitive processes of children and adolescents. Introspection (looking into one's own mind and inspecting one's own feelings) is a critical process that differentiates children and adolescents and contributes to differences in self-esteem.[4] Unlike young children, adolescents are more alert and responsive to their own thought processes.

Adolescents think of an idea and dismiss it as stupid. A teenager might reason, "I'd like to go to Harvard, but that's unrealistic because of my grades," and then argue with her own conclusions, "My grades may not be that bad and, besides, I have my sports and extracurricular activities that may help me get into Harvard." In order for introspection to occur, thought must first become conscious of itself. Young children are less likely to see themselves in terms of a psychological interior because they haven't developed the ability to introspect.

In addition to the increased use of abstract psychological terms, the self-evaluations of adolescents are more likely than those of young children to be integrated coherently and to include explanations for and qualifications of the evaluations offered. ("He's not very smart, but then again, he doesn't study.") Such evaluations are indicative of both a greater ability to organize one's thoughts and a greater recognition of the multidimensional nature of personality. Whereas younger children invariably evaluate themselves in terms of the immediate present, adolescents evaluate themselves in terms of their past and future.

Adolescents are capable of acknowledging that the self can be judged by traits and qualities that are opposites, for example, that one can be smart and dumb at different times. Another difference between young children's and adolescents' self-images is in the locus of self-knowledge. In children's view, the truth about the self tends to be vested in an external authority. The perceived locus of self-knowledge shifts from the other (especially the parent) to the self in adolescence. Adolescents now feel that they know themselves better than others do. These changes represent a qualitative shift in the structure of thoughts about self and others.

## Reorganization of Self-Esteem

Some theorists suggest that because of cognitive, physical, and social changes during adolescence, a considerable amount of reorientation of self takes place. As a result, self-esteem may be subject to a period of reorganization, characterized by a time of questioning one's values and goals and one's purpose in life, which may lead to a sense of discomfort and confusion. Does research support the premise that there is reorientation, reorganization, and disturbance in self-esteem? Several studies identify early adolescence as an apparently disturbing period. Disturbance does not connote psychopathology but, rather, any change in a direction presumed to be discomfiting for the adolescent. Not all studies report a decline in self-esteem during adolescence; none, however, have reported an increase. Most available evidence suggests that adolescents' self-esteem becomes less stable and more negative in early adolescence (the junior high years) compared to earlier and later periods, with females experiencing a greater decrease in self-esteem than males.[5]

On the basis of scores on various psychological scales, psychologist Robert Simmons and his colleagues concluded that the largest negative change seems to occur among 12-year-olds.[6] Girls who have reached puberty earlier, those who have embarked early on the new social behavior of dating, and those who have experienced a major environmental change by moving into a junior high setting are a particularly vulnerable group. The pattern of environmental change, early development, and dating, while a disadvantage for girls, appears to be an advantage for boys. Boys who mature faster, date earlier, and enter new junior high environments demonstrate higher self-esteem than their late-maturing, nondating, no-school-change counterparts.

Why is it that boys and girls react quite differently to the transition into early adolescence in terms of their self-esteem? Simmons makes the following conjectures. It may be that boys tend to focus more on inner sources of self-esteem (being competent) and girls tend to focus more on outer sources of self-esteem (receiving approval from others). As a result, girls have a tendency to value sociability or popularity and appearance. For example, when adolescents are asked to rank popularity, competency (being the best), and independence in order of importance, girls rank popularity first, while boys rate competency as number one. Thus, staking one's self-esteem on outer sources, others' opinions of oneself as popularity dictates, can cause girls' self-esteem to be especially vulnerable. Also, placing value on appearance or looks may also place girls' self-pictures in jeopardy, particularly because physical changes are more dramatic in adolescent girls compared to adolescent boys.

## Self-Esteem in Males and Females

Young adolescents, 13 to 15 years, tend to display stereotypic masculine and feminine ways of behaving. The idea that gender-appropriate behaviors intensify during early adolescence is referred to as the *gender intensification hypothesis.*[7] Researchers have noted, in support of this idea, that girls in early adolescence tend to become more self-conscious, more submissive, and demonstrate less interest in academic achievement. Socially, girls invest more time than boys in forming intimate friendships. Male adolescents, however, tend to act in a macho fashion and are very careful not to exhibit "weak" or feminine kinds of behavior.

Herbert Marsh of the University of Western Sydney found that sex differences in self-esteem are consistent with sex stereotypes.[8] Boys have higher self-esteem in "achievement/leadership" than girls and girls have higher self-esteem in "congeniality/sociability." Boys tend to describe themselves as more self-sufficient and achievement-oriented; girls describe themselves as more sociable and help-seeking. Marsh reports that boys have higher self-esteem in mathematics and girls have higher self-esteem in verbal skills.

Self-images of males tend to focus on athletic abilities, while females' self-images tend to center on physical appearance. Males are more satisfied with their bodies and experience them more positively than females. In addition, males are concerned more with task mastery and instrumental effectiveness than with physical appearance. Females are more concerned with physical attractiveness than males. Desire for social acceptance is also more important to girls than to boys. Girls tend to have higher self-esteem in relation to their reading and music abilities. Self-esteem differences are also found in the family domain. Females tend to emphasize connectedness (relationship, connection) to their family as being important. Males tend to emphasize separateness (power, independence, autonomy) from their families.

Moreover, the establishment of a separate sense of self seems to be more easily achieved by males than by females. As with most self-esteem sex differences, what is referred to here is not an absolute difference between males and females; rather, females on the average have more difficulty than males in experiencing an autonomous sense of self. The merging of one's self-esteem with others carries over into adulthood. To illustrate, self-definition for adult women has been characterized as being embedded in relationships and the emotional responses of others. In contrast, males tend to achieve a distinct and separate sense of self and as adult men are characterized as having more distinct boundaries between self and others.

Research indicates that women defer to the wishes of others, take on the interests and orientations of others, and experience greater difficulty than men in knowing their own needs or what they genuinely want or feel apart from what others expect or approve. Women's identity is anchored more deeply in relationships. Women have often been directed not toward pursuit of their own goals for themselves, but toward pursuit of their goals for others (for their children's achievement and success or their husbands' career aspirations). These goals may permit some gratification of the woman's wish to feel competent but robs her of recognition and direct reward, diverts her from her own pursuits and goals, and may arouse jealousy and resentment in the person she aims to help.[9] In addition, women are more in need of affirmation from others, and their assessment of their abilities is more vulnerable to criticism by others.

Some provocative arguments have been put forward that sex differences in the experience of a separate sense of self have their origins in infancy and early childhood. Boys, for example, are encouraged by their mothers to be more independent, to be adventurous, and to have more freedom and experience fewer restrictions than girls. In contrast, girls are encouraged to remain close to mother, receive more cuddling and closeness with their mother, have more restrictions, and are not given the latitude in exploration that boys are given. Separation from the mother and assertion of independence are crucial for the development of autonomy. Girls, however, are encouraged to remain in a matrix of emotional connectedness.

In partial support for the hypothesis that boys tend to separate from mother more so than girls, Rose Olver gave college-age men and women the Self–Other Differentiation Scale.[10] In addition, a questionnaire assessing the degree of maternal involvement and intrusiveness, with higher scores indicating more permeable boundaries between mother and child, was administered. The data indicate that men show a more separate sense of self than women. There is also clear support that mothers are more highly involved and intrusive in their relationships with their daughters' lives than with their sons' lives.

While mothers and sons form a close alliance, mothers depend more on their daughters for personal and familial needs than on their sons. Mothers and daughters are involved together with day-to-day household tasks such as shopping for food, preparing meals, and buying clothes. Daughters are being prepared for motherhood; so, if the daughter cannot learn to cook a simple meal, it's catastrophic. She cannot be lacking in these skills if she expects to be a wife and mother someday. Raising a daughter is about relationships, interpersonal achievements, homemaking, and affiliation. Parents, particularly fathers, may still see marriage as the main goal for their daughters. If they encourage their daughters to finish college, fathers generally do not perceive of them as engaging in demanding, high-paying careers; it is up to the daughter's future husband to take care of their daughter's financial needs.

While parents may believe that girls are being socialized to be independent and achievement oriented, many families continue to believe that daughters must learn to be sensitive, affectionate, nurturing, and self-sacrificing individuals. Raising sons is another story. Sons are not raised to be fathers. Rather, they are socialized more toward extrafamilial tasks such as earning money. For sons to achieve in this public world, they need to be detached, objective, autonomous, and aggressive.

## Feminine Girls and Masculine Boys

Do feminine girls and masculine boys feel better about themselves then? Are they happy, healthy, and well adjusted? Or would both sexes be better off if they adopted both feminine and masculine behavior, such as being nurturant to a child, assertive with employees, and sympathetic with a friend, as some psychologists suggest?

According to Sandra Bem at Cornell University, the combination of masculine and feminine characteristics is deemed to have desirable implications for an individual's behavior, regardless of sex.[11] Adolescents with desirable characteristics of both genders are more likely to develop a firm self-confidence, a broad range of adaptive qualities that transcend narrowly defined gender-role stereotypes, and have a wider range of capabilities. For example, such individuals can be as effective in a situation that requires assertiveness as in one that requires warmth.

In a series of experimental studies, Bem has found that older adolescents and adults who have a flexible gender-role identity that allows fluidity in various social situations and, thus, are capable of changing their behavior to suit the situation, exhibit higher levels of self-esteem and better adjustment.

In contrast, psychologists Marylee Taylor and Judith Hall report that adolescents whose behavior incorporates both masculine and feminine traits do not consistently exhibit higher self-esteem or better adjustment.[12] Rather, in both males and females, positive self-esteem is linked to masculine traits. Describing oneself as independent, assertive, and self-confident contributes to high scores on masculinity scales *and* self-esteem scales. Although girls who display both masculine and feminine traits feel better about themselves than either very masculine or very feminine girls, it is the masculine adolescent boys (not those who demonstrate masculine and feminine behavior) who show the highest levels of self-acceptance and overall high peer acceptance.

The findings of these two studies suggest, however, that it is easier for girls to behave, at times, in masculine ways during adolescence than it is for boys to act occasionally in feminine ways. Males, particularly during early adolescence, may be more likely to be criticized if they behave in feminine ways, but Bem maintains, as adults, males who have achieved a balance between masculine and feminine ways of behaving and consequently have achieved flexible and multiple interests and attitudes, will more successfully adapt to their surroundings than their more masculine counterparts.

Among adolescents, however, one can conclude from research that behaving in masculine and feminine ways is associated with high self-acceptance, high peer acceptance in females, better social relations, and superior adjustment for females more so than males. (Behaving in rigid, masculine ways, however, is not desirable for males.) Moreover, it is the masculinity component, more than the femininity component, that is associated with positive and psychological outcomes for females. These findings are interesting in that they suggest that it is more acceptable for women to adopt masculine traits than for men to adopt feminine traits. They also suggest that greater societal value is placed on masculine traits than feminine traits. Masculinity (assertiveness, independence, high achievement) appears to be the gender-role classification that is most associated with female adolescents' psychosocial well-being.

## Developing Inner Self-Esteem during Adolescence

Parental tasks that will enable adolescents to move through the adolescent period into young adulthood more effectively and smoothly include engaging in effective parenting styles and learning to communicate effectively with teenagers. In addition, there are several skills, behaviors, and attitudes that adolescents need to achieve (with the help of their parents), such as acquiring both masculine and feminine ways of behaving, developing a sense of separateness and connectiveness, developing a stable sense of identity, accepting and achieving a comfortable body image, and cultivating "outgrowing" minds.

## Effective Parenting Styles

Parenting style is a very important determinant of the extent to which adolescents are likely to achieve the aforementioned tasks and make a smooth and positive transition through adolescence. Obtaining the adolescent's cooperation is more crucial than obtaining their obedience. Adolescents who feel comfortable with their relationship with their parents are more likely to reflect their parents' values, to communicate their needs and feelings to them, and to cooperate with them. Moreover, when adolescents cooperate with their parents, obedience becomes a non-issue.

Parents who use authoritarian parenting styles characterized by high demandingness and low responsiveness may increase conformity and obedience in children in the short term, but such children are more at risk for depending on external controls (punishment, fear of getting caught) and not developing internal controls for their own behavior (doing what is right for its own sake). Adolescents with external controls are also more likely to blame others when things go wrong and are less likely to take responsibility for their own decisions and behavior. Authoritarian parenting can also lead to rebellion and a complete breakdown of the parent–adolescent relationship. Parents are likely to believe that the answer to their problems is to develop a "tough love" approach and become more and more controlling. The more strict and rigid they become, however, the lower the chances that the adolescent will do what the parents want.

Adolescents cope much better when they feel accepted by their parents, feel free to talk to parents about their problems, and are able to negotiate changes in rules and roles with their parents. Authoritative parenting involves reasoning with adolescents, parenting with flexibility and adaptability, firm but fair control, and a high degree of acceptance of the adolescent. These families are characterized by a high degree of democracy with the adolescent being given some opportunities to express opinions. Research consistently shows that authoritative parents have adolescents who are more cooperative and experience fewer adjustment difficulties; consequently, parents have an easier time parenting.[13] Research has also shown that adolescents who describe their parents as treating them fairly are more likely to develop positive attitudes toward and beliefs about their achievement, and as a consequence, they are more likely to do better in school.[14]

Parents need to emphasize to their adolescents that they are responsible for their own decisions and behavior and that they should not blame others or circumstances when they do something undesirable. Some teenagers continually blame their peers, for example, for their drunkenness or their teachers for their academic difficulties. Those teenagers with such an external locus of control, as was noted earlier, rarely accept responsibility for their behavior and subsequently don't change it.

Parents also need to be aware of the types of models they are presenting to their adolescents. Parents who drink excessively, are abusive in their relationship with their spouses, use drugs, and so forth, are poor role models. We cannot expect teenagers to accept the parents' rule of no drinking when the parents themselves abuse alcohol. Similarly, we cannot expect adolescents to respect others when spouses treat each other in abusive ways or accept such abuse as though they deserve it.

Rebellion or complete passivity is most likely to occur when the structure of authority is patriarchal and unequal, when discipline is excessive and inconsistent, and when demands are inflexible and arbitrarily made. Evidence seems clear that the best environment for adolescents involves firm but fair control combined with encouragement to be an autonomous individual. A good environment also means adjusting to the adolescent's needs rather than being rigid and inflexible. Adolescents who admire and respect their parents are much more likely to cooperate with them. Parents who overuse discipline and punishment are likely to minimize rather than increase their influence over their adolescents. When adolescents fear their parents, when they have no control over their lives, and when their relationship with their parents is negative, they become increasingly alienated from their families. They don't listen to their parents' advice or demands and don't respect their parents; thus, parents lose most if not all of their influence over their adolescents.

## Talking with Teens

Communication is a critical aspect of family life that affects the quality of the relationship between the parents and the healthy functioning of both individual family members and the family as a whole. Good parent–adolescent communication fosters a sense of independence in adolescents and, at the same time, increases the bonds of affection and closeness between the parent and child.

An examination of gender differences in communication patterns reveals that communication with mothers is more frequent than with fathers. Adolescents also tend to discuss a wider range of topics with their mothers. Similarly, daughters report stronger relationships with mothers than with fathers; mothers are seen as being more open, understanding, and accepting. Fathers are more likely to impose authority, and, as a result, adolescents tend to limit self-disclosure to fathers.

Daughters, more so than sons, communicate more frequently with their mothers about sexual attitudes and relationships. They tend to discuss their interests, their relationships with others, sexual problems, and general problems with mothers more so than with fathers. Because a daughter is often "Daddy's little girl" no matter what her age, she may attempt to protect her father's illusion on sexual matters. The amount of communication about sexual matters, however, is quite limited, especially with sons. Many adolescents report that they would like to have better sex-related communication with their parents, and many parents report that they want to be active resource agents for sex education. While parents want to talk about sexual matters, many report that they don't know how to do it. It seems apparent that we need more resources in helping adolescents and parents open up to one another on this important topic.

Adolescents tend to see their mothers as both initiating more discussion with them and recognizing and accepting their opinions more than fathers.[15] They describe their communications as more open, despite the fact that adolescents report more conflict with mothers than with fathers. The higher level of conflict with mothers is likely related to the fact that the adolescent tends to have more frequent and more meaningful communications with the mother than with the father.

Mothers and teenagers tend to argue more about personal matters, choice of friends, and clothes. Adolescents argue more with their fathers about money, use of leisure time, and attitude about school. Responsibilities within the home tend to be a source of conflict with both parents. Other areas of conflict relate to day-to-day living, relationships within the family, personal hygiene, chores around the house, social activities and friendships, disobedience, and conflicts with siblings. Interestingly enough, these are the same topics that parents and adolescents argued about 75 years ago.

Both boys and girls report that parents criticize them for being disobedient, breaking family rules, not being ambitious enough, and being messy and sloppy. The greater the level of parental criticism, the lower the adolescent's self-esteem. When communications consist mainly of criticism, a vicious cycle is perpetuated: Criticism leads to low self-esteem in adolescents, which leads to more negative behavior and subsequently more criticism from parents.

The most important aspect of language is communication, an interaction between two or more people that involves an exchange of information. Most of us tend to take communication for granted; it isn't until we experience some problem that we may begin to wonder how we can be more effective communicators. Parents sometimes remark that their teenagers just "clam up and don't say anything to us anymore." Adolescents may remark, "My parents boss me too much; My mom is always telling me what to do; Sometimes I want to plug up my ears when she opens her mouth." (Many do.) How can parents communicate effectively with adolescents? While effective techniques for communication are particularly important with adolescents, they are applicable to individuals of any age. In fact, the earlier we can apply effective communication strategies the better our relationship with our children will be.

### Typical Ways of Responding

Thomas Gordon, author of *Parent Effectiveness Training*, has pointed out typical ways in which adults respond to adolescents and the subsequent feelings they arouse in them.[16] Often adults simply order or command: "As long as you live in this house, you will do as you are told to do." Many adults moralize or preach: "When I was your age, my parents didn't help me with my homework. It was up to me to finish it." They judge and criticize: "You are such a messy kid; your room looks like the city dump." They advise and give solutions: "Listen to me; I know what's best. If I were you I would spend more time studying." These kinds of communiqués close the door to effective communication. They communicate unacceptance of the individual, produce fear of the parent's power, cause feelings of guilt, and make the adolescent feel inadequate and inferior.

The typical ways of responding are often used to send what Gordon calls a "solution-type message" to the adolescent. Adults may not wait for the adolescent to initiate appropriate behavior; they simply blurt out what the adolescent must, ought, or should do. To use Gordon's example, suppose a friend is visiting your house and he happens to put his feet on the rungs of one of your new dining room chairs. You certainly would not say to him, "Get your feet off my chair this minute!" This sounds ridiculous in a situation involving a friend, because most people treat friends with more respect. Most likely the chair owner would send some message, such as, "I am really worried that my new chair might get scratched by your feet." Adults send this type of message to friends but seldom to adolescents. We naturally refrain from sending a critical message to a friend, yet we do this every day with adolescents.

Adults tend to send "put-down" messages: "You lose everything; you're so irresponsible" or "John, you are never prepared for your math work; why don't you wake up?" It seems that most parents do not use these put-downs intentionally to wound adolescents and destroy their self-esteem; the statements are made with the hopeful expectation that they will somehow change the adolescent for the better.

Similarly, when parents ask too many questions, adolescents learn to respond passively in monosyllables.

"How was your day?"
"Fine."
"Anything exciting happen?"
"Nope."
"Are you going out tonight?"
"Yep."
"Where are you going?"
"Dunno."
"When will you be back?"
"Later."

When parents are always asking questions, adolescents learn to take very passive roles in the communicative process and simply wait for the next question without offering any information.

## Effective Communication

There are a number of techniques that parents can use to increase their effectiveness as communicators with children and adolescents (as well as with other adults). Being a good listener, engaging in active listening (reflecting the adolescent's feelings), and sending I-messages (reflecting the parent's feelings) are important techniques that will help establish a positive relationship between adult and adolescent and open the door to further communication.

There are two aspects to communication: output (the speaking and writing) and listening. Being a good listener is an integral part of effective communication. Be sure that you are really listening to the adolescent and not thinking instead of your own pressing concerns. When we are really listening, we are trying to make an honest effort to understand the adolescent's feelings and thoughts from his or her point of view.

One of the most effective and constructive ways of responding to adolescents is to offer them an invitation to say more and to share their own judgments, ideas, and feelings by giving responses that reflect their thoughts, a technique known as active listening. The listener restates, in his or her own words, the message the speaker has just sent. It involves paraphrasing the speaker's words, not parroting them. If the message is simply repeated verbatim, there is still a great chance that the listener might be misunderstanding what has been said. Amazingly enough, simply feeding back a person's ideas often helps them sort out and solve the problem.

In many cases you need to go beyond reflecting thoughts and also rephrase the often unspoken emotions that accompany the verbal message. For example, when your adolescent has just expressed, "I hate my job. Mr. Thomas treats me like I'm some kind of idiot, he never gives me important stuff to do," you may respond, "When you talk about all the petty tasks your boss gives you, it sounds as though you're saying that you're hurt and disappointed that he hasn't given you more responsibility." When your child says, "I hate Jimmy!", you may respond, "Sounds like you're pretty angry with your brother." These comments are phrased tentatively, not dogmatically. You are sharing an interpretation and allowing the speaker to decide whether or not it is correct. Active listening is a great way to get through the layers of hidden meanings.

Active listening is not used in all situations. Sometimes adolescents are just looking for information and not trying to work out their feelings. A teenager might say, "I can't decide if I should take Mary or Sue to the prom." At times like this, active listening would be out of place. In addition, active listening takes time. Therefore, if you're in a hurry and don't have time to listen, it is wise to avoid starting a conversation that you will not be able to finish. Set up a time that day when both of you will be able to talk at length.

I-messages are critical, because adolescents need to know how the adult feels. They are essential in keeping communication lines open and establishing healthy relationships. Sometimes when communicating with teenagers, parents send "you" messages, which imply a judgment, for example, "You are always picking on your younger brother" or "You are being inconsiderate when you blast your stereo like that." Try to rephrase these sentences to begin with an "I" plus a description of your feelings, for example, "I get upset with all this fighting" or "I cannot think straight when the music is being played so loudly." You simply say how the adolescent's behavior is making you feel. You take responsibility for and acknowledge ownership of your thoughts, opinions, and feelings. The message focuses on you, not on the adolescent. It does not blame. The tone of voice is important too. An I-message delivered in anger becomes a you-message conveying hostility.

## Developing Balanced Ways of Behaving

As noted earlier, rigid ways of behaving—highly masculine for males and highly feminine for females—are not regarded as the most desirable. Building healthy inner self-esteem in adolescents involves helping them develop more balanced ways of behaving. Adolescents who display flexible gender roles tend to make healthier adjustments to life and have higher self-esteem than males and females who rigidly cling to stereotypic ways of behaving. In our society, an adult needs to be independent, assertive, and self-reliant as well as nurturant, sensitive, and concerned about the welfare of others. These are all commendable human qualities; however, even in today's society, traditional concepts of appropriate behavior for males and females inhibit instrumental behaviors (competence-directed, achievement-oriented) in many women and expressive behaviors (nurturant, empathic) in many men.

Since males tend to exhibit instrumental behaviors and females tend to exhibit expressive behaviors, the developmental task of each is different. Adolescent males should learn to mitigate instrumental behaviors with expressive behaviors and adolescent females, the reverse. For example, males need to be socialized to be empathetic, more open, and affectionate and develop collaborative ties with others; women need to develop a sense of agency—being separate and self-sufficient and capable of pursuing autonomous, independent goals. Men and women who achieve a balance of agency and communion have the greatest satisfaction and mental health. Parents and other agents need to stop socializing children in ways that perpetuate these dichotomous areas of self-investment for boys and girls. Socializing agents, such as parents and teachers, can foster and help maintain expressive and instrumental behavior in boys and girls.

Perhaps the reason that we are not seeing educationally and occupationally liberated females and emotionally liberated males is that parents and other influential agents in the child's world have a hard time overcoming their own socialization histories and continue to reinforce children's traditional masculine and feminine ways of behaving. While more educated parents tend to be slightly more liberal in socializing their children along less traditional masculine and feminine lines, views of appropriate behavior for boys still tend to be dominated by beliefs that they should be aggressive, do well in such subjects as mathematics, and be nonemotional. Girls, more so than boys, are socialized to be passive, nurturant, and sensitive. It is apparent to some writers that we need to remove the burden of these stereotypes and allow individuals to feel free to express the best traits of men and women. We need to overcome these traditional gender-role polarities to reach a new level of synthesis.

The problem parents face today is how to help their daughters develop a strong sense of self so that they don't grow up expecting to "lose themselves" in relationships with other people because they never "found themselves" in relationships with their mothers. Daughters can gain a stronger sense of self, of their individuality and independence, if they receive their mothers' support in learning that separation from them is all right. There are indications that suggest that daughters stay close to their mothers' identities and that to some extent never achieve a clear sense of a separate self at all. Respect for separateness of females has never been very great, and it may be that this most basic aspect of identity has not usually been encouraged in girls.

This diffuse personal identification of daughter with mother, this lack of encouragement by the mother to separate from her encourages the merging of the self with the perspective of the other and a consequent diffidence about asserting one's own perspective. A girl's self-identity merges with that of others. Women have a tendency to live in and through other people, to behave as though there is no difference between self and others. Girls tend to rely more on their relationships with other people for a sense of safety and as a way of feeling they have an effect on the world.

A mother's role is a complicated one. She must be nurturing, but at the same time she must support the daughter's sense of autonomy.

The mother needs to help her daughter grow and develop as an individual in her own right. This is what mothers do for their sons, and it is important for them to do this for their daughters as well.

Daughters also need to receive support from parents in learning that roles labeled by society as masculine will not compromise their sense of themselves as women. The social definition of femininity must be broadened to include achievement and self-assertion. Exposure to nontraditional models, such as a strong, intelligent, competent female friend, boss, or mother is another influential factor in promoting more balanced ways of behaving. Daughters of working women, for example, conceive of the ideal woman in society as being independent and active—qualities traditionally associated with men.

Positive reinforcement from family and teachers for achieving academically is perhaps the most significant factor in producing more balanced feminine and masculine ways of behaving in females. Women with high self-esteem tend to describe themselves as coming from high-achieving, academically oriented families. These women report having fathers who encourage and reward achievement or assertiveness and mothers who also encourage them to be able to support themselves and advance in school. Daughters who identify with an affectionate and competent father tend to be more assertive and competent than daughters who do not.

Twenty-five top executive women had the following characteristics in common:

1. All were oldest or only children.
2. All had no more than two siblings, who were all girls.
3. All had a "typical" relationship with their mothers, that is, a good one.
4. All had an "atypical" relationship with their fathers, that is, father was highly involved with and supportive of his daughter.
5. Most of these daughters' mothers (92%) had education equal to the fathers, and 52% of them had superior educations.[17]

Expressive characteristics in males may be enhanced if parents encourage boys to communicate their emotions more freely. Girls are given much more freedom in expressing emotional kinds of behavior, but boys are given strong messages to suppress feelings, to "take it like a man." Showing feelings is seen as a mark of weakness. It's interesting that we socialize boys to behave in nonemotional ways only to criticize them later, as boyfriends, husbands, and fathers, for being emotionally insensitive and unable to communicate on a more emotional and intimate level. Males need to be socialized to express their innermost feelings. Relationships among males, as a result of not doing so, are rather superficial. Rarely does a male confide his innermost feelings to another person; consequently, they do not receive the maximum benefits from friendships.

Boys should not have to walk such a rigid tightrope in order to conform to masculine roles. Parents, as we have seen, put much more emphasis on their sons' masculinity than on their daughters' femininity. Inappropriate behavior for girls does not appear to carry with it the social stigma that inappropriate behavior for boys does.

One overwhelming factor in producing more balanced ways of behaving in males is the impact of key women in men's lives. Sensitivity toward gender-role equality appears to be influenced by exposure to competent, professional women, be it early in life with a mother figure or relative or in adolescence with a girlfriend.

## Emotional Separateness from Parents

Developing a sense of separateness from their families is another important step that helps adolescents increase inner self-esteem. There appear to be three phases of adolescence, each requiring a different mix of parental control, that encourage adolescents to develop separateness from the family. In early adolescence (the junior high school period), young people assume an exaggerated pseudo-independent stance, which parents should respond to by continuing to enforce age-appropriate limits (maintaining that homework be done before play, for example). During mid-adolescence (the high school years), children achieve cognitive and social gains that enable parents to increase both responsibilities and rights (money management, for example). It is only in late adolescence that the adolescent's emancipation becomes the central issue of development and a nearly symmetrical parent–child relationship becomes a meaningful possibility.

Separation or individuation implies that the growing person takes increasing responsibility for what he does and what he is, rather than depositing this responsibility on the shoulders of those under whose influence and tutelage he has grown up.[18] Individuality is self-assertion or the clear presentation of one's own point of view; separateness refers to the ability to differentiate one's point of view from those of one's parents.

Adolescence is a time when both males and females push for separateness and gradually develop the wherewithal to take that control. Adolescents often pour a great deal of emotional energy into relationships outside the home. The process of emotionally separating from parents involves two phases: practicing and rapprochement. In the practicing phase, adolescents revel in feelings of separateness and autonomy, defining themselves oppositionally to their parents and other authority figures. An adolescent who has always studied hard to do well in school and please his parents, for example, may become less conscientious about his studies.

In the second rapprochement phase, adolescents attempt to reestablish bonds with their parents. Provided that parents (mothers, in particular) recognize their adolescents' (daughters, in particular) autonomy, an amicable relationship can be restored.

The way in which the parent attempts to control the adolescent has an important bearing on whether or not the adolescent achieves a sense of autonomy. The authoritative parent, more so than the authoritarian or permissive parent, enables the adolescent to develop a sense of responsibility for his or her behavior. Parents and their adolescent tend to engage in conversations that are interactional and reciprocal, not unidirectional from parent to adolescent. While communication may be characterized by high levels of conflict, this may be a positive phenomenon. Conflict may be critical to helping adolescents analyze and evaluate their needs, values, and beliefs. While intense, prolonged conflict may result in problems for both parent and child, a moderate degree of conflict is important to the development of autonomy.

Adolescents who have achieved a sense of independence from parents experience satisfaction with who they are and with the directions they are taking for achieving goals. Self-confidence is evidenced by a stability in their relationships and self-presentation to others (family, friends, authority figures). Those who have not achieved a sense of independence tend to be extremely egocentric and narcissistic and lack self-criticism and assertiveness. An adolescent who wants to remain a child has excessive dependency needs, intense fear of the inability to assume responsibilities and demands of adulthood, intense fear of sexual impulses, low self-esteem, and poor peer relations. They tend to be academic underachievers and feel that adults are unacceptable role models.

Laurence Steinberg of Temple University suggests that there are four components of emotional autonomy:

1.  Extent to which adolescents de-idealize their parents    ("My parents are sometimes wrong.")
2.  Extent to which they see their parents as people ("My parents lose their temper sometimes, but they're only human.")
3.  Independence, or the degree to which adolescents depend on themselves rather than parents ("When I've done something wrong, I don't always depend on my parents to straighten things out.")
4.  Degree to which the adolescent feels individuated within the relationship with his or her parents ("There are some things about me that my parents do not know.")[19]

All four components of emotional autonomy increase throughout the adolescent period. De-idealization may be one of the first aspects of emotional autonomy to develop, because adolescents may likely shed their childish images of their parents before replacing them with more mature ones. Seeing parents as individuals, however, appears to develop much later, perhaps not until young adulthood.

## Emotional Connectedness

A significant task for parents of adolescents is to help them grow in autonomy while maintaining close ties with the family. Helping adolescents achieve individuation and autonomy while maintaining a sense of connectedness or closeness to the family is crucial to their development. Connectedness refers to the permeability or responsiveness to the views of others and mutual respect for the ideas of others. Family processes that balance expressions of individuality with expressions of connectedness are most effective in generating competence. Encouraging emotional "connectedness" to the family includes being open and responsive to adolescent's views, offering guidance and support, and being warm and accepting.

Adolescents develop their needs for connectedness with their peers as well. During this age period, adolescents form intimate relationships based on openness, sharing, mutual trust, respect, affection, and loyalty. Adolescents are able to establish and maintain relationships of greater intimacy, characterized by high levels of empathy, expression

of inner feelings, and responsiveness to another's experiences.[20]
Adolescents demonstrate concern for each other's well-being; a willingness to disclose private and occasionally sensitive topics; and a sharing of common interests and activities.

## Emotional Separateness and Connectedness

Emotional autonomy develops best under conditions that encourage both individuation and closeness.[21] The key word is balance.
Families characterized by a high degree of closeness have been called
enmeshed families. The involvement is so intense that the boundaries
between parents and adolescents are blurred, blocking emotional separateness. In enmeshed families, adolescents' feelings, thoughts, and
needs tend to become enmeshed with those of their parents. Moreover,
generally destructive family relationships are seen in enmeshed families, and adolescents in these families tend to engage in a great deal of
acting-out behavior such as defiance and noncompliance.

Similarly, when adolescents strive only for autonomy or independence without feeling connected to the family, adjustment problems may
occur. Laurence Steinberg claims that too much emotional distance from
parents results not in social competence but rather in heightened sus-
ceptibility to antisocial peer influences.[22] In other words, when adolescents don't feel emotionally connected to their families, they are more
likely to follow negative peer behavior (drinking, smoking, doing drugs,
truancy).

A subjective sense of self-reliance develops out of family relations
that are neither too close nor too distant. The effective family system
is one that avoids both enmeshment, in which individuality is discouraged in favor of exaggerated family harmony, and disengagement, in
which family members are so separate that they have little effect on
each other.

Emotional autonomy and connectedness is a process that begins
in infancy and continues through adolescence.[23] At each developmental
stage, parents need to meet their children's needs for dependency and
closeness as well as encourage them and give them emotional support
in their endeavors to become more independent.

In infancy, children's needs for closeness are met when strong emotional bonds are formed with caregivers. Caregivers must constantly
give infants confirmation and recognition by providing for their physical and psychological needs. At the same time, parents need to help chil-

dren develop their autonomy by helping them to see themselves as separate, causal agents.

In early childhood, children's closeness needs are met when parents can accept children's dependence. Letting go takes the form of recognizing their need to be self-sufficient and helping them learn self-help tasks. During middle childhood, children's needs for closeness is met when parents continually let them know they are praiseworthy and competent. Their need for autonomy is met by respecting their privacy and space in the home and by giving them control over their actions.

The best way to meet adolescents' needs for closeness is to avoid criticism and negative value judgments. Furthermore, it is important at this time to offer opportunities for the adolescent to share his or her inner feelings. By the same token, parents need to allow adolescents to assume responsibility for their own initiatives and behavior. Adolescents who have been successful in establishing a sense of individuation can accept responsibility for their choices and actions instead of relying on their parents. To help adolescents develop individuation, parents need to encourage assertion and freedom to disagree, help them assume responsibility for their behavior, and allow them to play an active role in decision making.

## Developing a Sense of Identity

Adolescents enter Erikson's fifth stage of development, "Identity vs. Role Diffusion," which continues into the early twenties.[15] According to Erikson, this is the most dynamic, complex, and significant stage of all. During this stage, adolescents try to figure out who they are. They either establish sexual, ethnic, and career identities or are confused about what future roles they will play. The process of self-definition is not some static end point; rather, it is an ongoing process reflecting change as needed throughout the life span.

Thus, according to Erikson, adolescents engage in an active search for a new understanding of self. This state has been referred to as the identity crisis—a sense of confusion about who one is and what one wants out of life. An important developmental task for adolescents, according to Erikson, is to bring together all the things they have learned about themselves as students, sons, daughters, friends, workers, and so on, and begin to develop a sense of who they are and where they are going—an identity. Identity is like a blueprint for future commitments and life choices. It is a set of beliefs and goals about one's relationship with family members, lovers, and friends; one's roles as a worker, citizen, and religious believer; and one's aspirations for achievement. As a psychosocial task, striving for a sense of unification and cohesiveness in the self provides meaning, direction, and purpose to one's life.

## Identity Statuses

Simon Fraser University professor James Marcia suggests four possible identity statuses.[24] An individual's position on these tasks can be described along two dimensions: commitment and crises. Commitment refers to a stable confidence in one's beliefs, and crises refers to the examination of alternatives with an intention to establish a firm commitment. Four identity statuses are derived from combinations of these two dimensions.

*Identity foreclosure* status exists when adolescents have not actively questioned alternatives but have made a commitment because it is what their parents want and not necessarily what they want. As such, this commitment is typically an extension of the values or expectations of significant others, which the adolescent has accepted without consideration of alternatives: "I will become an attorney like my dad, it's important to him" (but not necessarily to the adolescent). Hence, foreclosed commitments may be labeled premature and deemed developmentally unsophisticated. Foreclosed adolescents have a strong commitment to obedience, strong leadership, and respect for authority; their self-esteem is the most vulnerable of all groups.

*Moratorium* status exists when individuals are in the process of selecting among alternatives, actively seeking information and looking to make a decision: "I don't really know what to do. I'm not sure I want to become a lawyer. I've always been somewhat interested in teaching. I've got to check these occupations out." They are in crisis. The moratorium status is seen as an antecedent to the most sophisticated decision-making mode, identity achievement. The moratorium status is quite variable but closely resembles identity achievement.

*Identity achievers* refers to those adolescents who experience an optimal sense of identity. The most obvious concomitants of achieving a sense of identity are feeling at home in one's body, a sense of knowing where one is going, and an inner assurance of anticipated recognition from those who count. "After looking into these two occupations and taking a few classes in each, I think I will major in pre-law." If an adolescent is to function satisfactorily as an adult, a concept of "my way of life" or a sense of personal identity must be achieved. Adolescents who are in the identity achievement status demonstrate greater ego strength than the other three status groups; they also persevere and perform better on stressful concepts. Identity achievers are the healthiest of the four status groups in terms of general adjustment and relationship with peers and authority figures. They exhibit high levels of internal control and self-esteem and low levels of anxiety.

An individual's self-identity must be fairly consistent, or the personality will be fragmented and the individual will suffer from *identity diffusion*. This is the least sophisticated status. Individuals in this status have made no commitment nor are they attempting to arrive at a commitment in a given content area. Failure to accept one's self, crystallize one's goals, receive recognition from those who count, and experiment with various roles, according to Erikson, may lead to delayed commitment, prolonged adolescence, negative identity, or adjustment problems of varying degrees of severity. The identity diffusion status is characterized by the absence of any commitment to a system of values, a reluctance to accept the explanations, and a tendency to challenge authority. Adolescents experiencing identity diffusion appear unable to find a direction in life or define any goals, either educational or vocational. They may be avoiding making such long-term decisions out of fear or from psychosocial inability to explore and make decisions.

> The loss of a sense of identity is often expressed in a scornful and snobbish hostility toward the roles offered as proper and desirable in one's family or immediate community. Any aspect of the required role, or all of it—be it masculinity or femininity, nationality or class membership—can become the main focus of the young person's acid disdain.[25]

An adolescent boy, for example, whose parents have constantly stressed how important it is for him to do well in school so that he will be admitted to a prestigious college, may deliberately do poorly in school or quit school entirely and join a commune.

Those who successfully resolve the identity crisis have a strong sense of their values and directions and are at peace with whom they have become. Those who do not suffer from identity confusion and are directionless or merely adopt, without analysis, the roles imposed upon them.

## Parenting and Identity Achievement

Parents need to be supportive of their children and encourage them to explore their life goals. Identity achievement, particularly for females, appears to occur more readily in families who are not highly controlling. Females high in identity status report that their mothers encourage independence and autonomy. Adolescents in the identity diffusion status rate mothers high on control and regulation and, ironically, very high on encouragement of independence. Some parents want their adolescents to be independent but also want to control the process by which they achieve such independence. With this type of parenting, adolescents are less likely to engage in exploring identity alternatives and more likely to adopt external, rather than internalized life goals. Similarly, these adolescents are likely to have lower self-confidence and self-esteem and are likely to have problems in using their own judgment as a guide to behavior.

Different relationships with parents are seen in adolescents in different identity statuses. Adolescents in the identity foreclosure status, who have not actively questioned alternative life goals, have the closest relationships with parents, while those in the identity diffusion status, who have made no commitments, tend to be more distant from their families. These individuals see their parents as indifferent to them, not understanding them, and rejecting them. Conflict is more characteristic of the families of adolescents in the moratorium (actively questioning life alternatives) and identity achievement groups.

Families that best promote adolescent identity exploration are those that encourage independence and connectedness. In these families, parents and teenagers work together in redefining the parent–adolescent relationship as a more mutual and equal one. It is the balance between closeness in the family and the encouragement of individuality and autonomy that becomes the crucial factor.

The development of an integrated sense of self-identity is a complex and difficult task. Adolescents are expected to master many different roles in our culture. It is rare to find an adolescent who doesn't experience serious doubts about his or her capabilities in handling at least some of these roles competently.

Successful completion of the identity crisis is pivotal, because this allows young adults to develop mature relations with others, so that they can convey love and emotional security to them. If the identity crisis is not successfully resolved, the adolescent is faced with a sense of identity diffusion and an inability to cope with the demands of adulthood. Identity achievers have the highest evaluations of self, followed by those in the moratorium status, foreclosure, and lastly, identity diffusion. The adolescent's self-identity, then, is crucial in the development of high self-esteem and an integrated personality.

When parents adopt an inductive, democratic style of discipline, adolescents are able to make their own decisions and organize and adopt appropriate plans that are, interestingly enough, more satisfying to their parents. They also tend to seek guidance and advice from their parents. In democratic homes, adolescents strongly identify with their parents and, in turn, have internalized their parents' rules and values. In families where adolescents are encouraged to develop independence and autonomy, there is more possibility of identity exploration, especially for females.

Thus, in order for adolescents to develop an optimal sense of personal identity, adolescents must carry forward from middle childhood an inner confidence about their competence and ability to master new tasks. In addition, adolescents must have ample opportunity to experiment with new roles both in fantasy and practice, and they must get support in this effort from parents and adults.[26]

Moreover, the strength young people find in adults at this time— a willingness to let teenagers experience life, an eagerness to confirm adolescents at their best, consistency in correcting adolescents' excesses, and the guidance they give adolescents—will codetermine whether or not they eventually make sense or order out of their necessary inner confusion. Similarly, encouraging adolescents to express their own opinions and ideas, allowing them to take an active role in decision making in the family context, tolerating the adolescents' assertiveness, and allowing them to consider various alternative solutions to a problem are essential ways in which adults help adolescents achieve identity formation during the late high school years.

While family variables are important in helping adolescents achieve a sense of identity, adolescents also play an integral role in influencing parents' behavior. It is far easier, for example, to provide a warm, supportive, child-centered environment when the adolescent identifies strongly with his or her parents and is accommodating rather than rebellious. This bidirectional influence, while overlooked in research, should not be overlooked by parents. Adolescents have effects on parents as much as parents have effects on adolescents.

The journey toward self-identity is not an easy one; small progressions may be followed by regressions. There will be times when adolescents vacillate between the world of their childhood and the world of adulthood. Adolescents at times enjoy the safety and protection of home; at other times, they want to be free-spirited and independent.

## Acceptance and Achievement of a Comfortable Body Image

Inner self-esteem is enhanced when adolescents accept and feel comfortable about their body image. A certain amount of dissatisfaction and preoccupation with body image during adolescence are expected and normal. Good feelings about our physical selves, however, are important for comfort with body image. Adolescents' general appearance reflects their feelings about their body image. Cleanliness and good grooming, clothes in good repair and coordinated according to the current style, erect posture, and making eye contact as opposed to looking away all reflect a comfortable body image. It appears, however, that many teenagers are not happy with their body image. Girls tend to be pressured into thinking that they have to be thin; males want a more muscular body.

Early or late physical maturation is one factor that appears to relate to the adolescent's physical self-esteem. Early-maturing individuals tend to have a faster and more intense adolescent growth spurt than do late-maturing individuals.

### Early-Maturing and Late-Maturing Males

Early-maturing males are large for their age, more muscular, and better coordinated than late-maturing males, so they enjoy a considerable athletic advantage. They also enjoy considerable social advantages in relation to peers. Early-maturing males tend to have a more positive self-image.

Parents and others tend to rate early-maturing males as more physically attractive, more masculine, and more relaxed than late-maturing males. Parents tend to expect more of early-maturing males and expect adult behavior and responsibility. Thus, early-maturing males may have less time to enjoy the freedom that comes with childhood.

Late-maturing males may suffer socially induced inferiority because of their delayed growth and development. At age 15, the late-maturing male may be 8 inches shorter and 30 pounds lighter than his early-maturing counterpart. Accompanying this size difference are marked differences in body build, strength, motor performance, and coordination. Because late-maturing males tend to be shorter and physically weaker, they are less likely to be outstanding athletes in group sports such as basketball, baseball, soccer, and football.

Late-maturing males are seen by their peers as more childish; they are less popular and less likely to show leadership. On personality measures, late-maturing males exhibit stronger feelings of inadequacy, higher needs for autonomy, more negative evaluations of self, less control, and less self-assurance.

## Early-Maturing and Late-Maturing Females

While early maturation tends to be a plus for boys, this is generally not so for girls. It appears that early maturation has a negative effect on girls during the elementary school years. A physically mature fifth- or sixth-grader is at some disadvantage, because she is out of phase with the majority of her classmates. Early-maturing girls often find themselves towering over others, and many assume a slouching posture to conceal their height. Their advanced breast development seems to violate others' expectations of a young girl's petiteness and femininity. Since girls mature about two years earlier than boys, the early-maturing girl is not only more physically advanced than her female agemates but far more advanced than all her male classmates as well. By junior high school, however, early-maturing females come into their own, socially. They begin to look more like women, are envied by other girls, begin to attract the attention of older boys, and start dating. Such girls, however, may find themselves emotionally unequipped to deal with sophisticated social activities and sexual enticements.

Late-maturing girls tend to worry that they are not physically normal. During the early teen years, most adolescents want to be like their peers. While these concerns may seem trivial to some, they are very real and disturbing to the child who desperately wants to be grown up but whose body is just not cooperating, as the following quote from a popular teen novel suggests:

> Are you there, God? It's me, Margaret. Gretchen, my friend, got her period. I'm so jealous, God. I hate myself for being so jealous, but I am. I wish you'd help me just a little. Nancy's sure he's going to get it soon, too. And if I'm late I don't know what I'll do. Oh, please God, I just want to be normal.[27]

## The Ideal Masculine Physique

Another factor that affects adolescents' comfortableness with their body image is physical attractiveness. Most adolescents desire to be physically attractive, to have the "ideal body." In our culture, ideal most often means tall and muscular for boys and tall and slender for girls. Adolescents favor a muscular build for boys. In order to get bigger muscles, some boys may inject themselves with steroids. Today an estimated 10 percent of high school students, overwhelmingly boys, either take or have taken steroids. Many teenage boys say they take steroids not so much for improved athletic performance as for cosmetic purposes, to make them more muscular. Anabolic steroids come in many chemical forms, but essentially they are forms of testosterone, the chief male hormone. Some steroids may be taken orally in tablet form, but injection is actually preferred since it lessens the drugs' harmful effects on the liver.

Potentially severe side effects, the possibility of liver dysfunction, cancer, and damage to the reproductive system may result from long-term use or such practices as "stacking," taking two or three types of steroids simultaneously. Short-term effects are hair loss, severe acne, and high blood pressure as well as shrunken testicles and low sperm production. Women users, usually athletes, may be subject to masculine characteristics such as growth of facial hair and male pattern baldness; these effects tend to be irreversible.

Steroids may have a profound effect on behavior. Increased aggressiveness, known as "roid rage," often leads to violent, destructive behavior. Recovering steroid users can become extremely depressed when they try to give up the drug, which, in some cases, has led to suicide.

## The Ideal Female Physique

The importance of physical attractiveness in Western society is undeniable. There is great pressure on women to be thin. New diets proliferate for that segment of the population that wants to lose a few extra pounds. This turns out to be a large market, for it appears that the majority of young women are unhappy with their weight and want to be thinner. Some regard the cultural perception that "thin is chic" to be partially responsible for the eating disorders of anorexia nervosa and bulimia among women.

Anorectics use two different means of achieving thinness. Restricters rely on strict dieting. Bulimics alternate between dieting and binge eating followed by self-induced vomiting or purging. The central psychopathologic feature of anorexia nervosa and bulimia is an extreme fear of fatness. Anorexia nervosa is a disorder generally found in adolescent women but can also be seen in older women as well as men. It is characterized by self-induced starvation (intake of 300 to 600 calories a day), fear of fatness, amenorrhea (absence of menstruation) in women, and diminished sexual drive in men.

Estimates of the incidence of anorexia nervosa range from 1 to 3 percent, which is roughly one out of every 350 adolescent girls. The patients are predominately females; only 10 percent are men; the common age of onset is between 13 and 22 years of age.[28]

The highest probability of development of anorexia nervosa is found for a female who is highly perfectionistic and self-critical. Restricters tend to be conforming, reliable, insecure, and inflexible in their thinking. Typically, they go on a diet during their early teenage years to lose 5 to 20 pounds. Many of these individuals come from a family of upper or middle socioeconomic status. Exhibiting obsessive thinking about food and liquid intake, they are likely to have feelings of inferiority about their personality and appearance. They tend to show a disinterest in sexuality or fear of physical and emotional intimacy. Delusional thinking develops, especially with regard to body size and quantities of food ingested. Paranoid fears of criticism from others are often experienced, especially the fear of being seen as "too fat." Anxiety is alleviated only by weight loss and fasting. Restricters generally tend to deny their emaciated appearance, viewing others who are substantially heavier as thinner than themselves. Such individuals have a history of high achievement at school and are compliant and cooperative both in school and at home. They are often considered to be "model children" without associated behavioral abnormalities.

Bulimia is an eating disorder that occurs when an individual has repeatedly lost control of the impulse to binge and engages in the rapid ingestion of a large quantity of food, followed by attempts to avoid weight gain through self-induced vomiting. An anorectic eating pattern between binges is common. Some individuals starve all day only to eat for hours at night. Preferred foods are usually high in sugar and carbohydrates. While some individuals alternate overeating with extended fasting, most relieve it by vomiting. The typical bulimic is a white female who begins overeating at about 18 years of age and turns to purging by vomiting a year later.

Bulimics tend to be extroverted and sociable but unstable and tend to have problems with impulse control, such as stealing and substance abuse. While socially more skillful than restricters, their relations tend to be brief, superficial, and troubled. Their families tend to be more unstable than those of restricters; there is more discord, maternal and paternal depression, and impulsivity and substance abuse. Bulimic females have lower self-appraised problem-solving ability, lower sense of personal efficacy in successful performance of life tasks, and a tendency to attribute positive events to external, global factors.[29] Rachel Jacobson and Clive Robins found that bulimic females are characterized by a high degree of social dependency on men.[30] These women, for example, tend to depend on men to make decisions for them and are more obedient—they do what they are told to do.

Many factors have been cited as probable causes for the development of these eating disorders. Among those most frequently cited are factors related to family interaction pathologies, such as overprotectiveness, rigidity masking unconscious hostilities, parental occupation with appearance and success, and poor conflict resolution. The mother–daughter relationship is riddled with guilt, anger, and mutual overprotectiveness and characterized by mutual clinging that is devoid of trust.[31]

In families with children with eating disorders, the father has been described as nondemonstrative. That is, he finds it difficult to express or offer affection to his daughter. Some professionals maintain that fear of growing up and assuming adult responsibility is highly characteristic of anorectics. Failure to accept a more adult-looking body (that is, to be more separate from parents) leads the individual to diet as a means of gaining control over fears of inadequacy and rejection by others and other unidentifiable fears.

While it is possible that these two eating disorders have a single discrete cause, it is more probable that complex chains interact to precipitate these illnesses. In treating these disorders there must be simultaneous improvement in weight and the eating abnormalities, along with fundamental therapeutic attempts to uncover the underlying psychological conflicts and reverse the maturational arrests. Strict attempts of getting these patients to eat their way out of the hospital are not successful unless one deals with the underlying causes of the pathology as well. Approximately 40 percent of anorectics totally recover, 30 percent considerably improve, and 20 percent remain unimproved or seriously impaired by depression.[32]

The treatment of bulimia is less clearly defined. Hospitalization is less likely but may be necessary because of fluid and electrolyte imbalance, severe depression, threat of suicide, or resistance to intensive outpatient treatment. Inpatient treatment involves monitoring intake and purging behaviors and some combination of supportive, behavioral, group, individual, and family therapies.

Because of their extreme concern about fatness, all patients should be given the reassurance that they will not be allowed to gain too much weight. Otherwise, they may return to their rituals to bring about relief from unresolved fears. A major focus of treatment is the gradual identification by patients of uncomfortable mood states that trigger unconscious transformation of anxiety into abnormal weight control or an abnormal eating pattern. Families of these patients need to be involved in therapy as well.

Parents can help their anorectic or bulimic adolescent in the following ways:

1. Demand less decision making from the anorectic or bulimic adolescent.
2. Do not allow these adolescents to buy food and prepare meals for the family. When they cook the evening meal, through the preparation of the food, they believe that they have satiated their appetites for food. Moreover, this puts them in a nurturing role and allows them to deny their own need for food by feeding others.
3. Develop a parent–adolescent relationship on personal issues other than food or weight.
4. Do not demand weight gain or berate the adolescent for having an eating disorder.
5. Do not make statements such as, "Your illness is ruining the whole family" or "I can't take much more of this behavior from you." These statements put the adolescent in charge of the family's well-being and are received by her as dependent remarks, which throws her deeper into weight loss and illness.
6. Try to avoid abandoning statements such as, "Help me to help you" or "What can I do for you?" These statements request that the adolescent take charge of the family's behavior toward her. Because she doesn't know the answer to these questions, she feels like more of a failure.

7. It's best not to demand that she eat with you, but do not allow her eating problem to dominate the family's eating schedule or use of the kitchen.

## Developing "Outgrowing" Minds

The way adolescents think determines the way they behave. Many adolescents, unfortunately, tend to be rather critical of themselves. Instead of fortifying themselves with positive thoughts about self, they tend to be highly critical. We all have an inner voice that, from time to time, is rather unflattering in what it says to us about ourselves. Teenagers, particularly those with low self-esteem, have highly critical inner voices. One teenager commented that every time she asked a question in class, she would berate herself later. For *hours* after class she would say things like "How could you ask such a stupid question?" or "Everyone in the class must think you are super dumb" or "What a dope; I'll never ask questions again." But, she did, and the highly critical tape would rewind and play again. While adolescents have positive thoughts about themselves, more often than not they play this critical inner-voice tape that continually tells them that they are not adequate.

### Distorted Patterns of Thinking

David Burns, at the University of Pennsylvania School of Medicine, maintains that this kind of negative thinking is distorted.[33] Adolescents need to learn to refute self-critical thoughts, which tend to block positive behavioral actions. The following are some typical distorted patterns of thinking:

1. *All-or-nothing thinking:* One sees things in black and white categories. If performance falls short of perfect, one sees oneself as a total failure. A student fails an exam and thinks, "I am a total failure."
2. *Overgeneralization:* One tends to see a single negative event as a never-ending pattern of defeat. A shy, young adolescent male musters up his courage to ask a girl for a date. When she politely declines because of a previous engagement, he says to himself, "I'm never going to get a date. No girl will ever be serious about me."

3. *Mental filter:* One picks out a single negative detail and dwells on it exclusively so that one's vision of all reality becomes darkened, like the drop of ink that discolors the entire beaker of water. A depressed high school student hears some other students making fun of her best friend. She becomes furious because she thinks, "That's what the human race is basically like—cruel and insensitive."

4. *Disqualifying the positive:* One rejects positive experiences by insisting that they "don't count" for some reason or another. In this way one can maintain a negative belief that is contradicted by one's everyday experiences. A young woman receives praise for her appearance or work, and she automatically tells herself, "They're just trying to be nice." With one swift blow she mentally disqualifies the compliment.

5. *Jumping to conclusions:* One makes a negative interpretation even though there are no facts that convincingly support one's conclusion. A student asks a question in class and hears another student snicker. She immediately concludes that the student is laughing at her and her stupid question.

6. *Labeling and mislabeling:* This is an extreme form of overgeneralization. Instead of describing our error, we attach a negative label to ourself: "I'm a loser." When someone else's behavior rubs us the wrong way, we attach a negative label to him: "He's a liar." Mislabeling involves describing an event with language that is highly colored and emotionally loaded.

7. *Personalization:* One sees oneself as the cause of some negative external event which, in fact, we are not primarily responsible for. When a mother receives a note from her child's teacher indicating that the child is not doing well in math, the mother immediately decides, "I must be a bad mother. This shows how I've failed."

8. *Magnification (catastrophizing) or minimization:* One exaggerates the importance of things (such as a goof-up or someone else's achievement) or inappropriately shrinks things until they appear negligible (one's own desirable qualities or the other fellow's imperfections). A worker thinks, "I made a mistake, my reputation is ruined!"

9. *Emotional reasoning:* One assumes that one's negative emotions necessarily reflect the way things are: "I feel like a dud,

therefore, it must be true" or "I feel guilty, therefore, I must have done something wrong."

10.  *"Should" statements:* One tries to motivate oneself with "shoulds" and "should not's." "Musts" and "oughts" are also offenders. The emotional consequence is guilt. When one directs should statements toward others, one feels anger, frustration, and resentment. Should statements generate a lot of unnecessary emotional turmoil in daily life. When the reality of one's behavior falls short of one's standards, the shoulds and should nots create self-loathing, shame, and guilt.

Recognize some of these distorted thinking patterns in your adolescent? Try this. Start by having your adolescent write down some of his or her negative thoughts and cognitive distortions, followed by more rational responses for 15 minutes every day for two weeks. A sample exercise is shown in Table 8. To be fair, parents may want to do this exercise as well. Both of you should then take a close look at what both of you have to say about yourselves. This is an effective way to recognize cognitive distortions and learn to think in more rational ways and thus develop more "outgrowing" rather than "ingrowing" minds.

## Summary

Adolescents with ingrowing minds tend to engage in these types of cognitive distortions that block positive behavioral actions and lower their self-esteem. They tend to be inflexible thinkers and perceive themselves and their world in ways that are consistent to their distorted think-

**Table 8.**  Sample Cognitive Distortions Exercise

| Automatic Thought Response | Cognitive Distortion | Rational Response |
| --- | --- | --- |
| I never do anything right. | Overgeneralization | Nonsense! I get some things right. |
| This shows how stupid I am. | Labeling | Come on, so you forgot an assignment. This doesn't mean you're stupid. |

ing patterns. By helping adolescents become aware of their negative automatic thought responses and how to develop more rational ones, they can develop outgrowing minds characterized by more flexible and adaptive thinking patterns. Rational responses, characteristic of outgrowing minds, help adolescents to incorporate all kinds of new experiences into their self-pictures and help them to see themselves in more positive ways.

When children move from middle childhood to adolescence, we see a shift in their self-images from concrete, observable traits to more analytical, psychological, and abstract traits that sometimes involve a great deal of introspection. Girls tend to base their self-esteem on their physical appearance and popularity; boys tend to base their self-esteem on competence and athletic skills. Boys have higher self-esteem in achievement and leadership; girls have higher self-esteem in congeniality and sociability.

To enable adolescents to move through this period as smoothly and successfully as possible, parents need to engage in effective parenting styles (being authoritative as opposed to authoritarian or permissive; warm; and firm but fair) and communicate effectively with their teenagers (active listening, I-messages, being a good listener).

In addition, adolescents, with the help of their parents, need to master the skills and behaviors necessary for inner self-esteem, namely, developing both masculine (assertive, independent, and achievement-oriented) and feminine (nurturing, loving, and emotionally involved) ways of behaving; feeling a sense of separateness as well as connectedness with their family; establishing a stable sense of identity; achieving a comfortable body image; and developing outgrowing minds that are open to new experiences.

# PART II  Creating Home Environments that Foster Inner Self-Esteem

# CHAPTER 6  Mothers and Fathers as Disciplinarians

The chapters that comprise the second half of this book are designed to help parents create conditions in the home that promote the development of children's and adolescents' competencies in academic, social, physical, and moral domains. The information and suggestions offered are applicable to children of all age levels. We begin with how parents as effective disciplinarians can help their children develop inner self-esteem.

Socialization is "an adult-initiated process by which developing children, through insight, training, and imitation, acquire the habits and values congruent with adaptation to their culture."[1] A major part of children's socialization depends on helping them to develop social controls or adopt society's rules of behavior. In this sense, parents monitor their children's acts, offering approval or withholding it, in order to help shape children's future acts. While socialization does occur in the child's first year, the onset of socialization pressure or discipline generally comes in the second year.[2]

## Mothers and Fathers as Socializing Agents

In parenting, fathers tend to place more emphasis on child protection, self-sufficiency, initiative, and competition, while mothers tend to focus on concern for others and self-sacrifice. In accomplishing these goals, fathers are apt to use forceful techniques such as parental power and authority, whereas mothers stress more interpersonal techniques such as reasoning, nurturance, and praise.[3] Moreover, fathers are more likely to report encouraging independence and assertiveness in their children, whereas mothers are more likely to report encouraging appropriate interpersonal behavior (good manners and politeness). Fathers tend to use physical punishment and mothers rely more on material punishment. Parents are more punishing and less rewarding with same-sex children. For both mothers and fathers, reasoning and persuasion tend to increase as children get older.

In families with children who are difficult to control, mothers are likely to function as crisis managers who must cope on a daily basis with a range of dilemmas and conflicts. Often fathers in such families withdraw to avoid dealing with unpleasant situations. When fathers ignore their childrearing responsibilities, numerous ramifications fall upon the family system. Mothers feel unsupported and abandoned by their husbands, leading to feelings of anger, frustration, or resentment. Lack of participation by the father also deprives the child of an alternative role model and a source of nurturance.

The process of childrearing undergoes important changes as children develop. During each phase of children's development, different problems become foci for parental concern and subsequent action. Concerns in infancy center on irritability, illness, eating, and sleeplessness. During early childhood, toilet training, disobedience, inability to play cooperatively with others, delayed verbal skills, bedtime routines, control of temper tantrums, fighting with siblings or other children, eating and table manners, getting dressed by themselves, and attention seeking tend to monopolize parents' disciplining concerns. Some of these issues, for example, fighting and children's reactions to discipline, carry over into school age.

In middle childhood, parents tend to be concerned about their children's standards of performance, ability to entertain themselves, relationships with peers, whereabouts, problems at school, and achievement. During adolescence parents continue to be concerned about their children's social and academic performances, along with dating, sexual activities, and drugs.

A major influence regulating parenting behavior may be parents' beliefs and attitudes about children and children's behavior at different ages. That is, parents' disciplining techniques are likely to reflect their inferences about children's competence and responsibility for misconduct. When parents think misdeeds reflect an absence of competence, they prefer calm induction more and power assertion less. The parental attitude toward preschoolers tends to be predominantly indulgent and protective, while much more is expected of older children who are thought to be capable of conforming to nearly adult norms of behavior.

Parents certainly recognize that enormous advances in social skills occur with age and should therefore think that, in general, older children are more responsible. Studies suggest, at least in some respects, that transfer of power from parent to child occurs slowly with the major shift to genuine autonomy beginning at about age 12.[4] Parents tend to give children more responsibility for their behavior as they get older by replacing directive techniques such as forcing compliance and repetition of commands with less directive approaches based on reasoning and explanation.

It is argued that childrearing techniques depend to some extent on the nature of the types of competencies that adults are expected to have in a given population.[5] Consciously or unconsciously, adults try to inculcate in their children various cognitive, motivational, and social competencies that are considered relevant to their cultural milieu.

Thus, the parents' position in the social structure has an impact on how they discipline children. Parents of low socioeconomic status tend to emphasize respect, obedience, neatness, and staying out of trouble, because those are the attributes that they view as critical for success in the blue-collar economy. They stress obedience to external authority because this is adaptive in their existing social structure. Middle- and upper-class parents tend to emphasize less power assertion and more democratic modes of discipline. It has been suggested that middle- and upper-class parents value curiosity, consideration for others, independence, and self-control in their children because they want to prepare them for positions similar to their own that require them to make decisions and take responsibility.

## Disciplining Styles

Over the years, researchers have examined many different kinds of parental disciplining techniques. One prominent researcher, Diana Baumrind, has characterized two aspects of parents' behavior toward children: parental responsiveness and parental demandingness.[6] Responsiveness is the degree to which parents respond to children's needs in an accepting, supportive manner. Demandingness is the extent to which parents expect and demand mature, responsible behavior from children.

Because responsiveness and demandingness are more or less independent of each other, it is possible to look at various combinations

of these two dimensions. Labels have been given to the fourfold classification. A parent who is very responsive but not at all demanding is labeled *indulgent*, whereas one who is equally responsive but also very
demanding is labeled *authoritative*. Parents who are very demanding
but not responsive are *authoritarian*; parents who are neither demanding nor responsive are labeled *indifferent*.

What kind of disciplinarian are you? Answer the questions in Table
9 by circling 1, if you strongly disagree; 2, if you mildly disagree; 3, if
you're not sure; 4, if you mildly agree; and 5, if you strongly agree.

Scoring: Reverse the points for the following questions: 1, 4, 5, 7,
9, 13, and 14. That is, 5 = 1, 4 = 2, 3 = 3, 2 = 4, and 1 = 5. Then add up the
total points. A score of 60 to 75 points means that the parent is highly
authoritarian and controlling; lower scores indicate that the parent is
more democratic and authoritative.

The categorization proposed by Baumrind provides a useful way
of summarizing and examining some of the relations between parenting practices and children's psychosocial development. She notes that
children who are most responsible and mature tend to have parents who
establish consistent standards of behavior, negotiate with their children
concerning those standards, use explanations, and have warm relationships with their children—authoritative parents. Generally speaking, children raised in authoritative households are more psychosocially
competent than children raised in authoritarian, indulgent, or indifferent homes.

The authoritative parent expects mature behavior from the child.
These parents exhibit a high level of demandingness and a high level
of responsiveness to their children. They encourage children to be independent but still place limits, demands, and control on their actions.
Children from authoritative homes show greater social responsibility
(achievement orientation, friendliness toward peers, cooperation with
adults) and independence (social dominance, nonconforming behavior,
purposiveness).

Authoritarian parents exhibit high levels of demandingness and
low levels of responsiveness to their children. Rules in these homes are
not discussed in advance or arrived at by any consensus or bargaining
process. They are decided upon by the parents: Parents attach strong
value to the maintenance of their authority and suppress any efforts by
their children to challenge it.

Baumrind makes a distinction between firm control of authoritative parents and restrictive, punitive control of authoritarian parents.

**Table 9.** Parental Disciplining Styles

| | Strongly disagree | Mildly disagree | Not sure | Mildly agree | Strongly agree |
|---|---|---|---|---|---|
| 1. A parent and child should have warm, fun times together. | 1 | 2 | 3 | 4 | 5 |
| 2. The father's role is to provide the discipline in the family; mother's role is to give love. | 1 | 2 | 3 | 4 | 5 |
| 3. Parents must keep to their standards and rules no matter what their child is like. | 1 | 2 | 3 | 4 | 5 |
| 4. A child has to be treated differently as he or she grows older. | 1 | 2 | 3 | 4 | 5 |
| 5. Parents need to be sensitive to the needs of their children. | 1 | 2 | 3 | 4 | 5 |
| 6. Difficult children need to be punished. | 1 | 2 | 3 | 4 | 5 |
| 7. There is no one right way to raise a child. | 1 | 2 | 3 | 4 | 5 |
| 8. Punishment is the only way to keep kids in line. | 1 | 2 | 3 | 4 | 5 |
| 9. I discipline my child by taking away a privilege he/she otherwise would have had. | 1 | 2 | 3 | 4 | 5 |
| 10. No matter how hard a parent tries, some children will never learn to mind. | 1 | 2 | 3 | 4 | 5 |
| 11. The most important thing to teach a child is absolute obedience to whomever is in authority. | 1 | 2 | 3 | 4 | 5 |
| 12. A child must be trained early in life so he/she will be obedient to authority. | 1 | 2 | 3 | 4 | 5 |
| 13. I talk it over and reason with my child when he/she misbehaves. | 1 | 2 | 3 | 4 | 5 |
| 14. I encourage my children to be independent but still place limits on their behavior. | 1 | 2 | 3 | 4 | 5 |
| 15. High amounts of control are associated with good behavior in children. | 1 | 2 | 3 | 4 | 5 |

191

Firm control is not a measure of restrictiveness, punitive attitudes, or intrusiveness but, rather, a measure of strict discipline. She notes that it is not restrictive control *per se*, but the arbitrary, harsh, and nonfunctional exercise of firm control that has negative consequences for child behavior. Baumrind found that restrictive control that is arbitrary, harsh, and administered without the emotional caring component tends to produce children who display dependent, regressive behavior (crying and thumb sucking). Moreover, it seems that parents who are highly restrictive and who follow an absolute standard of conduct and control are likely to have children who fail to initiate activities.

While authoritarian parents make all the decisions, indulgent parents allow children to make all the decisions. Parents do not feel in control and do not exert control. Little or no parental control is associated with impulsive behavior in children. In addition, these children tend to be immature, dependent, regressive, the least self-reliant, and the poorest in self-control.

Children raised by indifferent parents are often impulsive and more likely to be involved in delinquent behavior and in precocious experiments with sex, drugs, and alcohol. In general, the effects of indifference tend to be slightly worse among boys than girls.

To summarize, authoritative parents are controlling but affectionate and encourage autonomy in their children; authoritarian parents are controlling but less affectionate; indulgent parents are minimally controlling but affectionate. Indifferent parents are neither demanding nor responsive.

On the basis of her findings, Baumrind conceptualizes parental discipline as being composed of two dimensions: warmth and control. Both are deemed essential for effective child management and children's acquisition of effective social skills. Firm parental control, when coupled with parental warmth (an attitude rather than a practice), promotes the development of such competencies as social responsibility, self-control, and independence. In addition, children who describe their parents as warm, democratic, and firm tend to develop skills and behaviors in academic, social, moral, and physical areas, which promote high inner self-esteem.[7]

Several studies have established that parental warmth is an important variable in the socialization process. Moreover, when parents are highly involved with their children, that is, when they frequently engage in joint task-related activities and high levels of playful, affectively positive interaction (playing interactive games, going to shows and concerts), children tend to be high in obedience.

## Punishment

Today, most parents who punish do not see that punishment is still retaliatory rather than corrective. A child, however, who is hit sees the punishing authority as trying to impose his or her will by brute force. Most children try to find ways of defeating the punishment because they resent the action and refuse to accept it. While in times past parents accepted the concept of their superiority and children's inferiority, and thus condoned punishment, today psychologists contend that punishment is not effective.

Punishment and discipline are not synonymous. The term discipline comes from the word disciple, meaning "one who gives instruction." Discipline goes beyond the confines of short-term, immediate behavioral gains. Discipline influences children's future behavior. Punishment, on the other hand, is causing children to pay some kind of price that is more painful than the forbidden behavior or activity in which they are engaging. The probability that the forbidden response will occur decreases. Parents erroneously think that punishment works and that its effects are long-term.[8]

No doubt, the immediate effects of punishment account for its popularity, but, as research points out, although it has an immediate effect in reducing a tendency to behave in a certain way, in the long run its effects are temporary. Moreover, when punishment is consistently used, the punishing agent must be present in order for it to be effective. For example, the children of mothers who resort to power-assertive disciplining techniques such as punishment tend to work on a task well as long as their mother is visible but do not continue to do so when she is not. Children whose mothers explain the importance of the task and do not resort to punishment persistently work on a task even in the mother's absence.[9]

Temporary control may be obtained at a rather high price. Although there are many ways that children can learn to respond to punishment, in general, they try to avoid contact with the punishing agent, which gives the parent less opportunity to socialize the child. When children are physically punished for inappropriate behavior, they are hurt from the experience, frustrated at not being understood, resentful that no one will help, helpless to retaliate directly, and fearful of further punishment. The result of all this is further negative feelings.

Deviant behavior (negativism for its own sake) is associated with parental control strategies that are highly power-assertive, such as anger, harshness, criticisms, and physical punishment. The most effective strategies appear to combine firm control and guidance for eliciting compliance. When control is combined with guidance, it provides the child with clear information about what the parent wants, but at the same time it invites power sharing. These techniques are reminiscent of Baumrind's authoritative pattern of parenting: Authoritative parents exert firm parental control, but they also listen to what their children have to say and can be influenced by them.

The important point to emphasize is that punishment does not teach a child self-discipline. Second, while fear of punishment may restrain the child from doing wrong, it does not make children wish to do right. Disregarding this simple fact is the great error that parents and educators make when they rely on these negative means of correction. The only effective discipline is self-discipline, motivated by the child's inner desire to act meritoriously in order to do well in one's own eyes and according to one's values, so that the child may feel good about himself or herself. Good behavior is based on values that children have internalized because they love, admire, and want to emulate their parents. It is not much of a conscience that tells children not to do wrong because they might be punished.

There are many other ways to discipline successfully. If parents think that they only have one arrow in their disciplining arsenal, that's the only one they will use. If, however, there are more arrows in their quiver, they may not have to use the one marked "spanking." There's an old saying: if all you have is a hammer, everything in the world is a nail. So it's wise for parents to develop alternatives to physical punishment. Some successful ones are diverting or distracting young toddlers, offering choices, and planning ahead. (When you know that your child is particularly difficult at a certain time of day, for example, you can plan activities that will help avoid many problems and frustrations.) Finally, have the right expectations for your child. Punishing a 2-year-old for being too energetic in church is setting an impossible standard.

## Reinforcement

From the very beginning, parents train their children in the Skinnerian fashion of rewarding or reinforcing them for certain kinds of behavior. To illustrate, young children receive positive attention when they begin to share with others. Rewarded responses become stronger and increase in frequency. Negative behaviors are sometimes ignored or punished. Simply put, parents generally reward children when they behave in socially approved ways (sharing with others) and show disapproval when their behavior is socially unacceptable (kicking Stanley in the shins and grabbing). When rewards are administered immediately, consistently, and genuinely, learning proceeds more rapidly than when reinforcement is delayed, inconsistent, and nongenuine.

Potential reinforcers may be rewards such as verbal praise, a hug, or a pat on the back or candy, toys, or money. Children are more likely to respond to these rewards if they are prudently used. In other words, if parents praise children for every little thing they do, praise tends to become rather meaningless. When praise is used sparingly and in meaningful ways, it is more effective. If rewards are given regularly, they come to be expected, their absence is experienced as punishment, and their presence may no longer stand out as rewarding.

Moreover, younger children tend to conceive right and wrong in terms of what they will be rewarded (and punished) for. With development, children shift away from this orientation and gradually tend to develop inner controls and behave in socially approved ways because they want to, not necessarily to receive a reward. Therefore, rewards may be more effective in shaping the behavior of young children and not too effective with older children.

It's best to offer your child encouragement rather than praise. This is praise: "You did a good job. You are a nice girl. What a great student you are! You are so smart. You're mommy's little helper." This is encouragement: "You are reading many words now. You worked a long time on this book report. You made real progress in both math and science this semester. You picked up your toys and went right to bed on time last night." Praise bestows external value for external qualities. Encouragement acknowledges effort while leaving appraisal to the artist. Praise is general; encouragement is specific and always more effective.

## Consistency

Another important element in the socialization of children is consistency in disciplining. Most parents are familiar with the fact that if they follow through with predictable and reliable actions toward their children's behavior, the results will be effective. Most parents are also aware that this, at times, is difficult to do. There are times when various family situations, interruptions, and diversions prevent parents from following through. If, however, parents make threats ("No television for a week!"), they should follow through. If they do not, children learn very quickly not to believe in their parents' authority. The use of idle threats is associated with high levels of disobedience. In addition, if there are wide fluctuations in the type of discipline children encounter, if some behaviors are punished one day and overlooked the next, children soon learn not to comply with parental requests. Consistent enforcement of rules is related to high levels of voluntary compliance by children.

Similarly, there should be a consistency in the number and type of rules. Parents can become more consistent by not creating too many rules and demands. If parents have numerous rules, there are too many areas of behavior that parents have to monitor, and they are liable to slip up and forget their own rules. Moreover, parental rules and requests need to be clearly stated and easy to remember and must deal with behaviors that can be regulated.

## The No-Lose Method

Thomas Gordon recommends that parents use the "No-Lose" method to resolve conflicts that cannot be avoided. There are six steps to be followed when using this method:

Step 1.   Identifying and defining the conflict
Step 2.   Generating possible alternative solutions
Step 3.   Evaluating the alternative solutions
Step 4.   Deciding on the best acceptable solution
Step 5.   Working out ways of implementing the solutions
Step 6.   Following up to evaluate how it worked[10]

In Step 1 parents want the child to become involved. They have to get their child's attention and then secure his or her willingness to enter into problem solving. The parent uses I-messages to identify and define the problem: "I feel it is unfair to me to do so much of the work around the house when you kids might help out."

In Step 2 a variety of solutions are generated. It's best not to evaluate, judge, or belittle any of the solutions offered. Accept all ideas for solutions. In Step 3, parents and children start to evaluate the various solutions. Generally, the solutions get narrowed down to one or two that seem best.

In Step 4, after all have expressed their ideas and honest reactions to the solutions, a superior solution often emerges naturally. Make sure everyone is satisfied with the solution. In Step 5 a plan is implemented. In conflicts around chores, questions such as "On what days?" and "What standards of performance are required?" need to be discussed. Finally, in Step 6, follow-up evaluations are done. Not all initial decisions turn out to be good ones. Consequently, parents sometimes need to check back with the children to see if they are still happy with the decision. Gordon maintains that using this method eliminates the parent's need to express power and encourages children to take responsibility for solving family conflicts. Because all family members have agreed on how to solve the problem and what needs to be done, solutions are carried out readily by the children and parents.

## Children's Influence on Parents

Controlling children is not something parents do *to* or *for* their children, but *with* their children. Children play an active role in their own socialization. It is apparent that what parents do with their children is determined by several factors, some of which are children's temperament, age, and birth order.

Mothers of children who have been classified as difficult (irritable and noncompliant) engage in more power-assertive strategies (use punishment, establish many new rules, primarily notice the child's negative behavior), which produce more conflict between the mother and child. Similarly, difficult behavior in children leads parents, over a period of time, to reduce their socialization pressure. That is, they tend to develop negative conceptions about their parenting skills, believe that what they do has little effect on the child, and thus, begin to spend less time and effort in disciplining the child. Moreover, when children tend to be hot-tempered and difficult to control in early childhood, their mothers tend, at a later time, to be somewhat tolerant toward their children's aggression.[11] For example, they tend to exert relatively little teaching pressure against their sons' aggression, resulting in further aggression.

Children's birth order also tends to have an effect on parents. With their firstborns, parents are inclined to expect more mature behavior at an earlier age and impose higher demands, which results in firstborn children being more conscientious, independent, and serious. With late-born children, parents tend to be more lax with their disciplinary efforts. These differences in ways of socializing firstborns and later-born children may occur because parents are inexperienced with their firstborns and may be more idealistic; thus, they may try harder to do just the right thing. Second, they usually have more time to spend with their firstborns compared to later-born children.

## Common Disciplining Problems

### Sibling Rivalry

Some of you may have had an overpowering sibling who consistently put you down. If you have had that experience then you know how it affects self-esteem. As a recipient of a sibling's nagging, criticism, and put-down comments, one tends to experience feelings of helplessness, a lack of self-confidence, and low self-esteem. For these reasons, it is important to help children master their feelings of jealousy and learn how to get along with their brothers and sisters.

Jealousy is a universal emotion and is thought to be unavoidable. One type of jealousy that is a thorn in many parents' sides is jealousy between siblings—one sibling's resentful suspicion of another sibling or that sibling's influence.

Jealousy actually has two faces, one of which is love—a side of jealousy that is sometimes neglected but extremely important. It indicates that jealousy includes a positive evaluation of, an attachment to, or commitment to the person one is jealous of. One can be jealous only of something that is highly valued. The second face of jealousy is fear of loss. In jealousy, there is always a rival, actual or imagined, and the loss of something is experienced as a loss to someone else. At the center of jealousy is fear of loss, fear of alienation of affections, and insecurity. Each child wants a good share of parental love, attention, and affection. It is not an unnatural reaction for children to want to be the most important, to be the best, and to come first. When children feel that they are not getting the lion's share of parental love and understanding, their disadvantaged feeling causes them to feel jealous.

The desire to be the mother's "one and only" is so strong that it tolerates no rivals. It hurts to share the mother's love. Sharing anything, to most children, simply means getting less of it and is charged with feelings of resentment, jealousy, and love. Children cannot understand that their parents have enough love to encompass more than one child.

The prospect of sharing is bad enough, but parental expectations that children should be happy and overjoyed at the arrival of a new sibling are beyond their logic. Sibling rivalry is based on being "dethroned," and young children feel displaced and resentful. However, many children also show increased maturity, concern for others, and independence after the birth of a sibling.

All people harbor some jealous feelings. A certain amount of jealousy is normal, but not in its extreme forms. It becomes debilitating when children are overloaded and constantly preoccupied with jealous feelings. As a result, they suffer from poor self-images and cannot form good peer relationships, and their school work is mediocre.

Jealousy comes in a thousand assorted disguises. It may show itself indirectly in overly dependent behavior, regressive behavior, or in constant demands for material objects and possessions. Jealous children may try to degrade and tear down others with criticisms in order to elevate themselves. They may become energetically obstinate, try to spoil the fun of others, or restrict another's freedom. Jealous children may brood and build unhealthy feelings toward themselves and resentment, anger, and hostility toward others. Repressed feelings of jealousy may express themselves in physical disorders (skin rashes, chronic coughing, minor infections, frequent colds) or nervous habits (nail biting, pulling one's hair). An obvious form of jealousy is striving for power and superiority. Jealous children feel that they have to show everyone that they are terrific; they are constantly pushing themselves in competitive situations in their attempts to outdo others. Or, they may totally shun competition and continually take a submissive back seat.

As a general rule, jealousy exists more in firstborn children than in others that follow. Perhaps this is because firstborns are the only ones to have had their parents' love and attention all to themselves for a period of time, and consequently it is more difficult for them to share these experiences with other siblings. The beginning of jealous feelings may occur when mother and father bring home the second child.

The arrival of the second child means a lot of changes around the house. With the arrival of the sibling, most children experience a decrease in maternal playful attention, an increase in confrontation, and a decrease in their mothers' initiating conversations with verbal games.

Parental expectations and demands toward the firstborn child increase, which brings about another problem older children face: losing dependency. Parents generally begin to demand more independent behaviors and are a little less tolerant of their firstborn's dependency.

Parents have a lot more to do after the arrival of the second child and they simply don't have the time to be overly accommodating and indulgent. Jealousy arises out of this dependence and the feeling of being deprived by someone else. Younger children are always enjoying what older children have had to relinquish. Although they may recognize the advantages and privileges of being older, they also want the advantages and privileges of being "the baby." Firstborn children resent the loss of whatever helpless, baby behaviors they enjoyed and may attempt to hold on to these previous behavior patterns that they associate pleasantly with dependency.

At first, older siblings will aim their anger at their parents. Anger, aggression, and noncompliance are directed at the parents, not at the infant sibling. There is a dramatic increase in mother–child conflict and confrontation in the immediate postpartum period, especially during the times when the mother is involved in feeding or caring for the baby. As the baby gets older, becomes mobile, and begins to attract more attention from outsiders, the younger sibling becomes the target for the older child's negative feelings.

Second-born children feel envious of the firstborn's skills. They encounter a sibling who is always ahead of them. Sometimes they try to copy the firstborn, and if they cannot do as well, they tend to feel resentful, inferior, and defeated. More often than not, however, second-born children develop their competencies and skills in areas of achievement different from those of their older sibling. The second-born's personality tends to differ from the firstborn's. Second-born children often become what their older sibling is not; they may become bold or shy, authoritarian or submissive, athletic or studious, neat or careless.

Middle children occupy a more complicated position, for they do not carry the strength or privileges of the oldest child, nor do they reap the advantages of being the youngest. The second-born is likely to feel a rivalry with the older child, who has more privileges and freedom and is likely to be jealous of the younger sibling who has displaced him or her. Middle children's lack of status may cause them to feel neglected or squeezed out. The oldest child is praised for accomplishment and the baby is always eliciting attention. They may maintain their middle-of-the-road status, or they may succeed in pushing both competitors down and gain superiority over both of them.

It is impossible to avoid feelings of jealousy, which may result in teasing, nagging, complaining about favoritism, bickering, and quarreling between brothers and sisters. Jealous feelings, however, are not entirely negative and undesirable. A reasonable amount of friction can help children learn to meet the demands of the outside world, can teach them how they must behave in order to be accepted by others, and can stimulate each child's creative interests. A little conflict helps children learn to share, compete, achieve, and respect the rights, privileges, and property of other people.

Some friction between siblings is common and natural. Gradually, the time will come when most siblings will live together on better terms. As children get older their relationships typically become less intense and less conflict-ridden. In fact, many children in later elementary grades report having a warm and close relationship with their older siblings.

Learning to get along with each other may be due, in part, to children's changing concept of love. Younger children, more so than older children, tend to have a quantum view of love, that is, the amount of love any individual has is limited. If someone he loves also loves someone else, that must mean that there is less love for him. The love for another is given at the child's expense. This is the presumption of a jealous child (and adult). Gradually many children learn that parental love is not a quantity but a quality and that the love they previously enjoyed is not taken away by the arrival of brothers and sisters. This is a difficult concept to learn, however, and often is not mastered until late in childhood. Thus, the following guidelines may help parents help their children to live together more harmoniously.

## Focus on the Positive

Older siblings serve as companions, attachment figures, role models, and teachers; younger children are help-seekers, pupils, imitators, and playmates. The emotional bond between siblings is almost always intense, with conflict between siblings the more salient aspect in the minds of many parents, despite the many positive features of sibling relationships. It is necessary for parents to focus on the positive aspects of sibling relationships. By doing so, parents build strong emotional bonds between siblings. For example, older children, at times, may protect, teach, and be a companion to their younger siblings.[12] When observing pairs of mixed-sex siblings in their homes, it was found that older siblings initiated 65 percent of the prosocial behaviors (explaining, taking turns, offering a toy). Similarly, when 3- and 4-year-olds were left alone with their younger siblings in a waiting room, more than half responded to their younger sibling's distress by providing reassurance and comfort. Some children hugged their siblings while explaining that their mother would return. Similarly, younger siblings displayed attachment behavior toward their older siblings, seeking proximity and contact with them and then using them as a secure base for play. So although it may seem that they are fighting all the time, siblings do have moments of playing well together. It is at these times that parents should take notice.

## Don't Be a Referee

In conflict situations between siblings, it is quite common for the youngest to flee to the parent for protection. When the second child comes to parents with cries of fright, parents may react by punishing the older child. After all, they are bigger, stronger, older, and should be able to control themselves. Eventually, in any situation in which an aggressive action takes place, parents punish their eldest and perhaps give a more lenient admonishment or do nothing at all to the younger child, the underdog.

Younger children, being smaller and more helpless, soon use these attributes to their advantage. They become the "subtle antagonist." They develop their own devices for getting back at their older sibling and do anything (just as long as what they do is not noticed by mother) to provoke their older sibling. Each child learns what irks the other child the most, and each delights in doing just those things.

Although older children cannot be allowed to physically abuse a younger sibling, parents can try not to attack their personalities by labeling them as mean or bad people. Parents can still protect their younger children without giving older children the feeling that they are not loved. Older children should be allowed to express their feelings, and parents should let their children know that they understand these feelings.

As children get older, there is less need for parents to intervene in sibling disputes. The older children should learn more control and resort less to physical attacks, and younger children become less helpless and more capable of protecting themselves. If parents are still playing the role of referee when their children are older, it is often because children's fighting and quarreling serve a purpose, mainly to keep caregivers occupied. Fighting annoys caregivers and makes them stop whatever they are doing so that they can come in and settle matters. A good brawl always brings caregivers to the scene. For children, it is a good, effective means of getting and keeping their parents' attention.

Whenever possible then, parents should stay out of fights and step out of children's problems. When parents interfere, children learn nothing about how to resolve conflicts on their own. Whenever parents take sides, one child is the winner and the other becomes the loser. The loser then tries to get even with the winner. Thus, as soon as one fight is over, another is brewing.

## Understand Your Own Feelings

Adults can minimize their children's jealous feelings by examining their own feelings about their children. Unwittingly, a parent's past experiences may influence how children are treated. Parents who were middle children, for example, and felt cheated out of parental privileges or indulgences may show favoritism toward their middle child. If babies of the family show certain characteristics that parents possess, parents may unconsciously overemphasize these qualities. Danger develops when parents, as a result of their past experiences and present needs, give preference to or punish one of their children.

## Treat Children as Individuals

Older and younger children should not be treated alike. Sometimes parents, in their zeal to be fair and just, forget that older children should be given privileges and responsibilities commensurate with their age. Older children should be allowed to stay up a little later, ride their bikes a little farther from home, or receive a little more allowance than their younger siblings. These same privileges will be accorded the younger children when they get older. As a result, younger children will look forward to growing up.

## Avoid Comparisons

In some homes, children are constantly being judged and pushed by comparisons between siblings: "Why aren't you neat like your sister?" Comparing of brothers and sisters is one of the most frequent causes of jealousy between siblings. It grows when favoritism, comparisons, or lack of respect for individuality are present.

**Arrival of the Baby**

Although there are no studies that examine the value of preparing a child for the new arrival, it seems to make sense that such preparation may help the child to be more accepting of and perhaps less jealous of the new baby. In announcing the arrival of the new baby, adults should tell the older child a short while in advance and avoid long, false explanations. No matter how well you prepare children for the arrival of the baby, however, and how clearly children seem to understand what the arrival will mean, as Anna Freud has pointed out, children may easily be emotionally overwhelmed by the real event. You should recognize, after all, that even as adults you may be rationally prepared for a change yet devastated by the experience of that change.

It is generally good advice to avoid saying that you will love both children equally. If adults say this, children will probably devote most of their time testing the parent's "equal love." More often than not, if their testing behaviors are negative (and they usually are), they will prove the parent wrong. It is better to explain to children that no one ever loves two people in the same way. We love people for different reasons. In this way, adults set the stage for explaining that their response to the new baby and to the older child will be different.

## Noncompliance

Another common disciplining problem is noncompliance, when children choose not to follow the requests and demands of their parents. Early noncompliance places children at risk for a chain of events, including coercive family interactions, poor social relationships, poor academic performance, delinquency, and problems later in life.[13] The function of nonproblematic levels of noncompliance is less understood, but it is clear that children in well-functioning families also engage in a considerable amount of noncompliance.[14]

Passive noncompliance involves children ignoring or not responding to a directive, and active forms of noncompliance involve signs of deliberate resistance. Passive forms of noncompliance may have positive functions in children's development of autonomy and social skill. Indirect commands (suggestions, requests, polite commands) as a way of initiating requests to children and the use of feedback in the form of verbal reprimands for inappropriate behavior are associated with high levels of compliance.[15] Punishment, however, is associated with frequent passive and active forms of noncompliance. Direct, power-assertive parental control strategies such as anger, physical punishment, or criticism often lead to less impulse control and less compliance. Family discord, particularly parental disagreement on disciplinary practices, has been associated with noncompliance in children.

The relationship between child compliance and parental behavior is clearly an interactional one, with children's past behavior influencing the nature of future parental prohibitions and with parenting behavior contributing to children's willingness to cooperate. Thus, the quality of the ongoing parent–child relationship appears to play a role. Young children who are securely attached to parents, for example, are also more compliant with maternal requests and less likely to refuse to cooperate with restrictions. Similarly, their parents are less likely, in turn, to be restrictive and less likely to set arbitrary or punitive limits. Thus, parents who have harmonious relationships with children have relatively cooperative children.

There are a number of positive strategies that parents can use to help children become more compliant. One of these strategies is anticipating trouble in order to avoid it. For example, you know that when your child comes home from school he is bursting with energy, so have him do some physical activities (shoot baskets), followed by a nutritious snack. Parents can also divert or redirect the child's behavior. ("You cannot play with Dad's saw, but you can use your toy saw.") Parents increase children's compliance when they provide choices. ("Would you rather have carrots or peas?") Finally, parents can suggest rather than demand compliance. ("I would appreciate it if you would turn down your radio.") These approaches are associated with child compliance, whereas physical restraints, threats, and negative prohibitions are more likely to elicit both immediate noncompliance and ongoing power struggles. Extreme noncompliance in early childhood often reflects inappropriate childrearing practices or failure of parents to establish firm, consistent, child-centered controls. It's best to phrase commands or requests in positive ways to increase children's compliance. Instead of saying, "No allowance until you clean up your room," say, "As soon as your room is clean, you may have your allowance." It may seem like this is a small semantic change, but in the child's eyes, the request is viewed in a more positive light and as a reward rather than a punishment; thus, the child is more likely to comply with your request.

## Temper Tantrums

Temper tantrums are quite common in the second year of life, and they make all parents feel that it's their fault. The intensity and passion that a toddler feels about each and every decision are reflected in his tantrum. Some parents wonder why these tantrums almost always occur in public places. The answer may be that the child is overloaded by excitement coupled with the fact that the parent's attention is diverted from them and they want it back; thus, they explode with demonstrations of negativism. Of course, a child thrashing about and turning blue always brings others to stop and observe the child's demonstration.

The best solution is to ignore the child; it's no fun turning blue when no one is there to observe. Parental attempts at soothing the child are only likely to prolong the temper tantrum. The more involved the parent is with the child, the longer the tantrum will last. If you are shopping at the local food store and the child throws a temper tantrum in the juice aisle, it's best to abandon the cart, take the child to the car, and say to her that you can continue shopping as soon as she is quiet and ready to return. When the tantrum is over, give the child a hug and say that you know how terribly upset she was.

Some experts suggest walking away from the child. As T. Berry Brazelton points out however, "some parents find it hard to leave the child because they are afraid the child will hurt himself. When he thrashes violently or bangs his head on the ground, it is frightening. It is unlikely that he'll hurt himself. If he seems too violent, he can be removed to a rug or bed. Fortunately, in most cases, he will stop before he loses control."[16]

## Effective and Ineffective Parenting

Is there one right way to bring up children? Unfortunately, no. There are no glib answers or easy-to-follow formulas, no simplified rules or pat advice. There are some guidelines, however, that will give parents effective methods of training their children to become accepted members of society.

### Words! Words! Words!

Usually parents become verbally active and physically lazy. Some parents continue putting words on words and commands on commands, even though they know their verbal barrages are ineffective. A parent may command the child to pick up his toys. Minutes go by and the toys are not picked up. Another command is followed by another waiting period. Finally, in desperation the parent says, "How many times do I have to tell you to pick up your toys!" Parents need to become physically active. They need to learn to say something once and then back it up with physical action. Just as the child may have learned that she doesn't have to mind unless her parents get to their full-volume yell, she will learn to obey the first command if it is known to be followed by action without being repeated. Calmly after telling the child to pick up his toys, take the child by the hand and ask him to pick up the toys. Calmly is the key word. If you do this in anger, the child refuses, and we have the beginning of a power contest.

## Be an Authority

The basic lesson for children, upon which all others stand, is to believe in the parent and to regard the parent as an authority—one who is dependable and means what he or she says. Parents begin to establish themselves as authorities by providing lessons accompanied by words and communicated by action.

## Maintaining Peace

Sometimes mothers will say they will do anything to maintain peace around the house. This also usually means that mother puts herself in a position of full-time maid service for her children. Some mothers may maintain that it is just not worth the hassle to nag the child to do chores.

A mother, for example, may nag her child to clean his room or feed the dog, and when, after several reminders, the child does not do the chore, the mother, who is tired of nagging, does the child's chore. The child learns that if he procrastinates long enough, mother will do the chore. In this case, mother needs to be an authority. Remind the child once, "Please feed the dog," and then calmly but firmly make sure that the child completes the task. When mothers do the child's chores they are creating a very demanding, self-centered child.

## Prioritize

A parent might think, "There are so many things my child does wrong, I don't know where to begin!" Parents then may concentrate on their child's harsh language one day, his manners the next, his sloppiness the next, and so forth. Parents need a consistent plan of action. If parents try to correct behaviors in random and accidental ways, trying to change everything at once, they limit their effectiveness. Make a list of everything the child does that bothers you. Then rank these behaviors from most to least serious and begin to concentrate your efforts on the most serious.

Parents who are able to prioritize have an easier time overlooking minor infractions of household rules in favor of more serious violations that involve safety hazards or impinge on the rights of others. Parents who have clear priorities about what is and what is not a serious transgression and who respond selectively to misbehavior, with strong prohibitions paired with explanations, have children who exhibit more prosocial behavior. Parents who use more frequent prohibitions and fail to pair them with explanations and reasons tend to have children who are more likely to ignore parental commands and who are less likely to behave in prosocial ways.

## Parental Agreement

An important factor in successfully disciplining children is the involvement of both parents in childrearing and whether they support each other in their childrearing efforts. Parental agreement has been seen as reflecting family organization, with high agreement indicating adaptive functioning and low agreement indicating disorganization. Parental agreement is also seen as one of the variables that characterize effective parenting, and parental disagreement is associated with negative interactive patterns. Successful couples are able to create a new, shared reality that both partners come to accept. Unsuccessful couples, by contrast, are unable to create this new reality; each member instead holds on to the one that he or she has brought to the relationship. Agreement between parents is generally seen by family researchers as an essential component of the marital relationship; as a positive correlate of marital adjustment, happiness, and satisfaction; and as having a positive impact on children.

## Keeping Your Cool

Parents have so much more power (and cognitive thinking skills) when they retain their emotional cool. Don't get out of control. Let's say that you are reading a book and relaxing for a few minutes and your children are playing rather noisily in the next room. For 15 minutes you listen as they get more boisterous; it's beginning to bother you, but you dismiss it and continue to try and read. Another 10 minutes go by and you are now quite angry and come into the den with clenched fists shouting at the children to be quiet. If the children are doing something that is upsetting you, act on it quickly before your anger gets the best of you. Or, if you've allowed yourself to become too angry, count to ten; it works.

## Building a Positive Relationship

Sometimes parents get so involved in "training" their children to behave appropriately that they overlook the most significant influence on the development of their children—the relationship they have with them. Some parents are so critical, negative, and fault-finding that their relationships with their children become very poor.

By constantly responding to children's negative behavior, whatever it may be, parents encourage it. The more parents fuss and punish, the more children retaliate, and the worse the relationship with children becomes. Build on the positive. Reinforce your children when they act independently (doing chores without being told or doing homework before watching television, for example) and lovingly (being nice to siblings or polite to other children).

## Summary

As socializing agents, fathers tend to place more emphasis on protecting children and helping them become self-sufficient, independent, and assertive. In accomplishing these goals, fathers tend to use more forceful techniques such as power and authority. Mothers, however, tend to emphasize interpersonal behavior such as good manners and being nice to other people and use more reasoning and praise in socializing their children to behave in these ways.

Parents tend to socialize their children in ways that will enable them to make a satisfactory adjustment to their environment as adults. In middle- and upper-middle-class families, behaviors that are valued and taught are curiosity, self-control, independence, and concern for others to prepare them for positions that will, in the future, require them to make decisions and take on responsibilities.

An authoritative parenting style promotes high self-esteem in children. These parents are warm, responsive, and more child-centered than parent-centered, and the control strategies they use are firm but fair and carried out in loving ways. When parents are authoritative disciplinarians, the environment created in the home is conducive to helping children develop socially approved skills and behaviors in social, academic, physical, and moral areas. Consistency, in terms of following through with what you say, establishing rules that don't change daily, not using idle threats, and incorporating the no-lose method, in which parent and child work together to solve conflicts, are also important to children's self-esteem. Common disciplining problems, such as sibling rivalry, noncompliance, and temper tantrums, and how parents can effectively manage children in these situations were discussed.

Finally, and most importantly, disciplining efforts should always be carried out and administered in ways that communicate love and concern for the child. As parents we should not lose sight of the most important aspect of parenting—establishing positive relationships with our children. Being a loving parent is pivotal in building and maintaining positive parent–child relationships and enhancing children's inner self-esteem.

# CHAPTER 7 Children with Special Needs

Some children, including emotionally handicapped children, physically handicapped children, mentally handicapped children, abused children, underachievers, children with learning disabilities, and gifted children, have special needs. Although children in each of these broad areas exhibit different handicaps and disabilities and each demands or imposes different challenges on family life, all need special opportunities to develop inner self-esteem.

## Emotionally Handicapped Children

Al, in his senior year of secondary school, obtained a certificate from his physician stating that a nervous breakdown made it necessary for him to leave school for 6 months. Al was not a good all-around student; his teachers found him a problem and he had a history of poor school adjustment. Al was a late talker and had no friends. Al also had odd mannerisms, made up his own religion and chanted hymns to himself. His father was ashamed of his son's lack of athletic ability and regarded him as "different."

This brief profile of Albert Einstein illustrates the danger of making snap decisions on the basis of superficial and incomplete evidence and the difficulties in defining mental health or disturbance. Albert Einstein didn't speak until he was 4 years old or read until he was 7 years old. Being different does not necessarily mean that one is in poor health or disturbed. Overwhelming evidence indicates that Einstein was a gifted and creative individual who had difficulty conforming to the requirements of school settings.

Parents need to be familiar with symptoms that may be indicative of unhealthy adjustment in children. Informed parents will be able to engage in early intervention and, thus, the child has a better chance of developing healthier adjustments. The sooner a parent can identify the child who is in need of professional help, the better the chances of helping that child as well as preventing other emotional overlays such as low self-esteem due to repeated frustrations, failures, and unhappiness. The purpose of early identification is to develop more effective learning and behavior programs for these children so they can develop competent behaviors and skills that lead to high inner self-esteem.

## Symptoms of Emotionally Handicapped Children

Emotionally handicapped children encompass children who are failing to function effectively in academic, personal, or social areas. I am excluding from this definition children with extreme emotional disturbances such as autism and child schizophrenia, which are beyond the scope of this book. Emotionally handicapped describes a child with *intrapersonal conflict*; these children are not at peace with themselves. Inwardly, they are in a state of turmoil; they are unable to cope with the stress of living, have a low opinion of themselves, and see themselves as disliked by others.

These children have *learning difficulties* despite having average or above-average intelligence. Because of inner conflicts and absorption with them as well as behavior difficulties, these children are potentially limited in learning capabilities.

Emotionally handicapped children have *interpersonal ineptness*. They are unable to form a good relationship with peers, teachers, and parents. They may be timid and passive or hostile and aggressive in their relationships with others. Finally, their behavior is limited, rigid, and inflexible. They exhibit extreme stubbornness and are generally not motivated by the usually effective motivational techniques (praise, reward, punishment) used to change their behavior.

## Identifying Children in Need of Professional Help

In general, closer scrutiny is warranted if the child is unable to learn, has unsatisfactory interpersonal relationships, inappropriate behavior, is continually unhappy, and suffers from repetitive illness. It may be said that the capacity to learn and keep on maturing behaviorally is the test of normality.

Some of the behavioral symptoms of children who may have serious problems and may need professional help are:

1. *Resistance to learning:* Some problems show up first in the form of academic failure, which cannot be explained by intellectual, sensory, or health factors.
2. *General unhappiness and habitual apathy:* Nothing seems to spark a glitter in these children's eyes; they are continually dissatisfied and depressed.
3. *Marked indifference to people's feelings:* These children are unable to show sympathy or warmth toward others.
4. *Excessive demands for attention:* Many of these children are not content unless they are the center of attention.
5. *Social ineptitude:* These children often steal, lie, pick fights, are harmfully sarcastic to others, and show little regard for hurting others.
6. *Refusal to accept any responsibility at home or at school for their behavior:* A child refuses to believe that he has acted inappropriately or that anything is his fault.
7. *Extremely negative view of self:* Children see themselves as unwanted and unacceptable to people or are unable to cope with people and see the world as unloving, unfriendly, threatening, rejecting, and perhaps persecuting.
8. *Excessive daydreaming:* Children live most of their time in a fantasy world, which interferes with their engaging in normal childhood activities.
9. *Intense sibling rivalry:* Children exhibit intense hatred toward their siblings, and jealousy pervades their whole personality and colors their whole life.
10. *Constant, open rebellion against authority:* These children are consistently overly defiant, selfish, stubborn, resentful, distrustful, and negativistic.
11. *Extreme tension and nervousness:* These children are highly excitable, may stutter, pull their hair out, bite their nails, and exhibit facial tics.
12. *Physical disturbances:* These children have excessive headaches, stomach aches, vague pains, and persistent and frequent illness.
13. *Bedwetting or soiling pants:* After the age of 5 or 6, children who exhibit these problems may be doing so as a form of re-

bellion against parental authority in general and against strict toilet training in particular.

In addition, children who seek out trouble, are predisposed to anger, are defiant, consistently seek immediate gratification, and fail to profit from experience may need help. At various developmental levels, children may exhibit certain symptoms that may require professional assistance. Preschoolers who have frequent nightmares or night terrors, children who masturbate excessively, children who totally disregard parental authority, and children who are unable to get along with others may need help. During middle childhood, truancy, bullying, cruelty to animals, depression, and prolonged lack of interest and enthusiasm may indicate an emotional disturbance. During adolescence, delinquency, acting out, stealing, sexual acting out, excessive drug abuse, and depression are indicators of disturbances that warrant professional help.

## Creating Conditions that Foster Emotionally Handicapped Children's Self-Esteem

One of the best things that parents can do for emotionally handicapped children is to know when symptoms are serious and to get professional help for these children as soon as possible. Many children may exhibit these symptoms in mild or moderate form. Our judgments of normalcy can be so finely calibrated that it appears that no child can measure up. Diagnosing behavior problems is a complex process; children's entire adjustment pattern, past history, and present responses must be carefully studied.

When are the aforementioned symptoms serious? It is not necessarily the number of symptoms; one symptom by itself or several symptoms do not necessarily mean the child is in trouble if his overall adjustment in other areas is good. But when a symptom gets in the way of the child's ability to function in academic and social situations, professional help should be sought. Second, if any one symptom becomes a persistent and permanent part of the child's personality, the child may benefit from help. For example, lying on occasion may not be too serious; chronic lying, however, represents a more serious problem. Repetitive disturbances can usually be interpreted as signs or symptoms of deeper underlying tensions.

Persistence of behavior, its resistance to change, is a useful gauge in determining its seriousness. When positive attempts and efforts to help children are employed and the behavior continues, outside help may prove useful. Most often, the greater number of areas in which the child causes a disturbance and the greater number of spheres in the child's life the problem reaches, the more serious the problem. A less disturbed child does not produce such uniform reactions in so many settings. Children, then, who exhibit problem behavior at home, at school, and in community groups, for example, likely need help.

When parents can no longer cope with the problem, feel emotionally exhausted by the child's behavior, and react with irritation and anger to the child's behavior, help is necessary. When children's behavior is potentially serious or life-threatening to self and others, outside assistance is necessary. Children who play with matches and children who harm or maim animals, for example, need psychological assistance.

When behaviors are impulsively driven, that is, children know they are alienating parents, friends, and teachers and yet continue to act the way they do and when usual motivation techniques are ineffective in helping these children change inappropriate behavior, help is needed. When children know exactly what they are doing, are aware of the correct behavioral response, but continue with the inappropriate behavior anyway, they may need assistance. Finally, when parents cannot understand a symptom or why the child is engaging in such behavior, they should seek professional help for their child.

## Physically Challenged Children

Parents of physically ill and handicapped children are likely to report experiencing stress more than any other group; they are followed by parents of deaf and blind children, parents of emotionally handicapped children, and then by parents of mentally handicapped children.[1] Each of these groups is more likely to report stress than parents of children with learning or speech difficulties. The physically challenged are those children who have physical defects or disorders that make it difficult for them to perform some of the everyday tasks and activities others of their age routinely perform. These children may have an incurable disease. They may be missing a limb; lack the ability to control parts of their body; suffer from complete or partial loss of vision or hearing; their hearts, lungs, muscles, bones, or nervous systems may be diseased, damaged, or deformed.

Physical challenges range from different degrees of blindness and deafness; to crippling conditions such as muscular dystrophy, and various kinds of paralysis; to disfigurements. Children may be born with physical challenges such as cerebral palsy, epilepsy, and hemophilia; or they may suffer a physical challenge because of a disease contracted during childhood, such as severe ear and eye infections leading to deafness or blindness, or meningitis, which can lead to paralysis. A third type of physical challenge may result from serious accidents.

When parents are first told that their child has a handicap, some display behaviors that are similar to bereavement. These parents suffer the loss of the normal baby they had expected. Some parents react to the discovery that their child is handicapped with anger, disbelief, and shock. They experience a feeling of uncertainty about the child's future outcome, which, in many cases, is impossible to predict. Some deny that their child is handicapped. Some may seek the opinion of other professionals. Denial postpones the process of adjustment and for this reason is maladaptive. Guilt is a common emotion, particularly for women. Was it something they did that caused this handicap? Could it have been prevented? In extreme cases, couples may abandon sexual activities, partially out of fear of producing another handicapped child.

Another sign of strain is depression among parents. Mothers with primary caretaking responsibilities often feel extremely fatigued, have difficulty sleeping, and complain that fathers fail to give them the sympathy and support they need. This is particularly true for low-income families.

In addition to coping with the handicapped child, some families must cope with the problems of material disadvantages as well. Physically ill children and handicapped children are more demanding of all parental resources—their time, energy, and financial resources. Costs for hospital stays, assessment, monitoring, and training, and alternate care to allow parents a break from parenting are all costly and financially draining.

## Creating Conditions that Foster Physically Challenged Children's Self-Esteem

All parents tend to conjure up images of what their baby will be like, and when their newborn child fails to match those images, they may feel a sense of anger, disbelief, denial, and loss. Once parents have adjusted to this loss, they are able to accept and appreciate these children, in their own right.

Families caring for children with physical handicaps have different demands made of them than do other families. These children require more care and attention to help them develop in physical, social, and cognitive domains. In actuality, it may not be the extra physical care that causes stress and strain but, rather, worrying about the child's future. The stress of adjusting to a handicapped child, regardless of the type of handicap, may place a strain on the marital relationship and the relationship with other family members as well.

Frequently mothers devote more of their time to the handicapped child and spend less time with the remaining children. The siblings of a handicapped child are expected to become less demanding and more independent. Girls, more so than boys, are expected to take over many domestic chores such as taking care of younger children, cooking, cleaning, and washing. Some siblings feel a strong pressure to excel because they believe their parents want them to make up for the handicapped child's limitations. While some siblings report that their handicapped brother or sister interrupts their sleep and their social lives (a view held for nonhandicapped siblings as well), most report that they are more mature and more attuned to the feelings and needs of others as a result of having a handicapped sibling.

Mothers usually assume the principal responsibility for the handicapped child, while fathers become more involved with the other children in the family. Fathers tend to spend little time with the physical care of a handicapped child, especially a severely handicapped child. Because they spend little time, however, does not mean fathers are not influential. Their influence may be more indirect in terms of helping mothers cope and care for the handicapped child and in influencing family cohesion and atmosphere. One of the father's greatest roles is to reassure the mother that she is doing an effective job with the handicapped child. Mothers of handicapped children, despite the amount of work they do, are, in general, well adjusted.

While physically handicapped children have a primary handicap, parents need to be cautious in the way they treat and interact with these children in order to avoid creating a "secondary handicap." Parents of a blind child, for example, may stop discussing things that are happening around the child because, after all, the child cannot see them. By doing so, parents are denying these children a rich linguistic form of stimulation. Some parents may be so protective and involved with their child that they fail to give the child opportunities to learn to do things by himself or herself. The goal in working with handicapped children is to make them as self-sufficient as possible, and this enhances their self-esteem. Give them chores around the house that contribute to the family. Assign them responsibilities, such as feeding the family pet, that they are able to carry out. Have them be in charge of their own pet—a turtle, bird, or goldfish—that is dependent on them for care. Teach them skills that will enable them to carry out self-help tasks such as dressing, bathing, and eating. All children take pride in being able to master their environment, and with their parents' help and guidance most children achieve this goal.

In helping your child develop inner self-esteem, the child's handicap should be viewed as an obstacle to be overcome, not an insurmountable problem. The parents' goal is to help their handicapped child be as much like a normal child as possible. Parents should be accepting and more relaxed about the child's handicap, so the child and those around him are accepting and relaxed as well. They should be viewed first as a child and secondarily as a child with a handicap. One of the most important goals for parents is to foster nondependency in their handicapped children by teaching them the necessary skills and competencies to enable them to live up to their fullest potential.

## Abused Children

### Physical Abuse

The sheer repugnance of the concept of child abuse draws deeply on the compassion of sensitive people. Researchers and policymakers have recognized the extent and severity of violence toward children. Physical child abuse involves *acts of commission* by the parent, characterized by overt physical violence, beating, or excessive punishment. The use of physical punishment against children seems to reflect a mixture of positive belief in force as a tool for shaping behavior, lack of effective alternatives to force, and emotional tension in the parent. Young children are more at risk of physical abuse than are older children; over half of the reported child abuse victims are under 4 years of age, with children under 2 years at the greatest risk.

### Emotional Abuse

It is recognized today that child abuse is not only confined to physical abuse, but also encompasses other forms of child maltreatment—emotional abuse, child neglect, and sexual abuse. One of the most cruel and long-lasting forms of abuse is emotional abuse—the systematic diminishing of another person. Emotional abuse is generally a lifelong process of destroying another person's self-esteem. The emotionally abused child suffers from a constant barrage of put-downs; this child never measures up. If he gets a B on a test, it's not good enough. They constantly receive negative remarks: "You're stupid," "You're fat," "You're ugly." They are negatively compared to others: "You'll never be a success like your older sister." Every area of their life is subject to constant disapproval. Emotional abuse occurs when parents fail to encourage normal development through assurance of love and acceptance. It involves verbal put-downs, labeling, humiliation, and unrealistic expectations. After a while, these children believe they are totally unworthy—unworthy of love, respect, friendship, and, in some cases, life.

While active emotional abuse involves thoughtless but constant belittling, passive emotional abuse is labeled neglect. Child neglect is maltreatment due to *acts of omission*, that is, when the parent fails to meet a child's physical, nutritional, medical, emotional, and other needs.[2] There are a large number of abused children for whom parents have very little affection or investment. These are the children who are likely to be kept in their rooms and their cribs as infants. These are children who are likely to be poorly fed and who have poor hygiene. Since the child is unloved, not cared for, and inadequately nurtured, psychological scars may be much more prominent than in other types of abuse.

Regardless of whether emotional abuse is active or passive, frequent or occasional, it is always painful—as painful as physical abuse and perhaps more devastating. A parent's love is so important to children that withholding it can cause irreparable damage. As with other forms of abuse, not all children in a family are emotionally abused by the parents. There is generally a target child who receives the humiliating abuse. The other siblings soon catch on and begin to emulate the parents' verbal abuse toward the target child.

Emotional abuse is the least studied form of abuse and consequently the least understood form of child maltreatment. The emotionally abused child has no visible wounds, and thus, this form of abuse is given a back seat to other more visible forms of abuse. While it is recognized that physically and sexually abused children need special care and time to heal, it is often thought that victims of emotional abuse will, as time passes, get over it. And, of course, this is not the case.

Because emotional abuse tends to be repetitive and begins at an early age, children do not have the cognitive sophistication to denounce or reject the negative remarks they hear. They often absorb these remarks like a sponge and come to believe they are as bad as their parents and siblings tell them they are. Many begin to belittle and humiliate themselves.

Many adults who were emotionally abused as children, spend their lives searching for love—love that they actually believe they don't deserve. Women who are physically abused by their husbands, for example, are convinced that they are at fault for this abuse ("I must provoke it somehow") and that they deserve this kind of treatment because they are so unworthy. Similarly, for emotionally abused individuals, intimate relationships with others are doomed, and the almost inevitable failure of adult relationships reinforces their feelings of unworthiness. Drug addiction, anorexia, bulimia, obesity, alcoholism, and depression are some of the self-destructive behaviors that adults who were emotionally abused as children may display.

## Sexual Abuse

Sexual abuse in families, or incest, involves dependent, developmentally immature children and adolescents in sexual activities they do not fully comprehend, which violates the social norms of family roles. The father–daughter dyad of sexual abuse constitutes 70 percent of all reported cases.[3] In incestuous households, daughters are frequently the dominant female figures. There is often a role reversal, with the daughter assuming a role of equal power to that of the mother. Both the incidence and type of abuse seem to change as the child matures. As a child, contact is often limited to genital stimulation. As a girl grows older, the chances of intercourse increase. The average incestuous affair lasts about $3\frac{1}{2}$ years, ending when the daughter struggles to establish autonomy from the family. Instead of reporting sexual abuse, more daughters choose to leave home as soon as possible through early marriage or running away. Sexually abused children have many misperceptions regarding different aspects of sexual abuse: This was his way of loving me; He did this because I was bad and I deserve it; I must have done something to make him think I wanted him to abuse me; He did it because he was drunk; He did this with me because my mother wouldn't have sex with him.

The mother is thought to condone her daughter's sexual role with her father. Such women may have a history of emotional deprivation and be ill equipped to protect their daughters. It appears that relatively few women actually take assertive action to protect their daughters once they find out about the abuse.[4]

Sexually abused children have low self-esteem and are often depressed and withdrawn. They often engage in fantasy and babylike behavior. They often have poor relationships with other children and are unwilling to participate in physical activities. At times, the sexually abused child engages in delinquent acts or runs away from home. Short-term effects of incest include regression to earlier behaviors such as thumb-sucking, eating disorders, sleep disorders, bed-wetting, tics, or excessive fears. It is difficult to disentangle the effects of sexual abuse from those of the disturbed environment in which it occurs. In general, the closer the relationship between the aggressor and victim, the more damaging the abuse. Other considerations include the age and developmental status of the child, the use of force, the degree of shame or guilt the child feels, and reaction of parents.

There are approximately 1 million abused and neglected children in the United States.[5] Of these, each year 100,000 to 200,000 are physically abused, 60,000 to 100,000 are sexually abused, and the remaining 700,000 to 840,000 are neglected. Sexual maltreatment has shown the greatest increase in reported abuse and neglect cases. Some researchers have suggested that the number of sexually abused children is underestimated due to the repression of traumatic memories by male children in particular and the negative societal messages that result from disclosure of sexual abuse.

## Characteristics of Abusive and Neglecting Parents

If anything conclusive can be said about a child abuser it is that the psychopathological model does not apply to the great majority of abusive parents. No "abusive personality" has been identified. Although abusers cannot be distinguished from nonabusers by individual psychological factors or by clusters of factors measurable by psychological testing, a number of characteristics are reported in the literature as occurring more frequently in parents who abuse their children than in parents who do not.

Mothers who abuse their children are more anxious, more suspicious of others, more dependent, less able to seek support from significant others, less nurturing, and less understanding of how to be a parent and interact less with their children than mothers who do not abuse their children. Abusive and neglecting parents show decreased self-esteem and lower satisfaction with family life. Abusers tend to be of lower intelligence and demonstrate aggressiveness, impulsiveness, immaturity, and self-centeredness.[6]

Abusive families are often characterized by deficient social skills, low social desirability, high anxiety, and lack of receptiveness and support-seeking behavior. Abusive families tend to use authoritarian control and fail to encourage a sense of autonomy in their children. Moreover, the family atmosphere is characterized by conflict and lack of cohesion.[7]

Physically abusive mothers tend to be controlling, interfering, and either covertly or overtly hostile. Neglecting mothers are unresponsive in that they tend neither to initiate interaction nor respond to their infants' initiatives. Infants of abusive mothers tend to be difficult, and infants of neglecting mothers tend to be quite passive.[8]

Physically abusive parents are said to interpret certain age-appropriate behavior in children as "willful disobedience" or intentional misbehavior when the children's actions do not conform to parents' commands.[9] Moreover, abusive parents tend to interpret noncompliant behavior as an indication of the child's "bad" disposition, often using such descriptors as "stubborn," "unloving," and "spoiled" as explanations for their contrary behavior. When abusive mothers respond to hypothetical vignettes in which their child behaves in ways that might be considered provoking, they report not only that they would administer greater levels of punishment in these situations than nonabusive mothers but also that their child is misbehaving to annoy them.[10]

One of the most frequently cited characteristics of physically abusive parents is that they, as children, were targets of violence from their own parents.[11] Some correlation between being abused as a child and being an abusive parent does exist. Parents abused as children do not necessarily become abusive; however, they do tend to adopt behavior patterns similar to those of their abusive parents, such as prosocial skill deficits (lack of sensitivity, empathy), social isolation, and deviant responses to stress (drug and alcohol abuse). Social isolation (few close friends, no interpersonal sources of emotional support, loneliness) is another frequently cited characteristic of the abusive parent. The picture described in research studies suggests a parent with few social gratifications, which leads to the feeling of being trapped alone at home with the child.

Four avenues of transmission of physical abuse have been suggested:

1. Persons exposed to high rates of aggressive discipline may develop a parenting philosophy that favors strict, physical discipline as an approach to childrearing.
2. Harsh parenting may foster hostile personalities that lead to aggressive behavior toward others, including the parent's own children.
3. Rather than promoting parenting beliefs favoring physical discipline, harsh parenting might result in the person learning a set of aggressive disciplinary behaviors that are used in a reflexive, rather unthinking way.
4. Harsh discipline is passed from one generation to the next because adult children tend to inherit the social class of their parents with its accompanying stressors and lifestyle.[12]

A large number of investigators have proposed a relationship between socioeconomic disadvantage and patterns of physical child abuse and neglect. It has been argued that the deprivations caused by poverty, including high-density living in deteriorating housing, limited financial resources, large numbers of children, absence of child-care alternatives, and inadequate support services, create chronic stress and frustration. These kinds of socioeconomic situations create a "triggering context" in which violence or neglect toward children is more likely to occur.

Many sexually abusive fathers are angry at their wives or women in general; they lack internal controls to respect the incest taboo; they have a marked history of emotional maladjustment.[13] There is often marital discord in incestuous families and sexual incompatibility between the spouses.[14] The father, however, is reluctant to seek a partner outside the family. Fathers who have had sexual contact with their children are more permissive and accepting of this behavior than normal men. They see more benefits resulting from sexual contact, greater complicity on the child's part, and less responsibility on the adult's part.[15] These factors, coupled with fears that the family will disintegrate, lead to incest, which paradoxically is seen as serving to keep the family together.

## Effects of Abuse and Neglect on Children

Children who have been abused exhibit a diverse set of problems. These include antisocial aggression, troubled peer relationships, impaired social cognitions, lack of empathy, and depression. As a group, abused children of all ages have been found to have a variety of psychological difficulties compared to nonabused children. The emotional impact of abuse of young children is predictable and occurs in a relatively orderly sequence:

1. Abused children search intensely for an explanation for being abused; many conclude that they are at fault and are responsible for the abuse because they are bad.
2. Abused children then respond to abuse with unconscious responses, including repression of anger, guilt, punishment-seeking behavior, and gratification in punishment.
3. Finally, denial and resignation occur in which children attempt to elicit positive responses from the abuser.[16]

## Creating Conditions that Foster Abused Children's Self-Esteem

Abusive parents need a great deal of help, and getting that professional help is the best thing that they can do to help their children. Abused children need to be totally safe from abuse, which may mean that foster care separation is the only approach. The need for therapeutic intervention on behalf of the child also needs to be recognized. We know also that unless both parents receive therapy they will not easily tolerate treatment for their child. However, removing the child from the abusive family and putting him or her in foster care is not enough for many reasons. While placement in some foster homes may be therapeutic, foster parents are not trained therapists. Further, the often abrupt removal from parents is in itself traumatic to the child, no matter how abusive his or her parents are. Separation from parents often generates feelings of rejection and abandonment on the part of the child. The needs of abused children are enormous, and a safe and supportive curative environment as well as therapy by a competent therapist need to be initiated at once.

Protective agencies must recognize that individuals closely involved in an abusive relationship require individual therapy. Group therapy sessions may be particularly helpful for sexually abused children, who tend to be more reluctant about disclosing sexual abuse to others. Group therapy, then, offers an alternative experience to the isolation, secretiveness, and shame that has become central to the sexually abused child. For this reason, the very act of sharing with others who have had similar experiences is likely to afford some emotional relief.

Children involved in long-standing abuse require more intensive work directed at easing a deep sense of guilt, responsibility, defilement, ambivalence, and unexpressed or inappropriately directed anger.

When a child tells someone inside or outside the family about abuse from another adult, it can be assumed that the child would like the secrecy surrounding that contact to be broken. It can also be assumed that he or she would like the abuse to cease. The role of the adult receiving the disclosure is initially to listen uncritically. Beyond gaining an understanding of the nature of the abuse, pressing for more details is not necessarily helpful at this point. At this time, an acceptance of what is being said and conveying that the story is believed and that the child is not in any way blamed for his or her involvement is most helpful to the child. Children should always be reassured that, despite inevitable misgivings, disclosure is the best course for them to have taken.

In particular, abused children need a predictable, nurturing environment in order to develop a sense of trust; they need adequate stimulation and support to develop their minds; they need to engage in play and experience the joys of having fun to recapture their capacity for pleasure; they need both physical and emotional support. Finally, abused children need to be taught how to play a more causal role in their environment. When children's self-esteem has been shredded, when they have been deeply injured and made to feel the injury is all their fault, and when they look for love and approval from others who cannot and will not provide it, they are playing the role assigned them by their abusers, which needs to change.

Abused victims frequently have distorted thinking patterns about the abuse. Many children think something they did elicited such abuse and that they deserve such abuse. These children need to be taught that it is not their fault and no child deserves to be treated this way. In the case of sexual abuse, children need to be educated about the self-centered behavior of the sexual offender (that is, that the abuse was carried out for the perpetrator's gratification), that the adult's behavior is what is inappropriate in the abuse situations, and that the adult has more power in the situation than the child (and thus, the abusing adult is the one responsible for the abuse). The child's thinking pattern needs to be restructured to recognize that hurting or exploiting the child is not a loving act and that having sex with a child is not an appropriate punishment for any misbehavior.

Diagnosis of the emotional damage to the physically abused, emotionally abused, and sexually abused child is imperative if reasonable treatment approaches are to be evaluated. The longer the duration of abuse, the greater the likelihood of negative effects in the form of emotional and behavioral trauma. While physical wounds may be devastating and lethal, the psychological and developmental injuries may be every bit as debilitating. The overwhelming majority of abused children, however, never come to the attention of child protection agencies. Explanations for the failure of many abused children to report their experiences have included a tendency to interpret the abusive treatment as deserved punishment and the use of "selective inattention" by suppressing the awareness of abuse and attending only to positive aspects of an experience. Protective agencies need to develop better ways of educating adults and children about abuse.

If children are placed in foster care, they need a stable environment to allow the child to develop a sense of trust and stability. Many abused children, however, experience four to ten moves in a short four or five years. A sense of impermanence in one's home is significantly correlated with emotional disturbance in abused children.[17] This pattern of repeated foster-home changes needs to stop. Similarly, we do not need to keep children in limbo for years while waiting to determine whether parents are fit to raise their children. The importance of developing attachment bonds with caregivers was pointed out earlier, and abused children need this as much as children raised in normal homes. If we understood the importance of the miseries of abused children and their need to develop strong attachment to a permanent caregiver, we would not take years and years to decide if the child should or should not be with his or her biological family.

## Mentally Retarded Children

Developmental disabilities range from retardation to learning disabilities. Mentally handicapped children vary widely in intellectual ability from those who must live their lives under continuous medical supervision to mild forms of retardation. A mentally challenged child is one who has subaverage general intellectual functioning. In most states, children with IQs below 70 are regarded as mildly mentally retarded. While low academic competence is a necessary attribute in describing a mentally challenged child, low IQ alone does not equal mental retardation. Other factors, which are amenable to change, such as having few friends, poor adjustment to school, feeling unhappy, and self feelings of incompetence are often characteristic of the mentally challenged child.[18]

Down syndrome is the common cause of mental retardation. The behavior of a Down syndrome baby is similar to that of any other baby during the first six months of life. After six months, however, their rate of development slows down. While continuing to pull ahead, the handicapped child does so at a slower pace.

The child with Down syndrome has distinctive facial features: large, protruding tongue, broad skull, and slanting eyes. After birth, the rate of growth continues to be slow, with shortness of stature common. These children generally show poor balance. Sexual maturity is rarely attained.

Children with Down syndrome have difficulty communicating with others and sometimes have a hard time maintaining eye contact. Vocalizations tend to be brief and intermittent and require greater stimulation to elicit a response. Their skills at taking turns while conversing are poor, which may cause more interactional clashes between parent and child.

## Creating Conditions that Foster Mentally Handicapped Children's Self-Esteem

Having a mentally handicapped child presents many challenges to parents, but there are positive consequences as well. Because parents engage in a very demanding role, they may lose contact with some of their friends. Many parents of mentally handicapped children, however, form new and deep social relationships with other parents of handicapped children. The experiences that they have in common provide strong social support.

How family members cope is largely determined by how they perceive the mentally challenged child and their family situation. Families who have positive perceptions of their handicapped child have children with high self-esteem, and these children make a much better adjustment to life. Parents need to take pleasure and pride in the special individual they are raising. If parents see their children as hopeless and fear for their future, the children will do the same. If, however, they see their children as capable and able to meet the demands of life, children will do the same.

Most emotional upsets experienced by mentally handicapped children are expressed in fear and rage. These outbursts must be treated with understanding, firmness, and sympathy to an even greater extent than with "normal" children. As with all children, mentally handicapped children require a lot of attention. But parents of handicapped children must recognize the needs of other children in the family. If mother spends an inordinate amount of time with the handicapped child, siblings will become resentful and suffer emotional problems of their own.

Mentally handicapped children need contact with normal children as well as children of their own mental level. Participation in groups is a wonderful experience for them. These children should be afforded opportunities to visit children's concerts, plays, and amusement parks. Mentally handicapped children can be provided with colored paper, crayons, pegs, blocks, and finger paints, which, under adult supervision, will help them learn the fundamentals of color, size, and numbers. Listening to music has a calming effect on children, even those who are high-strung and irritable. Moreover, music helps to keep the child's interest and helps him or her concentrate.

The ultimate goal in the education of mentally handicapped children is to help them learn to help themselves. Parents must not do everything for the child. Let them do as much as they are capable of doing. No matter how slow they are, parents need to be patient. Mentally handicapped children can learn to do simple chores around the house (make their bed, set the table) and often take pride in their helping-out skills. Parents should praise their achievements and take pride in every task these children master. Supporting the child with encouragement and emphasizing positive aspects and strengths of his or her personality are effective ways to build inner self-esteem and are crucial to the child's long-term educational and social progress.

## Children with Learning Disabilities

A learning disability refers to a specific disorder in one or more of the following areas: language (technically known as aphasia), perception, behavior, reading (known as dyslexia), spelling, writing (dysgraphia), mathematical reasoning or computation (dyscalculia). Learning disabilities comprise a heterogenous group of disorders manifested by significant difficulties in the acquisition and use of listening, speaking, reading, writing, reasoning, or mathematical abilities.

A few generalizations can be made from this definition. The learning disabilities concept provides a canopy for all those children who are not performing as expected. The learning-disabled child is affected in different areas of function, not with a generalized inability to learn. Most definitions incorporate a significant discrepancy between these children's estimated intellectual potential (in the average range) and their actual level of performance. These children are achieving considerably less than the composite of their IQ, age, and educational opportunity. Children who are severely brain-damaged (mentally retarded, cerebral palsy) are excluded from the learning-disabled category.

Estimates of the number of learning-disabled children vary considerably but are in the 10 percent range. learning-disabled children are usually diagnosed in the primary grades when lags in reading and writing become apparent. Early identification is important for early treatment.

## Causes of Learning Disabilities

Possible causes for learning disabilities fall into three categories: (1) neurological damage, (2) genetic, and (3) environmental. Neurological damage can be caused by low birthweight or deprivation of oxygen at birth. Genetic causes have received some support from family studies, which have shown that there is a higher rate of learning disabilities among twins than for singletons. Because family analysis confounds genetic and environmental factors, no conclusions can be derived from these studies. In general, genetic factors should be considered as contributing to learning disabilities in certain cases. For example, there is some evidence that children with severe reading disabilities have a genetic vulnerability that makes them prone to develop this disorder. Environmental causes range from impoverished learning environments to poor teachers.

## Characteristics of Learning-Disabled Children

The following characteristics may indicate a learning-disabled child:

1. Restless in the "squirmy" sense
2. Makes inappropriate noises when he or she shouldn't
3. Acts "smart" (impudent or sassy)
4. Temper outbursts
5. Distractability or attention span problem
6. Submissive attitude toward authority

7. Excitable, impulsive
8. Appears to be easily led by other children
9. Appears to lack leadership
10. Denies mistakes or blames others
11. Childish and immature
12. Difficulty in learning
13. Excessive demands for teacher's attention
14. Restless, always "up and on the go"

learning-disabled children display difficulty in abstract thinking, have poor organizational skills, are unable to pick out significant information, have difficulty with concepts of right and left and time relationships, and have trouble getting their ideas on paper. These children generally lack good judgment. They make snap judgments, reach conclusions that don't follow from the facts, and fail to use problem-solving skills.

Behavioral disorganization is one of the prime characteristics of the child with learning disabilities. The child exhibiting behavior disorganization is continually in motion (hyperactive) and may display erratic and inappropriate behavior on mild provocation. The child is abnormally responsive to environmental stimuli and tends to react randomly without logical predictability. Other behavioral manifestations of a learning-disabled child are perseveration (inability to discontinue an activity on command), distractability, restlessness, purposely disruptive behavior, withdrawal from others, low self-esteem, and a lack of awareness of the consequences of one's own behavioral actions.

learning-disabled children have low self-esteem in the academic and social domains. They do not do well in school and many, because of their annoying behavior, alienate their peers. learning-disabled children may have a number of behavior problems that interfere with their meeting the demands of a traditional classroom. learning-disabled children may be nervous, irritable, defiant, disobedient, and an annoyance to other children. They are unable to concentrate for any length of time and are readily distracted or found daydreaming. Most of the time learning-disabled children act before they think. These children simply cannot organize materials and thoughts the way normal children do.

Frequently, the learning-disabled child is clumsy. He stumbles and falls frequently and has a difficult time playing certain sports, riding a bike, or playing running games. Printing, writing, and drawing may be poor.

While the learning-disabled child may flit from activity to activity, at times, she conversely may become so absorbed in a certain activity that she will spend hours at it. Finally, the child tends to be confused about space and time. These children have difficulty understanding right and left and up and down and have difficulty identifying the parts of the body. They may also find telling time an impossible task to learn.

## Behavior in the School Setting

Primarily because the learning-disabled child's IQ is in the average range, he or she, in most school systems, is in the regular classroom. learning-disabled children are characterized by high rates of off-task behavior (not working on an assignment when they are supposed to, bothering others, talking out of turn), inattentiveness, poor concentration, and a lack of persistence when faced with difficult tasks. They tend to be overly active and appear to be more interested in everybody else's activities rather than their own. They are often overstimulated by the wealth of interesting material on hand and by the spontaneous, lively activity of their classmates. The stimulation, which is appropriate and right for normal children, overloads learning-disabled children's nervous systems and leads to immature or objectionable behavior that is disturbing to the group. They seem to make little or no progress in the classroom no matter what devices the teacher may employ.

## Behavior in the Home Setting

Parents often describe their learning-disabled child as one who often doesn't understand the consequences of his actions or elicits certain responses in others through his behavior. He frequently exhibits immature behavior such as temper tantrums and can be lazy or rebellious.

One aspect of behavior that is confusing to parents is that the child may do some things very well on one occasion and on another occasion perform the same task quite poorly. For example, the child may respond quickly and adequately to a verbal instruction from her parents at one time and yet be confused at another time by the same instruction. Her written work for school may be neat and quickly done one time; the next time the product may be scrambled and illogical.

No explanation has been given for the child having such random and fleeting moments of achievement. The child's performance variability may make things more difficult for her. The parents as well as the school may be convinced that she could do the work if she tried. Any failure on her part may be viewed purely in terms of her behavior and poor attitudes. Increased impatience and blame from the parents or teachers only magnifies the child's anxious and frustrated behavior.

## Creating Conditions that Foster Learning-Disabled Children's Self-Esteem

There are several things that parents can do to help children with learning disabilities develop positive evaluations of self. An important thing for parents and teachers to remember is that so much of the irregular and often irritating behavior that these children exhibit is beyond their control. The knowledge that the child is not merely being rebellious and uncooperative can produce positive changes in attitude toward the child, which, of course, is of paramount importance if therapeutic endeavors are to produce maximum results.

It has been suggested that an environment should be as free from extraneous stimulation as is reasonably possible. At home, this may mean using soft, neutral colors on the child's bedroom walls. It means giving the child short, simple directives. Parents can sequence learning for their child. The child may be taught a new activity by breaking the activity into simple, sequenced steps. The child may need to go over and over these steps until the actions become a habit.

It's not that learning-disabled children are not paying attention; on the contrary, they are paying too much attention to too many things. Parents need to be aware that many learning-disabled children are overwhelmed with stimuli, such as the number of words, numbers, or problems found on one page of written material. Work sheets need to be clear, simple, and not overloaded with stimuli. Similarly, the environment should be simplified and structured in such a way as to produce a predictable, regimented, consistent, everyday life pattern for the child. Such routines become a stabilizing influence for the child.

At home, a definite sequence of activities can be established starting when the child wakes up in the morning. Some definite warning (We will pick up Dad from the train in five minutes) may be provided as a signal to get ready to move to the next activity. The child may then be adequately prepared for any change in routine or for new experiences.

One can expect great variability in the child's day-to-day performance. A bit of knowledge or skill apparently mastered one day may be completely strange to the child the following day. Because the learning-disabled child generally comes from a family and cultural background that is congruent to academic achievement, and because these children have average intelligence and do quite well in some academic subjects, parents (and teachers) may assume that these children are simply lazy and could do better academically if they just tried harder. Consequently, these children may be continually pressured by increasingly irritated and exasperated adults to improve a situation they are helpless to change. As a result, emotional or behavioral problems frequently compound the child's already existing learning disability. The parents' efforts to understand and accept this inconsistent behavior can be sensed by the child and will do much to relieve his or her anxiety and insecurity.

Finally, parents need to look beyond the frustrating and annoying symptoms of some learning-disabled children. If they look deep enough perhaps they will be able to help illuminate a child's special talents, for many learning-disabled children have them. The sculptor Rodin and Harvey Cushing, the famous brain surgeon, had dyslexia. Thomas Edison never did learn to spell and his grammar and syntax were appalling. Woodrow Wilson was 13 before he learned to read. Albert Einstein failed the entrance examination for college. Abbott Lowell, president of Harvard from 1909–1931, had no visual memory and spelled the way he heard words. And William James, psychologist and philosopher, could seldom recall a single letter of the alphabet.

## Underachievers

Sometimes underachievers are labeled as daydreamers, lazy, uncooperative, and unmotivated. The absence of achievement in individuals where it is expected has drawn considerable attention. When there is a discrepancy between children's actual performance and their predicted performance (assumed or measured potential), we call them underachievers. Underachievers are children who perform markedly below their capacities to learn.

Underachieving children have superior ability and score roughly in the top quarter on measured academic ability, but their grades are significantly below their high measured aptitudes or potential for academic achievement. In short, they could do better in school if they tried, but don't or won't.

The onset of underachievement differs for males and females. Male underachievers begin receiving lower grades from first grade on, and the differences become significant in third grade. Females who become underachievers actually exceed the achiever group during the first five years of school but begin a sharp decrease in achievement in grade 6, and their achievement continues to remain low. This fact is particularly bewildering to the parents of girls who have achieved relatively well throughout the early years of education then suddenly begin to get poor grades and evidence little concern over this in the junior high school years.

## Characteristics of Underachievers

Most parents are quite familiar with academically resistant children who act oblivious to their academic surroundings, thus avoiding active participation in the learning situation. Their lazy indifference, nonresponsiveness to motivational techniques, apathetic passiveness, and their general "I don't care" attitude permeates their personality.

While underachieving children are likely to have their own peculiar causes and identifying characteristics, researchers and educators have agreed on a number of specific characteristics. There are more boys with this problem than girls. Aggressive, hostile, boisterous behavior is usually not exhibited by underachieving children. Underachievers are not a problem because of what they do but, rather, because of what they don't do. There is a more pronounced tendency toward passivity in underachievers; their overt behavior is submissive and docile. This seemingly docile nature makes the underachiever easy to be with. Underachievers follow a path of nonresistance; they do not rebel at given assignments, usually follow school regulations, and generally are quiet but nonparticipating members of the classroom.

Some underachievers are described as having passive–aggressive personality. These children do not express their inner aggressive feelings and anger openly; they are unable to express direct hostility and therefore use indirect means. They are terrified by the idea of feeling anger and fear what may happen to them if they openly express their anger. Therefore, their aggressive tendencies are stored up, and resentments are expressed secretly and deviously. They seek hidden and passive ways to express their inner anger, for example, through the development of an educational problem.

Typical underachievers have a low capacity to function under pressure and are easily frustrated. Frustrating incidents, however, occur with high frequency because underachievers are unconsciously geared to look for trouble. They start several projects, but complete few. They stay with a project or an assignment until things get tough and then quit.

Generally, underachievers demonstrate behavior patterns that are considered to be less mature than that shown by their achieving peers. Often, this immaturity is manifested in the inability of underachievers to undertake and complete tasks which they find personally unpleasant and in their lack of self-discipline. Similarly, underachievers have a difficult time in working for distant, long-range goals. They like (and perhaps need to experience) success quickly.

Underachievers can sit for a few minutes and study for a short time only. They are unable to maintain a concentrated line of thought in class. Their distractability often makes it difficult for them to attend and concentrate in class. Finally, there is one overriding interest in their life. They appear to focus all their motivation and desire for achievement on one area, for example, electronics, music, cars, and so forth.

## Causes for Underachievement

Many reasons are given for the discrepancy between capacity and school achievement: physical factors, measurement factors, sociological factors, pedagogical factors, emotional factors, and home factors. Physical factors include children's state of health, poor hearing, and inadequate vision. Measurement factors involve the adequacy of the measuring instrument and the fact that these children may do well on standardized tests (which take relatively little time to complete) but are unable to keep up a sustained effort on a day-to-day basis in the classroom. Moreover, because underachievers tend to have an above-average general knowledge, they tend to do well on tests, but because they do not participate in class assignments, they do poorly on teacher-made tests, which are specific to the class assignment.

Sociological factors relate to the influence of peers on the underachiever's academic performance. If their peer group rejects or devalues education, underachievers may internalize these behaviors and attitudes. Children want to be like other children; no child wants to be taunted with names like "brain" or "egghead." Motivational factors have been discussed quite frequently as the cause of underachievement. Nonachieving children are not motivated to exert themselves. To these children, school is dull, books are unexciting, and academic activities are boring. No matter what teaching technique is tried, children remain their usual uninvolved, unstimulated, bored selves. But, we cannot say that the underachieving child lacks motivation. The student's nonachievement syndrome does not arise from an incapacity to achieve; rather, poor achievement is the student's choice. It is an active but not necessarily conscious choice that does require the exertion of a great deal of the child's motivational energy, but in a negative direction.

Pedagogical factors may influence the underachieving child. A teacher who is bored, unenthusiastic, and tired of the same old teaching routine, for example, may communicate this negative attitude to students. In these situations, those children who have already lapsed into underachievement may feel no compulsion to get out of it.

Factors at home may involve subtle and indirect influences. Parents may engage in few intellectual activities and provide an impoverished home climate in which the child is not stimulated academically or exposed to challenging learning situations. Many underachievers, however, come from homes that are privileged or at least average. Parents of underachievers do not appear to be poor parents. They provide homes that are materially comfortable. The fault, then, is generally not an obvious material one. It follows, then, that the atmosphere and climate of the home is likely the culprit.

The parent–child relationship may be a contributing factor. The relationship between the parent and child is likely to be a more distant one emotionally. The most frequent pattern is that the parent takes successes for granted and notices the child's failures. The contact between the parent and child is through failure. Parental modes of communication take the form of nagging, pressuring, urging, pushing, and threatening.

## Creating Conditions that Foster Underachieving Children's Self-Esteem

Underachievers are not a homogeneous group, and it is not justifiable to treat them as such. Each underachiever has his or her own developmental stage, personality structure, and needs. Therefore, children must be viewed from their individual needs and a program worked out that best meets these needs. The following suggestions, however, should help parents by providing a general framework of how they can create environments that will help these children acquire the skills and behaviors needed to achieve academically.

If the causes for academic underachievement are physiological, the recommendations are rather clear-cut. If the child has a vision problem, she should receive glasses. If the causes are sociological, the child can be encouraged to join clubs and community organizations that display a positive attitude toward education. If the primary causes appear to be pedagogical, a remedial educational program should be planned. Children should receive additional instruction to provide them with the necessary prerequisite knowledge they need in order for the child to accomplish more complex learning skills.

Parents should try not to nag, scold, plead, and coerce the child to study. Underachievers should not be compelled or commanded to achieve. Underachieving children's intrinsic pleasure of accomplishment is lost, because the ulterior, unconscious motive of frustrating their parents is their primary goal. Let children assume the responsibilities for their academic successes and failures. This is not accomplished by an increased pressure to achieve or indifference to their achievements. Parents should try to value the child's academic accomplishments but not directly pressure the child to attain them. These children need to see the separateness of their own lives, and that may bring back the desire to do well by those lives. Parents should encourage the child to study, but it should be clear that studying is for the student's sake and not the parents'.

When the child brings home a good grade, parents need to avoid making comments such as "I told you so" or "I knew you could do it." When parents make such comments, the child has little incentive to continue to do well because this shows that they have not tried previously. Success indicates that the parents are vindicated and the child has been the guilty party all along. Improvement, then, actually means a type of punishment.

Underachieving children may be harboring intense feelings of anger. They need to feel more comfortable with their own angry feelings. The underachieving child's parents should be encouraged to help the child express his or her hostilities and still have the love, guidance, and support of a trusting parent. Underachievers need to see that their parents' love is unconditional and so solidly based that the child's successes or failures in the academic situation cannot influence it profoundly. Underachieving children need to receive their parents' attention in a wide variety of areas, not only those related to competition and academics.

These suggestions are all ways of helping underachievers develop a better understanding of themselves, giving them more purpose and direction in their lives, and opening the door toward better achievement in the classroom, which helps them develop higher inner self-esteem.

## Gifted Children

The identification of gifted children has changed in recent years. In lieu of standardized tests and IQ tests with specific cutoff scores (usually 130 and higher) to identify gifted students, a multiple criteria approach is now used to gather as much information as possible about the child from a variety of sources. Schools are likely to use group intelligence tests, individual IQ tests, standard achievement tests, and teacher nominations to identify gifted children.

The traits most significantly associated with intellectual giftedness are a large vocabulary, complex thinking skills, unusual capacity for symbolic thought (mathematical skills), insight (capacity to see relationships), early physical and social development, and sensitivity.[19] The following are some general and subjective characteristics that parents can use in determining whether their child is gifted.

- Verbal facility
- Good memory
- Flexibility of thought
- Energy
- Creativity, imagination
- Curiosity
- Range of information
- Aesthetic interests or talents
- Outstanding performance
- Leadership
- Social responsibility
- Enthusiasm
- Facility in writing
- Ability to learn easily
- Abstract reasoning
- Planning and organizational ability
- Originality
- Sense of wonder
- Broad range of interests
- Attention to detail
- Scholastic achievement
- Attention and concentration
- Cooperation
- Sense of humor

Any or all of these signs may be positive indicators but cannot accurately predict or guarantee the presence of giftedness later in life. Similarly, the absence of any or all of these indicators doesn't mean a child is not gifted. While this sounds a bit noncommittal, remember that we have no infallible method to measure giftedness; we can only describe its manifestations.

Parents' recognition of giftedness and other, more "objective" measures, however, are fallible. Since there is so much more to children than an IQ, many potentially gifted children may miss being identified by group or individual IQ tests. Moreover, with standard achievement tests, which are designed to measure knowledge or proficiency in something learned or taught, one's potential is not being measured. Finally, teachers may rely on outward features such as how the children are dressed or their verbal skills in identifying gifted students and overlook the creative, divergent thinkers.

Insight *skills* are particularly important criteria for identifying intellectual giftedness.[20] Significant and exceptional intellectual accomplishments—for example, major scientific discoveries, new and important inventions, and new and significant understandings of major literary, philosophical, and similar works—almost always involve major intellectual insights. The thinkers' gifts seem to lie directly in their capacities for creative insight rather than in their IQ test abilities or abilities to process information rapidly.

Moreover, the gifted child should be expected in a more sophisticated way to deal with new kinds of tasks and situations in general. Similarly, gifted individuals should be particularly adept at applying their intellectual skills to the task or situation at hand.

When gifted boys and girls are screened separately according to personality factors, certain differences between gifted and nongifted children seem to emerge.[21] The most prominent differences are that gifted boys show more dominance, more individualism, and less group dependency than the norm for their age and sex. Gifted girls seem to be more outgoing, more conscientious, and curious than the norms for their age.

Another guideline for recognizing giftedness is that gifted children, even as young infants, tend to be very alert and observant. They appear to be more absorbed than others in what is going on around them. Other early signs of giftedness in infancy through age 2 include longer attention spans, demonstration of faster learning, and a great appetite for books and pictures. They are able to grasp and hold objects accurately, while other infants will not even make an effort to do so. Children whose strong skills are in nonverbal areas are often early walkers. Gifted children tend to find more ways to use toys, tools, and puzzles; imagine more creative situations; and demonstrate a deeper understanding of questions and answers from adults.

In early childhood, many gifted youngsters are precocious talkers; they use complex phrases and sentences, along with an advanced vocabulary. Although precocious academic skills do not necessarily single out the gifted child, it is estimated that many gifted children read before coming to school.[22] In most instances, the parents have done little formal instruction other than pointing out the letters of the alphabet. Basic arithmetic skills also appear at an early juncture. Many gifted children seem to possess remarkable memories. Gifted preschoolers are very curious creatures and ask endless questions. They almost appear driven to explore their environment. Gifted children usually read above grade level and have good memories and large vocabularies, long attention spans, and complex ideas. They are well informed, are curious, learn easily, understand relationships, and develop cognitive skills earlier than their peers.

Gifted children can learn material faster. They can think new information through and grasp its meaning more quickly than their peers. They have the ability to generalize, to see connections, and to use alternatives.

## Creating Conditions that Foster Gifted Children's Self-Esteem

Gifted children are often aware that they are above-average students. Acknowledging giftedness by placing them in a special program usually does not give them a big head, as many parents might fear. However, if a child has been misdiagnosed and placed in a fast or high track only to be removed to a lower, slower-paced track, this could be rather hard on the child.

Parents should encourage their children to be well rounded, kind, and friendly. Some parents have the mistaken notion that gifted children are unpopular children. Others excuse gifted and bright people as being so intelligent that they simply don't think about being socially polite to others. Being gifted does not mean (nor does it excuse) being socially inept. Gifted children need to be encouraged to develop social skills and learn the art of getting along with others, including those who are not as intellectually advanced as they are.

Generally it's not a good idea for parents to overemphasize or continually label their child as "gifted." There's no heavier burden than a great potential. Parents should be aware of the difficult time a gifted child might have when he or she grows up labeled as a "genius." Predictably, parents and other adults have very high expectations for their gifted child, which often results in intensified pressure on the child. A significant portion of this pressure is self-imposed by the gifted child and he certainly doesn't need more pressure from parents or school. Similarly, these labels contribute to children developing their IQ as *the* measure of their self-worth; consequently their self-evaluations become too narrow and focused, and their self-esteem becomes too wrapped up with outer self-esteem, that is, others' expectations. When parents continually resort to this special labeling, children have a tendency to form less favorable images of themselves; become more prone to stress, anxiety, and depression; develop behavior problems; and become conceited and less liked by their peers.

By the same token, parents should avoid comparing other siblings to their intellectual star. For parents of gifted children, the comparison of one child with another is the most flagrant misuse of parental persuasion and the least effective. When Cynthia is reminded of her older brother's accomplishments, she tends to experience either resentment (of parents, self, or sibling) or loss of worth and status in the family, both of which are highly detrimental to her self-esteem.

Some parents feel that because the child is so bright he or she will naturally have high self-esteem, but this is not always the case. Positive self-esteem may be difficult to maintain because of excessive self-criticism and sensitivity to criticism from others. Moreover, as Barbara Clark of California State University comments, it is not uncommon for gifted children to have an ideal of what they think they should be that does not match what they think they are.[23]

Also, comments made to gifted children are often less than positive and can lower their self-esteem. Statements such as "If you are so gifted, figure it out" or "Of course, you don't need any help, you know everything" or "You're capable of better work than Bs" are not supportive of healthy self-esteem.

Gifted children should be encouraged to develop *their* special areas of interest, not the parents' areas of interest. Parents need to respect their child's interests even when they do not coincide with their own.

It is obvious to many parents that their child is gifted even when he or she is very young. Parents should not plan every minute of every day programming their child for greatness. Children need to be kids as well. Some parents feel compelled to get their child into the right nursery school so that the young child is on the right track for an Ivy League education and the Nobel Prize later on; this can deprive children of their needed childhood. Play is crucial to the gifted child's self-esteem. Play encouraged for its own sake enhances personal expression and encourages creative approaches to work later in life.

Gifted children are often perfectionists, and for this reason they need to learn how to deal with limitations (we all have them) and failure (it happens to the best of us). Some gifted children, for example, view getting one B on a paper as catastrophic; parents can help them get over viewing these kinds of incidences as total failure. Some gifted children's fear of failure may keep them on a perpetual treadmill of exceptional achievement. These children need to see their limitations. If a gifted child is a very creative writer but an atrocious speller, the parent can inform the child that this is a skill that he or she can learn to master.

One myth surrounding gifted children needs to be mentioned. Many parents and educators believe in the notion that gifted children can make it on their own no matter what. The cream, however, does not always rise to the top. The best conditions for building self-esteem in gifted children are for the parents to be informed about giftedness and then pave the way, enrich the surroundings, and open doors. In addition, let the child find joy in learning and develop his or her keen sense of curiosity and inquisitiveness. Respect the child's ideas, even the seemingly outlandish ones. Encourage questioning and open-ended discussions. Refrain from always judging the worth of the child's activities and products, particularly those that may appear uninteresting or nonproductive to you. Create a safe and comfortable atmosphere for discovery.

## Summary

Special children require special conditions for enhancing their inner self-esteem. Emotionally handicapped children are those who exhibit intrapersonal conflict (not at peace with self), learning difficulties (despite average intelligence), and interpersonal difficulties (cannot get along with other children). Once parents recognize the symptoms and identify children with emotional handicaps, they can begin effective treatment for them. Physically handicapped children should be encouraged to be as self-sufficient as possible, which helps develop their inner self-esteem.

Characteristics of physically, emotionally, and sexually abused children and how their parents can create conditions that foster their self-esteem are examined. All abused children and their abusive parents need professional help. Parents of children with learning disabilities can help them develop inner self-esteem by making their learning environment in the home as free from distracting stimuli as possible, planning a definite sequence of activities each day, expecting great variability in day-to-day performances, and knowing that the frustrating and annoying behavior of some learning-disabled children is not intentional. Underachievers need to learn to be responsible for their own academic achievement. Parents should not coerce or compel the child to achieve but, rather, should let children assume the responsibilities for their academic successes and failures. These children need encouragement, support, and guidance from their parents. Most importantly, they need to see the separateness of their own lives, and that may bring back the desire to do well by those lives.

Parents can help their gifted children develop inner self-esteem by appreciating their talents, not labeling them as gifted or geniuses, not comparing them to siblings, exposing them to many exciting new experiences, encouraging their creativity and curiosity, developing their social skills, and helping them develop a good sense of humor.

# CHAPTER 8  Changing Family Lifestyles

## Divorced Families

Do you agree or disagree with the following statement: When there are children in the family, parents should stay together even if they don't get along. In the 1950s a majority would have agreed; however, in the 1990s, the majority would probably disagree. During the past few decades, Americans have come to place a greater value on personal satisfaction and self-fulfillment. The rise of personal fulfillment as the main criterion for evaluating marriages is due to two developments: the weakening of religious and other moral constraints and the demise of the breadwinner–homemaker family. It is estimated that one out of every ten children will experience two divorces of the custodial parent before the child turns 16 years old.

The divorce rate, although high, has reached a plateau. What impact does divorce have on children? It appears that the initial period of divorce and parental separation is profoundly difficult for all children. Even when parents have been caught in severely unhappy marriages, their children usually do not want the divorce to occur and suffer as a result of it. In recent years, researchers have moved away from viewing divorce as a static event that has pathogenic effects on children. Rather, current investigators are viewing divorce as a process of events. They are focusing on the diversity of children's responses prior to, during, and after the dissolution of marriage and on the factors that facilitate or disrupt children's adjustment during the parents' marital transition. There are several factors that appear to relate to whether children adjust to their parents' divorce with their self-esteem intact: children's age, the quality of the ex-spouses' relationship, custody arrangements, the quality of the parent–child relationship, children's gender, and the support systems available to the family.

## Children's Age

Short-term reactions of children to the separation of their parents vary as a function of their age. Preschool children are most likely to worry about their own contribution to their parent's departure, to believe that the separation is temporary, and to be confused by a parent assuring the child of his or her love yet still moving away. These children tend to be the most frightened and confused. Children between 6 and 8 years of age can understand that their parents might be incompatible and incapable of living together. They want to see their parents reconciled but also realize that this is unlikely and can see the benefits of the reduction in family conflict. Children ages 9 to 12 years are most likely to experience conflicts of loyalty and also to be ambivalent about both parents and view their home and family environment negatively. Divorce strikes young adolescents (13–16 years) as a personal affront and has a disturbing effect on them. Older adolescents, however, can see some positive outcomes of the divorce in terms of their own increased sense of self-reliance and responsibility and positive personality changes for parents. Although divorce tends to be difficult for all involved, children of varying ages respond somewhat differently to their parents' divorce.

### Effects of Divorce on Infants

The results of a handful of recent studies indicate that even infants and toddlers react negatively to parental stress and conflict. While infants $1\frac{1}{2}$ to 2 months old react to naturally occurring and simulated instances of interparent conflict with distress,[1] 3-month-olds have been found to respond negatively to simulated acts of maternal depression.[2]

### Effects of Divorce on Children in Early Childhood

Children in early childhood tend to become frightened and confused, rendering them especially vulnerable. The most frightened children are those who have not received any explanation of the events in the family. Unfortunately, the majority of young children of divorced parents do not receive sufficient explanations for the divorce, and it is these children who most frequently regress and show fear.[3]

Young children, as a result of their parents' divorce, tend to exhibit intense need for physical contact with adults. They tend to worry that their mother will abandon them; they are afraid that they will awaken in the morning and find their mother gone. Often, when mothers return from work or retrieve their children after school, they are greeted with angry tears, crankiness, and sometimes tantrums by these children who are so relieved by the parent's return to express the anguish and frustration they have suffered during the parental absence.

Acute regressions (playing with recently outgrown toys, carrying around a security blanket, whining, crying, general fearfulness) are often observed in young preschool children ($2\frac{1}{2}$ to $3\frac{1}{2}$ years) after a divorce. Such behavior tells parents that the child needs to go back in development and mark time for a while in order to gain strength for the next step forward. Regression is not the favored initial response for older preschool children. Many, however, become irritable, whiny, and tearful.

Divorce seems to have a substantial effect on the children's play and their ability to get along with peers. Disruptions are found in both play and social relations for boys and girls.[4] These adverse effects largely disappear in girls two years after the divorce but are more intense and enduring for boys. The play patterns of children from divorced families are less socially and cognitively mature, they show less imaginative play, and they also do less playing and more watching than children from intact families. In the year following divorce, both boys and girls show high rates of dependent, help-seeking behavior and acting-out behaviors (temper tantrums, physical aggression toward other children). This, again, is more enduring in boys than in girls.

Although these children are distressed and frightened and represent the age group most severely troubled by family crisis, the results of follow-up research paint a different picture. When this same group of preschool children was studied later at 12 to 18 years of age, most had no memories of their intact, predivorce families. The cognitive immaturity that created profound anxiety for children who were young at the time of their parents' divorce appears to prove beneficial over time. Ten years after the divorce, these children have fewer memories of either parental conflict or their own fears and suffering, and they typically have developed a close relationship with the custodial parent. What emerges is the very interesting possibility that children who are very young at the marital breakup are considerably less burdened in the years to come. They carry fewer memories of unhappiness and conflict between the parents and almost no memories of the intact family or their fights and suffering at the time of divorce. In addition, they appear to be very optimistic about the future.[5]

## Effects of Divorce on Children in Middle Childhood

Like their younger counterparts, older children experience considerable initial pain and anger when their parents divorce. Children who are between the ages of 6 and 12 no longer feel that they are personally responsible for their parents' divorce, but they still feel abandoned and rejected. They appear, however, to be better able to receive, sift through, and absorb the shocking news that their parents are going to separate. In fact, these children exhibit presence, poise, and courage and seem to display an ease and comfortableness in talking about their parents' divorce. One of their major concerns is that they will not be able to continue in activities that they value and will have to give them up because of the financial stresses of divorce. Children in middle childhood tend to define divorce in psychological terms and frequently cite parent incompatibility or changes "on the inside" as a reason for the divorce. Unlike young children, school-age children usually tell friends about the divorce, which can be helpful to them.

## Effects of Divorce on Adolescents

Some parents feel that it may be best to wait to get a divorce until their children are older, in their teens. Divorce at this time, however, has a profoundly disturbing effect on adolescents. The event strikes them as a personal affront in every way. Adolescents contemplate the loss of face the divorce might inspire among their peers. They become acutely aware of money difficulties when their parents divorce. They are angry and feel powerless to change what is happening; they often strike back at the parent whom they feel is responsible for the divorce. They report feelings of emptiness, fearfulness, difficulty in concentrating, chronic fatigue, and troubled dreams.[6]

Because the marital rupture occurs at an age when the adolescent is preoccupied with sex and the search for a partner, these issues become centers of anxiety. A number of adolescents become overtly anxious about their parents' sexuality—suddenly now visible—where before the divorce it could be denied. The relative invisibility of sex in the intact family reinforces the adolescents' capacity to deny that their parents have sexual needs. Parental dating prompts adolescents to see that their parents are sexual beings, and this produces a great deal of discomfort and anxiety for many of them (it's comforting to think of parents as old and sexless).

Both sons and daughters in divorced families tend to be given more responsibility, independence, and power in decision making than those in intact families. Divorced mothers tend to monitor their children less closely than do mothers in intact families. In other words, these children tend to grow up faster.

Few adolescents believe their parents offer them a good explanation of the reasons for the breakup of the marriage. Adolescents often talk about being angry at being "kept in the dark." When the breakup finally happens, they are surprised, hurt, and embarrassed about not being told about what was happening. Rather than feeling protected, adolescents report that they wish their parents had confided in them.

One thing is clear—divorce can affect children of all ages in adverse ways. But, if the marriage is characterized by strife and strain, isn't it better for the children if parents do divorce? Do children in one-parent households feel better about themselves than those in intact families characterized by marital discord? This is a critical question, and the answer is particularly relevant because it bears on issues such as whether parents should stay together or separate for the sake of the children.

University of Virginia's E. Mavis Hetherington reports that in the first year following divorce, children in divorced families function less well than children from intact families with high marital discord.[7] In this period, children from divorced families are more oppositional, aggressive, lacking in self-control, distractable, and demanding of help and attention both at home and in school than children in intact families with high rates of marital discord. Two years after the divorce, however, more acting-out, aggressive behavior and less prosocial behavior (helping, sharing, and cooperation) is found in boys in homes of marital discord than in boys living with one divorced parent.

The impact of divorce seems more pervasive and long-lasting for boys than for girls. Differences between the social and emotional development of girls from divorced and "regular," low-conflict, intact families have largely disappeared by two years after the divorce. Although the behavior of boys from divorced families greatly improves over the two-year period following divorce, they are still more disruptive than boys from reasonably stable intact homes. There is still considerable conflict between mothers and sons. At school, the boys from divorced families are more socially isolated, verbally aggressive, immature, and less constructive in play.

Thus, it appears that divorce, in the long run, may be more advantageous when the marriage is characterized by a high degree of conflict. This remains true, however, only if the divorce results in a termination of conflict between the parents.

## Quality of Ex-Spouses' Relationship

Conflict between the parents often survives the legal divorce by many years. In fact, a rather high proportion of divorced couples continue to experience open parental discord even ten years after the dissolution of the marriage.

Current evidence suggests that interparental conflict, whether in intact families or in divorced families, is the most salient factor in creating childhood behavior problems.[8] Children from divorced or intact families characterized by interparental conflict are at a greater risk for developing low self-esteem and adjustment difficulties than are children from divorced or intact families that are relatively harmonious. The existence of a correlation between ongoing parental conflict and childhood emotional problems has been well documented. High levels of interparental conflict have been shown to be related to increases in the behavior problems of toddlers,[9] school-age children,[10] and young adolescents.[11]

Therefore, another significant factor influencing children's adjustment is whether parents engage in cooperative behavior or in combative interchanges (quarrels, sarcasm, demeaning the other parent, physical abuse). Continuous parental discord has an extremely negative influence on children and seems to lead to consequences that adversely affect feelings of security, healthy adaptive behavior, healthy self-esteem, and developmental progression.[12] Children in families fraught with high parental conflict exhibit significantly higher levels of adjustment difficulties.[13] These difficulties include academic problems, internal problems (high anxiety, withdrawal), and external problems (conduct disorders).

Repeated exposure to parental discord has been associated with the development of problems of control (aggression, conduct disorders) in boys.[14] One mechanism through which adults' angry behavior might influence aggressiveness is through increasing arousal or stress, particularly in boys. Adults' angry behavior is emotionally stressful and arousing for children and is linked with increasing aggressiveness in play between children following exposure.

Parental conflict may produce lax parenting, particularly maternal monitoring of the child's behavior. As parental conflict escalates, parents become increasingly absorbed in the marital problems and begin to pay less attention to the child. The child may learn that acting out is a new and effective attention-getting strategy to be used in response to perceived parental withdrawal.

## Custody Arrangements

For nearly a century, child custody decisions in the United States have been guided by the stereotypic notion that mothers are, by nature, uniquely suited to care for children. The child will suffer irreparable damage, so the argument goes, if separated from the mother during the "tender years." When there is a custody dispute, it has been the practice of the courts in the United States to award custody to fathers only when the mother is proven unfit. Thus, in the large majority of current divorces, spouses agree that the mother should be the custodial parent. Only around 15 percent of divorces are associated with custodial conflicts that are brought to court. Currently, then, the vast majority of divorced fathers are noncustodial parents by choice. Though these fathers want their former wives to have the primary custodial responsibility for their children, they still, by and large, want to maintain a significant relationship with their children. The noncustodial father who is sensitive to the children's plight in adjusting to divorce and how divorce affects children will want to maintain a positive, close relationship with his children, even if they're not living in the same house.

Similarly, the mother, in the best interest of her children, should facilitate visits between the children and their father that are free of conflict. Children cannot be divided surgically, psychologically, or emotionally, as King Solomon wisely reminded us. In the best interest of the child, noncustodial fathers need to support the custodial mother's authority, help provide an emotionally and financially secure environment for their children, and become a trusting and supportive father and ex-spouse. By doing so, he is providing the best service to his children and developing a significant, satisfying relationship with his children.

The extent to which fathers visit children after the divorce depends upon the father's attitudes toward the divorce, the age of the children, and the children's attitudes toward his visits. Typically, fathers see their children in frequent short visits, usually every second weekend. Preadolescent boys, in particular, seem to gain from frequent contact with their fathers after the divorce. The positive effects of fathers' visits do not apply, however, in cases where the level of postdivorce conflict between parents is high.

A few studies have reported that school-age children adapt better in the custody of a parent of the same sex.[15] Boys in the custody of their fathers are more mature, social, and independent; are less demanding; and have higher self-esteem than do girls in their fathers' custody. There may be some limitations to these studies because all the fathers in the studies were awarded custody of their children and, as a result, one may conclude that they may be especially good parents. Boys do tend to be less communicative and less affectionate. However, boys in the custody of either mothers or fathers show more acting-out behaviors than girls.

A small but growing number of largely well-educated, relatively affluent fathers are deeply involved in sharing custody of their children. But far more fathers still fade out of their children's lives. All across the United States tonight, one third of the nation's children will go to bed without their biological fathers in the next room. And most of them will not see him the next day either. In fact, about 40 percent of the children who live in fatherless homes haven't seen their fathers in over a year.[16] Why do many men feel compelled to pull away from their children? Perhaps it is because many fathers relate to their children primarily through their wives—marriage and parenthood are a package deal. Ties to children and their feelings of responsibility for their children depend on ties to their wives. If the marriage breaks up, the indirect ties between father and children may also seem broken.

In the 1980s, California pioneered a great innovation in custody—joint custody. There are two types: joint legal custody and joint physical custody. The argument usually given for joint legal custody is that by giving the father continuing authority over his children, the court increases the chance that he will continue to remain a part of their lives and will continue to support them. Under joint physical custody, children alternate between mothers' and fathers' residences according to an agreed-upon schedule. If successful, it can reduce conflict over who has custody and provide children with a continuing relationship with both parents. But joint physical custody requires a great deal of communication and cooperation between the parents. Joint physical custody can merely prolong and deepen conflict between parents unless they can work well together.

Some studies have shown that children benefit from contact with both parents after the divorce, provided there is a low level of conflict between the parents. A child's adjustment to the divorce is related not to the type of custody (joint, father, or mother) but to the quality of the current relationship between parents. Joint custody in and of itself may not benefit children's adjustment. When parents continue to engage in acrimonious battles, joint custody may just prolong the children's involvement in hostility and conflict, thus making their adjustment to divorce much more difficult. There is no evidence that encouraging or mandating joint custody and frequent visitation through the legal system either diminishes hostility between those parents who are severely disputing such arrangements or increases their cooperation in parenting their children.

Some studies, however, have found that children who have more frequent access to both parents during custody and visitation disputes are more emotionally troubled and less well adjusted. More verbal and physical aggression appears to be generated between parents when children have more frequent access arrangements. The higher incidence of parental conflict to which children are exposed is associated with their increased vulnerability to being caught in the middle and used in the parental disputes; this, in turn, partially explains the higher incidence of emotional and behavioral problems.[17]

## Children's Gender

As noted, one of the most consistent findings is that boys are more negatively affected by divorce than girls. Girls tend to recover faster from the divorce of their parents. Boys, on the other hand, take longer to recover from the initial effects, and they show greater problems in social, emotional, and academic areas. Boys are likely to show more sustained, noncompliant, aggressive behaviors even two to three years after the divorce. As was mentioned, disturbances in social and emotional adjustment in girls have largely disappeared two years after the divorce.

Girls tend to show their negative behavior prior to the separation, and their behavior does not appear to decline further after the divorce.[18] The marital disruption itself does not appear to create more negative consequences for girls than they have already experienced. For boys, however, the main consequences appear to occur after the divorce. Boys may be able to buffer themselves emotionally during the stressful pre-separation period, but can no longer sustain this emotional distance after the divorce.[19]

Why do boys make a poorer adjustment to divorce than girls? One reason may be that in many studies children's adjustments are measured by having parents and educators fill out behavioral checklists, and the adjustment variables on these checklists tend to focus on acting-out behaviors (noncompliance, aggression, difficulty in getting along with others, and so forth). Boys tend to show more acting-out behaviors in divorce situations and thus receive higher scores on adjustment difficulties. Girls, however, tend to show more internalized reactions to divorce (withdrawal, depression), and these types of behaviors do not receive much emphasis on the checklists; thus, girls receive lower scores on adjustment difficulties.

Second, parents tend to argue more in front of males than they do in front of females. Perhaps this is so because parents believe that boys are more sturdy and less sensitive to and better able to handle conflict than girls. Another explanation as to why boys experience more difficulties following a divorce is that they tend to receive less support and nurturance from their caregivers and are viewed in a more negative way by mothers and teachers in the period immediately following the divorce than are girls. Divorced mothers of boys report feeling more stress and depression than do mothers of girls and may reflect this in their treatment of sons.

Finally, some researchers have suggested that boys from divorced families may not be doing as well as boys from intact families because of "diminished parenting."[20] Divorce may reduce the parental attention and supervision available to children, particularly to children who are more difficult and demanding to care for, which, in general, may apply more to boys than to girls.

## Social Support Systems

Support systems can serve as sources of practical and emotional support for both parents and children experiencing divorce. Schools and day-care centers, for example, can offer stability to children by providing warm, structured, predictable environments. School personnel can validate feelings of self-control and competence. Children who are experiencing high levels of stress as a result of their parents' divorce tend to perceive social support in a positive way. Similarly, these children report few adjustment problems as a result of the social support they receive. Children who are experiencing low levels of stress as a result of their parents' divorce, however, view social support in a negative way and report more adjustment problems as a result of the social support they receive. In these situations, high support from nonfamily adults may be associated with more adjustment problems, because these children may view this aid as a message that they have problems, which may influence children's assessments of their functioning.

## Conditions that Foster Children's Self-Esteem in Divorce Situations

As noted earlier, children of various ages experience the separation of their parents in different ways. Infants and toddlers show their distress by becoming irritable and fearful. These children need to have secure and stable caregivers who provide lots of love and regular feeding and sleeping schedules. Preschoolers, who tend to be frightened, confused, and tend to blame themselves for their parents separating, need to be assured that they are not to blame and need to be told about the impending divorce.

When children do not receive adequate explanations, they are at the mercy of their own conclusions. They are apt to believe that they are personally responsible for their parents' separation. This belief of being responsible for the parents' divorce may be the result of the child's special, magical kind of thinking. For example, young preschool children believe that they can cause things to happen just by thinking them. Similarly, they believe that events that happen together cause one another. A child will become attached to a blanket or teddy bear that brought comfort once, because the child now believes that it causes or necessarily brings about comfort. Similarly, children may feel that Daddy has left because they did not clean up their room or brush their teeth often enough. Preschoolers need to be assured and reassured that they did not cause their parents to separate as well as being given adequate explanations about the divorce. This helps to reestablish the child's fractured world.

Both parents should talk to the children together. This reduces the tendency to blame the other parent, and children will feel more secure.

Children should be told about one or two weeks before one parent moves out of the home. To tell the children too soon is to foster reconciliation fantasies. The longer the parent remains, the more the child believes the event will never happen. Telling the child a few days before does not allow enough time to adjust. Be honest with children and explain the reasons for divorce appropriate to the age of the child. You might begin by saying, "Maybe you've seen that Mom and Dad haven't been too happy with each other for some time." You don't have to elaborate the minute details that children won't understand. Parents need not fear openly expressing their emotions. Don't be afraid to cry. Tears are an expression of love. When adults cry in front of children they're giving their children permission to cry as well. Let children express anger and resentment. This reaction is normal; children should not be punished for it. Explain what life may be like in the future as best you can. If you know you're going to sell your home, share that information. By supplying details of common, everyday experiences, children can feel a sense of stability about their future.

Children in middle childhood, who appear to be quite willing to talk about their parents' divorce, need ample opportunities to do so in order to recognize and work through the feelings they are experiencing. Adolescents, who tend to be embarrassed and uncomfortable when their parents begin dating and perhaps openly showing their affection for others, need to practice a little discretion so that the adolescent will feel more comfortable with the new dating arrangement.

One of the major factors that affects children's self-esteem in negative ways and impedes their adjustment to divorce is interparental conflict. When parents continue to engage in bitter battles, children, at all age levels, feel unable to master the resulting stress and psychic pain. The ability of parents to handle differences in their relationship through appropriate conflict management and communication skills contributes to their children's well-being.

Conflict occurs to some extent in all marriages, yet most children do not develop emotional or behavioral problems; in fact, observing their parents resolve disagreements may even be beneficial for children. It is important to understand, then, the conditions under which marital conflict is likely to be harmful for children. Children's interpretation of the conflict is one factor. When children evaluate parental discord as an event that threatens their own security, they are likely to be adversely affected. Similarly, when children believe that they are responsible for the parental discord, it will significantly affect their behavior. Parental conflict is stressful to children when the topic of the parental argument is child-related. Disagreements about parenting strategies may be more problematic for children than those about non-childrearing issues such as finances. Parents who argue about non-childrearing issues but agree about childrearing are less likely to have children who are aggressive and who display behavior problems. Child-related conflict leads to greater fear of the child being drawn into the conflict and feelings of shame and self-blame. Marital conflict that is hostile or aggressive and poorly resolved is also destructive.

The greater the animosity between parents, the more likely parents will attempt to form an alliance with the child against the other parent. The higher the conflict between parents, the more children feel caught in that conflict. The extent to which a child feels caught between parents, practically and emotionally, may predict difficulty in adjusting to divorce. Feelings of being caught are related to higher levels of depression, anxiety, and more deviant behavior in children. Girls may be more vulnerable to feeling caught between parents than boys, because they are more concerned with maintaining harmonious interpersonal relationships and with resolving conflict in a harmonious way. If parents knew how devastating parental conflict is to children, they would, despite their anger and animosity, try to be more civil toward their ex-spouses.

While a good relationship with both parents is the optimal situation for children, a positive relationship with the mother has a particularly strong effect on children's self-esteem and overall adjustment. The quality of the relationship with the mother is a stronger indication of children's adjustment than that with the father. Because mothers are likely to spend more time with the child, it makes intuitive sense that disturbances in that relationship may be more destructive to the child.

In talking about divorce, the overriding tendency is to highlight the negative consequences of a family breakup. There are, however, some positive features. In the long term, children from divorced families frequently see themselves as more mature and sensitive and as having benefited from the extra responsibility they took on. Another advantage may be that the children and their custodial parent may develop a close and confiding relationship as they rely on each other for emotional and social support. Siblings can also become close. Divorce can also provide the impetus for growth in each of the separating parents. Among these benefits are, for women, the development of a satisfying career, which is usually associated with increased self-confidence and a sense of maturity. Men may become more emotionally sensitive to the needs of others.

## Single-Parent Families

Divorce involves that transition from a two-parent to a single-parent household. The number of single-parent households has more than doubled since 1970, and the majority of children in single-parent households (90 percent) live with their mothers. About three quarters of the single-parent households result from divorce or separation of married couples, although a growing minority are composed of never-married mothers and their children. The distribution varies according to race. Among whites, half of the single-parent families are a result of divorce, one fourth are a result of separation, and fewer than one tenth have never-married mothers. Among African-American single mothers, one third are never married, one third are separated, fewer than one fourth are divorced, and fewer than one tenth are widowed. Among Hispanic single mothers, one third are separated, fewer than three tenths are divorced, one fifth are never married, and fewer than one tenth are widowed. Thus, although the most frequent cause of single-parenting for whites is divorce, it is out-of-wedlock births for African Americans and marital separation for Hispanics. It is estimated that approximately 50 percent of the children born in the 1990s will experience their parents' separation or divorce and will spend an average of five years in a single-parent home before their custodial parent's remarriage.[21]

Some single-parent households are headed by unmarried mothers. There is a substantial rise in the number of births occurring to unmarried mothers. Approximately 14.5 percent of all white children and 60.1 percent (3 out of 5) of nonwhite children are born to unmarried mothers.[22] The incidence of marriage increases substantially with increasing age for women who were never married at the time of the child's birth: 19 percent in the 15–19 age group will marry; 42 percent in the 20–24 age group; 61 percent in the 25–29 age group; and 80 percent in the 35 and older age group.

Currently, of the 60.1 percent of African-American children who live in female-headed households, 70 percent are poor, compared with 24 percent of African-American children who live in two-parent families.[23] Furthermore, African-American children spend more time than white children in a single-parent family before making the transition to a two-parent family and are much more likely to remain in a single-parent family for the duration of childhood.

## Children's Adjustment

Because only one parent is present in the home, children from single-parent families have been thought to be at risk for problems. In the past, the common belief was that children from broken homes tended to have more academic, emotional, and behavioral problems. The single-parent household was assumed to be the cause of the child's low self-esteem, achievement problems, inappropriate gender-role behavior, and immaturity. A one-to-one causal relationship was assumed between single-parent lifestyles and all kinds of psychological problems found in children.

The major problem with the results of these early studies is that they failed to control for important variables, such as socioeconomic status, the custodial parent's access to social supports, the involvement of the noncustodial parent, or the relationship between the parents before and after the breakup. Research today is studying single-parent families while controlling for these important variables.

Despite the common misconception that in any group of disturbed children a large number of them will be from single-parent homes, research indicates that intervening variables play a more significant role in determining single parents' and their children's self-esteem and adjustment than the absence of one parent. Economic deprivation appears to be an important variable.

The greater the financial hardship following a family breakup, the harder the adjustments for all family members and the greater the adjustment problems shown by children. Parents who are preoccupied with family finances will find it harder to be attentive and responsive to their children. Children who suffer minimal loss of material resources and who are able to maintain predivorce routines do not show impairment in their cognitive, emotional, and social functioning.

If the change in the working status of the parent occurs soon after the breakup, this presents another change in routines for families. The total income of single-mother families with children, including sources such as public assistance, alimony, and child support, is considerably lower than for single-father families and two-parent families. The median annual income of single-mother families is about one-third that of two-parent families. Among those with children under 6 years of age, the income of single-mother families is about one-fourth that of two-parent families.[24] The average child in single-mother families lives in an economically disadvantaged environment relative to his or her counterpart in a married-couple family. Three out of every five Hispanic and African-American single mothers live below the poverty line due to the mother's low earning capacity, lack of support from the nonresidential father, and few benefits provided by the state. In addition to income insecurity and erratic work patterns, these stressed single mothers change residence more frequently, leading to less social integration and potential support from neighbors. Although relatives provide physical support, they also are likely to interfere with the mother's parenting role, leading to conflict that may increase her stress.

Moreover, economic variables appear to play an important role in determining children's social and academic achievement. When children from one-parent and two-parent homes in similar economic circumstances are compared, little difference is found in children's school performance and their social adjustment.[25] Thus, living with one parent may not necessarily be the most important factor that affects a child's development but, rather, the economic difficulties encountered by single parents. A combination of factors, not just the absence of a parent, may produce psychological problems in children.

## Parents' Adjustment

It may also take time for parents to adjust to a single-parenting situation. Parents tend to experience three stages following the actual divorce: aftermath, realignment, and stabilization.[26] In the aftermath period, which lasts for about two years, single parents tend to feel highly defensive, feel little control over life events, and feel less competent. Generally speaking, in the first two years following the divorce, custodial mothers make few demands on their children; they communicate with them less, show fewer signs of affection, and are inconsistent in their disciplining. This inconsistent disciplining takes the form of restrictive rules that are seldom enforced. The more stressed the custodial parent is in the aftermath of the breakup, the more inconsistent she is likely to be in setting and enforcing rules and the more antisocial children's behavior becomes. In the realignment stage, single parents tend to feel less defensive and undergo an "emotional divorce" in which they become more accepting of their situation. The last stage, stabilization, which occurs three to four years after divorce, is characterized by more positive attitudes about themselves, feelings of control, and an ability to develop more favorable attitudes toward remarriage.

Divorce can more generally provide women with new opportunities for personal growth. Many women have often operated in the traditional role of dependency in the marriage relationship. With the divorce, some women may experience a sense of powerlessness or helplessness. Some women, however, do not respond to divorce or separation with these feelings but, rather, take on a more active and instrumental role in their lives. They begin to look to themselves, not their ex-husbands, to define and implement new roles and careers. It is these women who, through their own instrumentality, experience a strong sense of independence, personal growth, competence, and high self-esteem. This newly found freedom and independence may cancel out some of the negative effects of divorce (less money, less free time, and more demands made on mother's time.)

## Conditions that Foster Children's Self-Esteem in Single-Parent Families

Single mothers and single fathers have similar as well as different hurdles to overcome. Mothers, more so than fathers, experience economic disadvantages, and it is this factor rather than the absence of the father that contributes to children's low self-esteem and adjustment difficulties. In addition, single mothers generally report being less happy than single fathers, which is generally attributed to economic factors. Men typically do not lose economic support, as is the case with many women. If mother does not have to worry incessantly about financial matters, she, in turn, is able to parent her children more effectively, and they, in turn, have higher self-esteem. The noncustodial father can help alleviate the mother's economic disadvantages and help her devote more of her energy to meeting her children's needs if he continues to support his children's mother financially.

The addition of new tasks that father may have previously taken care of are now added to the single mother's tasks. Taking care of the car, paying bills, and lawn chores, for example, may be a few of her new responsibilities. Some mothers, who may have looked to their spouses as controlling, disciplinarian figures, may have to develop a more authoritative stance when disciplining their children.

In single-parent families, there is one adult who has primary responsibility for keeping the family together, providing care, and maintaining order. Children's self-esteem is enhanced when single parents do not see this as a disadvantage but, rather, an advantage—this single line of authority is simpler and more streamlined than before. In single-parent families there is only one parent who now has dual roles: nurturing and managing, providing care and functioning in an executive capacity, giving leadership and promoting well-being, and fostering autonomy while encouraging interdependence. A basic threat to the successful functioning of a single-parent family is the deeply ingrained belief that these functions are, or must continue to be, gender-defined and differentiated. (Fathers carry out instrumental behavior and do masculine things with and for their children, and mothers are nurturing and do feminine things with and for their children.) The two roles can and must be integrated in the single-parent home.

Single mothers may experience greater social disadvantages than their spouses. For single custodial mothers who take care of the house and children, there isn't much time, and, in many cases, not much of an opportunity to be very active socially. Taking time for oneself is often overlooked by single parents, particularly single mothers. It *is* possible to find a few minutes each day and a few hours each weekend to devote to oneself. Whenever the schedule gets too busy, the first thing many single parents tend to do is omit self-indulgent activities. They simply don't have the time to exercise, take in a movie, or read a few chapters in a good book. The best way to be an effective parent is to take some time for oneself and engage in some type of activity that is enjoyable— this adds to the parent's mental health and, in turn, to the health of his or her children.

While single mothers' major concerns center on economic problems, single fathers tend to experience most of their difficulties in the emotional domain and in managing household tasks such as meal preparation. Some fathers may need to learn to relate to their children in a more sympathetic, warm, and nurturing way, which may take some time. Mastering domestic tasks, however, is accomplished relatively easily for most fathers. Some bring in outside help, some fathers enlist the aid of their children, and some become skilled domestic engineers through trial and error. The best transitions are made by fathers who have previously participated in childrearing and who have been actively engaged in household management chores before the divorce. There is nothing in the genes, however, that prevents fathers from becoming competent parents. Those who are motivated to do so become very skilled at their new custodial parent role.

In single-parent families, there is a greater expectation that everyone, including young children, needs to contribute to the maintenance and welfare of the family. A positive outcome of this is that children recognize that their family genuinely depends on them for their contributions to the family system. A wonderful thing for children's self-esteem is knowing that they are valued and needed, that they are continually growing by helping the family, and that they have the ability to be self-sufficient.

Both single mothers and fathers need to establish stable family routines. Some of these routines, however, may be somewhat different from those before the divorce—family members need to be flexible and open to change. Both spouses need to resolve their feelings of "failure"—the marriage may have failed, but this does not mean that the parent is a failure. Joining support groups such as Parents Without Partners may be helpful in rediscovering feelings of self-worth and forming new attitudes and behaviors as single parents. The attributes that lead to successful single parenting are the same attributes that are applicable to effective parenting in all types of families, namely, being empathetic, sympathetic, flexible, loving, and nurturing and, of course, maintaining a good sense of humor.

## Blended Families

Each year in the United States about one-half million children are directly affected by remarriage, adding to the 7 million stepchildren under 18. About 10 percent of children at any given point are living with a stepparent as well as one of their biological parents, but it is thought that 30 percent of children spend some part of their childhood living in this type of family.[27] Because mothers most frequently have custody of children, stepparent families are usually stepfather families. There are more than four times as many stepfather families as stepmother families. The composition of stepmother and stepfather families is somewhat different. For instance, families headed by a biological father and a stepmother are more likely to include boys than girls, whereas families headed by a biological mother and a stepfather have equal numbers of boys and girls.

Estimates show that 30 percent of remarriages do not involve children at all. Another 49 percent to 56 percent include children from one spouse's prior marriage, and 7 percent to 12 percent include children

from prior marriages of both spouses. Approximately 3 percent of remarriages are the most complex in that they involve the father's children, the mother's children, and children in common.[28]

The average age of children at the time of parental remarriage is 2
to 5 years for about one third of the children. Because about 60 percent
of remarriages eventually terminate (half of these do so within $5\frac{1}{2}$ years)
one can conclude that both adults and children will encounter a series
of changes in family structure within a brief period of time. By the time
a child reaches the teen years, he or she could have been part of an original, first-marriage family; then spent time in a single-parent household;
then resided in a stepfather family; and finally, live again in a single-parent household.

Stepfamilies cannot operate as traditional families—it takes more
flexibility and dedication. Approximately 75 percent of divorced mothers and 80 percent of divorced fathers remarry, and the divorce rate in
remarriages is about 50 percent higher for second marriages than for
first marriages. Thus, many children are exposed to a series of marital
transitions and household organizations following their parents' initial
separation and divorce.

## Frailties in Blended Families

Second marriages frequently falter and the most common cause of
difficulties is that the demands of parenting allow too little time for the
couple to get to know one another. As a result, parents tend to view the
marriage as less cohesive, more problematic, and more stressful than
do parents in first marriages.

There are several challenges that confront stepparents. A major
problem in remarriage situations appears to be difficulties with the children. Sometimes it is hard for children to adapt to the new situation,
which may make life difficult for the parents. For example, children may
have a special bond with the solo parent following the marital dissolution and feel betrayed when he or she remarries. If the parent marries
too soon, the child may not have had enough time to adjust to the divorce before having to adjust to the remarriage. Some children continue
to harbor wishes that their "real" parents will get together—a new marriage obviously undermines this possibility.

With remarriage the behavior of the custodial parent toward his or
her children changes. Mothers become warmer in their interaction with
their children and more consistent in their behavior but also more de-

manding of good and mature behavior from children. Stepmothers tend to experience intrapersonal conflict and have more feelings of anger, anxiety, and depression. Stepmothers experience an inordinate amount of such stress compared to mothers in other family structures.

The arrival of a stepmother may be particularly disruptive for boys who seem to be functioning in socially competent ways in father-custody families. The difficulties may be much more apparent in the interaction of the son with his father than with the stepmother. It may mean that the son now has less time to spend with his father and has to share his father with the stepmother and her children. Gaining a same-sex parental model may be more advantageous for girls.

It takes most stepfathers quite a while to become effectively involved with their stepchildren. Initially, they show little warmth and low involvement. They do not attempt to monitor the child's activities or control them and make fewer disciplinary demands. At the outset, stepfathers appear like polite strangers. Later, in an attempt to become more involved, they discuss things with children and grow relatively warm. Because the response of their stepchildren to such overtures is more often negative than positive and because stepchildren exhibit higher levels of problem behavior, it appears that many stepfathers eventually give up attempting to form a close relationship with stepchildren. Stepfathers who initially spent time establishing relations with stepsons by being warm and involved but not asserting parental authority may eventually be accepted by their stepsons. Acceptance of the stepfather by the stepdaughter, however, is uncorrelated with his behavior toward her and is more difficult to obtain.

Nevertheless, there is evidence that many stepfathers achieve better relationships more quickly than stepmothers with stepchildren of all ages.[29] Stepmothers have more difficulty with adolescent stepchildren but fewer problems with younger stepchildren, who need an authority figure to feel secure. One explanation might be that stepfathers play an important supportive role to the mother rather than a direct one with their children. Thus, stepfathers are less likely to be directly involved in demanding certain behaviors from their adolescents or in open conflict with them.

A stepfather has to adjust not only to having a mother for his children, but also to being a husband again. Stepfathers try to avoid, withdraw from, or deescalate conflict and try to conceal feelings in the face of acrimonious exchanges. Stepmothers tend to be more eager to confront and discuss problems and more willing to tolerate, provoke, or escalate conflicts.

Discipline is a thorny issue. Some children resent having a stepfather or stepmother telling them what to do. Both remarried mothers and fathers report poor family communication, less effective problem resolution, less consistency in setting rules, less effective discipline, and less family cohesion in the early months of remarriage than couples who are married for the first time. Experiences with hostile children may be so negative that they offset any pleasures that the couple may find in each other's company, swinging the balance against continuing the relationship. Causes of conflict often center on the children, their behavior, how to respond to them, and money spent on them.

## Creating Conditions that Foster Children's Self-Esteem in Blended Families

Children have to cope with developing a relationship with the stepparent and learn to share their custodial parent's attention with the stepparent. The children have to recognize that the custodial parent is a sexually active and desired figure. Moreover, children sometimes have to adjust to new step-siblings. With so many adjustments to make, children in blended families are likely to experience some adjustment problems.

Within the first five years of their parents' remarriage, stepchildren exhibit more behavioral problems than other groups of children, and this is true even when the children have good relationships with the stepparent. Younger children, however, appear able, eventually, to form an attachment with a competent stepparent and to accept the stepparent in the parenting role. Most younger children in supportive homes with "normal" conflict levels eventually accept a warm and caring stepparent. Developmental tasks facing adolescents, however, may make them especially vulnerable and unable to adapt to the transition of remarriage. In addition, because older children have more confidence and resources for fighting back, they may confront or question some aspects of family roles and functioning that younger children would not.

Do stepchildren differ from their counterparts in intact families? It appears that the entrance of a stepfather into a previously single-mother home has a positive effect on boys' cognitive and personality development.[30] The entry of a stepfather tends to trigger excitement, growth, and rapid attachment. (A similar process may occur for girls when a stepmother arrives in a previously single-father home.) As noted, girls in stepfather families, however, show more anxiety than girls in intact homes.

Whereas boys experience more pervasive problems in postdivorce adjustment, girls have more problems adjusting to remarriage. Girls, who often have close relationships with their custodial mothers and considerable independence, may find stepfathers disruptive and constraining and view them as intruders or competitors for their mothers' attention. Even two years into the marriage, girls still show unhappiness; mothers have less control over them, and conflict with daughters increases. Daughters become demanding, hostile, and coercive to both their mother and the stepfather. Thus, boys tend to show more pervasive effects of divorce (than girls) except in postdivorce family forms in which a stepparent is present. Boys benefit from remarriage, but most of the benefit comes from an improved relationship with the custodial parent and not from the new relationship with the stepparent.

Although mothers and stepfathers view sons as extremely difficult, the son's behavior improves over time. Boys whose mothers had been remarried for over two years show no more aggressive, noncompliant behavior in home and school than boys in intact families. Daughters tend to exhibit more demandingness, hostility, and coercion and less warmth toward both remarried mothers and stepfathers. While their behavior tends to improve, two years after the remarriage girls are still more antagonistic and disruptive with their parents than girls in two-parent families.[31]

One of the most difficult issues for stepchildren is loyalty conflicts. Some stepchildren feel guilty if they start to get close to their stepparent. Children adjust better to their stepparent and to having two homes if their biological parents refrain from fighting with each other. Parents can emphasize to their children that it takes time to feel comfortable in a stepfamily. They need to listen to children's concerns and make sure that they understand them correctly. Support for the spouse should be demonstrated in front of the children.

Support for the noncustodial biological parent is important to children's inner self-esteem as well. Loyalty conflicts between stepparents and biological parents can occur. When the biological parent is demeaned and considered unworthy by the new stepparents or by the other biological parent, stepchildren experience loyalty conflicts. Boys are better at maintaining good relationships with their stepmothers and their biological mothers. When they have contact with their mothers, girls tend to have worse relations with their stepmothers. Stepmothers are most readily accepted when the biological mother has died, or, if she is still alive, when children do not see her. The acceptance of the stepfather is not influenced by these considerations, reflecting his more peripheral role in most households.

A stepfather's income can reverse the economic slide that afflicts many divorced mothers and their children. Generally speaking, children in second marriages are as well off economically as children in first marriages. Second, the addition of a new parent helps relieve the demanding existence of single parents. Someone else is around to share the burden of housework and the supervision of the children. These factors are certainly beneficial to children and their future adjustments.

Stepparents quickly discover that they have been issued a limited license to parent. Some accept and even appreciate the limits, draw back, and disengage from their parenting role. Others feel rejected and insist on trying to extend their mandate. Children's self-esteem is enhanced when the stepparent does not make an active attempt to initiate, shape, and control children's behavior, but rather is supportive of the biological parent. Later, the stepparent may become more authoritative, which leads to constructive long-term outcomes. Stepparents who are authoritative in their parenting style appear to have fewer negative encounters with their stepchildren, and their relationships improve over time. In contrast, stepparents who use permissive or authoritarian styles have stepchildren who exhibit negative behavior that continues over time.

It has also been recommended that the biological parent should be in charge of setting and enforcing limits and in carrying out negative sanctions for his or her own children. This means that each spouse, in conjunction with his or her ex-spouse, takes primary responsibility for raising or disciplining his or her own biological children. It is a dangerous assumption to make that mothers should be responsible for disciplining children. Either father or his new wife or both of them may simply assume that she will be in charge of his children (as mothers are "supposed to be"). This results in endless resistance to that arrangement from the children and their mother. When the biological parent is not able to do so, he or she should make it clear to the children that the stepparent is in charge and needs to be obeyed. It is particularly important in blended families for the biological parent and stepparent to present a united front, at least in the initial stages of parenting. When a stepparent requests or presents an unpopular decision, stepchildren are likely to use this as a wedge between the parents and this becomes a constant source of friction. ("She's unfair; she's always picking on me" or "He doesn't care about me; I'm not his real son.") By being united, parents can insulate themselves from these attempts to separate them.

Creating conditions that foster children's self-esteem involves planning how to handle everyday practical problems, ranging from major issues such as finances to more minor concerns such as what to call the stepparent. (It's best not to introduce a new spouse as your child's new father or mother. This tends to put children off when first meeting the stepparent. Stepparents should make it clear that they do not intend to replace the biological parent.) As soon as possible, the couple should talk about division of labor and finances, how they will handle child discipline, and so on, so that they have a plan for coping with daily issues. Advanced planning helps to avoid misunderstanding. The more preliminary planning that is done, the smoother the transition will be. It's also helpful to schedule weekly family meetings to talk about the previous week and any problems or misunderstandings that may have occurred. Rotate leadership of the meeting among all family members.

Even when plans are carefully made questions will continue to arise, and stepparents need to address these questions, whenever applicable, with their children. Open communication is important in order to handle new problems or concerns. The issue of where to live, if there is a choice, may be one that needs to be discussed by both parents and children. To move or not to move is a difficult decision. Moving may mean that the children will have to change schools, which may be hard on them. Moreover, it may be financially better to stay in the same house rather than incur the expense of moving. The stepparent, however, may feel that he or she is trespassing on someone else's property and it may be better to move to a neutral area. Should the stepparents have their own baby? This decision is based on the needs and wishes of the parents. All issues need to be discussed between the parents, and children need to be included as well in decisions that involve them.

A new marriage is difficult enough without an instant family. So it is particularly important for the new couple to work on establishing a strong husband–wife bond. In first marriages, there is usually some time for spouses to establish a close relationship with each other; in blended families, there is no time. A serious problem in marriages, not just in blended-family marriages, is that relationships are sometimes taken for granted and very little time or effort is expended on nurturing the relationship. It's interesting to note that individuals who are trying to succeed at work or become better at tennis, for example, know that if they are to be successful they have to put in a lot of time and energy to achieve their goals. Many, however, spend very little time working, really working, on building a strong relationship with their spouse. Nurture and enrich the couple relationship by demonstrating affection, supporting each other's emotions, and spending time together. In good marriages, the couples are best friends; they know how to handle conflict; they can deal with negative emotions; there is trust; they share interests and have interests of their own that they pursue; they have fun together and are honest and flexible. The new couple needs to spend some time together without the children so that their relationship is solid enough to withstand the beginning adjustment period.

Similarly, relationships between parents and children need to be nurtured, and this enhances children's self-esteem. But in an instant family, these relationships have to be discovered and developed, which takes time and patience. Love is not essential, but respect and concern for each other are. Good relationships between stepparents and stepchildren are a result of perseverance, self-sacrifice, and hard work. While family activities can help to establish relationships between stepparents and stepchildren, it's also important to have individual time—time alone away from other family members. For this reason, a private and individual space, no matter how small, should be created in the home for each family member.

Conditions that foster children's self-esteem are created when cordial relations between ex-spouses are developed and maintained. When there are children involved, a complete separation from the ex-spouse is a rare occurrence so it may as well be a friendly relationship. It's best if one can make peace with an ex-spouse and resolve any residual feelings of loss, pain, or anger. Begin your own special family traditions. While keeping some of the family traditions that each spouse may bring to the new family is important, it is equally important to begin new family traditions that will help to bond members of the blended family.

The Stepfamily Association of America has noted that new stepfamilies may need several years to develop a smooth, acceptable life. While the road to a fully integrated stepfamily may be long, it is not impossible. Although there may be a temporary period of disruption and an increase in conflict and negativity between parents and children immediately following the remarriage, these aversive interactions diminish over time. Generally two years after the remarriage, few differences are found between the relationships of nondivorced parents and their children and the relationships of remarried parents. Successful blended families, once they have established rules, have an organized family life, and have agreed upon major and minor issues through careful planning, can concentrate on developing relationships that will contribute to the growth of the parents and the self-esteem of their children.

## Less Traditional Families

As noted, a decreasing number of American families fit the traditional definition of family. Fewer than 7 percent of families now reflect the two-parent, first-marriage model with husband as breadwinner and wife as homemaker.[32] Despite that, researchers have typically studied two-parent, white, middle-class families in which the father is engaged in outside employment and mother is a full-time homemaker. Prevalent beliefs hold that the traditional family constellation is normative and thus has an inherent superiority over other family patterns, which may be a questionable belief. Even if it were superior, reality does not mirror that standard. Given that the configurations of families have changed dramatically over the years, we need to study less traditional families, such as those with same-sex parents, teenage parents, parents with only one child, and adoptive parents.

### Same-Sex Parents

In the wake of increasing openness among lesbian and gay adults, a number of family forms are emerging in which one or more of a child's parents identifies themselves as gay or lesbian. Despite the fact that more homosexuals are "coming out," they still tend to be an invisible population, and accurate statistics are impossible to maintain. Because of the fear of discrimination, gay and lesbian parents conceal their sexual orientation; thus, the number of gay and lesbian parents is at best an approximation. Among homosexuals, fear of losing child custody or visitation rights if their sexual orientation were to be known is the major reason for concealing their sexual preference. The reluctance of the courts to grant custody or even visiting rights to lesbian mothers and gay fathers centers on the belief that children will become homosexuals if raised or influenced by homosexual parents and that children raised in homosexual households will be harassed by peers because of their parents' sexual preference.

Estimates of the number of lesbian mothers generally run from about 1 to 5 million. Estimates of the number of children of gay and lesbian parents range from 6 million to 14 million. Recent estimates hold that 5,000 to 10,000 lesbians have borne children after coming out.[33] The number of lesbians who are bearing children is also believed to be increasing. Whatever the precise figures, it is clear that the numbers of children of gay or lesbian parents are substantial.

Most of these families are composed of children who were born in the context of a heterosexual relationship between the biological parents. These include families in which the parents divorce when the husband or wife comes out as homosexual. Approximately one third of lesbians have been heterosexually married compared to one fifth of gay men. Custody of the children has been awarded to lesbian mothers, as long as the mother's homosexuality is not disclosed to the court. Both single and coupled lesbians are increasingly giving birth to children. The majority of such children are believed to be conceived through donor insemination. It is relatively recently that donor insemination with known or unknown sperm donors has become widely available to unmarried heterosexual women and to lesbians.

The lesbian woman's reasons for becoming pregnant, as opposed to adopting a child, include a desire to have her own child, the personal experience of giving birth, the difficulty of adopting, and the desire to raise a newborn. Regulations governing foster care and adoption in many states have made it difficult for lesbians and gay men to adopt children or serve as foster parents.

A number of gay men have also sought to become parents after coming out. Options pursued by these gay men include adoption and foster care of children to whom they are not biologically related. Through donor insemination or through sexual intercourse, gay men may also become biological fathers of children whom they intend to coparent with a single woman (whether lesbian or heterosexual), with a lesbian couple, or with a gay male partner.

## Conditions that Foster Children's Self-Esteem in Same-Sex Parent Homes

Homosexual parents can create conditions that foster their children's self-esteem by providing their children with opposite-sex role models, and it appears that they generally do. Fathers appear to make a more concerted effort than mothers, however. Lesbian mothers attempt to raise their children in nonsexist ways and to bring their children up without the constraints of traditional gender roles. Lesbian mothers, however, have more adult male family friends and include male relatives more often in their children's activities than heterosexual mothers.

A common concern is that children brought up by gay fathers and lesbian mothers will show disturbances in sexual identity. It is feared that children brought up by same-sex parents will themselves become gay or lesbian or be confused about gender-related sex roles when they are not provided with gender-differentiated models by parents. Studies have shown that about 8 percent of the offspring of homosexual parents are lesbian or gay in orientation,[34] a figure that is within expected percentages in the population at large. Thus, the myth that homosexuality is communicable has little support.

Moreover, most of these parents report that their children seem to be developing "normal" gender-role identification; they also report that they think their children are similar to other children of the same age and gender. Providing quality family interactions and relationships is important. Research seems to confirm that the home environments provided by gay and lesbian parents are as likely as those provided by heterosexual parents to support and enable children's psychological growth.[35] Parental sexual orientation may be less important in influencing children's self-esteem than variables such as quality of family interactions and relationships.

Children's self-esteem is enhanced when gay parents identify their sexual preference to their children. Fathers, for example, who have publicly identified themselves as gay tend to be less authoritative, use less corporal punishment, and experience stronger desires to rear children with nonsexist, egalitarian standards than closeted fathers.[36] Closeted fathers tend to spend less time with their children since looking for or maintaining homosexual liaisons takes time away from the family. Moreover, father–child interactions seem to be filled with tension and workaholism, which undermines children's self-esteem. In addition, closeted fathers tend to be more authoritarian and are more likely to use physical punishment when disciplining their children. Openly gay fathers place greater emphasis on nurturance of their children, describe themselves more positively as parents, place less emphasis on the economic provider role, and are less traditional in their overall attitudes about parenting than closeted gay fathers.

It appears that children who are informed of their parents' sexual preference are able to cope better than children whose parents have not disclosed their sexual preference. Children who are told of parental gay, lesbian, or bisexual identity in early childhood or late adolescence are more well adjusted and find the news easier to cope with than those who first learn of it during middle childhood or early adolescence. Early adolescence is a particularly difficult time for children to learn about a gay or lesbian parent.

It seems that most gay and lesbian parents do inform their children of their sexual preference. Only a small percentage of parents do not inform their children for various reasons. Many feel that the knowledge would damage the children, the children would not understand, and that their children would be rejected by other children. Young children informed of their parent's sexual identity have been taught by parents to accept social and personal variance in others. In some cases, children have been introduced to the subject of homosexuality through reading, informal discussions, and meeting family friends. Thus, they have learned to view the world in less prejudicial and conforming ways.

While research shows that most children do not feel stigmatized by having a lesbian or gay parent, it is true that some children with lesbian or gay parents may be stigmatized by their peers and may, on occasion, be embarrassed by having less traditional parents. To create conditions that foster children's self-esteem, parents should talk to their children's teachers to see how they are getting along with their classmates and if there are problems, they can discuss what may be done to help alleviate the teasing and taunting that their children may be experiencing.

## Parenting Only Children

While a growing number of families are currently having only one child, the norm in the United States is still 2.3 children per family. The presence of siblings has been presumed to be essential for a child to develop normally, and a child's position among his or her siblings has been thought to have profound effects on the child's future. Early research concluded that only children are not as healthy or vital as children with siblings; they do not do well academically (their success in school work is below average) or socially (their social relations are more frequently characterized by friction); and they compensate socially by forming imaginary friendships more often than do children with siblings. Based on these findings, it was concluded that "being an only child is a disease in itself." Recent research, however, has found that only children are similar to children with siblings in terms of adjustment and sociability.[37] In fact, in terms of achievement and intelligence, only children do better than children with siblings, particularly those children from large families.

## Myths about Only Children

There are several myths about only children that need to be clarified:

*Only children prefer more solitary, noncompetitive amusements because they are alone a great deal of the time.* Some only children would actually rather read, engage in a favorite hobby, or listen to music. These interests tend to arise from the parents' values and the home environment of middle- or upper-middle-class families, which are more likely to have only children.

*Only children are antisocial and, therefore, lonely.* Only children, today, are hardly lonely. Current research on only children paints a picture of a child who is highly active in clubs and extracurricular activities.[38]

*Only children are four-eyed intellectuals and eccentric child prodigies.* Only children do have higher academic skills and a higher need to achieve. Only children, however, are not exclusively bookworms.

*Only children are spoiled.* While it may be true that only children may have more access to the latest toys and computers and that their parents may take them to several interesting places, most only children are not self-centered, egotistical, or manipulative, that is, "spoiled."

*Only children become too mature, too quickly.* It does appear to be true that only children seem more grown up than their peers who have siblings. The reason for this is that only children tend to spend a lot more time with adults; children with siblings relate and talk with their peers rather than their parents. Secondly, the only child's primary role models tend to be his or her parents, not other children. For these reasons, only children tend to be more mature than children with siblings.

## Conditions that Foster the Only Child's Self-Esteem

The conditions that promote healthy self-esteem for only children are quite similar to those that are recommended to parents with more than one child, namely, a balance between receiving and giving and teaching the child to share and respect others; setting boundaries that define acceptable behaviors, and not doing for the child what she can do for herself. A few suggestions, however, may be particularly meaningful to parents with only children.

Parents of only children may put too much psychic energy in raising their only child, and thus, parents need to be aware of intensity; the parents' and the child's lives can become too intertwined. Parents need to set aside time for themselves. A healthy balance of involving yourself with your child and disengaging yourself from your child's life, of spending time with your child and having time alone, of fostering independence and freedom of expression and adhering to the rules, is particularly vital for successful rearing of only children.

Parents of only children may have more resources available and may shower their children with material things. If the child receives too much for too long, eventually he or she will demand his or her anticipated rewards, and parents will have the stereotype of the impatient, spoiled only child. Parents need to teach their child that he or she is not exempt from caring and making contributions to the family.

Parents may have extremely high expectations for their only child and subsequently may exert too much pressure on the child to meet these expectations. Watch for danger signals that indicate the pressure is too great—not doing well in school or not wanting to play with others, for example. That extra push that parents may think is helping their child may be counterproductive.

Finally, the likelihood of a child ruling the roost is far greater when there are no siblings. Rebellion against the parents is one of the most obvious indications that the child is trying to seek control. Parents need to set boundaries for their child. In an atmosphere of love and warmth, they need to communicate that they are the ones running the show, not the child.

## Adoptive Parents

Adoptive parents undergo the same experiences as biological parents; they experience the same happiness, contentment, difficulties, and disappointments; have hopes and dreams for their adoptive children; worry when they get sick; and want them to succeed in life as much as biological parents do.

The principal reason that leads couples to become adoptive parents is infertility. It is interesting to note, however, that approximately 8 percent to 14 percent of adoptive parents have biological children of their own after adopting a child.

A variety of experiences related to parenthood are unique for adoptive parents. These include evaluation by a social agency, court, or other authorities within the United States or overseas with the power to deny them the opportunity to be parents; in most cases, they do not have the experience of a completed pregnancy and live birth and they do not have control over when the child will come into the family. In addition, adoptive parents must go through a trial period before court finalization, during which time the child may be removed from the adoptive parents. And, finally, they must contend with the stigma of adoption and respond to some of the unique aspects of raising an adopted child. All of these are thought, by some, to add to the conflicts and problems associated with being adoptive parents.

## Conditions that Foster Adopted Children's Self-Esteem

Conditions that contribute to adoptive children's self-esteem are marital stability; a degree of warmth, empathy, and security; tolerance of differences; flexible roles and rules; an open communication system; acceptance of the child and his or her membership in the family; being open and receptive to seeking and accepting support and help from outside postadoption support services; and accepting the adopted child's family of origin, background, and past links.

Ambivalence of adoption is resolved when the child, if older, emotionally separates from the biological parents after mourning their loss, frees himself from the self-accusation that he was a bad person and that is why he was not wanted, and adopts the adoptive family. It is at this point that the adoptive parents may also feel more secure and confident about their parenting capabilities and the love of the adopted child. Adoptive parents should be reassured by research findings that adoptive children, even when they meet their biological parents, nearly always return and choose the adoptive family as their true family.

If adopted children display somewhat more emotional problems in early adolescence it may be related to the fact that this is the stage when they are beginning to grasp and integrate their adoptive status. No significant differences between adopted and nonadopted children on overall measures of identity and adjustment have been found. Similarly, there is no evidence that adoptees are more prone to psychological disorders compared to the rest of the population. Adoptees and their adoptive parents tend to be more satisfied when they are able to perceive or imagine likeness between them; the major cause of their dissatisfaction is an absence of this link and the child's failure to acquire the family's value system.

Children's satisfaction with adoption is optimized if they are under 10 years of age at the time of placement and do not exhibit behaviors that are too problematic; form an attachment to their new family within the first 15 months or so; receive information about their origins and circumstances of adoption; have not been subject to physical or sexual abuse; and, if old enough, have been well prepared before placement.

Earlier laws cloaked adoption in security and mystery. These laws were partly aimed at protecting single parents and their offspring from the stigma of unwanted parenthood and illegitimacy and ensuring that natural parents would not interfere in the relationship between the child and his adoptive family. It is now recognized that although this practice may have served the needs of the adoptive parents and birth parents, it does not necessarily serve the needs of the adoptee. Uncertainty about one's origins is assuming more importance now compared to the past. Because of the diversity of lifestyles and different methods of "conception" an increasing number of children are now being reared in families where one or both parents are not biological parents. For those children, clarity about their past and the circumstances of birth will be important for their sense of well-being. Accessibility to both sets of parents would clearly help to diminish the destructive aspects of an adopted child's split loyalties.

Today, the meaning and importance to all children and adults of their genealogy and circumstances of upbringing are recognized. The sharing, in a positive way, of genealogical information is now seen as a step that promotes a sense of identity, aids in personality development, and satisfies curiosity. Truth about backgrounds and the sharing of information does not undermine relationships with parents or substitute parents; on the contrary, it seems to strengthen and cement them. People who matter most to children are those who care for them and not necessarily those who gave birth to them—blood is not always thicker than water. The truth helps them know who they are and where they stand.

The less people know about their ancestry, the more likely it is that they will want to seek out this information. Continued ignorance of vital information about one's background or the sudden discovery in adult life that one is not the child of people one had come to look upon as "parents" can be extremely distressing. The term "genealogical bewilderment" is used to convey the distress displayed by people who are ignorant or confused about their origins.

Most experts recommend that children should be told of their adoptive status between the ages of 4 and 7 years. It is up to the adoptive parents to take the initiative and explain things to the child without waiting for the child to ask. It is not surprising that some parents would like to protect adopted children from the harsh reality of having been unwanted by not telling the child or postponing the revelation until the child is in late middle childhood or adolescence. Most mental health professionals and adoption experts do not agree with this approach. Between the ages of 4 and 7, children are able to comprehend, in simple terms, that they are adopted. They are able to understand that their biological parents were not able to care for them but that they still loved them. Telling the child that he was unwanted by the biological parents only breeds feelings of anger, resentment, and rejection. It's best to tell them that their biological parents loved them so much that they wanted to make sure that they had a good home—a better home and circumstances than they could offer at the time the child was born.

## Summary

There are several conditions that are important in helping children develop positive evaluations of themselves in divorce situations. Telling the child about the divorce; having both parents explain the impending situation in terms that children can understand; not giving them too much responsibility, independence, and decision-making power; not quarreling with or demeaning the ex-spouse; maintaining a good relationship with the child; and receiving social support from family and friends are some of the conditions that enable children to develop competent behaviors that foster inner self-esteem.

Children's inner self-esteem is stronger in single-parent families when the custodial parent does not feel intensely guilty and blame all the child's problems on their being raised in a single-parent family. It isn't the absence of a parent (usually the father) that contributes primarily to lower self-esteem and lower adjustment levels in children of single-parent families but, rather, economic deprivation and the resultant problems. For this reason, it is important for the father to continue to give the custodial mother child support. In this way, the mother, now less preoccupied with family finances, will find it easier to create an environment that optimizes children's inner self-esteem. Children's self-esteem is fostered when the single parent sees the advantage of his or her single-parent role. This single line of authority is simpler and more streamlined. Finally, the notion that only fathers can be instrumental, only mothers can be nurturing, and that children need both parents in order to fulfill these roles is simply not true. The two roles can and must be integrated in the single-parent home.

Creating conditions that promote children's inner self-esteem in blended families involves planning ahead of time how everyday problems from division of labor to finances to disciplining strategies will be handled. It's best when the biological parent is the disciplinarian. It's important for the new couple to have time together so that their relationship is solid enough to withstand the beginning adjustment period (generally two years after the remarriage). Children's self-esteem is enhanced when they are not involved in loyalty conflicts between biological parents and stepparents.

Less traditional parents, such as same-sex parents, can help their children feel good about themselves when they provide their children with role models of the parent's opposite sex, when they disclose their sexual preference to their children, when they are warm and loving with their children, and when they receive help for children who might be stigmatized by other children.

Parents of only children can promote healthy self-esteem in their children by not becoming too enmeshed in their child's life, not giving material things to an excess, having appropriate expectations for their child, setting boundaries and firm but fair rules for their child to follow, and creating an atmosphere of love and acceptance. Adopted children's self-esteem is strengthened when they are adopted before the age of 10, when they are told about their adoption in a positive way, when they are helped to integrate their adoptive status, and when they receive information about their origins and the circumstances of their adoption.

# CHAPTER 9  Mothers in the Work Force

Just a generation ago experts would more than likely have recommended that a woman contemplating work outside the home should consider the answers to these questions: Will my working result in a happy child, a satisfied husband, a good home life, and a better community? Or, will my working cause my youngster to feel deprived of a normal, happy childhood or my husband to feel he is an inadequate provider? Because of my decision to work, will the community eventually have to deal with a broken home or a potentially delinquent child? Three decades ago, the working mother, especially one with younger children, was considered selfishly derelict in her maternal responsibilities, and her husband was considered an inadequate provider and weak, because he "permitted" her to go to work.

Current attitudes toward maternal employment are more accepting. For example, although society has long recognized the importance of work as a validating activity for men, evidence suggests that it is now becoming increasingly significant for women as well. Studies of employed mothers have shown that they express higher levels of self-esteem, competence, and a general satisfaction with life than mothers not engaged in paid employment.[1]

Employment is strongly associated with women's increased sense of accomplishment, independence, and self-esteem. This is especially true for professional women in better-paying jobs. Working in outside paid employment can provide women with additional opportunities to experience agency (self-direction and independence) and communion (collaborative ties with others). Further, women who have developed a sense of independence, mastery, and self-esteem at work may carry over these feelings into their homes, which, in turn, enhances their children's self-esteem.

At the same time, mothers' employment has presented special challenges and concerns for both women and men and for society at large. The special challenges and problems faced by employed women include multiple roles. Working mothers, in addition to their responsibilities at work, are also involved in childrearing responsibilities and domestic chores, which can lead to role conflict and role overload. Some women may believe in deeply rooted cultural values, which, for the most part, still maintain that women retain almost total responsibility for the care and rearing of their children, despite their employment status, financial necessity, or personal preference.

Other potential negative effects for mothers who are engaged in outside paid employment include the possibility that they have less time to monitor their children's behavior, which may increase the risk of negative peer influences. Children in families with mothers who stay home tend to perceive their mothers as having greater control than children in families with employed mothers.[2]

Going back to work is much more complicated than signing a W-2 form. There are several problems faced by dual-career families. There is a scarcity of time for relaxing, socializing, intimacy with spouse, and interaction with children. There is the financial stress of having to pay for and find supplemental child care. Working mothers can expect to pay $80 to $100 per week for full-time day care on a national average.

An urban single mother of two preschoolers must earn about $20,000 to cover expenses such as day care, taxes, transportation, and clothing. The Current Population Survey, conducted annually by the U.S. Bureau of the Census, reports that 8.7 million women with children under the age of 6 who are employed full-time year-round earn median incomes of $20,553. Approximately 3.2 million female heads of household, however, earn less than $20,000. For example, the average earnings for married women with children under 6 years who are working full-time total $12,160. Such women earn less than married women with older children ($13,070); in contrast, mothers with no children below the age of 18 earn an average of $14,260. The overall earnings of married women with young children are the lowest of all married workers, reflecting not only the general wage gap but also the effect of age and lack of education and skills on the dismal economic circumstances of this group.[3]

While the media may give women the impression that they are liberated souls, the research on women indicates that educationally and occupationally, women have a long way to go. Although stereotypic conceptions of men and women have been gradually crumbling over the years, they are by no means gone. Most female workers remain segregated in relatively low-status, low-paying, female-dominated occupations—so-called pink-collar jobs.

A survey of the federal government's *Dictionary of Occupational Titles*, which rates the complexity of tasks in some 30,000 jobs (which also influences many public and private compensation plans), ranks foster mother, nursery school teacher, and practical nurse in the lowest category—all of these occupations are ranked below and considered to be less demanding than that of a parking lot attendant. Employed women are far more likely than men to be administrative support workers (a category that includes clerical workers) and service workers; in fact, almost half of all women (46 percent) can be found in jobs in these broad occupational groupings. Nonetheless, the occupational distribution of female workers has been changing. Just under 11 percent of all women are now in managerial positions, more than double the percentage in 1972. Women in the 1990s are also slightly more likely to be professionals than women in the 1970s.

Some improvements have been made in formerly male-dominated professions such as law, medicine, and management, where women's representation ranged between 3 percent and 14 percent in the early 1960s and has increased to levels of 20 percent to 40 percent in the 1990s.[4] However, while female lawyers in the mid-1990s comprised 25 percent of all associates, only 6 percent of female attorneys are partners in law firms.

Similarly, women have a much higher representation in the teaching profession than men but only one quarter of all school principals and superintendents are women. According to the Census Bureau, there are 2.9 million women-owned businesses in the United States. In business, it is still unusual to see women in the bastions of financial power. Only 1.7 percent of the executives in the top 500 American companies are women. Most wealthy women in our country acquire their money by marrying it or inheriting it, not by earning it.

In terms of salary, what is a woman worth? Among full-time workers, the average female college graduate still earns less than the average white male with a high school diploma. Given the low wages of women, it has been economically rational for working couples to give priority to the husband's career, relocate in accordance with the husband's job prospects, and assign a disproportionate share of domestic obligations to women.

Characteristics such as education and experience cannot account for more than half of current gender disparities in earnings. On the whole, women who make comparable investments in time, preparation, and experience still advance less far and less quickly than men do. Although women have made substantial inroads in a number of male-dominated occupations, it has been estimated that at current rates it would take between 75 and 100 years to achieve complete occupational integration in the work force.[5]

On the positive side, a working mother and a father who helps with childrearing may provide more effective role models and socialize their children in ways that emulate their parents' nonstereotypic behaviors. Not long ago, the socialization experiences of boys and girls reflected the expectation that girls would spend most of their adult lives as mothers and boys would be breadwinners. The fact that children of employed mothers tend to be more egalitarian and less stereotyped in their gender-role concepts would have been interpreted as an adverse effect of maternal employment—not so today.

## Prevalence of Working Mothers

It needs to be mentioned that *all* mothers work. The labels "at-home mothers" and "working mothers" are not meant to imply that mothers who choose to remain at home do not work. The labels are meant to differentiate between mothers who are full-time homemakers and mothers who are homemakers and engage in employment outside the home. When a woman combines motherhood and employment, she faces a difficult task. Although mothers who stay at home and care for their children are supported by the dominant culture, they may also be challenged. While we give lip service to the important role that mothers play in raising competent, well-adjusted children, in actuality, some in our culture may demean this role—apparent in remarks such as "She's only a housewife!" Similarly, working mothers must confront the dilemma of integrating two seemingly contradictory tasks—working outside and inside the home.

The rate of working mothers has steadily increased among women of all ages. The current rate of maternal employment for two-parent families with school-age children is 73 percent.[6] This rate increases modestly each year. In the early 1970s, mothers typically waited until their children were in school to return to paid employment. In contrast, in the 1990s, 57 percent of married mothers of infants and preschoolers are employed outside the home. Employment figures for single mothers is even higher: 84 percent of single mothers of school-age children and 70 percent of single mothers of children under the age of 6 are employed outside the home.[7]

The most impressive recent change in maternal employment rates has been among mothers of infants and preschool children. Employed mothers of infants under 1 year of age represent the fastest growing subgroup, escalating from 31 percent of all women with infants under 1 year in 1976 to 52 percent in 1990.[8] In the United States, there are roughly 20 million children under the age of 16 whose mothers are in the labor force.

Assuming that the present labor force trends continue, it is predicted that by 1997, two thirds of all preschool children and three fourths or more of all school-age children will have mothers in the work force.[9] That is, 15 million infants and preschoolers and 34 million school-age children will have mothers who work outside the home.

## Why Mothers Work

Why are so many women engaged in paid outside employment? Thirty years ago, most women could assume they would marry for life, that their husbands would support them economically, that male employers would deny them upward mobility in male-dominated fields, and that men would support feminine domesticity and aggressively oppose other alternatives. Women, and men, face a different situation today. A changing structure of gender relationships is slowly eroding the structural supports for feminine domesticity and uncontested male dominance.

The decline in the stability of heterosexual partnerships, rising divorce rates, separation, cohabitation, postponed marriage, and even permanent singlehood means that a growing proportion of women find themselves outside the permanent, legal structure of marriage. This change represents a chance for increased economic independence outside of a traditional marriage.

Moreover, there is a decline in the ability of a single breadwinner to support an entire family, making it necessary for women to bring home a paycheck upon which the family depends. Most women in the labor force work primarily because the family needs the money and secondarily for their personal self-actualization.[10] Although sizable earnings disparities exist between males and females, working wives bring increased economic power to their families. Although significant barriers to workplace equality remain, employers can no longer blatantly discriminate with impunity against women workers.

## Effects of Mother Working on Infants and Toddlers

Not surprisingly, with the increased number of women working outside the home, a substantial number of children need supplemental care.[11] Of the 10.5 million children of working mothers, 37 percent are cared for in someone else's home by relatives or nonrelatives; 31 percent are cared for in their own homes by relatives or nonrelatives; 23 percent are in day-care centers or preschools; and 8 percent are cared for by their mothers while they work at home.[12] Approximately 13 percent of the infants of employed mothers are cared for by nonrelatives, while 7 percent attend day-care centers.

As infants of women who are employed full-time move into toddlerhood, there is a 15 percent decline in care by relatives, with a corresponding increase in reliance on other types of care, generally day-care centers.[13] For infants of mothers employed part-time the trend is different. There is a 33 percent increase in the proportion of care provided by relatives and a 10 percent decrease in the proportion of care provided by nonrelatives.

Fathers provide the care for about one third of the preschool children who are cared for by their relatives. Usually these working mothers and fathers work different shifts allowing one parent to always be home with the child. Use of organized child-care facilities (nursery schools, day-care centers) by employed mothers, however, has increased substantially and sharply from 16 percent in 1983 to 23 percent in 1988. According to the U.S. Bureau of the Census, only 24 percent of all preschool children can be accommodated in approved facilities. Socioeconomic status and child-care arrangements are closely related. Poor parents cannot afford high-quality programs and tend to use either low-quality care or informal arrangements with nontrained persons.

Current research is focusing on the association between infants' participation in day care and the quality of the infant–parent attachment. An infant's attachment to the mother emerges at approximately 7 months of age, its quality being a product of the preceding months of interaction. It is widely held that forming secure physical and emotional bonds of attachment between the infant and principal caregiver are vital to children's healthy adjustment and positive self-esteem. The results of studies addressing the short- and long-term effects of the mother working full-time and subsequent full-time day care on the infant have been unclear enough to allow varied interpretations.

The major index used to assess the infant's attachment to his or her mother is known as the Strange Situation Test. This test, as noted earlier, is a structured observation involving a mother and her infant entering a small room. The mother interests the infant in some toys and allows him or her to explore or play freely. This is followed by a series of 3-minute periods of separations and reunions. First, an unfamiliar adult enters the room, talks to the mother, and interacts with the infant. Then, the mother leaves the room, often resulting in a distressed infant. In a short while, mother returns, and once again the infant's reaction to mother returning is observed.

Some investigators find a higher incidence of insecurely attached infants among those mothers who are employed and whose infants are in full-time day care. In examining the results of several attachment studies, Jay Belsky finds that infants in full-time day care are more likely to have insecure attachment bonds than infants in part-time day care and infants who remain at home with their mothers. According to Belsky, "a strong and reliable association exists between extensive nonmaternal care in the first year of life and an elevated risk of insecure infant–mother attachment."[14]

This statement has provoked a number of rebuttals. Alison Clarke-Stewart from the University of California at Irvine has concluded that there is insufficient evidence to support Belsky's claim.[15] She criticizes the selection of studies upon which Belsky bases his conclusion and suggests that a more comprehensive assessment can be made. Clarke-Stewart finds less dramatic differences than those reported by Belsky; 38 percent of the infants in full-time day care are classified as insecure compared with 29 percent of the infants whose mothers are employed part-time or are not employed. While acknowledging an elevated "risk" of insecure attachment among infants in day care, Clarke-Stewart emphasizes the need to explore a variety of factors that may explain these differences in attachment classifications.

In another attempt to clarify this controversy, the same data were reexamined by a different team of investigators.[16] The reanalysis yields no evidence that day-care enrollment systematically affects the quality or security of infant–parent attachment. The rates of secure attachment for children younger than 15 months and older than 15 months in day care are 66 percent and 58 percent, respectively; rates for children in the exclusive care of their parents are 72 percent and 67 percent. These are not significantly different.

Recently, University of Miami's Tiffany Field observed infants, toddlers, and preschoolers before, during, and after separations from their mothers.[17] Her data indicate that children in her study seem to adapt to repeated separations; that is, they no longer exhibited stressful reactions to mother leaving, which lends support to the suggestion that the Strange Situation Test may not produce anxiety in children whose mothers work and who may be more accustomed to separations from their mothers.

Belsky does not agree with the propositions advanced by Field and Clarke-Stewart. He found that infants with extensive day-care experience whimpered, fussed, and cried more and engaged in object play less in each reunion episode than their counterparts with little or no day-care experience. Consequently, Belsky concludes that it is untenable that infants of working mothers with extensive day care are less stressed by separations from their mothers during the Strange Situation Test than are infants who are reared at home by their mothers.[18]

Overall, the research yields little conclusive evidence that infant day care sharply affects the security of infant–parent attachment as assessed using the Strange Situation Test, which suggests that other factors may explain these differences in attachment classifications. There is some evidence that variables like role strain, mother's feelings of guilt, and maternal separation anxiety may be important variables that may have a stronger effect than day care on the attachment between mother and infant.

## Role Strain

Role strain occurs when the mother feels overwhelmed by the amount of responsibilities and the limited time in which she has to accomplish all that is expected of her. There is some indication that role strain may adversely affect the parenting practices of employed mothers. For example, mothers with higher role strain set more limits on their children's behavior than mothers with less role strain.

The number of hours a woman works may contribute to role strain. Belsky found that only infants of mothers who work more than 20 hours a week are at increased risk for developing insecure attachment.[19] Part-time employment at less than 20 hours a week had no such detrimental correlates. Mothers who work 35 hours or more per week give the least enthusiastic description of their children. Part-time mothers who are working 5 to 34 hours describe their children more positively—more positively, in fact, than at-home mothers. Full-time maternal employment during the early months may be a stress, which when combined with other stressors, leads to role strain and subsequently affects the mother–infant relationship.

## Mother's Guilt

Maternal guilt may also be an important mediator of the effects of maternal employment. Working mothers may feel guilty for leaving the children, more so perhaps, for leaving infants and toddlers. Infants displaying more conflict in reunions, for example, are more likely to have employed mothers who believe that infants deserve exclusive maternal care.

Guilt is often experienced throughout an entire pregnancy; many women feel that anything that goes wrong is entirely their fault and these guilt feelings may continue after the child is born. For some mothers, any problem the child may encounter may be, in some measure, linked to mother working. Thus, while guilt is something all mothers seem to share, working mothers may experience more.

## Maternal Separation Anxiety

Maternal separation anxiety is defined as an unpleasant emotional state reflecting a mother's apprehensions about leaving her child. A mother's expressions of maternal separation anxiety include feelings of sadness, worry, or uneasiness about being away from her child. The degree to which the mother experiences anxiety about separation from her child has implications for both the child's emotional development and the mother's mental health. The traditional cultural belief that a woman's place is in the home still seems prevalent enough to instill doubts in the minds of mothers in our culture who return to work. These mothers who experience doubts about their working may feel inadequate as a mother, which, in turn, influences the quality of childrearing or interferes with the mother's relationship with her child. Each mother who considers employment outside the home must also consider her own feelings about separation from her infant and her beliefs about how nonmaternal care will affect her child.

Women who are employed, but prefer to stay home, show significantly more maternal separation anxiety (evidenced by symptoms of depression and higher levels of stress) than mothers who want to be employed and are.[20] Mothers who have a strong investment in motherhood, but prefer to be employed, exhibit less apprehension about separating from their infants and leaving their infants with alternative caregivers. These women believe that their children will not be negatively affected by separation and have less intense concern about leaving their infants. Women who work and desire to work may have achieved a psychological balance between their own needs and their infant's needs that allows them to act without guilt and anxiety.

The overwhelming impression of attachment studies is that maternal employment and full-time infant day care may not be such robust variables that they can be related to mother–child attachment. As one researcher states, "The distance between maternal employment and subsequent day care for her child and a child's attachment classification is too great to be covered in a single leap."[21]

## Effects of Mother Working on Preschoolers

The available evidence indicates that for middle-class preschool children, day care has neither beneficial nor adverse effects on intellectual development (as measured by standardized tests). For economically disadvantaged children, however, day care may have positive effects. Children from lower-class families who are in day care perform significantly better than youngsters from lower-class families who remain at home. Moreover, when the intellectual levels of these children are assessed semiannually, day-care children continue to outscore home-reared children.[22] Thus, quality day care helps prevent the decline in intellectual performance typically observed in socioeconomically disadvantaged families, and quality day care positively affects the overall preschool cognitive level of socioeconomically disadvantaged children.

Clarke-Stewart studied 2- to 4-year-old children from a mixture of socioeconomic backgrounds and a variety of care arrangements, including being at home with parents or babysitters, day-care centers, nursery schools, and day-care homes.[23] The children were tested on various measures of intellectual competence such as remembering numbers, identifying photographs of objects, using play materials, solving problems, and copying designs. On all these measures of intellectual competence, a clear difference was found between lower-class children in home care (with parent, sitter, or home day-care provider) and lower-class children in center care (nursery school, day-care centers), favoring those in center care. This occurred for both boys and girls from the lower classes, after as little as six months in day care, thus giving support to the results of previous research.

In terms of children's social development, day care has both positive and negative effects. On the positive side, children who have experienced day care are more peer-oriented than home-reared children. Full-day preschool children, for example, interact more with their peers and display more prosocial behavior than half-day preschool children. On the negative side, however, these children also display more aggressive and acting-out behaviors. Increased interaction may provide greater opportunities for conflict, leading to more aggressive behaviors.

Children with extensive day-care experience tend to be less cooperative with adults, more active, and somewhat more aggressive toward their teachers. Children with intensive child-care experiences since infancy are, as toddlers, rated by teachers and parents as having poor peer relationships, work habits, and emotional health and as being more difficult to discipline.

## Effects of Mother Working on Older Children

Research on the effects of mother's employment on school-age children and adolescents presents a fairly consistent finding that daughters of working mothers are higher achievers than daughters of nonworking mothers and show more positive adjustment on several indexes.[24] Sons of working mothers, as with daughters, are less stereotyped in their view of what each gender is like; they see women as more competent than do sons of nonworking mothers, and they see men as warmer.

There is some evidence suggesting that the effects of maternal employment differ according to the sex of the child. Detrimental effects of maternal employment occur for middle-class boys, whereas positive effects are seen for girls. It is possible that differences in the behavior of employed mothers toward sons and daughters might account for these differences.

Maternal employment may have more positive effects on girls than boys because boys tend to be more physical. Many boys "test" mother's patience regardless of whether mother is at home or working outside the home. At the end of a long day, working mothers, however, may not be flexible and patient enough to deal with their sons' energetic and non-compliant behavior.

During early and middle childhood, full-time working mothers tend to give less enthusiastic descriptions of their sons than their daughters. Research indicates that parental behavior and attitudes may be less favorable toward boys than girls in families with employed mothers, whereas the opposite pattern may be seen in families with nonemployed mothers. Russian psychologist Urie Bronfenbrenner and his colleagues found, for example, that in families in which the mother works, daughters get more attention than sons and are described very positively by their mothers.[25] Their sons are described in less positive terms. The most positive pictures are given for daughters of mothers employed full-time. The opposite pattern is found for nonemployed mothers. This is a rather different picture from the traditional favoring of sons that is found in homes where mother does not work.

Very few studies of maternal employment during adolescence have found negative effects, and most have found positive ones. Daughters of working mothers tend to be more outgoing, independent, active, and highly motivated and appear better adjusted on social and personality measures. Both sons and daughters of working mothers show competent social behavior, have a strong sense of self-esteem, and have good family relations and interpersonal relations at school.[26]

## Creating Conditions that Enhance Self-Esteem of Infants and Toddlers of Working Mothers

Contrary to the mixed results on the effects of day care on children's social development in the United States, Swedish children who enter day care as infants (prior to their second birthday) are more socially competent (more cooperative, more persistent, more independent) than late-entry (after age 2) and home-reared children.[27] These socially competent ways of behaving are very stable. When these children were studied again at age 13, for example, those who entered day care prior to their second birthday were again rated as being the highest in social competence compared to home-reared or late-entry children. The cognitive effects of day care in Sweden have also been examined. It appears that children who enter day care before age 2 are, at ages 8 and 13, more cognitively competent (perform better on verbal tests and in school subjects) than late-entry day care children and home-reared children.[28]

In support of these conclusions, researcher Carolee Howes studied the effects of early entry (before first birthday) and late entry (enrolled between 12 and 48 months) and high-quality and low-quality day care on children's subsequent social and cognitive development during kindergarten on a group of American children.[29] She found that those children who enter low-quality child-care centers as infants have the most difficulties with peers as kindergartners and are rated by their teachers as more distractable and less task-oriented. Those children who enter high-quality child-care centers as infants (early entry), however, do not appear different from home-reared children. These data suggest that children who enter day care as infants are not disadvantaged if they are enrolled in high-quality day-care centers.

Similarly, when preschoolers who start high-quality day care within the first six months of life are compared with preschoolers who start later (but still in the infancy period), no differences in attachment behavior is found. Interestingly, the children with more months of day-care experience are more socially interactive with their peers. Teachers and parents give those children who receive more quality infant day care higher ratings than children who do not attend day care on self-esteem, emotional well-being, attractiveness, and assertiveness.[30]

Thus, there appears to be a growing consensus that the quality of day-care programs is a salient factor in influencing children's adjustment. It appears also that the high quality of Swedish day care accounts for the differences found in social development cross-culturally. Analysis of the current research on day care in the United States also suggests that the amount of day care and age of entry may not be as important to children's social and cognitive competence as the *quality* of day care.

Finding high-quality, affordable, reliable child care, however, is hard to do, and it is one of the most serious problems faced by employed mothers. Child-care concerns not only increase a mother's level of stress but make her less productive at work. The severity of child-care problems faced by employed mothers is perhaps most vividly indicated by the finding that 47 percent of female employees with children age 5 years and under have considered quitting because of child-care problems.[31]

Clearly, the whole country benefits if all children have access to quality early childhood care.

Studies have shown that when young children are enrolled in high-quality day care, which has steady caregivers, caregivers trained in child development, and more adult caregivers per child, they become more academically and socially adjusted than children enrolled in day-care programs of lower quality.

Other factors that contribute to day-care quality are health and safety factors. Floors should be carpeted or have nonskid covering; at least one adult should be present at all times to supervise children; detergents, medicines, and drugs need to be kept out of children's reach; and records (emergency phone numbers, medical information) need to be kept on each child. The physical space of the day-care center should include the following: individual space (locker, drawer, cubicle) for each child to store personal belongings; dark and quiet space to allow children to nap; and a toileting area that is easy for children to get to. There should not be overcrowding (too many children or too much large equipment). There should be lots of materials, equipment, and activities: attractive and well-written story and picture books and materials and equipment for quiet play (books, puzzles) and for active play (riding toys, climbing structures). In outdoor play, the area should be safe and inaccessible to outsiders. Teachers and adult staff are also a factor. There should be enough adults to provide individual attention (probably at least one for every six children, more for children under 3 years); caregivers and teachers should use encouragement, suggestion, and praise rather than orders, commands, prohibitions, and criticism; and teachers should have some training in child care and child development.

One of the pertinent issues then is how the majority of working mothers can enroll their children in high-quality day care. The cost is prohibitive for most working mothers in the United States. Sweden stands at the forefront of advanced, industrialized societies in its recognition of the dilemmas of employed parents and sees providing quality day care as a public rather than private problem. Phyllis Moen, author of *Working Parents*, considers some of Sweden's policies.[32]

In Sweden, parental insurance permits the father or mother to take a six-month paid leave of absence on the birth of a child and receive, typically, 90 percent of their normal wage. The parental leave benefit is paid for by the Riksforsakringsverket (Social Insurance Board) rather than by employers directly. Swedish couples have 156 months of job-guaranteed paid leave to share between them. A father is legally entitled to half of the leave. The policy was instituted with radical social change in mind. It sought to break the tradition of women having the primary responsibility for caring for infants. The policy was designed to promote women's employment and to liberate men from traditional roles. The typical pattern with the shared leave is for mother to take the first five months; the father then takes the rest of the time and the wife returns to work. In the United States, approximately 70 percent of fathers take short leaves of five days or less, 90 percent take some leave (one day or more), and 20 percent take more than five days. Most often the leave days fathers take are vacation days or sick days and are therefore paid.

Moreover, in Sweden, parents of children under 8 years of age have the right to reduce their working time to 6 hours a day with proportional reduction in wages. Two thirds of mothers with preschoolers work part-time; however, they receive all the fringe benefits of full-time employees. There is a high degree of flexibility and discretion available over work schedules.

Maternity leave benefits in the United States are seriously inadequate. The mandatory provision of temporary disability insurance for a pregnant worker is usually determined by individual states, with only five states currently providing such compensation. Aside from this small provision for maternity leave, until 1993, with the passage of the Family and Medical Leave Act, the United States was the only major industrial nation without a national policy on parental leave.

Another basic support for working parents is the option of some kind of care when children are sick, which alleviates another major concern of working mothers. In the United States, providing care for sick children is the number one problem that female employees with children chose out of a list of 15 concerns.[33] Parents often find it difficult to arrange for substitute care for sick children, especially on short notice. The most frequent arrangement to care for sick children is for the mother to stay home. Approximately 66 percent of married working mothers stay home with their sick children, compared to 21.3 percent of married fathers.[34] Currently, few day-care centers and even fewer workplaces have a special room dedicated to meet the needs of sick children, and these are by far the most popular out-of-home options with parents.

The lack of adequate, affordable child-care provisions in the United States creates critical problems for women workers and their children. Not only are individual women left with the responsibility of finding and paying for child care, but many women are simply unable to work when such services are not available. There is extreme variation in the quality of child care available in this country. As part of the National Child Care Staffing Study, 227 day-care centers in five metropolitan areas in the United States were examined, and only 12 percent of the sample classrooms received a rating of good.[35] It is impossible to overemphasize the fact that, compared to other nations, the child-care policies of the United States are woefully inadequate and do not reflect the current realities of American families.

The United States tends to take a negative view of government-supported programs (and higher taxes); Sweden, however, views the absence of adequate parental support and child care as harmful. Studies have shown that problems with child care can reduce productivity, increase absenteeism, and contribute to low morale and high levels of stress among workers. Providing more public and private resources for quality child care is regarded by many people as one of the most important issues in the 1990s. When parents know that their child is well taken care of, they can relax, feel less guilty, become more productive at work, and become happier and better parents—all of which allow parents to create conditions in the home environment that enhance children's inner self-esteem.

Expert discussions on the effects of day care on children are superfluous; maternal employment is a reality. Parents need to know how to make their children's experiences at day care and at home supportive of children's adjustment and self-esteem and of their parents' peace of mind. Society needs to agree that every child of working parents has a right to a day-care environment conducive to his or her optimal growth and that every mother and father has a right to the peace of mind that such an environment is provided for their child.

Another factor that will help parents and their children feel more secure about day care is keeping the communication lines between school and home open. In order to bridge the gap between home and day care, parents need to exchange information with the teacher about things that are happening at home and have the teacher keep them informed about what is happening at school. This way parents and teachers can be knowledgeable about children's experiences. Sometimes children feel more secure and comfortable if they bring something from home, a stuffed animal, blanket, or pillow, for example, to day care. It's also a good idea for parents to spend a few minutes at the day-care center when they drop off the child before leaving and to spend a few extra minutes before leaving.

It is also important to remember that several studies provide evidence of possible intellectual benefits in high-quality day care for high-risk populations. The cultural ideal we have in the United States that young children should be cared for in their own homes by their own mothers can be a costly one for economically disadvantaged families. Staying home with mother can deprive families of the financial wherewithal to escape from poverty. Staying home can result in low-income families being less able, because of their economic or emotional circumstances, to provide their children with an environment that fosters healthy inner self-esteem.

## Creating Conditions that Foster Self-Esteem in Older Children of Working Mothers

School-age children may need care while their parents are working, but programs for school-age children are not widely available, nor are they used by the majority of parents. By the time children reach 8 years of age, reported use of "self-care" rises sharply. About 50 percent of the children in grades K–3, about 66 percent of those in grades 4–6, and about 80 percent of those in grades 7–8 are home alone or with siblings after school. Only 26 percent of working parents are able to be home after school with their 5- to 11-year-old schoolchildren. When the parents are not home, in 11.3 percent of cases the child is home alone, and in 27.7 percent of cases the child is home with an older sibling.[36] In fact, in the business world a new term is being widely used, the "three o'clock syndrome," referring to the reduced productivity and higher error and accident rates as employees' minds turn to their children around the time when school lets out. The need for care before and after school is apparent.

There are positive and negative aspects for latchkey or self-care children. On the positive side, they may be more independent and responsible, and they are learning some practical household skills. However, these children are often by themselves, isolated from their friends. Many spend their time after school in sedentary activities such as watching television and playing video games. If possible, mother or father should call children after they are home to chat for a few minutes about what happened in the child's day. This phone call should not be to remind children of the chores they have to do.

Also, children and adolescents of employed mothers may feel rejected or overburdened by household chores. To illustrate, the self-reports of children with working mothers reveal that they carry out moderate to high levels of family responsibility (taking care of younger children, preparing meals, working in the yard, doing laundry) and moderate to high levels of personal management tasks (doing homework without being reminded, earning own money, getting to school on time) compared to a group of young adolescents from homes in which mothers are not employed. Responsibilities and fun need to be balanced with giving children and adolescents time to participate in what is meaningful and important to them as well as what is meaningful and important to the family.

While it is critical for parents in a two-paycheck family not to overburden their children with responsibilities, it is also important not to be too indulgent as a way of lessening their guilt. Mothers may be reluctant to ask for their children's help; even "super moms," however, need some help in taking care of the house. Similarly, parents should not be overindulgent and let the child get away with immature behavior.

Finally, children, no matter what their age, need some special quiet time with their parents—a quality time when the parent is "all there" or focused on the child. During infancy this may mean actively playing with the baby; during preschool it may mean special trips to the zoo; during middle childhood it may mean being involved with the child's clubs, such as Boy Scouts or Girl Scouts, and their school activities; during adolescence it may involve listening to the adolescent's problems. Parents also need some time for themselves—together and by themselves.

Experts will agree that happy, well-adjusted mothers with high self-esteem tend to have children who are also happy and well adjusted, with high self-esteem. What are some of the factors that promote these behaviors in mothers and, in turn, their children?

One important factor that contributes to mothers' satisfaction, emotional health, and self-esteem is 50–50 parenting. Society, however, still views the father's role as primary breadwinner and the mother's primary responsibility as home and hearth, even if she is working outside the home. Many women, career women included, carry this "cultural dicta" with them and thus experience strong feelings of guilt about leaving their children.

Working women also tend more to feel guilty about not doing more around the house than do fathers. Women do about 75 percent of housework and men pick up the remaining 25 percent. Perhaps men do not feel guilty about the amount of work they are doing around the house because they are comparing themselves to their own fathers and the amount of household and childrearing chores they did, which was negligible in most cases. With this as their comparison base, men feel that they are doing their fair share and, thus, experience very little guilt. Women, on the other hand, tend to compare themselves with their mothers. Their mothers, however, most likely did not work; made breakfast, lunch, and dinner from scratch; canned their own peaches; ironed every article of clothing; and disinfected the entire house every other day. With this as a comparison base, many working mothers feel guilty about not doing more around the house, despite the fact that they are working in outside paid employment.

While we shall discuss the father's role in more detail in the next chapter, we should note here that some men may not be participating more in family chores and childrearing tasks because their wives cling wholeheartedly to traditional roles, which doesn't leave much of an incentive for fathers. Women may feel threatened about giving up their centrality at home and not allow fathers to trespass into their domain. While women may verbally acknowledge that they want more help, in subtle (and not so subtle) ways, they may sabotage their husbands' efforts at domestic chores. After Dad has cleaned the bathroom, for example, the mother may ridicule his efforts or simply reclean. Mothers need to refrain from recleaning and redoing; this only undermines change.

Some fathers are quite aware of the "strategic delay" technique; that is, fathers know that all they have to do is wait long enough and their wives will ultimately break down and clean up messes. The sooner fathers assume responsibilities for chores and childrearing, the better.

Most important, the mother's satisfaction with her role, whether employed or not, is vital to her self-esteem as well as her child's.[37] Regardless of employment status, some women are in their preferred role and others are not. Given today's economic conditions, many women are working out of necessity to supplement the family income. Other women are working for more personal reasons and would choose to work even without the financial need. Women who are homemakers may choose to be at home because of their strong investment in their role as primary caregivers to their children. Others may feel obligated to remain at home because of prevailing social norms about motherhood, even though they would rather be employed. The effect of employment status is different in these various situations.

It does appear that mothers who prefer employment but remain home show higher scores on depression and stress inventories than mothers whose employment status is consonant with their preferences. Employed mothers who choose to work show their children more affection and sympathy, discipline less severely, and feel less hostility during situations when their school-age children are noncompliant than employed mothers who do not want to work. Employed mothers with low role satisfaction use more negative control than do employed mothers with high role satisfaction. Employed mothers use more power-assertive discipline techniques (spanking and inflexible rules, for example) than nonemployed mothers only when they are dissatisfied with their work role. The effect of role satisfaction on parenting is greater for employed mothers than for nonemployed mothers.

Family socioeconomic status may also interact with employment to affect maternal behavior and child outcomes. Women with less education may have less interesting jobs as well as less lucrative ones. Mothers with higher levels of education express more favorable views of children than mothers with no education beyond high school.

Evidence indicates that low-income women may be more likely than women with higher incomes to work out of necessity, to work longer hours, and be less able to buy services and labor-saving devices that reduce demands on time and energy at home. Moreover, there is evidence that low-income women as a group experience less role satisfaction and less social support than higher income women,[38] and as a consequence, their parenting may be more adversely affected when they are employed.

Mother's satisfaction with her role, be it employed mother or full-time homemaker, is associated with more effective childrearing experiences and outcomes. Mothers who are dissatisfied with their roles show more rejection of their children and, in turn, have more difficult children with low self-esteem. Along the same lines, maternal job satisfaction is associated with children's higher self-esteem and fewer conduct problems.

Women who are in their preferred roles, whether at home or work, feel more positive about their lives and are able to respond more positively to all their roles, including motherhood. These women have higher self-esteem and tend to be more satisfied and less anxious than women who are not in their roles by choice; consequently, these feelings of satisfaction and self-esteem are seen in their children as well.

# Summary

The number of mothers entering the work force increases daily. Maternal employment has its advantages. Women who work outside the home, for example, develop a sense of independence and self-direction and experience of sense of accomplishment. There are, however, some disadvantages as well—scarcity of time for relaxing, socializing, intimacy with spouse, and interaction with children.

The largest number of women returning to work are those with infants. Research has studied the effects of the mother's working on the infant's attachment classification. As noted, building strong bonds of attachment with the principal caregiver is vital to children's future adjustment and healthy self-esteem. There have been mixed results in interpreting these studies. Some find that day care causes insecure attachment and others find no such correlation. In analyzing current research results, it appears that other variables, such as role strain, role conflict, guilt feelings, and maternal separation anxiety, may be more potent factors than day care *per se* in influencing infant–caregiver attachment.

Research studying the effect of mother's working on preschoolers has focused on how maternal employment affects their cognitive and social development. Cognitively, a mother's working has no effect either positively or negatively on middle-class children, but it has a big positive effect for lower-class children. Children from lower-class families who are in day care perform significantly better than youngsters from lower-class families who remain at home. In terms of social development, researchers note that children in day care are more prosocial. On the negative side, however, these children are also more aggressive and defiant toward authority figures.

Among school-age children, daughters of working mothers consistently show higher self-esteem and feelings of mastery. Girls often receive more favorable treatment than boys in homes where the mother works. The contrary is true in families in which the mother does not work outside the home. In these situations, boys receive better treatment (more attention and positive descriptions) than girls. Most studies of adolescents of both sexes show positive effects of mother working.

In creating conditions that foster children's self-esteem in infancy and early childhood, finding quality day care is of supreme importance. Studies conducted on infants and preschoolers who are enrolled in quality day care find no difference socially and academically between these children and children who are reared at home by their mothers. Other factors such as keeping open the communication lines between school and home, spending time with the child at the day-care center before leaving him or her, talking with the child about what is happening at school, and spending quality time with the child each day are also conditions that will enable the child to develop positive self-esteem. For older children of working mothers not giving them too many responsibilities, not being overindulgent, making sure that they have time for fun and friends, calling them from work, leaving recorded messages for them on a tape recorder, and, again, quality time, are conditions that foster self-esteem.

When mothers are satisfied and happy, their children tend to be satisfied and happy. Working mothers are happy when there is a 50–50 delineation of childrearing and household chores. Mothers who are in their preferred role (either full-time mother or mother employed outside the home) have the highest satisfaction and the highest self-esteem, and consequently, their children tend to be that way too.

# CHAPTER 10  Father's Role in the Childrearing and Domestic Domains

Fatherhood, history reminds us, is a cultural invention. Michael Pleck of the University of Illinois at Urbana-Champaign notes that from colonial times through the early nineteenth century, mothers provided most of the caregiving chores, much as they do today.[1] Fathers, nonetheless, were thought to have more influence on their children, particularly in the moral domain. Fathers were viewed as the family's ultimate source of moral teaching. The emphasis on father's influence was rooted in this period's conceptions of the nature of men and women, namely, that men were thought to have superior reason, which made them less likely than women to be misled by "passions" and "affections."

During the nineteenth century, new conceptions of fathers arose. Fathers were seen as playing an indirect role in the parenting process while women played a greater role. Mothers were thought to have a special influence on infants and young children. Fathers were viewed as distant breadwinners. This image was brought about, in part, by the Industrial Revolution, which meant that fathers were separated from their wives and families for a considerable part of each day. Fathers, however, continued to set the official standard of morality and to be the final arbiters of family discipline. Fathers were often respected but feared and remained invisible, distant, and aloof in their parenting roles.

By the end of the nineteenth century and the start of the twentieth, maleness was defined more and more in terms of ambition and achievement. There was a change in the social environment: work experience and domestic experience became even more distinct for greater and greater numbers of men. Moreover, the late nineteenth century brought the first great boom in suburban living, as street railways (and later buses and private automobiles) opened new vistas to com-

303

muting. Suburbs would soon become the epitome, in spatial terms, of the work–home dichotomy. "The suburban husband and father," noted one writer as early as 1900, "is almost entirely a Sunday institution."[2] Since such fathers spent so little time at home, they could not and would not acquire savvy and skills in the domestic arena.

During and following World War II, a new perception of father was ushered in: father as a sex-role model. Many fathers had gone to war and many had not returned. As a result, there was a postwar interest in the effects of the father's absence. The absence of fathers was linked to a number of phenomena from homosexuality to juvenile delinquency. Consequently, a new view of father as the principal transmitter of culturally based conceptions of masculinity and femininity emerged. While mothers were encouraged to be expressive (nurturant) with both sons and daughters, fathers were encouraged to be instrumental (competence-oriented) with their sons and expressive with their daughters.

Today, yet another image of father has emerged, a "softer" sort, summed up by the term "the new father." Today's father attends Lamaze classes, attends the child's birth, participates in child-care routines, washes dishes, and perhaps prepares an evening meal a few times a week. But remnants of fathers' past images as a moral overseer, ultimate authority, and family provider are still apparent as well. The newly expanded image of father has not totally freed him from the past, traditional roles. In a time of changing values and changing parental roles, what is father's primary role and how can he best enhance his children's self-esteem? Fathers play a pivotal role directly in building children's sense of independence and self-esteem in academic, social, and moral areas and indirectly by influencing mothers' self-esteem, satisfaction, and happiness.

The mere presence of a father is not enough to accomplish this. The bottom line is that children whose fathers are functionally absent are at a greater risk for developing problems. All children benefit from the love, caring, and economic support that a father can provide.

## Fostering Independence

Fathers, more so than mothers, play with their children and consequently through their physically stimulating behavior tend to foster independence in their children. Fathers tend to be more active and aggressive, abrupt, daring, and distant than mothers, which fosters independence in children. Mothers are found to respond to, stimulate, express positive affection toward, and provide more basic care for their children in all situations. A mother's traditional and continuing family role is the expressive specialist or relationship expert—the person in charge of handling all family members' feelings and emotional needs.

Fathers tend to be more "abrupt" and mothers tend to be more "gradual" in their interactions with their offspring. When children are infants, for example, fathers frequently hold their newborns on their folded arms at waist height, whereas mothers will keep them close to their breasts or faces. Fathers are more inclined than mothers to hold babies with the baby's face facing forward. Fathers also tend to toss their children up in the air, further increasing the distance between themselves and their children, a practice that serves as an exercise in separation between caretaker and baby.

Fathers participate less in caregiving but spend a greater percentage of time available for interaction in play activities than mothers do.[3] When mothers play with their young children they tend to play visual games, maintaining a form of interactive play in conventional motor games such as pat-a-cake and peek-a-boo. Mothers often play watching games in which a toy is presented and made obvious by shaking or moving it. Fathers play tactile and limb movement games; they engage in more bouncing and lifting games. Fathers do not often introduce toys when interacting with their children. They engage in rough-and-tumble types of play, while mothers tend to be more verbal when playing with their children, a pattern that continues after infancy and toddlerhood as well. Physical play between father and his children is highest when children are 2 years old; between 2 and 10 years there is a decreased likelihood that they will engage their children physically.

Several possible benefits of fathers' play for children have been proposed. It encourages curiosity and exploration, and this, in turn, encourages the intellectual development of children. Fathers' play also encourages children to become more independent and adventurous. Fathers' play tends to be nonrepetitive and variable; it's hard to predict what fathers will do next. This kind of play presents children with problems to try and solve, and to do this they have to be alert to any cue that fathers may present. The striving for understanding that is involved in the father's play helps to develop children's problem-solving skills. While fathers encourage intellectual development by their playful behavior and by their encouragement of independence, mothers encourage the same skills by their linguistic stimulation and their focus on rule-bound, intellectually stimulating games and their use of objects.

Mothers are typically more expressive (nurturant, empathic) in dealing with their children. Their role appears to be to give warmth and understanding. Mothers tend to keep the family subsystem functioning smoothly by performing the expressive, integrating, supportive functions. Mother's responsibility is to care for the family members. Fathers are consistently more likely to take an action-oriented role with their children, whereas mothers more often provide emotional support and encouragement.

## Fathers and Children's Academic Self-Esteem

The father's support and affection for his children as shown in his physical and verbal responses to them and his positive regard for himself and his children seem to have a strong influence on children's level of achievement.[4] These supportive attitudes tend to release the child's ability to concentrate on mastering learning tasks. It is possible that the variables of paternal nurturance, high academic expectations, sex-role attitudes, quality of cognitive facilitation, and marital compatibility with spouse may interact in subtle and complex ways to foster children's intellectual competencies.

A number of studies have demonstrated that fathers can have a positive impact on their children's cognitive development. For example, infants' mental test scores are positively associated with the amount of contact with their fathers.[5] Similarly, paternal involvement is positively associated with preschool cognitive performance, especially among boys. Conversely, the absence of the father has been associated with poorer behavioral and cognitive function in younger and older children.

A number of studies suggest a relationship between the cognitive development of children and the father's *style* of interaction. Paternal hostility, restrictiveness, and authoritarian control tend to be negatively related to cognitive development in children. An extensive literature on the absence of the father tends to show that boys from families in which father is physically or psychologically absent have problems in the areas of school performance and control of aggression.

Children with nurturant fathers tend to emulate these types of fathers and their modes of thinking and problem solving.[6] Similarly, children who perform well academically appear to value their fathers' companionship. The children perceive themselves as similar to their fathers; fathers of high achievers are more accessible to their children and are democratic in dealing with their children.[7]

More often than not, paternal nurturance has been found to be positively related to children's high achievement. High-achieving students, for example, report that their fathers are more accepting and somewhat less controlling than fathers described by low achievers.[8] It has also been found that low-achieving students have fathers who feel that children should make only minor decisions, should always believe their parents, and should be under their parents' complete control and that it is wicked to disobey parents.[9]

In divorced families, a child's academic competence is associated with the father's child support payments.[10] It is not surprising that child support appears to be a weighty factor in how well the child does in school. Many studies have shown a positive link between measures of socioeconomic status and academic achievement. The economic value of child support might have a prismic effect—it could directly increase the resources available to the child. More money could be spent on educational activities and materials. The extra money might allow the child to receive better health care or live in a better neighborhood, where academic achievement is valued. A strong cognitive home environment is positively associated with a child's intellectual development and it can compensate for the negative effects of father absence.[11]

Several American scholars have attempted to explain why the father's involvement has a critical impact on children's academic competence. Michael Lamb has studied fathers extensively and explains that particularly in the area of cognitive competence, children with two highly involved parents benefit from the diversity of stimulation.[12] The child learns from two enthusiastic teachers, not just one. Second, high paternal involvement allows both parents to engage in diverse and meaningful activities; for example, fathers have an opportunity to satisfy a desire to become closer to their children in addition to pursuing a career. Mothers can retain close relationships with their children while following their own career goals. In other words, increased paternal involvement in the family is likely to make both parents feel more satisfied with their lives. Although the quantity of paternal involvement is crucial, the quality of such involvement will also likely have a significant effect on children and fathers.

## Fathers and Children's Moral Self-Esteem

Fathers tend to play a major role in helping children develop in morally competent ways. Through the standards he sets, his own rule-abiding behavior, and establishment of rules, a father conveys to his children a set of values and expectations for the way they should act. Children with democratic, nurturant, but firm fathers tend to experience more guilt than children with authoritarian fathers when they have done something wrong. This guilt acts as a deterrent to engaging in undesirable behavior in the future and promotes morally competent behavior.[13]

Thus, fathers' involvement with their children is important, and the lack of such involvement leads to numerous behavior problems, such as juvenile delinquency, mental health problems, and suicidal behavior. Urie Bronfenbrenner paints a dire picture, stating that when fathers are uninvolved their children are at "greater risk for experiencing a variety of behavioral and educational problems, including extremes of hyperactivity or withdrawal, lack of attentiveness in the classroom, difficulty in deferring gratification, impaired academic achievement, school misbehavior, suicide, vandalism, violence and criminal acts."[14]

## Fathers and Children's Gender-Role Development

The father's involvement with his offspring sometimes depends on the child's gender. Fathers tend to be more engaged with their sons than with their daughters. Fathers may feel that it is important to teach their son appropriate, masculine ways of behaving, and therefore, they are more involved with their sons. Moreover, as boys grow older and more competent, fathers' interest in them increases. Fathers have more contact with children and display more interest in their sons as they get older and become more competent. In contrast, their contact with daughters declines as they get older.[15]

When the father is the sole breadwinner in the family, the pattern of involvement is more gender-typed, with fathers spending almost three times as much time with sons as with daughters. The pattern for dual-earner fathers is a bit more egalitarian. The number of children in the family also affects father's involvement. The larger the number of children in a family, the fewer parental resources for each child. Thus, a father's interaction with children on an individual basis is reduced in families with more children. Firstborns and perhaps second-born children may reap the benefits of less dilution of parental energies. For children born later, older siblings often serve as a substitute for parents.

Mothers are less likely to be concerned with sex-type behavior. This is not to say that mothers do not value or encourage sex-appropriate behavior. Mothers do share common cultural values with fathers concerning appropriate masculine and feminine behavior, but they do not ordinarily make as sharp a distinction in their attitudes toward their sons and daughters as fathers do.[16]

While the mother has a primarily expressive relationship with both boys and girls, the father rewards his male and female children differently. He encourages instrumental behavior (competence-directed, achievement-focused) in his son and expressive behavior in his daughter. For example, with his son the father plays roughly and invites aggression and assertive responses, whereas he is flirtatious and pampering with his daughter, encouraging her to be affectionate and docile.[17] There is a greater differentiation on the part of the father toward children of both sexes, even among parents who believe in non-sexist childrearing.[18] Fathers prefer that sex distinctions be easily recognized, so they exert a strong and dogged influence on their children's development.

Many fathers want their daughters to be pretty and likeable and their sons to be achievement- and competence-directed. Fathers think their sons should show an ability to hold their own in a man's world. In each case, the father's reaction is representative of the gender-role demands that the outside world still continues to make on children. This pattern of fathers expressing affection for their daughters and encouraging their sons to achieve may be the earliest indicator of dichotomous masculine and feminine self-evaluations.

Although fathers encourage cognitive growth in both their sons and daughters, many focus their direct teaching on sons, not daughters. In addition, fathers tend to set higher standards for their sons and place greater emphasis on their sons' achievement. With their daughters, fathers focus more on interpersonal aspects of the teaching situation—encouraging, supporting, joking, and protecting. The father is more demanding with his sons, often playing the role of the mentor or taskmaster.

Sons and daughters also perceive that they are treated differently by their fathers. High school boys, for example, perceive their fathers as being more concerned with stereotypic gender-role enforcement than do high school girls. The boys also report that their fathers are stricter and more critical, less positive, and less protective than do the girls. Boys, more so than girls, indicate that their fathers are less affectionate and nurturant than their mothers.[19]

It is difficult to determine whether fathers' differential treatment of sons and daughters is a result of their own preconceived notions about how boys and girls should act or whether children themselves, through their behavior and attitudes, socialize their fathers. The data suggest that both fathers and children contribute to different socialization strategies for boys and girls. For example, young boys have been observed to be more active and disruptive in their behavior than girls; they are more likely to show greater resistance to control and are less likely to be responsive to adult directives both at home and at school, thereby more frequently eliciting critical, negative reactions from adult caregivers.

Some research suggests that lack of warmth in the father–daughter and father–son relationships correlates with negative outcomes. Delinquent adolescents, for example, report that they are not close to their fathers, that their fathers are not very interested in them, and that they perceive their fathers as cold, rejecting, and uninterested.[20] Too much paternal warmth and support, however, is associated with passivity in children. For both sons and daughters, a warm relationship with their fathers is important to healthy self-esteem. Fathers who encourage both their sons as well as their daughters to pursue academic and occupational goals and who are warm, challenging, and nurturing raise the most socially competent children who are high in self-esteem and self-determination.[21]

## Fathers and Mothers' Satisfaction

Father's involvement in childrearing may have its strongest effects in an indirect way. His deeds and actions may influence the mother, whose behavior then affects the child. The father who compliments the mother and communicates to her directly and indirectly that she is doing a good job helps her to gain more self-confidence in her parenting skills and, in turn, engage in more effective parenting. Perhaps the most crucial factor for children is the overall impact of the father–mother mode of interaction. The quality of communication, respect, and cooperation between fathers and mothers has a strong effect on the child's developing conceptions of male–female relationships.

Current research reinforces the important role that fathers play in providing social support for their wives, which, in turn, positively affects mothers' behaviors toward their children.[22] It appears that the father's ability to be supportive is influenced by the quality of the marital relationship. The impact of marriage on parenting may be greater for fathers than for mothers.[23] Father's satisfaction with his marriage also relates to his degree of participation. The happier and more satisfied the father is with his spouse, the more likely he will help with domestic and childrearing chores. Unhappily married men give less social support to their wives; some withdraw from them and also distance themselves from their children. Both the fathers' psychological adjustment and the status of the marriage affect the ability to predict fathers' attitudes toward their children and their roles as parents.

Highly involved fathers may play a beneficial role in their children's development directly by providing cognitive and social stimulation or indirectly by alleviating strain on the mother, thereby improving the family's overall dynamics. They may also exemplify a more egalitarian division of roles, which could benefit children in the long run. Although an involved father may have a significant, positive impact, available evidence suggests that too few fathers show this high degree of involvement.

Mothers are happiest when they perceive fathers as partaking in childrearing and domestic chores—a 50–50 parenting situation. Unequal sharing of responsibility for family management is the single most important cause of marital conflict.[24] In contrast, a husband's willingness to share responsibility has been shown to be directly related to a decrease in stress for working mothers, which leads us to ask, do fathers and mothers engage in 50–50 parenting?

## Degree of Father's Involvement

The changes in women's roles, particularly their increased participation in work outside the home, have been accompanied by ideological changes concerning fathers' roles in child care and childrearing.

Research has increasingly recognized fathers and has addressed various aspects of their role. The father of the 1990s is (or should be) very involved in the daily care and rearing of his children. However, there is not a great deal of empirical evidence that supports this image.

Fathers spend, on average, 26 minutes per day in direct interaction with children below the age of 6. As children get older, the time decreases to 16 minutes a day,[25] which is an improvement over times past. In 1971, for example, fathers spent 37-1/2 seconds a day interacting with their children.[26] A national survey found that fathers in single-earner households, on an average, spend 3 minutes per day on weekdays and 19 minutes per day on weekends on family work including feeding, bathing, helping, and playing with their children. On average, fathers spend less than 1 hour a week with children, whereas they spend approximately 54 hours a week at work.[27]

Consider these figures concerning the degree of fathers' involvement in two-parent families in which mothers are not employed outside the home. According to Michael Lamb, fathers tend to spend about 20 to 25 percent as much time as mothers do in "engagement" (direct, one-to-one interaction) with their children.[28] In terms of being accessible to their children (available whether or not interaction is actually taking place) fathers spend about one third as much time as mothers do. Perhaps the biggest discrepancy between paternal and maternal involvement is in responsibility, defined as providing appropriate care at all times. Fathers, reports Lamb, tend to help out when "it is convenient."

The picture does not significantly change when we view fathers' engagement and accessibility when mothers are employed outside the home. The figures for direct interaction and accessibility average 33 percent and 65 percent, respectively. (The proportion cited here goes up, not because fathers are doing more, but because mothers are doing less.) As far as responsibility, the fact that mother works outside the home doesn't affect father's level of involvement with his children. Even when mother works over 30 hours a week in paid employment, the amount of responsibility assumed by fathers appears negligible. The frequency with which fathers actually engage in child-care activities seems largely unaffected by the changes in ideology and women's work patterns.

While many fathers may give lip service to the importance of 50–50 parenting, the sad truth is that only a small percentage of fathers are responsible for any regular household tasks and childrearing activities.

While many may believe that fathers should be actively involved with their children, it appears that this is the case only if it does not jeopardize father's paramount role as breadwinner.

## Fathers Who Are Involved

Since fathers play an important role in developing children's sense of independence and academic and moral self-esteem and contribute to mothers' feelings of competency, happiness, and self-esteem, their involvement in childrearing and domestic chores matters. The consequence of father's involvement is the children's well-being, that is, the degree to which children are able to engage successfully and appropriately in interpersonal relationships and in work or play activities with relative freedom from noxious social behavior, burdensome emotions, and poor physical health.

A factor that is highly influential in determining fathers' child-care involvement is that fathers may believe that their principal way of being involved is not through active participation with their children and helping with domestic chores but, rather, through their monetary contribution to the family. They feel that money provides security and the material things their families need. Fathers and society, as we shall see, need to revise this limited view of involvement.

The father's personality also determines his level of commitment to family chores and responsibilities. Research in the United States, Australia, and Europe shows that engaged fathers are less subject to physical illness, have marriages in which their spouses are more satisfied, and have children who are better able to adapt to life stresses. Similarly, fathers who are more mature, are occupationally stable, have high self-esteem, and are more sensitive to the feelings of others are also more responsive and involved. The father's emotional stability affects how he organizes his parenting relationships. Fathers who are depressed and anxious interact less often than fathers who are not in these emotional states.

The mother's preference and beliefs also influence the level of father's involvement. The mother's preferences for father–child contact and her regard for his parenting abilities affect the father's involvement. Father's involvement is more highly correlated with spousal support than is the mother's. Mothers who encourage fathers to become involved generally become more involved. When fathers are encouraged to help, their participation in chores and childrearing tasks is more frequent and of higher quality. Still, when fathers are forced to be highly involved without wishing to be so, the quality of fathering may not be as high. It is interesting to note that a high percentage of mothers do not want their husbands to take a greater part in raising their children.[29] Some may fear that greater involvement would change the power balance and other attributes of the marital relationship.

Knowledge of children's development enhances the father's involvement. Involvement may have more effect on knowledge, in fact, than vice versa; that is, fathers more involved in social interaction will acquire basic knowledge and that type of parenting is related to knowledge.[30] Fathers' perceived skills and self-confidence in carrying out child-care chores or relating to their children will affect their willingness to continue in these roles. Many fathers do not believe they have the knowledge, skills, or support to do so. They feel alone in their experience and feel they lack the necessary parenting skills.

As Allen Hawkins of Brigham Young University points out, mothers tend to become highly involved with their children from birth onward; fathers, however, may or may not become immediately involved with their infants.[31] Faced with the nine-month gestation of a child in her body and then the demands of caring for a newborn infant in the first few postpartum months, a mother is challenged quickly to develop a commitment to her dependent infant. Of course, not all mothers develop this bond. For fathers, however, the transition to parenthood is usually different. Whereas women's active participation in the daily care of their infants is virtually universal, men's involvement is still viewed as optional. For men, significant, direct involvement with the children may not occur right away or at all.

Caring for newborns by fathers is limited by a number of factors: lactation, infant activity, employment/caregiving arrangements, the economics of unequal salaries, residual societal attitudes about men's roles, and some women's ambivalence about "making room" for fathers in the domestic role. Consequently, it is not difficult to see how fathers often come to view themselves as relatively inadequate caregivers compared to mothers, which results in many men giving up. This profile of relatively little involvement by fathers is shown even in families that before the child's birth were egalitarian and avoided division of homemaking chores along traditional sex-stereotyped lines.

In particular, fathers need to perceive that they are able to read their children's signals, know what they want, and know how to respond appropriately and also realize what expectations are realistic. Contrary to the notion of maternal instinct, parenting skills are usually acquired "on the job" by both mothers and fathers. Because mothers are on the job more than fathers usually are, they become more sensitive to their children, more in tune with them, and more aware of each child's characteristics. Fathers often overlook the fact that the mother, too, is undergoing on-the-job training and sometimes feels inadequate as well. Many fathers think that their spouses know a great deal about parenting, when, in reality, most first-time mothers don't.

One of the most consistent predictors is fathers' motivation or the extent to which *he wants* to be involved. Fathers who want to take part usually do. The father's attitude toward the quality of fathering he has received is a pivotal factor affecting his involvement. In many cases, this involves negative modeling—fathers want to be close to their children *because their own fathers were not.*[32]

One of the major reasons given for why fathers have been slow to change is lack of exposure to appropriate paternal role models. Traditionally, mothers have acted as a central parental role model for their adult children with one consequence being that small boys often do not have a clear picture of who their father is. Typically, fathers are shadowy figures difficult to understand and typically unavailable to provide confident, rich models of manhood. Moreover, in light of changes in father's role in recent years, how do men reconcile the "good provider" model of their fathers' generation with the current societal expectation of the "new, nurturant father?"

Although these men are clear about not wanting to be like their fathers, they frequently express respect for the way that they carried out their roles. At the same time that they deliberately seek to construct for themselves fatherhood roles that are different from their own fathers, they are frequently preoccupied with some of the same symbols of good parenting, such as standards of conduct and control over their children.

Most fathers today see their fathers as conveying a set of values and expectations for the way children should act. These standards are rooted in father's commitment to his work. One of the implications of feeling that they have no known models to emulate is to feel unprepared for parenthood and uncertain about what is required in the job of being a father.

Thus, the way to increase father's role is to expand society's limited view of father as financial provider to include nurturing caregiver as well. Wives should encourage fathers' involvement. Mothers should help fathers feel confident about their parenting skills and encourage their on-the-job training so that they are able to read their children's signals and know what their children want. Fathers need to be given a clear picture of what is expected of them in their "new father" roles so that they, unlike the previous generation of fathers, can become good role models for their own children.

## When Father Is Not Around

Children's academic and intellectual performance suffer more when the father's absence is due to divorce, separation, or desertion than when his absence is due to death. As noted, boys are damaged more by fathers' absence than girls are. When the father's absence is not because of death, the age of the child at the time of father's leaving is important. Generally, before the age of 5 a father's absence is more damaging to children than when the absence occurs between the ages of 6 and 11 years. When the father's absence is because of death, however, the most vulnerable age for boys is 6 to 9 years. There is no evidence of cognitive impairment in boys whose fathers died before they were 2 years old. There is even a trend for such boys to be superior in their academic performance to peers who have fathers.[33]

Death of the father may bring the realization that one has truly lost the opportunity to obtain what a father might have given had the relationship been different or had he lived longer. This is particularly apparent when the father did not or could not show any affection or emotion toward the child. Some older children lament their lost chance to "undo" ambivalences, earn the father's respect, or express feelings of simple compassion. During the dying and death of a father, a son may feel a special urgency to set things right. A frequently encountered wish is that fathers would verbalize not only their vision of their world, but also their concept of what their son had meant to them, conveying directly or indirectly, "I love you. It was worth having you."

When fathers' absence is due to divorce, it's important to understand how these fathers view their responsibilities to children and how they view the costs and benefits of their relationships with children. Fathers' attitudes toward involvement with their children in postdivorce situations depend on the current family arrangements; relationships with their former spouses and children; social background, including education and other aspects of fathers' social placement; and involvement with nonresident children. Current family arrangements include whether the nonresident father has remarried or is living in a nonmarital union, whether he lives with other children, and the characteristics of these children (biological or stepchildren). Other factors that influence the father's involvement with children after a divorce are his satisfaction with parenting, his perceptions of his influence on his children's development, and his geographic proximity to his children. When fathers experience positive relationships with their children, believe that they have a direct influence over their children's behavior, and live close to their offspring, their involvement tends to be high.

When nonresident fathers remarry, they decrease their involvement with children from a previous relationship, perhaps because the new relationship competes with earlier ones for their time and attention. Some fathers who remarry, however, may do so because they hold strong family values that lead to their continued commitment to paternal responsibilities to children after divorce. If their new wives share these family values, they may encourage continued involvement with their children. A significant number of fathers, however, cease to nurture and provide for their children after divorce, and this has a debilitating effect on children's self-esteem.

## Effects of Father's Absence on Girls

Among girls, early absence of the father appears to be more disadvantageous, even though the effects may remain unobserved until adolescence. Adolescent girls who have lost their fathers before they are 5 years old seem uncertain about their actions around males.[34] Fatherless girls report feeling anxious around males. Another crucial factor affecting girls' adjustment in the absence of a father is the reason for the absence. Daughters of widows appear shy and uncomfortable when around males, while daughters of divorced mothers are more assertive around male peers and men. When girls age 13 were observed at a dance, for example, the daughters of widows stayed with other girls and frequently hid behind other girls. Some even spent most of the evening hiding in the rest room. Daughters of divorcees behaved very differently, spending more time at the boys' end of the hall, often initiating encounters and asking male peers to dance.

How can these patterns of behavior be accounted for? All of the mothers under study were equally "feminine" and reinforced their daughters for sex-appropriate behaviors. It has been suggested that daughters of divorced women may view their mothers' lives as unsatisfying and feel that for happiness it is essential to secure a man. In contrast, daughters of widows may have idealized their fathers and feel that few men can compare favorably with them or, alternatively, may regard all men as superior and as objects of deference and apprehension. One experimenter concludes:

> Father absence is highly associated with impaired development for boys and less so for girls. . . . Father-absent girls, unlike boys, still have a parent of their own sex as a model. Hence, although being negatively affected, girls have less difficulty in continuing to progress toward psychological maturity.[35]

One word of caution is in order when interpreting these studies. All of the girls were deprived of contacts with males in general, not just fathers. None of the girls had brothers or stepfathers in their homes.

## Effects of Father's Absence on Boys

For boys, as noted, the age at which separation from the father occurs is a critical factor affecting children's adjustment. Early separation could prevent masculine identification from occurring and could create a disruptive effect on learning masculine gender-role behaviors. A variety of studies have shown that fathers' influence on children's gender-role development tends to be more traditional because, when compared with mothers, they more routinely differentiate between masculine and feminine behaviors and encourage greater conformity to conventional gender roles. Later separation may have little effect or could result in an overemphasis on masculine behavior that was learned through identification with the father prior to his absence.

The dividing point between early and late separation is usually regarded as roughly 5 years of age, both in theoretical discussions of gender-role development and in a sizable number of studies that have explored the knowledge of children of various ages about the appropriateness of various kinds of behavior for males or females in general. Nursery school boys from father-absent homes are observed to be emotionally more dependent, show more separation anxiety behavior, and exhibit less autonomous striving for achievements. The boys from father-absent homes are less socially adjusted, have more difficulties in peer interactions, and tend to be significantly more dependent on peers. In ratings of aggression, boys from homes with fathers and those who are separated from their fathers after the age of 6 are significantly more aggressive than those who are separated from their fathers earlier. In addition, early-separation boys play fewer physical games involving contact (boxing, football) than do the late-separation or father-absent boys. The early-separation boys spend more time in nonphysical, noncompetitive activities (reading, working on puzzles) than boys from intact homes. In general, research indicates that boys who are separated from their fathers at the age of 5 or earlier are less masculine in some areas of behavior, while boys who are separated after 6 are similar to those from intact homes. The effects of the father's absence on older boys is less clear. Some investigators find no differences between homes with fathers and those without. Others find a pattern called compensatory masculinity in boys separated from their fathers. In this pattern, the boy displays excessive masculine bravado and at other times shows feminine behavior, such as dependency. Children whose fathers are psychologically absent (present in the home, but distant and inaccessible) suffer consequences that are similar to, although not as extreme as, those suffered when fathers are physically absent.

The absence of the father may not be the only variable that can cause differences in these children. Other factors, such as the altered family structure and the qualitatively different maternal behavior vis-à-vis the child, can increase or decrease the impact of the father's absence. The age of the child at the time of the father's departure, the child's opportunities for exposure to other male role models, length of the father's absence, age and sex of siblings, and socioeconomic status of the family may operate singly or in concert with other factors. Thus, delineating the "true" causal agents of the child's development may be impossible.

Some research findings, however, document the direct correlation between father's absence and higher rates of aggressive behavior in sons, sexually precocious behavior in daughters, and more rigid sex-role stereotypes in children of both sexes. Other research, however, suggests a minimal impact of fathers beyond their contribution to the economic well-being of the family.[36] These findings are in keeping with prior findings that the effects of fathers' presence on young children's cognitive and behavioral adjustment are minimal once family economic status is controlled. In families without fathers, maternal characteristics such as IQ and educational attainment appear to be more influential to children's well-being than the father's absence.

Thus, although some evidence indicates that the father's absence is not good for children's development, absence *per se* may not be the actual cause of certain problems—economic deprivation appears to be the greatest overriding factor affecting children. A host of variables may mediate the negative effects of father absence. Exposing children to male role models (relatives, coaches, teachers, leaders in organizations such as Boy Scouts, for example); making sure they spend some quality time with an older, male friend or companion; and engaging in "masculine" activities are a few of the ways to help children when father is not around.

## Reinventing Fatherhood

Judging from contemporary media coverage, fathers have been moved from their aggressive positions in the conference room and on the ball field to the warm ambiance of the nursery. In the United States there has been an explosion of interest in fathers and fatherhood. Yet, in spite of this interest and signs of widespread support for an expanded role for father, the rate of change has been slow. As women have evacuated homes, however, men have not rushed in to fill the vacuum. Dominant images of fatherhood from the past have left their mark on contemporary attitudes. The old verities about hard, striving, emotionally aloof men seem problematic in the face of a new world.

The optimal situation in the 1990s is for the child to have an engaged mother and father. Children are then exposed to a wider range of adaptive characteristics. As Henry Biller points out, children who are both mothered and fathered are likely to have positive self-esteem and feel good about being a male or female.[37] Unfortunately, relatively few children enjoy this well-rounded nurturance since researchers have found little evidence of a shift toward a more active father role. Active parenting is expected only of men whose jobs allow it, and fathers are seldom negatively sanctioned by society if they spend little time with their children because of long work hours or frequent travel. This conditional feature of the father's role generates variability and provides a rationale for men to escape even moderate parenting duties. But, this rationale seems less tenable as mothers continue to enter the labor market.

Fathers are still entrenched in the norms of traditional masculinity in the following ways: (1) Fathers often feel bothered by participating in nontraditional child-care tasks; (2) those who partake in personal direct child-care activities still avoid other domestic roles such as cooking and cleaning; (3) they rarely mention favorite tasks related to the affective dimension of child care (nurturing and comforting); and (4) they seem quite satisfied with their basic paternal roles in child care.

Society could do much more to help the transition of the father in dual-career families toward a more equal parenting role. The structures of the workplace are steeped in the traditional values of masculinity, often totally ignoring a man's family life. Employers in America, for example, lag far behind such progressive countries as Sweden in making the workplace changes to accommodate involved fathers. The workplace remains basically the same as it always has been. In other words, it is an environment developed by and for competitive men that incorporates their values of the battlefield and continues to be an environment in which family issues are ignored. "Currently, there is nothing in this society to make us believe that employers will drastically change the workplace into one more cognizant of the needs of working parents of both genders. . . . the business policies and practices that do support women and men as parents with family concerns are few and vanishing."[38] Fathers take care of their children more when they have flexible or alternating work schedules.

In addition to job constraints, a major reason for men's lack of equal parenting is that our society has not expanded an identity for fathers beyond that of a good provider and it needs to do so.

> Until our culture includes nurturing and attachment as highly valued qualities in male gender-identity formation and defines child care as central to fathering, the achievement of equality within the confines of heterosexual marriage will remain elusive. Government needs to begin developing legislation to support rather than to deprive and mistreat one of our society's most important institutions, the family. Families are endangered because legislators and corporate policy makers are so out of touch with reality of the American family and how it functions in the 1990s.[39]

The mainstream definition of father's role is that he is the family founder, breadwinner, protector of wife and children, and model for character development and behavior. If a father spends too much time at home he is considered lazy, unmasculine, and unsuccessful—not a very good example for his children. Although family, friends, and coworkers often find something "cute" in father being more involved, they often consider the commitment unprofessional or even unmanly.

James Garbarino, Director, Family Life Development Center, Cornell University, points out that many traditional fathers have set goals in business, industry, government, the arts, and academia over investing time and care in their children. Others simply have ignored the paternal role. Traditionally, men's "work" in the family has focused on assertion of authority and power.[40]

Perhaps the reason that men continue to invest in the male occupational role is simply because a man's occupation and success in that occupation identifies him. The provider role is intimately linked with a man's sense of self and self-esteem. Some men who are unable to fulfill their roles as economic providers to the family become unstable emotionally. Men, then, may have a lot to lose if they "give up" their provider role. Similarly, women may center their sense of self on being a nurturing mom and a good housekeeper. Traditionally, the role of housewife/mother has offered women their greatest sense of worth. Having a strong commitment to a work identity does not necessarily preclude men from having a similar commitment to nonprovider family roles and vice versa for women.

Children value fathers who spend time with them. They want access to their father and to sense his personal investment in them. To have high inner self-esteem, children need to be esteemed by their fathers, which means more than only economic support. More than half of the children born today will spend some or all of their childhood without a father in residence, either physically, psychologically, or both. Thus, even when the traditional, noninvolved, nondiapering, distant father is present, he is absent from many children's lives.

As James Garbarino points out, in years past, the nurturing and available mother made traditional fatherhood work, at least passably well, in the lives of children.[40] But the many changes in the roles, opportunities, and interests of women have altered this balance in ways that require reinventing fatherhood. A few decades ago, most kids took for granted that their mothers would be available to them on a full-time basis; this is not true today. More and more women are working and we have not seen a corresponding change of more and more fathers being involved with home and hearth. Consequently, we have seen a continuing decline in the amount of time parents spend actively with their children. When women enter the work force, their time investment in family work and time spent with children declines. Some experts have urged women to stay home for the children's sake. Even if every woman had a choice about working, is that the answer? Is a better solution for men to become more involved with family, chores, and childrearing?

Garbarino continues by saying that as mothers change and fathers don't, children are caught in the middle or, worse, left out in the cold. The needs of children haven't changed amid the many social changes that have swept through adults' lives. They still need to be mothered and fathered. If in the past we could sustain a culture in which fathers were distant, preoccupied, and authoritarian because mothers "made up the difference," today we cannot. If fathers and mothers don't contribute equally to household chores and childrearing tasks, children will be left holding the bag.

To develop a new kind of father, we must encourage a new kind of man. What does reinventing fatherhood mean? It means developing new roles for fathers that better reflect the needs of children in this modern era of changed roles for mothers. This means restoring fathers to the lives of the many children who live without them. Reinventing fatherhood, according to Garbarino, will require men to know their children, change their diapers, kiss their hurts, spoon out the applesauce, throw and catch balls, read their stories, and hear their confidences. It will require men to communicate their love clearly and unconditionally.

## Summary

Judging from what research has learned about fathers, it appears that father plays an important role in fostering independence and enhancing children's academic and moral self-esteem, as well as contributing to his wife's happiness and their marital success. For sons and daughters, a warm relationship with their fathers is important so that they can develop healthy self-esteem in cognitive and moral domains. Children who are punished or who have rejecting or passive fathers are less secure, less well adjusted, and have lower academic and moral self-esteem. Fathers more than mothers vary their behavior as a function of the sex of their children. They appear to play an especially important role in encouraging masculinity in sons and femininity in their daughters. They encourage instrumental behavior (achievement, independence) in their sons and expressive behaviors (nurturing, caring, sensitivity) in their daughters. Both of these behaviors need to be encouraged in their sons *and* their daughters. Father's absence has a more debilitating effect on sons than on daughters; however, economic deprivation as a result of father's absence seems to have a greater impact on children than father's absence *per se*.

We have seen, in the 1990s, the influx of mothers into the work force. We have not seen the majority of fathers, exceptions notwithstanding, engaging in 50–50 parenting. Because the majority of mothers are working, they are spending less time with their children. Reinventing fatherhood involves changing our perceptions of men to see them as breadwinners and, equally important, as nurturing, loving, helping husbands and fathers.

# Epilogue

There are two sources of self-esteem: an outer and an inner source. The outer source of self-esteem develops through children's perceived reflections of how their parents esteem and value them. Outer self-esteem is enhanced when parents communicate through their words and deeds that their children are worthy and loved. Parents' arbitrary praise given unconditionally initially promotes the development of healthy, outer self-esteem. Inner self-esteem, which has been overlooked in self-esteem literature, is the second and equally, if not more, important component of self-esteem. As children get older, parents, children themselves, and others base their evaluations and approval of children on their actual competencies and skills. Self-esteem then can no longer be supported by positive evaluations arbitrarily bestowed on them by parents; it must be earned. Thus, children need to develop inner self-esteem by developing socially valued skills, behaviors, and attitudes and integrate *self*-evaluations with others' evaluations of them.

Parents can help their children develop competencies that will enable them to have high inner self-esteem in physical, social, academic, and moral domains. Each developmental level requires cultivating different skills and ways of behaving. During infancy, for example, foundations for developing inner self-esteem are laid when infants and parents develop strong physical bonds of attachment and when parents foster children's feelings of trust and encourage their infants to develop a sense of self as a distinct, separate, causal agent. During early childhood, parents can enhance children's inner self-esteem by helping them acquire independent ways of behaving, become more self-sufficient, and reason and behave in morally competent ways.

Children in middle childhood need to develop social competencies (getting along with others) and academic skills (doing well in school), which gives rise to inner self-esteem. Parents with adolescents can foster their teenagers' inner self-esteem by encouraging them to separate from parents while retaining emotional closeness or connectedness, helping them achieve a comfortable body sense, and assisting them in formulating a clear sense of personal identity.

The term "inner self-esteem" is synonymous with "competency." The parents' role in enhancing children's inner self-esteem is to help their children acquire these socially valued skills, which leads to children's positive self-evaluations (as well as positive evaluations from others). Inner self-esteem is more solid and stable than outer self-esteem because it has a solid base in children's actual skills, characteristics, and behaviors and has been established by previous successes.

In addition to helping children develop social, physical, academic, and moral competencies, parents can promote children's inner self-esteem by creating conditions in the home environment that enable children to develop valued skills and competencies, thus promoting inner self-esteem. Being effective disciplinarians translates into children's having high self-esteem. With parents who are consistent, firm but fair, authoritative, warm and loving, and flexible disciplinarians, children are able to develop competent ways of behaving. Some children have special needs, which require creating special conditions for developing inner self-esteem. Parents can create environments conducive for building healthy inner self-esteem for emotionally, mentally, and physically handicapped children, abused children, children with learning disabilities, underachievers, and gifted children.

Family lifestyles have changed significantly in the past decade as parents divorce and children live in single-parent homes and blended families. Children's inner self-esteem can be optimized in each of these different lifestyles. Moreover, in the 1990s, we have seen a growing trend of less traditional family lifestyles; same-sex parents, parents with one child, adoptive parents, and foster parents can establish environments that promote children's inner self-esteem in these situations as well.

Another significant change in the 1990s is the number of mothers who are working outside the home. The fastest growing group consists of working mothers with infants and preschoolers. We have looked at how mother's working affects her children at various age levels and how parents in a two-paycheck family can best foster children's inner self-esteem. Finally, we must encourage fathers—the new fathers—to discover what an integral role they can have in this process of creating environments that promote healthy inner self-esteem in children.

Inner self-esteem is vital to children's adjustment, health, and success. Because self-esteem literature has placed its emphasis on outer sources of self-esteem, that is, the "looking-glass self," the inner, more salient component of self-esteem has been ignored. Inner self-esteem is not bestowed upon children; it is earned by children. There are two important objectives of this book: the first is to illustrate the skills that are needed in our society that promote inner self-esteem and how parents can help their children acquire these valued ways of behaving; the second is to show parents how they can create conditions in the home under which children's inner self-esteem will flourish. It is my hope that reading the information and following the suggestions offered in this book will enable parents to help their children become responsible, resilient, well-adjusted, self-directing, self-reinforcing, and positive-thinking individuals—children fortified with inner self-esteem.

# Notes

## Introduction

1. Cooley, C. H. 1909. *Social Organization*. Schocken Books, New York.
2. Rogers, C. 1961. *On Becoming a Person*. Houghton-Mifflin, Boston, Massachusetts.
3. Shavelson, R. J., J. J. Hubner, and J. C. Stanton. 1976. Self-concept: Validation of construct interpretations. *Review of Educational Research* 46: 407–441.
4. James, W. 1950. *The Principles of Psychology*. Dover, New York (Original work published 1890), p. 350.
5. Wylie, R. 1979. *The Self-Concept: Theory and Research on Selected Topics*. University of Nebraska Press, Lincoln, Nebraska.
6. Watson, J. B. 1928. *Psychological Care of Infant and Child*. W. W. Norton, New York.

## Chapter 1

1. Cole, J. G. 1991. High-risk infants: Prenatal drug exposure (PDE), prematurity, and AIDS. In: *Readings in Child Development* (N. Lauter-Klatell, ed.). Mayfield, Mountain View, California, pp. 36–42.
2. Fantz, R. 1961. The origin of form perception. *Scientific American* 204: 66–72.
3. Schaal, B. 1986. Presumed olfactory exchanges between mother and neonate in humans. In: *Ethologie et Psychologie de l'Enfant* (J. LeCamus and R. Campan, eds.). Prival, Toulouse, France pp. 100–110.
4. Lipsitt, L. P. 1969. Learning capacities in the human infant. In: *Brain and Early Behavior* (R. J. Robinson, ed.). Academic Press, New York.
5. Gunnar, M., and S. Malone. 1985. Coping with aversive stimulation in the neonatal period: Quiet sleep and plasma cortisol levels during recovery from circumcision. *Child Development* 56: 824–834.
6. Tanner, J. M. 1978. *Education and Physical Growth*. Hoddler and Stoughton, London.
7. Bates, E. 1979. *The Emergence of Symbols*. Academic Press, New York.
8. Hartup, W. W. 1989. Behavioral manifestations of children's friendships. In: *Peer Relations in Child Development* (T. J. Berndt and G. W. Ladd, eds.). Wiley, New York, pp. 46–70.

9. Tronick, E. A. 1989. Emotions and emotional communication in infants. *American Psychologist* 44: 112–119.

10. Mahler, M., F. Pine, and A. Bergman. 1975. *The Psychological Birth of the Human Infant*. Basic Books, New York.

11. Rubin, J. Z., F. J. Provenzano, and Z. Luria. 1974. The eye of the beholder: Parents' views on sex of newborns. *American Journal of Orthopsychiatry* 44: 512–519.

12. Fagot, B. I., and R. Hagan. 1991. Observations of parents' reactions to sex-stereotyped behaviors: Age and sex effects. *Child Development* 62: 617–628.

13. Bowlby, J. 1980. *Attachment*. Basic Books, New York.

14. Spitz, R. 1945. Hospitalism: An inquiry into the genesis of psychiatric conditions in early childhood. *Psychoanalytic Study of the Child* 1: 53–74.

15. Ainsworth, M. 1982. Attachment: Retrospect and prospect. In: *Review of Child Development Research* (B. M. Caldwell and H. N. Riccioti, eds.). University of Chicago Press, Chicago, Illinois, pp. 3–30.

16. Erikson, E. 1968. *Identity: Youth and Adolescent in Crisis*. W. W. Norton, New York.

17. Belsky, J., R. Lerner, and G. Spanier. 1984. *The Child in the Family*. Addison-Wesley, Reading, Massachusetts.

18. Bates, J. E., C. A. Maslin, and K. A. Frankel. 1985. Attachment security, mother-child interaction, and temperament as predictors of behavior-problem ratings at age three years. In: *Growing Points of Attachment, Theory and Research* (I. Bretherton and E. Waters, eds.). *Monographs of the Society for Research in Child Development* 50.

19. Belsky, J. 1988. The "effects" of infant day care reconsidered. *Early Childhood Research Quarterly* 3: 234–272.

20. Waters, E., K. Kondo-Ikemura, G. Posada, and J. Richters. 1990. Learning to love: Mechanisms and milestones. In: *Minnesota Symposia on Child Psychology* (M. Gunnar, ed.). Erlbaum, Hillsdale, New Jersey, pp. 217–255.

21. Fraiberg, S. 1974. Blind infants and their mothers: An examination of the sign system. In: *The Effect of the Infant on Its Caregiver* (M. Lewis and L. A. Rosenblum, eds.). Wiley, New York.

22. Ainsworth, M. 1973. The development of infant-mother attachment 1973. In: *Review of Child Development Research* (B. M. Caldwell and H. N. Ricciuti, eds.). University of Chicago Press, Chicago, pp. 1–94.

23. Malatesta, C. Z., C. Culver, J. R. Tesman, and B. Shepard. 1989. The development of emotional expression during the first two years of life. *Monographs of the Society for Research in Child Development* 54.

24. Greenberg, M., and N. Norris. 1974. Engrossment: The newborn's impact upon the father. *American Journal of Orthopsychiatry* 44: 520–531.

25. Peterson, G. H., L. E. Mehal, and P. Leiderman. 1979. The role of some birth-related variables in father attachment. *American Journal of Orthopsychiatry* 49: 330–338.

26. Parke, R. D. 1981. *Fathers*. Harvard University Press, Cambridge, Massachusetts.

27. Seitz, V., L. K. Rosenbaum, and N. H. Apfel. 1985. Effects of family support intervention: A ten-year follow-up. *Child Development* 56: 376–391.

28. Dweck, C. S., and E. S. Elliott. 1983. A model of achievement motivation: A theory of its origins, and a framework for motivational development. Unpublished

manuscript, Harvard University, Cambridge, Massachusetts. Reported in P. H. Mussen (ed.), *Handbook of Child Psychology*. Wiley, New York.

29. Tronick, E. Z., and J. F. Cohn. 1989. Infant-mother face-to-face interaction: Age and gender differences in coordination and the occurrence of miscoordination. *Child Development* 60: 85–92.

# Chapter 2

1. Stipek, D. H., H. Gralenski, and C. Kopp. 1990. Self-concept development in toddler years. *Developmental Psychology* 26: 972–977.

2. Piaget, J. 1970. *Science of Education and Psychology of the Child*. Orion Press, New York.

3. Eder, R. A. 1989. The emergent personologist: The structure and content of $3\frac{1}{2}$-, $5\frac{1}{2}$-, and $7\frac{1}{2}$-year-olds' concepts of themselves and other persons. *Child Development* 60: 1218–1228.

4. Lytton, H., and D. M. Romney. 1992. Parents' differential socialization of boys and girls: A meta-analysis. *Psychological Bulletin* 109: 267–296.

5. Burns, A. L., G. Mitchell, and S. Obradovich. 1989. Of sex roles and strollers: Female and male attention to toddlers at the zoo. *Sex Roles* 20: 308–317.

6. Pomerleau, A., D. Bolduc, G. Malcuit, and L. Cossette. 1990. Pink or blue: Environmental gender stereotypes in the first two years of life. *Sex Roles* 22: 359–365.

7. Caldera, Y. M., A. C. Huston, and M. O'Brien. 1989. Social interactions and play patterns of parents and toddlers with feminine, masculine, and neutral toys. *Child Development* 60: 70–76.

8. Snow, M. E., C. N. Jacklin, and E. E. Maccoby. 1983. Sex of child differences in father-child interaction at one year of age. *Child Development* 54: 227–232.

9. Cooley, C. H. 1909. *Social Organization*. Schocken Books, New York, pp. 145–146.

10. Thomas, A., S. Chess, and H. Birch. 1980. *Temperament and Behavior Disorders in Children*. Brunner/Mazel, New York.

11. Goldsmith, H. H., and J. J. Campos. 1990. The structure of temperamental fear and pleasure in infants: A psychometric perspective. *Child Development* 61: 1944–1964.

12. Korn, S. J. 1978. Temperament, vulnerability, and behavior. Paper presented at the Louisville Temperament Conference, Louisville, Kentucky.

13. Elkind, D. 1988. *The Hurried Child: Growing Up Too Fast, Too Soon*. Addison-Wesley, Reading, Massachusetts.

14. Winn, M. 1983. The loss of childhood. *Forecast for Home Economics* 5: 38–46.

15. Erikson, E. 1980. *Identity and the Life Cycle*. W. W. Norton, New York.

16. Baumrind, D. 1989. Rearing competent children. In: *Child Development: Today and Tomorrow* (W. Damon, ed.). Jossey-Bass, San Francisco, California, pp. 349–375.

17. Brazelton, T. B. 1979. Behavioral competence in the newborn infant. *Seminars in Perinatology* 27: 532–545.

18. Hoffman, M. L. 1984. Interaction of affect and cognition in empathy. In: *Emotions, Cognition, and Behavior* (C. E. Izard, J. Kagan, and R. B. Zajonc, eds.). Cambridge University Press, Cambridge, England.
19. Walker, L. J., and J. H. Taylor. 1991. Family interactions and the development of moral reasoning. *Child Development* 62: 264–283.
20. Hoffman, M. L. 1983. Empathy, guilt and social cognition. In: *The Relationship between Social and Cognitive Development* (W. F. Overton, ed.). Erlbaum, Hillsdale, New Jersey.
21. Hoffman, M. L. 1977. Moral internalization: Current theory and research. In: *Advances in Experimental Social Psychology* (L. Berkowitz, ed.). Academic Press, New York.
22. Harris, S., P. H. Mussen, and E. Rutherford. 1976. Some cognitive, behavioral and personality correlates of maturity of moral judgment. *Journal of Genetic Psychology* 128: 123–135.
23. Stapley, J. C., and J. M. Haviland. 1989. Beyond depression: Gender differences in normal adolescents' emotional experiences. *Sex Roles* 20: 295–301.

# Chapter 3

1. Livesley, W., and D. B. Bromley. 1973. *Person Perception in Childhood and Adolescence*. Wiley, New York, p. 238.
2. McGuire, W., and A. Padawer-Swinger. 1976. Trait salience in the spontaneous self-concept. *Journal of Personality and Social Psychology* 33: 743–754.
3. Damon, W. 1983. *Social and Personality Development*. W. W. Norton, New York.
4. Rosenberg, M., and F. Rosenberg. Psychological selectivity in self-esteem formation. In: *Self-Concept: Advances in Theory and Research* (M. Lynch, A. Norem-Hebeisen, and K. J. Gergen, eds.). Ballinger, Cambridge, Massachusetts.
5. Signorielli, N. 1989. Television and conceptions about sex roles: Maintaining conventionality: The status quo. *Sex Roles* 21: 341–346.
6. Lott, B. 1989. Sexist discrimination as distancing behavior. *Psychology of Women Quarterly* 13: 341–355.
7. Janman, K. 1989. One step behind: Current stereotypes of women, achievement, and work. *Sex Roles* 21: 209–216.
8. Weitzman, N., B. Birns, and R. Friend. 1985. Traditional and nontraditional mothers' communication with their daughters and sons. *Child Development* 56: 894–898.
9. Mills, R. S. L., and K. H. Rubin. 1993. Parental ideas as influences on children's social competence. In: *Learning about Relationships* (S. Duck, ed.). Sage, Newbury Park, California, pp. 98–118.
10. Booth, C. L., L. Rose-Krasnor, and K. H. Rubin. 1991. Relating preschoolers' social competence and their mothers' parenting behaviors to early attachment security and high-risk status. *Journal of Social and Personal Relationships* 8: 363–382.
11. Miller, J. 1993. Learning from early experience. In: *Learning about Relationships* (S. Duck, ed.). Sage, Newbury Park, California, pp. 1–29.

12. Hartup, W. W. 1985. Relationships and their significance in cognitive development. In: *Social Relationships and Cognitive Development* (R. A. Hinde, A. Perret-Clermont, and J. Stevenson-Hinde, eds.). Clarendon, Oxford, United Kingdom, pp. 66–82.

13. Rubin, K. H., S. Hymel, R. S. L. Mills, and L. Rose-Krasnor. 1991. Conceptualizing different developmental pathways to and from social isolation in childhood. In: *Rochester Symposium on Developmental Psychopathology: Vol. 2, Internalizing and Externalizing Expressions of Dysfunction* (D. Cicchetti and S. L. Toth, eds.). Erlbaum, Hillsdale, New Jersey, pp. 91–122.

14. Parke, R. D., K. B. MacDonald, A. Beitel, and N. Bhavnagri. 1988. The role of the family in the development of peer relationships. In: *Social Learning and Systems Approaches to Marriage and the Family* (R. De V. Peters and R. J. McMahon, eds.). Brunner/Mazel, New York, pp. 17–44.

15. Russell, A., and V. Finnie. 1990. Preschool children's social status and maternal instructions to assist group entry. *Developmental Psychology* 26: 603–611.

16. Cohen, J. S., and E. Woody. 1991. Maternal involvement in children's peer relationships: The contributions of mothers' experiences, values, and beliefs. Paper presented at the biennial meeting of the Society for Research in Child Development, Seattle, Washington, April.

17. Rubin, K. H., R. S. L. Mills, and L. Rose-Krasnor. 1989. Maternal beliefs and children's competence. In: *Social Competence in Developmental Perspective* (B. H. Schneider, G. Attili, J. Nadel, and R. P. Weissberg, eds.). Kluwer, Dordrecht, Netherlands, pp. 313–331.

18. Ladd, G. W., and C. H. Hart. 1991. Parents' management of children's peer relationships: Patterns associated with social competence. Paper presented at the biennial meeting of the International Society for the Study of Behavioral Development, Minneapolis, Minnesota, July.

19. Bullock, J. 1992. Children without friends: Who they are and how teachers can help. *Childhood Education* 69: 92–96.

20. Coie, J. D., and K. A. Dodge. 1988. Multiple sources of data on social behavior and social status in school: A cross-age perspective. *Child Development* 59: 815–829.

21. Whiting, J., and B. Whiting. 1975. *Children of Six Cultures.* Harvard University Press, Cambridge, Massachusetts.

22. Roff, M., S. B. Sells, and M. M. Golden. 1972. *Social Adjustment and Personality Development in Children.* University of Minnesota Press, Minneapolis, Minnesota.

23. Volling, B. L., C. Mackinnon-Lewis, D. Rabiner, and L. P. Baradaran. 1993. Children's social competence and sociometric status: Further exploration of aggressive, social withdrawal, and peer rejection. *Development and Psychopathology* 5: 459–483.

24. Zimbardo, P. G. 1978. *Shyness: What It Is and What To Do about It.* Addison-Wesley, Reading, Massachusetts.

25. Kagan, J. J., S. Reznick, and N. Snidman. 1988. Biological bases of childhood shyness. *Science* 240: 167–171.

26. Plomin, R. 1990. *An Introduction to Human Behavioral Genetics.* Brooks/Cole, Pacific Grove, California.

27. Volling, B. L., C. Mackinnon-Lewis, D. Rabiner, and L. P. Baradaran. 1993. Children's social competence and sociometric status: Further exploration of aggressive, social withdrawal, and peer rejection. *Development and Psychopathology* 5: 459–483.
28. Sameroff, A. J., and R. Seifer. 1990. Early contributions to developmental risk. In: *Risk and Protective Factors in the Developmental of Psychopathology* (J. Rolf, A. S. Masten, D. Cicchetti, K. H. Nuechterlien, and S. Weinstraub, eds.). Cambridge University Press, New York, pp. 52–66.
29. Cairns, R. B., and B. Cairns. 1984. Predicting aggressive behavior patterns in girls and boys: A developmental study. *Aggressive Behavior* 10: 227–242.
30. Patterson, G. R., B. D. DeBaryshe, and F. Ramsey. 1989. A developmental perspective on antisocial behavior. *American Psychologist* 44: 329–335.
31. Parke, R. D., K. B. MacDonald, A. Beitel, and N. Bhavnagri. 1988. The role of the family in the development of peer relationships. In: *Marriage and Families: Behavioral Treatments and Processes* (R. D. Peters and R. J. McMahon, eds.). Brunner Mazel, New York, pp. 17–44.
32. Coie, J. D. 1990. Toward a theory of peer rejection. In: *Peer Rejection in Childhood* (S. R. Asher and J. D. Coie, eds.). Cambridge University Press, New York, pp. 365–401.
33. Eron, L. D. 1982. Parent-child interaction: Television, violence, and aggression in children. *American Psychologist* 37: 197–211.
34. Thomas, M. H., R. W. Horton, E. C. Lippincott, and R. S. Drabman. 1977. Desensitization to portrayals of real-life aggression as a function of exposure to television violence. *Journal of Personality and Social Psychology* 35: 450–458.
35. Guerra, N. G., and R. G. Slaby. 1990. Cognitive mediators of aggression in adolescent offenders: Intervention. *Developmental Psychology* 26: 269–277.
36. Dodge, K. A., J. D. Coie, G. S. Pettit, and J. M. Price. 1990. Peer status and aggression in boys' groups: Developmental and contextual analysis. *Child Development* 61:1289–1309.

# Chapter 4

1. Harter, S. 1983. Developmental perspectives on the self system. In: *Handbook of Child Psychology* (P. H. Mussen, ed.). Wiley, New York, pp. 275–385.
2. Covington, M. V. 1985. The role of self-processes in applied social psychology. *Journal for the Theory of Social Behavior* 15: 355–392.
3. Rotter, J. 1966. Generalized expectancies for internal versus external locus of control reinforcement. *Psychological Monographs: General and Applied* 80: 1–28.
4. Findley, M., and H. Cooper. 1983. Locus of control and academic achievement: A literature review. *Journal of Personality and Social Psychology* 44: 419–427.
5. Dreikurs, R., and V. Soltz. 1964. *Children: The Challenge.* Hawthorn Books, New York.
6. Gordon, T. 1970. *Parent Effectiveness Training: The Tested New Way to Raise Responsible Children.* David McKay, New York.

7. Robinson, F. 1941. *Effective Behavior*. Harper & Row, New York.

8. Beneson, J., and C. S. Dweck. 1986. The development of trait explanations and self-evaluations in the academic and social domains. *Child Development* 57: 1179–1187.

9. Stipek, D. J., and L. Tannatt. 1984. Children's judgments of their own and their peers' academic competence. *Journal of Educational Psychology* 76: 75–84.

10. Stevenson, H. W., and S. Lee. 1990. Contexts of achievement. *Monographs of the Society for Research in Child Development* 55, nos. 1–2.

11. Lynn, R. 1982. IQ in Japan and the United States shows a growing disparity. *Nature* 297: 222–223.

12. Miller, A. 1985. A developmental study of the cognitive basis of performance impairment after failure. *Journal of Personality and Social Psychology* 49: 529–538.

13. Chapman, M., E. A. Skinner, and P. B. Baltes. 1990. Interpreting correlations between children's perceived control and cognitive performance: Control, agency, or means-ends beliefs? *Developmental Psychology* 23: 246–253.

14. Keith, T. 1982. Time spent on homework and high school grades: A large-sample panel analysis. *Journal of Educational Psychology* 74: 248–252.

15. Stevenson, H. W., S. Lee, C. Chen, M. Lummis, J. Stigler, L. Fan, and F. Ge. 1990. Mathematics achievement of children in China and the United States. *Child Development* 61: 1053–1066.

16. Rosenthal, R., and L. Jacobson. 1968. *Pygmalion in the Classroom*. Holt, Rinehart, & Winston, New York.

# Chapter 5

1. Buhrmester, D. 1990. Intimacy of friendship, interpersonal competence, and adjustment during preadolescence and adolescence. *Child Development* 61: 1101–1111.

2. Elkind, D. 1988. *The Hurried Child: Growing Up Too Fast, Too Soon*. Addison-Wesley, Reading, Massachusetts.

3. Piaget, J. 1975. *The Development of Thought* (A. Rosin, trans.). Viking Press, New York.

4. Rosenberg, M. 1985. Self-concept and psychological well-being in adolescence. In: *The Development of Self* (R. Leahy, ed.). Academic Press, New York, pp. 205–246.

5. Blyth, D., and C. Traeger. 1991. The self-concept and self-esteem in early adolescents. In: *Readings in Child Development* (N. Lauter-Klatell, ed.). Mayfield, Mountain View, California, pp. 130–135.

6. Simmons, R. G., D. A. Blyth, E. F. Van Cleave, and D. M. Bush. 1979. Entry into early adolescence: The impact of school structure, puberty, and early dating on self-esteem. *American Sociology Review* 44: 948–967.

7. Hill, J. P., and M. Lynch. 1983. The intensification of gender-related role expectations during early adolescence. In: *Family Puberty* (J. Brooks-Gunn and A. Petersen, eds.). Plenum Press, New York.

8. Marsh, H. W. 1989. Age and sex effects in multiple dimensions of self-concept: Pre-adolescence to early adulthood. *Journal of Educational Psychology* 81: 417–430.

9. Koff, E., J. Rierdan, and M. L. Stubbs. 1990. Gender, body image, and self-concept in early adolescence. *Journal of Early Adolescence* 10: 56–67.

10. Olver, R. R., E. Aries, and J. Batgos. 1990. Self-other differentiation and the mother-child relationship: The effects of sex and birth order. *Journal of Genetic Psychology* 150: 311–321.

11. Bem, S. L. 1985. Androgyny and gender schema theory: A conceptual and empirical investigation. *Nebraska Symposium on Motivation* 32: 179–226.

12. Taylor, M., and J. A. Hall. 1982. Psychological androgyny: Theories, methods, conclusions. *Psychological Bulletin* 92: 347–366.

13. Baumrind, D. 1989. Rearing competent children. In: *Child Development: Today and Tomorrow* (W. Damon, ed.). Jossey-Bass, San Francisco, California, pp. 349–375.

14. Baumrind, D. 1980. New directions in socialization research. *Developmental Psychological Monographs* 4, Pt. 2.

15. Youniss, J. 1980. *Parents and Peers in Social Development.* University of Chicago Press, Chicago, Illinois.

16. Gordon, T. 1970. *Parent Effectiveness Training: The Tested New Way to Raise Responsible Children.* David McKay, New York.

17. Henning, M., and A. Jardin. 1978. *The Managerial Women.* Doubleday, New York.

18. Blos, P. 1967. The second individuation process of adolescence. In: *Psychoanalytic Study of the Child* (R. S. Eissler, ed.). International Universities Press, New York, p. 168.

19. Steinberg, L. 1985. *Adolescence.* Knopf, New York.

20. Hunter, F., and J. Youniss. 1982. Changes in functions of three relations during adolescence. *Developmental Psychology* 18: 806–811.

21. Grotevant, H. D., and C. R. Cooper. 1985. Patterns of interaction in family relationships and the development of identity exploration in adolescence. *Child Development* 56: 415–428.

22. Steinberg, L. 1985. *Adolescence.* Knopf, New York.

23. Ryan, R. M., and J. H. Lynch. 1989. Emotional autonomy versus detachment: Revisiting the vicissitudes of adolescence and young adulthood. *Child Development* 60: 340–356.

24. Marcia, J. E., 1980. Identity in adolescence. In: *Handbook of Adolescent Psychology* (J. Adelson, ed.). Wiley, New York, pp. 159–187.

25. Erikson, E. 1980. *Identity and the Life Cycle.* W. W. Norton, New York, p. 173.

26. Hauser, S. T., S. I. Powers, G. Noam, A. M. Jacobson, B. Weiss, and D. J. Follansbee. 1984. Familial contexts of adolescent ego development. *Child Development* 55: 195–213.

27. Blume, J. 1990. *Are You There, God? It's Me, Margaret.* Bradbury Press/Macmillan Child Group, New York.

28. Yates, A. 1989. Current perspectives on the eating disorders: II. Treatment, outcome, and research directives. *Journal of the American Academy of Child/Adolescent Psychiatry* 29: 1–9.

29. Etringer, B., E. Altmaier, and W. Bowers. 1989. An investigation into the cognitive functioning of bulimic women. *Journal of Counseling and Development* 68: 216–219.
30. Jacobson, R., and C. Robins. 1989. Social dependence and social support in bulimic and nonbulimic women. *International Journal of Eating Disorders* 8: 665–670.
31. Pallazzoli, M. S. 1978. *Self Starvation*. Aronson, New York.
32. Silber, T. J. 1986. Approaching the adolescent patient: Pitfalls and solutions. *Journal of Adolescent Health Care* 7: 31–40.
33. Burns, D. D. 1980. *Feeling Good*. William Morrow and Co., Inc., New York.

# Chapter 6

1. Baumrind, D. 1980. New directions in socialization research. *American Psychologist* 35: 639–652, p. 640.
2. Kegan, R. 1982. *The Evolving Self*. Harvard University Press, Cambridge, Massachusetts.
3. Power, T. G., and J. A. Shanks. 1989. Parents as socializers: Maternal and paternal views. *Journal of Youth and Adolescence* 18: 203–208.
4. Dix, T., D. Ruble, and R. Zambarano. 1989. Mothers' implicit theories of discipline: Parent effects and the attribution process. *Child Development* 60: 1373–1399.
5. Ogbu, J. 1988. Black education: A cultural-ecological perspective. In: *Black Families* (H. P. McAdoo, ed.). Sage, Beverly Hills, California, pp. 169–186.
6. Baumrind, D. 1980. New directions in socialization research. *American Psychologist* 35: 639–652.
7. Steinberg, L., J. Elmen, and N. Mounts. 1989. Authoritative parenting, psychosocial maturity, and academic success among adolescents. *Child Development* 60: 1424–1436.
8. Patterson, G. R. 1975. *Families: Applications of Social Learning to Family Life*. Research Press, Champaign, Illinois.
9. Chapman, M. 1979. Listening to reason: Children's attentiveness and parental discipline. *Merrill-Palmer Quarterly* 25: 251–263.
10. Gordon, T. 1970. *Parent Effectiveness Training: The Tested New Way to Raise Responsible Children*. David McKay, New York.
11. Olweus, D. 1980. Familial and temperamental determinants of aggression behavior in adolescents: A causal analysis. *Developmental Psychology* 16: 644–660.
12. Abramovitch, R., C. Corter, and B. Lando. 1979. Sibling interaction in the home. *Child Development* 50: 997–1003.
13. Patterson, G. R., B. D. DeBaryshe, and E. Ramsey. 1989. A developmental perspective on antisocial behavior. *American Psychologist* 44: 329–335.
14. Forehand, R. 1977. Child noncompliance to parental requests: Behavioral analysis and treatment. In: *Progress in Behavior Modification* (M. Hersen, R. M. Eisler, and P. M. Miller, eds.). Academic Press, New York.
15. Kuczynski, L., and G. Kochanska. 1990. Development of children's noncompliance strategies from toddlerhood to age 5. *Developmental Psychology* 26: 398–408.

16. Brazelton, T. B. 1992. *Touchpoints: Your Child's Emotional and Behavioral Development.* Addison-Wesley, Reading, Massachusetts.

# Chapter 7

1. White, D., and A. Woollett. 1991. *Families: A Context for Development.* Falmer Press, New York.
2. Friedman, R. M., J. Sandler, M. Hernandez, and D. A. Wolfe. 1981. Child abuse. In: *Behavioral Assessment of Childhood Disorders* (E. J. Mash and L. G. Terdal, eds.). Guildford Press, New York.
3. Coleman, H., and D. Collins. 1990. Treatment trilogy of father-daughter incest. *Child and Adolescent Social Work Journal* 7: 339–355.
4. Coleman, E. 1987. Child physical and sexual abuse among chemical dependent individuals. *Journal of Chemical Dependency* 1: 27–38.
5. Cohen, J. A., and A. P. Mannarino. 1993. Sexual abuse. In: *Handbook of Prescriptive Treatments for Children and Adolescents* (M. Hersen, ed.). Allyn and Bacon, Boston, Massachusetts, pp. 347–367.
6. Hotaling, G. T., D. Finkelhor, J. T. Kirkpatrick, and M. A. Strauss. 1988. *Family Abuse and Its Consequences: New Directions in Research.* Sage, Newbury Park, California.
7. Trickett, P. K., J. L. Abner, V. Carlson, and D. Cicchetti. 1991. Relationships of socioeconomic status to the etiology and developmental sequelae of physical child abuse. *Developmental Psychology* 27: 148–158.
8. Crittenden, P. 1985. Social networks, quality of child rearing and child development. *Child Development* 56: 1299–1313.
9. Trickett, P. K., and E. J. Susman. 1988. Parental perceptions of childrearing practices in physically abusive and nonabusive parents. *Developmental Psychology* 24: 270–276.
10. Plotkin, R. D., and C. T. Twentyman. 1982. Cognitive mediation of child abuse. Unpublished manuscript, University of Rochester, New York.
11. Milner, J. S., K. R. Robertson, and D. L. Rogers. 1990. Childhood history of abuse and adult child abuse potential. *Journal of Family Violence* 5: 15–34.
12. Simons, R. L., L. B. Whitbeck, R. D. Conger, and W. Chyi-In. 1991. Intergenerational transmission of harsh parenting. *Developmental Psychology* 27: 159–171.
13. Coleman, H., and D. Collins. 1990. Treatment trilogy of father-daughter incest. *Child and Adolescent Social Work Journal* 7: 339–355.
14. Mitnick, M. F. 1983. Family sexual abuse and custody evaluation. *Conciliation Courts Review* 21: 89–94.
15. Sternac, L., and A. Segal. 1990. Adult sexual contact with children: An examination of cognitive factors. *Behavioral Therapy* 20: 573–584.
16. Van Dalen, A. 1989. The emotional consequences of physical child abuse. *Clinical Social Work Journal* 17: 383–394.
17. Martin, H. P., and P. Beezley. 1976. Foster placement: Therapy or trauma. In: *The Abused Child* (H. P. Martin and C. H. Kempe, eds.). Ballinger, Cambridge, Massachusetts, pp. 189–199.

18. Dolce, L. 1994. *Mental Retardation*. Chelsea House, New York.

19. Alvino, J. 1989. *Parents' Guide to Raising a Gifted Toddler*. Little Brown and Company, Boston, Massachusetts.

20. Sternberg, R. 1985. *Beyond IQ: A Triarchic Theory of Human Intelligence*. Cambridge University Press, New York.

21. Odom, J., and M. Shaughnessy. 1989. Personality and mathematical achievement. *Psychological Reports* 63: 1195–1201.

22. Perino, S., and J. Perino. 1981. *Parenting the Gifted: Developing the Promise*. Bowker, New York.

23. Clark, B. 1992. *Growing Up Gifted*. Macmillan Publishing Company, New York.

# Chapter 8

1. Cohn, J. F., and E. Z. Tronick. 1983. Three-month-old infants' reaction to simulated maternal depression. *Child Development* 54: 185–193.

2. Cummings, E. M., R. J. Iannotti, and C. Zahn-Waxler. 1985. Influences of conflict between adults on the emotions and aggression of young children. *Developmental Psychology* 21: 495–507.

3. Wallerstein, J. S., and J. B. Kelly. 1980. *Surviving the Breakup: How Children and Parents Cope with Divorce*. Basic Books, New York.

4. Hetherington, E. M. 1979. Play and social interaction in children following divorce. *Journal of Social Issues* 35: 26–49,

5. Wallerstein, J. S., S. G. Corbin, and J. M. Lewis. 1988. Children of divorce: A ten-year study. In: *Impact of Divorce, Single-Parenting and Stepparenting on Children* (E. M. Hetherington and J. D. Arasteh, eds.). Erlbaum, Hillsdale, New Jersey, pp. 198–214.

6. Wallerstein, J. S., and J. B. Kelly. 1980. *Surviving the Breakup: How Children and Parents Cope with Divorce*. Basic Books, New York.

7. Hetherington, E. M. 1989. Coping with family transitions: Winners, losers, and survivors. *Child Development* 60: 1–14.

8. Zill, N. 1988. Behavior, achievement, and health problems among children in stepfamilies: Findings from a national survey of child health. In: *Impact of Divorce, Single-Parenting and Stepparenting on Children* (E. M. Hetherington and J. D. Arasteh, eds.). Erlbaum, Hillsdale, New Jersey, pp. 325–368.

9. Jourdes, E. N., L. J. Pfiffner, and S. G. O'Leary. 1988. Marital conflict, parenting, and toddler conduct problems. *Journal of Abnormal Child Psychology* 16: 197–206.

10. Shaw, O. S., and R. E. Emery. 1987. Parental conflict and other correlates of the adjustment of school-age children whose parents have separated. *Journal of Abnormal Child Psychology* 25: 269–281.

11. Long, N., R. Forehand, R. Fauber, and G. Brody. 1988. Self-perceived and independently observed competence of young adolescents as a function of parental marital conflict and recent divorce. *Journal of Abnormal Child Psychology* 15: 15–27.

12. Cummings, E. M., D. S. Pellegrini, C. I. Notarius, and M. Cummings. 1985. Children's responses to angry adult behavior as a function of marital distress and history of interparent hostility. *Child Development* 60: 1035–1043.

13. Long, N., and E. Slater. 1988. Continued high or reduced interparental conflict following divorce: Relation to young adolescent adjustment. *Journal of Consulting and Clinical Psychology* 56: 467–469.

14. Block, J. H., J. Block, and P. Gjerde. 1986. The personality of children prior to divorce: A prospective study. *Child Development* 57: 827–840.

15. Camara, K. A., and G. Resnick. 1988. Interparental conflict and cooperation: Factors moderating children's post-divorce adjustment. In: *Impact of Divorce, Single-Parenting and Stepparenting on Children* (E. M. Hetherington and J. D. Arasteh, eds.). Erlbaum, Hillsdale, New Jersey, pp. 169–195.

16. Easton, J. J. 1994. Life without father. In: *Annual Editions of Child Growth and Development* (E. N. Junn and C. J. Boyatzis, eds.). Dushkin Publishing Group, Inc., Guilford, Connecticut, pp. 178–184.

17. Kline, M., J. M. Tschann, J. R. Johnston, and J. S. Wallerstein. 1989. Children's adjustment in joint and sole physical custody families. *Developmental Psychology* 25: 430–438, p. 437.

18. Wierson, M., R. Forehand, R. Fauber, and A. McCombs. 1989. Buffering young male adolescents against negative parental divorce influences: The role of good parent-adolescent relations. *Child Study Journal* 19: 101–112.

19. Block, J. H., J. Block, and P. Gjerde. 1986. The personality of children prior to divorce: A prospective study. *Child Development* 57: 827–840.

20. Hetherington, E. M. 1989. Coping with family transitions: Winners, losers, and survivors. *Child Development* 60: 1–14.

21. U.S. Bureau of the Census. 1988. *Statistical Abstract of the United States, 1988.* U.S. Government Printing Office, Washington, D.C.

22. Furstenberg, F. F., and A. J. Cherlin. 1991. *Divided Families: What Happens to Children When Parents Part.* Harvard University Press, Cambridge, Massachusetts.

23. White, D., and A. Woollett. 1991. *Families: A Context for Development.* Falmer Press, New York.

24. Emery, R. E. 1988. *Marriage, Divorce, and Children's Adjustment.* Sage, Newbury Park, California.

25. Dornbusch, S. M., J. M. Carlsmith, S. J. Bushwall, P. L. Ritter, H. Leiderman, A. H. Hastorf, and R. Gross. 1985. Single parents, extended households, and the control of adolescents. *Child Development* 56: 326–341.

26. Dreman, S., E. Orr, and R. Aldor. 1990. Sense of competence, time perspective, and state-anxiety of separated versus divorced mothers. *American Journal of Orthopsychiatry* 60: 77–85.

27. Reid, W. J., and A. Crisafulli. 1990. Marital discord and child behavior problems: A meta-analysis. *Journal of Abnormal Child Psychology* 18: 105–117.

28. Bray, J. H. 1988. Children's development during early remarriage. In: *Impact of Divorce, Single-Parenting and Stepparenting on Children* (E. M. Hetherington and J. D. Arasteh, eds.). Erlbaum, Hillsdale, New Jersey, pp. 279–298.

29. Smith, D. 1990. *Stepmothering.* Harvester Wheatsheaf, Hemel Hempstead, England.

30. Santrock, J. W., and R. A. Warshak. 1979. Children's and parents' observed social behavior in stepfather families. *Child Development* 53: 472–480.

31. Reid, W. J., and A. Crisafulli. 1990. Marital discord and child behavior problems: A meta-analysis. *Journal of Abnormal Child Psychology* 18: 105–117.

32. Ricketts, W., and R. Achtenberg. 1990. Adoption and foster parenting for lesbians and gay men: Creating new family traditions. In: *Homosexuality and Family Relations* (F. W. Bozett and M. B. Sussman, eds.). Harrington Park, New York, pp. 83–118.

33. Bigner, J. J., and F. W. Bozett. 1990. Parenting by gay fathers. In: *Homosexuality and Family Relations* (F. W. Bozett and M. B. Sussman, eds.). Harrington Park, New York, pp. 155–176.

34. Ricketts, W., and R. Achtenberg. 1990. Adoption and foster parenting for lesbians and gay men: Creating new family traditions. In: *Homosexuality and Family Relations* (F. W. Bozett and M. B. Sussman, eds.). Harrington Park, New York, pp. 83–118.

35. Kweskin, S. L., and A. S. Cook. 1982. Heterosexual and homosexual mothers' self-described sex role behavior and ideal sex role behavior in children. *Sex Roles* 8: 967–975.

36. Bozett, F. W. 1987. Children of gay fathers. In: *Gay and Lesbian Parents* (F. W. Bozett, ed.). Praeger, New York, pp. 39–57.

37. Newman, S. 1990. *Parenting an Only Child: The Joys and Challenges of Raising Your One and Only Child.* Doubleday, New York.

38. Falbo, T. 1984. *The Single-Child Family.* Guilford Press, New York.

# Chapter 9

1. Hoffman, L. W. 1986. Work, family, and the child. In: *Psychology and Work: Productivity, Change, and Employment* (M. S. Pallak and R. O. Perloff, eds.). American Psychological Association, Washington, D.C., pp. 173–220.

2. Moore, T. W. 1975. Exclusive early mothering and its alternatives. *Scandinavian Journal of Psychology* 16: 256–272.

3. Weitzmand, L. M., and L. F. Fitzgerald. 1993. Employed mothers: Diverse lifestyles and labor force profiles. In: *The Employed Mother in the Family Context* (J. Frankel, ed.). Springer Publishing Company, New York, pp. 7–31.

4. American Bar Association (ABA). 1988. *Commission on Women in the Professions. Report to the House of Delegates.* Chicago, Illinois.

5. Rhode, D. L. 1990. Gender equality and employment policy. In: *The American Woman: 1990–1991* (S. E. Rix, ed.). W. W. Norton, New York, pp. 132–169.

6. Vandall, D. L., and J. Ramanan. 1992. Effects of early and recent maternal employment on children from low-income families. *Child Development* 63: 938–949.

7. U.S. Bureau of the Census. 1988. *Statistical Abstract of the United States, 1988.* U.S. Government Printing Office, Washington, D.C.

8. See note 7.

9. Hofferth, S. L., and D. A. Phillips. 1989. Child care in the United States, 1970–1995. *Journal of Marriage and the Family* 49: 559–571.

10. Scarr, S., D. Phillips, and K. McCartney. 1994. Working mothers and their families. In: *Annual Editions of Child Growth and Development* (E. N. Junn and C. J.

Boyatzis, eds.). Dushkin Publishing Group, Inc., Guilford, Connecticut, pp. 163–170.

11. Lamb, M. E., and K. J. Sternberg. 1990. Do we really know how day care affects children? *Journal of Applied Developmental Psychology* 11: 351–379.

12. Hofferth, S. L. 1989. What is the demand for and supply of child care in the United States? *Young Children* 4: 28–32.

13. Lerner, J. V., and N. L. Galambos. 1988. The influence of maternal employment across life: The New York longitudinal study. In: *Maternal Employment and Children's Development* (A. E. Gottfried and A. W. Gottfried, eds.). Plenum Press, New York, pp. 59–83.

14. Belsky, J. 1988. The "effects" of infant day care reconsidered. *Early Childhood Research Quarterly* 3: 234–272.

15. Clarke-Stewart, K. A. 1989. Infant day care. *American Psychologist* 44: 266–273.

16. Lamb, M. E., K. J. Sternberg, and M. Prodromidis. 1990. Nonmaternal care and the security of infant-mother attachment: A reanalysis of the data. Unpublished manuscript, National Institute of Child Health and Human Development.

17. Field, T. 1991. Quality infant day care and grade school behavior and performance. *Child Development* 62: 863–870.

18. Belsky, J., and J. M. Braungart. 1991. Are insecure-avoidant infants with extensive day care experience less stressed by and more independent in the strange situation? *Child Development* 62: 567–571.

19. Belsky, J. 1988. The "effects" of infant day care reconsidered. *Early Childhood Research Quarterly* 3: 234–272.

20. Hock, E., and K. K. DeMeis. 1990. Depression in mothers of infants: The role of maternal employment. *Developmental Psychology* 26: 285–291.

21. Hoffman, L. W. 1974. Effects on child. In: *Working Mothers* (L. W. Hoffman and F. I. Nye, eds.). Jossey-Bass, San Francisco, California, p. 128.

22. Burchinal, M., M. Lee, and C. T. Ramey. 1989. Type of day care and preschool intellectual development in disadvantaged children. *Child Development* 60: 128–137.

23. Clarke-Stewart, K. A. 1989. Infant day care. *American Psychologist* 44: 266–273.

24. Armistead, L., M. Wierson, and R. Forehand. 1990. Adolescents and maternal employment: Is it harmful for a young adolescent to have an employed mother? *Journal of Early Adolescence* 10: 260–278.

25. Bronfenbrenner, U., W. Alvarez, and C. R. Henderson. 1984. Working and watching: Maternal employment status and parents' perceptions of their three-year-old children. *Child Development* 55: 1362–1378.

26. Scarr, S., D. Phillips, and K. McCartney. 1994. Working mothers and their families. In: *Annual Editions of Child Growth and Development* (E. N. Junn and C. J. Boyatzis, eds.). Dushkin Publishing Group, Inc., Guilford, Connecticut, pp. 163–170.

27. Andersson, B. 1989. Effects of public day care: A longitudinal study. *Child Development* 57: 1024–1033.

28. Andersson, B. 1992. Effects of day care on cognitive and socioemotional competence of thirteen-year-old Swedish school children. *Child Development* 63: 20–36.

29. Howes, C. 1990. Can the age of entry into child care and the quality of child care predict adjustment in kindergarten? *Developmental Psychology* 26: 292–303.

30. Field, T., W. Masi, D. Goldstein, S. Perry, and S. Parl. 1988. Infant day care facilitates preschool behavior. *Early Childhood Research Quarterly* 3: 341–359.
31. Benin, M., and Y. Chong. 1993. Child care concerns of employed mothers. In: *The Employed Mother and the Family Context* (J. Frankel, ed.). Springer Publishing Company, New York, pp. 229–245.
32. Moen, P. 1989. *Working Parents*. University of Wisconsin Press, Madison, Wisconsin.
33. Fernandez, J. P. 1986. *Child Care and Corporate Productivity*. Lexington Books, Lexington, Massachusetts.
34. Googins, B. K. 1991. *Work/Family Conflicts*. Auburn House, New York.
35. Whitebook, M., C. Howes, and D. Phillips. 1989. *Who Cares? Child Care Teachers and the Quality of Care in America*. Child Care Employee Project, Berkeley, California.
36. Friedman, D. E. 1986. Child care for employees' kids. *Harvard Business Review* 65: 28–34.
37. Crockenberg, S., and C. Litman. 1991. Effects of maternal employment on maternal and two-year-old child behavior. *Child Development* 62: 930–953.
38. Crockenberg, S. 1988. Stress and role satisfaction experienced by employed and non-employed mothers with young children. *Lifestyles: Family and Economic Issues* 9: 97–110.

# Chapter 10

1. Pleck, J. H. 1988. Men in domestic settings. In: *50–50 Parenting* (G. Kimball, ed.). Lexington Books, Lexington, Massachusetts, pp. 83–97.
2. *Harper's Bazaar*, 1900, p. 200.
3. Johnson, M. M. 1982. Fathers and femininity in daughters: A review of the research. *Sociology and Social Science Research* 67: 15–27.
4. Dornbusch, S. M., P. L. Ritter, P. H. Leiderman, D. F. Roberts, and M. J. Fraleigh. 1987. The relation of parenting style to adolescent school performance. *Child Development* 58: 1244–1257.
5. Osofsky, J. E. 1979. *Handbook on Infant Development*. Wiley, New York.
6. Dweck, C. A. 1983. Achievement motivation. In: *Handbook of Child Psychology* (P. H. Mussen, ed.). Wiley, New York.
7. Radin, N., and G. Russell. 1983. Increased father participation and child development outcomes. In: *Fatherhood and Family Policy* (M. E. Lamb and A. Sagi, eds.). Erlbaum, Hillsdale, New Jersey, pp. 191–218.
8. Cross, H. J., and J. Allen. 1989. Relationship between memories of parental behavior and academic achievement. Proceedings of the 77th Annual Convention, American Psychological Association, Washington, D.C.
9. Teahan, J. E. 1963. Parental attitudes and college success. *Journal of Educational Psychology* 21: 345–348.
10. King, V. 1994. Nonresidential father involvement and child well-being: Can dads make a difference? *Journal of Family Issues* 15: 78–96.

11. Mott, F. 1990. When is a father really gone? Paternal-child contact in father-absent homes. *Demography* 27: 499–517.
12. Lamb, M. E. 1977. Father-infant and mother-infant interaction in the first year of life. *Child Development* 48: 167–181.
13. Hoffman, L., and H. D. Saltzstein. 1967. Parent disposition and the child's moral development. *Journal of Personality and Social Psychology* 19: 45–57.
14. Bronfenbrenner, U. 1991. What do families do? In: *Family Affairs*. Institute for American Values, New York, p. 4.
15. Radin, N., and R. Harold-Goldsmith. 1989. The involvement of selected unemployed and employed men with their children. *Child Development* 60: 454–459.
16. McHale, S. M., W. T. Bartko, A. C. Crouter, and M. Perry-Jenkins. 1990. Children's housework and psychosocial functioning: The mediating effects of parents' sex-role behaviors and attitudes. *Child Development* 61: 1413–1426.
17. Lamb, M. E. 1981. *The Role of the Father in Child Development*. Wiley, New York.
18. Stattin, H., and I. Klackenberg-Larsson. 1990. The short- and long-term implications for parent-child relations of parents' prenatal preferences for their child's gender. *Developmental Psychology* 27: 141–147.
19. Hochschild, A. 1991. *The Second Shift*. Viking, New York.
20. Hetherington, E. M. 1989. Coping with family transitions: Winners, losers, and survivors. *Child Development* 60: 1–14.
21. Hetherington, E. M. 1988. The role of individual differences and family relations in coping with divorce and remarriage. In: *Advances in Family Research: Family Transitions* (P. Cowan and E. M. Hetherington, eds.). Erlbaum, Hillsdale, New Jersey.
22. Hartup, W. W. 1989. Behavioral manifestations of children's friendships. In: *Peer Relationships in Child Development* (T. J. Berndt and G. W. Ladd, eds.). Wiley, New York, pp. 46–70.
23. Parke, R. D., and B. J. Tinsley. 1987. Family interactions in infancy. In: *Handbook of Infant Development* (J. Osofsky, ed.). Wiley, New York, pp. 579–641.
24. Hochschild, A. 1991. *The Second Shift*. Viking, New York.
25. Gottfried, A. E., and A. W. Gottfried. 1988. *Maternal Employment and Children's Development*. Plenum Press, New York.
26. Rebelsky, F., and C. Hanks. 1971. Fathers' verbal interaction with infants in the first three months of life. *Child Development* 42: 63–68.
27. Ishii-Kuntz, M. 1993. Work and family life: Findings from international research and suggestions for future study. *Journal of Family Issues* 14: 468–490.
28. Lamb, M. E., and D. Oppenheim. 1989. Fatherhood and father-child relationships: Five years of research. In: *Fathers and Their Families* (S. Cath, A. Gurwitt, and L. Gunsberg, eds.). Analytic Press, Hillsdale, New Jersey, pp. 11–26.
29. Grossman, F. K., W. S. Pollack, and E. Golding. 1989. Fathers and children: Predicting the quality and quantity of fathering. *Developmental Psychology* 24: 82–91.
30. Bailey, W. T. 1993. Fathers' knowledge of development and involvement with preschool children. *Perceptual and Motor Skills* 77: 1032–1034.
31. Hawkins, A., S. L. Christiansen, K. P. Sargent, and E. J. Hill. 1994. Rethinking fathers' involvement in child care. *Journal of Family Issues* 14: 531–549.

32. Daly, K. 1993. Reshaping fatherhood: Finding the models. *Journal of Family Issues* 14: 484–509.

33. Santrock, J. W. 1972. The relation of type and onset of father absence on cognitive development. *Child Development* 43: 455–469.

34. Lamb, M. E. 1986. The changing role of fathers. In: *The Father's Role: Applied Perspectives* (M. E. Lamb, ed.). Wiley, New York, pp. 3–27.

35. Levy-Shiff, R. 1982. The effects of father absence on young children in mother-headed families. *Child Development* 53: 81–86.

36. Crockett, L. J., D. J. Eggebeen, and A. J. Hawkins. 1993. Father's presence and young children's behavioral and cognitive adjustment. *Journal of Family Issues* 14: 355–377.

37. Biller, H. B. 1985. The father and sex role development. In: *The Role of the Father in Child Development* (M. E. Lamb, ed.). Wiley, New York.

38. O'Reilly, P., and F. Brisco. 1993. Social support for working families. In: *The Employed Mother and the Family Context* (J. Frankel, ed.). Springer Publishing Company, New York, pp. 260–271.

39. Garbarino, J. 1993. Reinventing fatherhood. *Families in Society: The Journal of Contemporary Human Services* 74: 51–55.

40. See note 39.

# Index